DiD iT!

Pat Thomas

FANTAGRAPHICS BOOKS

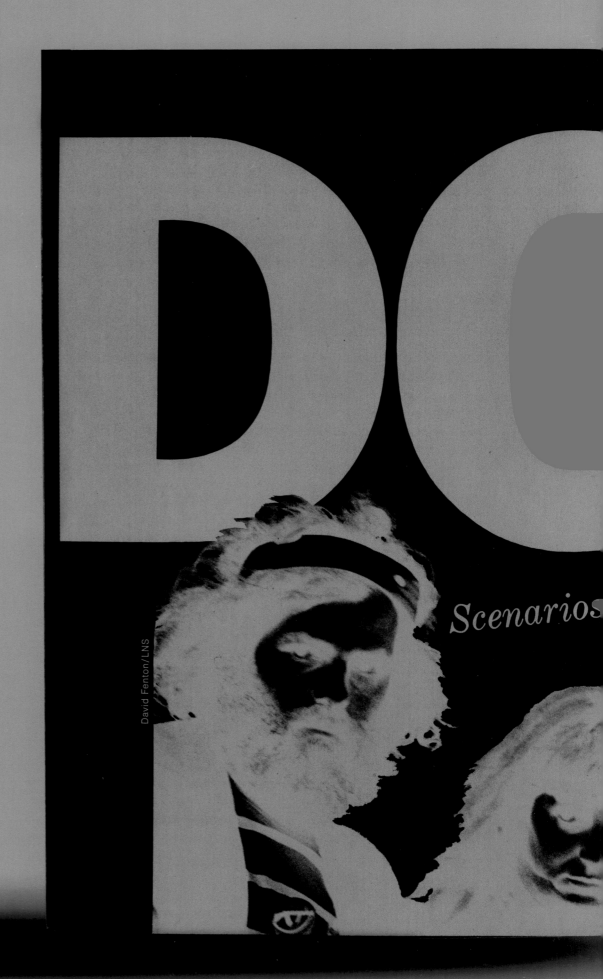

Scenarios

DID IT!

From Yippie to Yuppie

*Jerry Rubin,
an American Revolutionary*

Written by Pat Thomas

Yipped by Kathy Wolf

Zapped by Jacob Covey

Fantagraphics Books   Seattle

& Revolution
y Jerry Rubin

Introduction by Eldridge Cleaver
Designed by Quentin Fiore
Yipped by Jim Retherford
Zapped by Nancy Kurshan
Simon and Schuster   New York

Nearly everyone on this list was interviewed in detail either in person or by telephone—a handful were done by email whereby they submitted just a few short comments.

Michael Simmons	Jonah Raskin
Gil Rubin	Dana Beal
Mimi Leonard	Leni Sinclair
Bennett Samuels	James Lato
Rabbi Barton Shallat	Jim Retherford
Sheldon Greenfield	Mark Kramer
Michael Lerner	A. J. Weberman
(The "Other") Jerry Rubin	David Peel
Martin Kenner	Craig Pyes
Marilyn Milligan	Gary Van Scyoc
Barbara Gullahorn	Larry Yurdin
Stephen Smale	Gabrielle Schang
Moe Hirsch	Kathy Streem
Country Joe McDonald	Lee Weiner
Michael Ochs	Diane Rose
Ron Davis	Rona Elliot
Frank Bardacke	Suzanne Peck
Jack Kurzweil	Sharon Skolnick-Bagnoli
Nancy Kurshan	Jerrelle Kraus
John Sinclair	Roger Ressmeyer
Rex Weiner	Stuart Samuels
Robert Friedman	Jay Levin
Tom Miller	Leslie Meyers
Judy Gumbo	Tiffany Stettner
Stella Resnick	Stevanne Auerbach
Kate Coleman	Adam Ippolito
David Spaner	Steve Whitman
Jim Fouratt	Anne Weills
Ratso Sloman	Werner Erhard
Gerald Lefcourt	Robin Morgan
Paul Krassner	Bobby Seale
Lola Cohen	Daniel Ellsberg
Sam Leff	Ed Sanders
J. Michael Lennon	Todd Gitlan
Abe Peck	David Fenton
Rennie Davis	Al Goldstein
Walli Leff	

Written and Directed by Pat Thomas
with Co-conspirators:
Editor, Curator, Additional Text
and Production Assistance: Kathy Wolf
Art Direction and Book Design: Jacob Covey
Production Assistant and Transcriber: Kevin Uehlein
Research Assistant and Transcriber: Katie Westhoff
Executive Producer for the Jerry Rubin Estate: Mimi Leonard
Executive Publisher: Gary Groth
Associate Publisher: Eric Reynolds
Proofreader: Conrad Groth
Indexer and Copy Editor: Kari Pearson
Production Assistants: Pat Barrett and Beth Hetland

Fantagraphics Books
7563 Lake City Way NE
Seattle, Washington 98115

Our books may be viewed—and purchased—on our web site at fantagraphics.com, and by phone by calling 1-800-657-1100. Follow us on Twitter @fantagraphics and on Facebook at facebook.com/fantagraphics.

ISBN: 978-1-60699-892-2
Library of Congress Control Number: 2016911486
First Edition: May 2017
Printed in China

Gil and Jerry Rubin with Louise and Nancy Kurshan, Chicago, November 3, 1969.

Photograph by Richard Avedon

Copyright © The Richard Avedon Foundation

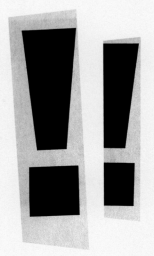

PAT THOMAS

The Author's Introduction

Jerry Rubin was a sellout. That's why you don't like him. He didn't live up to your nostalgic 1960s dream, but he couldn't live in the past. He was bored being a counterculture hero like his former comrade, Abbie Hoffman. To use a cliché, Jerry was ahead of his time. When you listen to his debates with Abbie in the 1980s, he was already speaking of a world that we take for granted today. He told a jeering audience that someday a baby boomer would be president. He spoke of environmentally conscious entrepreneurs, and about these newfangled things called computers how they might even be used for social networking! Sadly, all the audience could hear was Abbie's insistence that by wearing a tie, Jerry had sold his soul.

To see the man on a podium in 1985, wearing a Brooks Brothers suit, one would never guess that he had been the cofounder of The Yippies—one of the most radical, revolutionary organizations ever to shake the foundations of the United States government. Jerry Rubin helped invent political theater, and exhibited a brand of media savvy previously unseen by the New Left. Other anti-Vietnam War activists thought the only way to fight the system was by giving dogmatic speeches and grassroots canvassing door-to-door; they criticized him.

Yippie contact sheet © John Jekabson

Yuppie photo courtesy of Rubin Estate

Contemporary activist groups like Occupy and Pussy Riot should give Jerry his due for creating the kind of outrageous scenarios that are now their stock in trade. Jerry and his partner, Abbie Hoffman, revolutionized political activism in the 1960s. The stunts they pulled are infamous. They shut down the New York Stock Exchange by dropping dollar bills onto the floor, which traders fought over, and they turned a march on Washington into a psychedelic happening at the Pentagon in October '67. When Jerry was federally indicted as part of the Chicago 8—which includes Abbie, Tom Hayden, Rennie Davis, Lee Weiner, and Bobby Seale—for "The whole world is watching" riots that took place during the 1968 Chicago Democratic Convention, he described that moment as winning "the Academy Award of protest." He was a celebrity for actually doing something meaningful over a period of several years, rather than being instantly trumpeted via social media for doing absolutely nothing. American humor was built on Jewish humor, stretching from vaudeville to Harpo Marx to the sociopolitical Lenny Bruce. Certainly, the Yippies were part and parcel of that provocative lineage.

This is the first-ever biography of Jerry Rubin. Though Abbie Hoffman is more famous in the twenty-first century thanks to *Steal This Book*, Jerry was more ubiquitous in the twentieth—and turned up in many more books in his lifetime than Abbie ever did. Given their mutually successful partnership, which lasted three decades—both as friends and supposed enemies—it's always puzzled me that multiple Abbie biographies have failed to explore their complex relationship. It's like writing about Paul McCartney and leaving out John Lennon. In this book, Abbie is not a bit player; he's a key participant in Jerry's life. (Speaking of Lennon, longtime Beatles fans will be surprised to read the much-neglected story of Jerry's musical involvement with John & Yoko, as well as several first-person accounts of Rubin's personal rapport with the couple.) In 2012, I was given complete access to Jerry's personal archives (untouched since his death in 1994): thousands of photos, letters, journals, clippings, and diaries that spanned from the 1950s to the 1990s. Amongst the treasure trove was a March 1968 letter to the notorious mayor of Chicago, Richard J. Daley, signed by Jerry, Abbie, Paul Krassner, Jim Fouratt, and other Yippies, asking for his cooperation for a Festival of Life. (After I showed it to him, a UCLA professor exclaimed, "This should be in the Smithsonian!") There was Yoko Ono's 1972 psychological analysis of Jerry, on Apple Records stationery, and a 1969 communiqué from Eldridge Cleaver in Algeria, agreeing to write the foreword to Jerry's book *Scenarios of the Revolution*.

I crisscrossed the country, tracking down nearly a hundred people, many of whom had never been interviewed before, including Jerry's childhood friends and his brother Gil. Jerry's close relationships with Allen Ginsberg, Timothy Leary, Norman Mailer, and Phil Ochs are detailed in depth here, as is his lifelong friendship with Yippie Stew Albert, who was more important in Jerry's private life than Abbie. This is not just the story of Jerry Rubin. The voices of over seventy-five others are heard throughout—friends and comrades, lovers, and enemies. Some of these voices have been heard before: Paul Krassner, John Sinclair, Rennie Davis, Country Joe McDonald. Other voices have not been heard, including those of key women in Jerry's life: his Yippie partner Nancy Kurshan, Gestalt therapist Stella Resnick, and his wife (and partner) Mimi Leonard. Women's voices are often overlooked in histories about the turbulent '60s, so Judy Gumbo, Leni Sinclair, Kate Coleman, and others from the Free Speech Movement, Vietnam Day Committee, Yippies, White Panthers, and New Age Movement, speak their minds here.

One thing that nearly all those voices agree on: no matter who Jerry was at any given moment—Yippie, New Age enthusiast, Yuppie—it was never a put-on. He was always sincere. Jerry's arc echoed many baby boomers', but boomers often criticized him for spearheading their own trajectory. In the '60s, he was a revolutionary activist writing several books. The best known is *DO iT!*, published in 1970 as the Chicago 8 trial came to a close. (The phrase "Do it!" was co-opted decades later by Nike for their ad campaigns.) In the '70s, he was part of the "me" decade and into self-help, est, and health food. In the '80s, he was an entrepreneur and a Yuppie spokesman. He pioneered

social networking by throwing public parties to bring like-minded people together for personal and professional gain—the prototype for LinkedIn and Facebook. He shifted from fighting the military industrial complex to embracing complex vitamins. The United States was built on revolution, individualism, and capitalism—making Jerry the quintessential American.

Digging through the various obits in the Rubin Estate's archives, I was stricken by one written by Bill Kunstler, the Chicago 8's defense attorney, which appeared in the London newspaper *The Independent*, just days after Jerry's passing. It stated, in part:

Frequently, I have been asked about my reaction to Jerry Rubin's transformation from an unreconstructed rebel into a highly visible exponent of capitalist society. My response has always been the same—Jerry fully paid his dues in the 1960s and early 1970s and the fact that his life had later changed should not be allowed to detract one whit from the enormous contributions he made during the struggle to end American military involvement in Vietnam and white racism at home. In my opinion, he has more than earned, along with his perennial partner, Abbie Hoffman, a prominent place in history.

Several months before he was fatally injured, he had demonstrated that the fires that had burned in him years earlier had not been extinguished. Jerry had been incensed by a talk-show host who had urged that homeless people "should be put to death," and he brought these remarks to the attention of the Santa Monica City Council. As a result, that body wrote a scathing letter to the offending station and is now preparing to file a complaint with the Federal Communications Commission.

In the last analysis, it is difficult to gauge accurately any public figure's place in history. However, as far as Jerry Rubin is concerned, he deserves much more than a mere footnote . . . He was the epitome of youthful protest during one of the most turbulent eras of our times. Along with his sidekick, Abbie, he brought young people into the demonstrational process and inspired them to risk their lives, undergo police brutality, and jeopardize their futures in what proved to be a highly successful effort to end the war in Vietnam and eliminate overt racism in America. Now that the United States has turned to the right, his legacy may be more needed than ever before.

Jerry lived the mythological American dream: be whoever you want to be. In Jerry's case, he succeeded in both of our nation's most popular dream-myths: Revolutionary-Patriot and Entrepreneur-Capitalist. *Do it!* he cried, and he *Did it!*—like no one else had done before, or since.

Handwritten list:

Daniel Ellsberg	Bob Greenblatt
Stew Albert	Mike Smith
A. Hoff.	Kate Coleman
Nancy Kurshan	Robin Palmer
Paul Krassner	Sharon Krebs
Martin Kenner	Bobby Seale
Bob Fitch	Mark Scheer
Mario Savio	Marvin Garson
Anita Hoffman	Bob Fass
Ken Kelley	Barbara Gullahorn
Steve Smale	Abe Peck
Moe Hirsch	Ed Sanders
Tim Leary	Keith Lampe
Eldridge Cleaver	Bob Scheer
Tom Hayden	Steve Weisman
Rennie Davis	Jack Weinberg
Dave Dellinger	Bee Axelrod
Tom Forcade	Allen Ginsberg
Judy Gumbo	Bella Abzug
Bob Cirese	Lee Weiner
Fred Halstead	Peter Camejo

LOVE LETTER TO JERRY RUBIN

Who, if they were sane, would care?
Only a century of Egyptian slaves
    could get your raving skull to comb out straight,
    strand parallel to strand,
    in some geometrical mummy helmet of utter neatness.
    "Face it, baby," as Janis Joplin whispered to a mirror,
    "you've got ratty hair."
And what other perennial nonstudent has
--made free speech popular, filthy, and worth enjoying
--blocked troop trains like a wised-up Tonto
--poured ketchup on General Taylor
    to the accompaniment of elevator Muzak
--run for mayor to reaffirm (too close for comfort)
    his absolute unelectability
--flaunted burning money in the faces of outmoded leftists
--stripped naked to deliver speeches he double-talked
    silent and clothed
    from the back row of a lecture hall
--worn Minuteman silk breeches and the battle dress
    of the American Revolution
    to the same televised third-degree
    that set liberals once to slitting each
    other's throats in public
    like true-to-form thieves gloating over
    a treasure chest of newly minted guilt
--taught teenyboppers for free that the
    pop bottle at their Lolita lips
    can also be fun for throwing,
    give or take a good target and a little gasoline
--climbed a wall like Batman
    during the Battle of Morningside Heights
    to infiltrate the Mathematics Building commune
    hours before the police bust--only to freak out
    even those students with his impolite contempt for property.
Who else praises sheer laziness and joy,
    yet can never be found at rest and always remembers
    to be a little worried for his brothers;
who else rejects the joyless masochism of prison terms
    yet looks through bars so frequently
    you might as well
    write him in care of
    America's jails.

Who, if it were true and they humane, would mind?
For no detail can be beaten thin enough
    to cover the mere facts
    that make legends out of heroes and vice versa.

OPPOSITE: In the 1990s, Jerry made a list of the important people in his life during the 1960s.

THIS PAGE: Anonymous love letter to Jerry, circa 1970; Yuppie as Revolutionary image from The Realist.

DID IT!

norman lear

May 23, 1972

Dear Jerry,

Thank you for your wonderful, warm note
regarding ALL IN THE FAMILY. If it's
half as good as you say it is, I'm very
pleased indeed.

We have talked about your notion
regarding an appearance as "a real live
activist", and if the need arises, you
can be sure we'll keep it in mind.

Meanwhile, I wanted you to know how much
we all appreciated hearing from you.

Sincerely,

Mr. Jerry Rubin
Apartment 1D
156 Prince Stree
New York, New Y

Mr. Jerry Rubin
Apartment 1D
156 Prince Street
New York, New York 10012

Live From New York, It's Saturday Night!

On October 18, 1975, Jerry appeared as "himself" in a comedic sketch in the second episode of *Saturday Night Live's* debut season. Paul Simon, who brought Art Garfunkel on to sing duets of "The Boxer" and "Scarborough Fair," hosted the show. Here's a play-by-play of the skit. It's a fake TV commercial for decorative home wallpaper, featuring iconic protest slogans of the '60s. Dylan's "Blowing in the Wind" plays in the background, as Jerry stands in front of red-brick wallpaper covered in yellow spray-painted graffiti with slogans. **AVENGE ATTICA; SMASH THE STATE; WHITE PANTHERS; ON TO CHICAGO; OFF THE PIG!; BLACK POWER; BURN BABY BURN.**

"Hi, I'm former Yippie leader Jerry Rubin, and I lived those years with you burning draft cards, liberating the administration building, and, of course, scrawling revolutionary slogans on the walls in spray paint. Now, the Berkeley Collection has captured those colorful years, and the graffiti that tells it like it was, on these pre-trimmed, pre-pasted rolls of durable decorator-approved wallpaper, perfect for your den or recreation area. Join me in a protest march down Memory Lane, with the pattern we call 'The Dissident.'"

The camera cuts to the slogans listed above.

"Too heavy for you? I understand. Perhaps 'The Peacemaker' is more your bag." Jerry unrolls a new pattern of orange-on-green wallpaper accompanied by John Lennon's "Give Peace a Chance." The slogans include: **SNOOPY FOR PRESIDENT; THE MAN CAN'T BUST OUR MUSIC; HELL NO, WE WON'T GO; GIRLS SAY YES TO BOYS WHO SAY NO; DRAFT BEER, NOT STUDENTS; MAKE LOVE, NOT WAR!**

"But no matter where your head is at, being free turns everyone on, right? That's why we chose this fit-any-mood freedom motif for our borders and trim. We call it 'The Digger.'" Jerry unrolls yet another wallpaper pattern. Puce on a pink background, while an instrumental version of "Born Free" plays. The slogans include: **FREE ERIKA HUGGINS; FREE JOHN SINCLAIR; FREE THE PANTHERS!; FREE BOBBY SEALE; FREE LOVE; FREE ANGELA DAVIS; FREE THE CHICAGO 8** (with 8 crossed out and replaced by 7).

Out of nowhere, yellow paint splatters across the wallpaper that Jerry's holding. An anonymous hand appears, holding a white rag, cleaning off the mess. "Oops! No hassle! This wallpaper is vinyl-acrylic-coated, to make it scuff and stain resistant. Wipes clean with a damp cloth. Isn't this out of sight? So take it from me, Jerry Rubin, when I say [*raising his fist in a militant power salute*]: 'Up against the wallpaper, [bleep]!'"

MICHAEL SIMMONS, MUSICIAN/JOURNALIST: The concept of the *SNL* piece recalls the Bob Dylan parody by Christopher Guest on the 1972 *National Lampoon* LP, *Radio Dinner*. Michael O'Donoghue cowrote the *Lampoon* album, and was head writer at SNL early on, so the Rubin parody was probably O'Donoghue recycling himself. I know he was close to Abbie, and got him to pose for the cover of the *Lampoon* (wearing the American flag shirt of *Merv Griffin Show* infamy) during the magazine's first year [October 1970] surrounded by Nixon and Agnew puppets.

Writer Anne Beatts, who was living with O'Donoghue then, confirms that he "came up with the concept of 'Off the Wallpaper,' and then filled in the blanks. Getting Jerry to do it was icing on the cake but the joke came first, as I well remember."

On Sunday, February 15, 2015, NBC broadcast a three-hour primetime special celebrating *SNL's* fortieth anniversary. The show combined new comedic routines with snippets culled from hundreds of previous sketches. Of the countless things that they could have chosen, it was surprising to see that they still consider Jerry relevant, with a funny (yet tasteful) joke about his death, which originally ran the week he died in 1994. "Weekend Update" newscaster Norm Macdonald said, "*YIPPIE!* Jerry Rubin died this week . . . Oh sorry, that's 'Yippie Jerry Rubin.'"

All in the Family. The *SNL* episode was Jerry's only television appearance as a scripted comedic actor, but in spring 1971, the enterprising Rubin penned a letter to producer Norman Lear. The first season of *All in the Family* had just made its debut. Jerry suggested that he appear as "a real live activist" (i.e., as himself). Given Archie Bunker and Meathead's bickering over controversial politics, Jerry's idea was inspired. Although Norman's response is dated May 23, 1972, the postmark on the envelope is May 24, 1971, which is more likely and informs Lear's tone (as the first season had just ended). Though it became one of the most talked-about shows of the decade, initial response was lukewarm.

"My life's nothing. All I do is entertain drunken conventioneers in Las Vegas. At least you are trying to change the world."
— *WOODY ALLEN, SPEAKING TO JERRY CIRCA 1970*

Woody Allen. In the 1971 film *Bananas*, Woody Allen plays a Latin American revolutionary who is arrested and put on trial in the United States. The judge orders him to be bound and gagged. Woody's character is conducting his own defense, so he has to cross-examine witnesses by mumbling through the gag, leading to some hilarious onscreen moments. It's obviously inspired by Judge Hoffman's gagging of Bobby Seale during the Chicago trial. The year after, Jerry's daily calendar lists several meetings with Allen at the former's Manhattan residence. My guess is that they were discussing the McGovern campaign, since Allen participated in that. In interviews, Allen said he was a liberal Democrat against the Vietnam War.

The 112th Congress. After all these years, Jerry and the Yippies are still referenced on popular television shows. In 2012, during the third episode of HBO's dramatic series *The Newsroom*, Sam Waterston's character (Charlie Skinner), the old-school producer of a current-day news show, is debating the Tea Party with his younger anchorman Will McAvoy (played by Jeff Daniels), when the conversation turns to this:

Will McAvoy: Back in 1968, when Rennie Davis and Hayden and their guys organized the SDS, it was specifically to end the Vietnam War, but that movement got eaten by Abbie Hoffman and Jerry Rubin and the Yippies.

Charlie Skinner: Hoffman and Rubin were a lot more charismatic [than the Tea Party].

Will McAvoy: Yeah, but it was impossible to define what the Yippies were protesting! They were about giving the finger to anyone over thirty, generically hating the American establishment, dropping out and getting high.

Charlie Skinner: And?

Will McAvoy: That's how the Progressive Movement would be painted for the next forty years: people passing out daisies to soldiers and trying to levitate The Pentagon.

Charlie Skinner: I was there, that damn near worked!

Will McAvoy: No it didn't. The Pentagon is a really big building. You can't levitate it.

NEW YORK POST

SATURDAY, JUNE 25, 1983

PAGE SIX

Rubin's right in the thin of it

IF it's trendy, you can be sure Yippie-turned-Wall Street broker-turned public relations entrepreneur Jerry Rubin will try to cash in on it. Latest object of Rubin's seemingly inexhaustible enthusiasm: fat, and how to get rid of it. The battle of the bulge has brought together ex-Yippie Rubin with Monty Hall, whom you'll remember from his days greeting people dressed as pickles and ketchup bottles when he was host of the TV game show *Let's Make a Deal*. Jerry and Monty have cooked up a program for marketing a line of diet products developed by a California-based nutrition company under the label, the Genesis Program. The slimming stuff, said to be similar to the popular Cambridge Diet, will be sold through Rubin's "Networking" salons, those weekly gatherings at Studio 54 where young urban professionals trade business cards and phone numbers. Says Jerry: "I tasted the food [diet drinks, candy bars and six low-cal 'gourmet' meals] and I decided that I'd discovered something with tremendous potential for serving people and making money." Diet edibles aren't Jerry's only new road to low-fat bucks. He'll also offer exercise tapes "a la Jane Fonda" and "behavior modification instruction tapes" narrated by Monty Hall.

For information on private seminars on this fantastic business opportunity call: 245-6555

Mother Simpson. In 1995, in the eighth episode of *The Simpson's* seventh season, Homer's mother Mona shows up (having been absent from all the previous episodes thus far). She's been underground since 1969, when she helped bomb Mr. Burns's germ warfare lab in the town of Springfield. The character is loosely based on Bernadine Dohrn, and voiced by Glenn Close. At one point she's shown reading a copy of *Steal This Book*. She's resurfaced after all these years. Marge says, "Sorry I misjudged you, Ma. You had to leave to protect your family."

Lisa Simpson chimes in. "How'd you survive?"

Mona replies: "Oh, I had help from my friends in the Underground, Jerry Rubin gave me a job marketing his line of health shakes. I proofread Bobby Seale's cookbook, and I ran credit checks at Tom Hayden's Porsche dealership."

Godard & Rosset. Rubin has been portrayed by actors in docudramas as well as appearing in documentaries himself. The oddest movie is a 1971 Jean-Luc Godard film titled *Vladimir and Rosa*, which is a "fictionalized rendering of the Chicago 8 Trial." If that wasn't strange enough, the film was recut by Barney Rosset (of Grove Press and *Evergreen Review*) with the insertion of real-life footage of Jerry and Abbie mocking the film then re-released as *Vladimir and Rosa and Jerry and Abbie*.

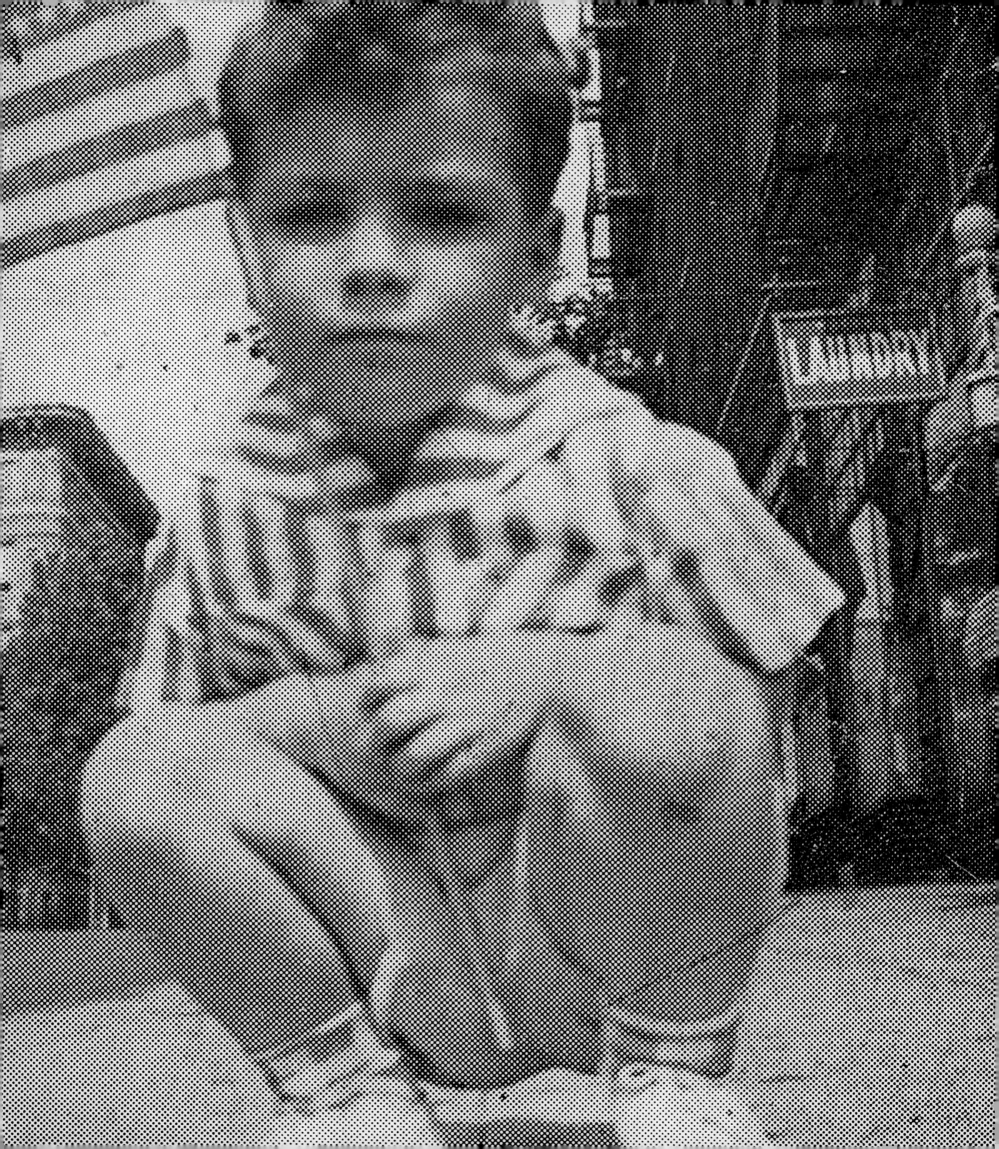

From Kiev to Kentucky: Esther Meets Bob.

In 1902, a family of Russian Jews named Katz left Kiev and emigrated to Kentucky. They opened a dry goods store in Covington—right across the river from Cincinnati. Over time, they had four sons and one daughter named Esther, born in 1908. As was the custom back then, the sons married young and assimilated into the family business. Esther remained unmarried. Considered an "old maid" at twenty-eight, her parents sent her to Florida in hopes she'd meet a nice lawyer or doctor. Instead, she met and fell in love with a grocery store clerk named Robert Reuben. Robert was born in 1911, and was raised in the Bronx.

Like Esther, Robert's family had Russian roots and had recently changed their name from "Reuben" to "Rubin" around the time that "Bob" (as he was known to most people) met Esther. They married in Jacksonville, Florida, in January 1936, and moved back to Cincinnati to be closer to Esther's family.

Growing Up

Life with the In-Laws. Esther's parents—instead of being thrilled that Esther was no longer a spinster—felt strongly that Bob wasn't good enough for their daughter. Living under the same roof as his in-laws, Bob was made aware of their opinion on a daily basis. This put a damper on the young newlyweds, but on July 14, 1938, the couple gave birth to Jerry Clyde Rubin. It was the perfect birthdate for the future revolutionary—the 149th anniversary of the French Revolution, which began with the storming of the Bastille.

Unlike his grandparents, Jerry's parents were strictly working class. After serving in WWII, Bob began driving a delivery truck for a bakery and Esther worked as a secretary. Esther's four brothers ribbed Bob with their own ethnic in-jokes and wisecracks, which often went over the head of the "earnest bakery driver from New York" (as was told to Milton Viorst).

Jerry recalled to J. Anthony Lukas that perhaps his "father may have seemed a little threatening—the Katz side of the family always had this feeling of kind of being on the edge, that they hadn't really been accepted into America, that only when they had money and a big house and a big bank account and good ties would they be accepted. They were always afraid of scandals, of being embarrassed." They were concerned that Bob Rubin would embarrass them by becoming a financial burden.

With the birth of Jerry's brother Gil in November 1947, there were now four mouths to feed. Esther's brothers suggested that Esther, Bob, and their two kids move in with their aging parents, who were in need of constant care. This handshake arrangement called for the Rubins to inherit whatever money was left when the parents died in exchange for caretaking. Esther looked forward to spending more time with her family; Bob felt emasculated. While his wife doted on her father, Bob had to contend with his disapproval around the clock.

They shared a two-story house in a Jewish section of Cincinnati known as Avondale. Whenever Esther's brothers would visit, Jerry's dad would camp out on the second floor knowing that he was the black sheep. Meanwhile, Bob's working week was tough, six days a week; he had to leave the house by 4 a.m. for the morning delivery route. With the route completed by noon, he returned home to relax. After dinner, he retired early.

Many of the tactics I now use I learned at home.

—Jerry Rubin

Raising a Rebel. In 1970, Jerry told J. Anthony Lukas that he felt his parents

had total dedication to me. And that's kind of a key as to why I could become so rebellious. My father would put his foot down. He'd punish me—turn me over his knee or even slug me. But he didn't really mean it. I knew they loved me so much that if I cried, I'd get my way. If I screamed, I'd get my way. If I insisted, I'd get my way. It was really total toleration, total permissiveness. Many of the tactics I now use I learned at home. I learned just how far to push before you got totally wiped out. I learned how to play one parent off against the other, because my mother didn't approve of some of my father's methods. Living in that home was like an education in psychological warfare. I'm really convinced that the whole of my recent activity in the movement has been a playing out on a massive political scale of the things I learned in the family.

Jerry's aunt Mildred recalled, "I remember once when Jerry was little, he lay down in the street and kicked his heels, saying he wouldn't go any farther. Maybe the first sit-in."

While Jerry was surrounded by Jewish customs during his formative years, he mostly ignored them. His parents were not Orthodox, and they silently supported his religious ambivalence. In contrast, Jerry's grandfather tried to force Orthodox Judaism on him. According to Gil, their grandfather "didn't answer the phone on the Sabbath, kept a kosher table, and warned Jerry not to marry a shiksa!" Recalling all the Saturdays his grandfather made him to go to temple, Jerry said "All those old men shaking their gray heads under their yarmulkes, I hated it. I became a Communist right then!"

Jerry's mother was the only one in the Katz bloodline to graduate from college. She had attended the University of Cincinnati and loved to read and play the piano. She and Jerry enjoyed "deep conversations," and he credited her for "the gentle side of me, the intellectual side." But he was dismissive of her vulnerability and loyalty to her family, which allowed her to live with her parents.

GIL RUBIN: My mother was well read, there were always books around the house . . . and she was always reading on the couch, and that was unusual to see a housewife doing that.

He credited his father's strong personality for his own rebellious nature; Jerry described himself as a "bratty, rebellious, screaming kid."

GIL RUBIN: I remember we weren't the kind of family that had dinner around the dinner table; there really wasn't a lot of room in our apartment for a dinner table. And it was a pretty volatile group, between my brother and my father; they were both very strong people . . . it's funny because there would be arguments that were so loud that my uncle who lived four doors down the next day would come by and say, "Wow, that was some argument between Jerry and Bob last night." I spent much of my growing-up years underneath the bed, just hiding.

MIMI LEONARD [WHO WAS MARRIED TO JERRY]: Jerry had a few funny stories about his parents, and one of them was that around the dinner table at night, the one surefire question that would bring a pause and great attention to the group would be, "But is it good for the Jews?" So every political discussion somehow evolved into that question. And so we would occasionally joke around, and say, "But is it good for the Jews?" even if we were having an unrelated political conversation, just because it was funny.

Even as a preteen, Rubin was conscious of racism and injustice. When a black family moved into his neighborhood, he saw the difference in his upper-middle-class relatives' and his more tolerant, working-class parents' attitudes. Eventually the Rubins moved out, away from Esther's oppressive parents. Jerry recalled those years as happy ones, "because his father finally felt like a master in his own home." From around the age of nine until he was fourteen, Jerry and his father bonded over sports. Bob founded a Boosters Club for the city's hockey team, jumping up and down in his seat to cheer them on. Jerry was a typical 1950s All-American Boy who loved baseball. He attended local games when he could, listened on the radio when he couldn't, collected baseball cards, and read the sports section of the paper.

When Jerry was a teenager, his grandmother suffered a stroke, and the Rubins were obliged to live under the Katzses' roof again to care for her and her husband. Again, Jerry felt the class differences between him and his Katz cousins—who "had better cars, they had better furniture, and they went to better restaurants." Arguably, this could be the seed of both Jerry's Yippie and Yuppie years. Rebelling against the upper classes as a youth (typical, whether you come from money or not), then wanting a better standard of living later in life— most people do. As several of his friends pointed out, even Abbie Hoffman, Jerry's future Yippie cohort, secretly consulted investment advisors later in his life.

High School.

Jerry's insecurity and ambition heightened during his high school years, where he found himself surrounded by rich kids in an upper-class high school. In 1970 Jerry remembered, "I came from the lesser part of town. They were just richer and there was like an inferiority relationship there. I had to prove myself."

BENNETT SAMUELS, HIGH SCHOOL FRIEND: We went to Walnut Hills High School, which was a college preparatory school. The people that went to our school were James Levine, from the New York Metropolitan Opera, and way back, Miller Huggins, who managed the New York Yankees, when Lou Gehrig and Babe Ruth were there. Some physician that won the Nobel Prize for medicine, and we had Jerry Rubin.

When we had our twenty-fifth reunion at Walnut Hill, he wasn't invited. They voted not to invite him, because it would have created too much of a conflict—first of all, nobody liked his ideas or wanted him there. They felt with the police, the security, they didn't want the attention. But at the fiftieth reunion, that's all they talked about, was Jerry Rubin as a great hero. Everything was about Jerry as one of the great people of the class.

— RABBI BARTON SHALLAT, HIGH SCHOOL FRIEND

The *Chatterbox*: Jerry Rubin, Cub Reporter.

Jerry began to make his mark via the weekly student newspaper, the *Chatterbox*. He covered sports and quickly rose through the ranks to become the paper's sports reporter. By his junior year, he became sports editor, a position usually held by a senior. Jerry began branching out, covering the news and even writing the occasional gossip column. In his senior year, he became co-editor of the *Chatterbox*—dwarfing the efforts of his fellow editor and most of the other writers. He was known amongst the staff as "a perfectionist, a taskmaster, a bug on accuracy and details." "He could be terribly intolerant of somebody who wasn't as good as he was," Alexander Gleason, the paper's faculty adviser, remembered two decades later. But as Gleason also pointed out, "Mind you, he was good. He'd been elected on the basis of his drive, his devotion to the paper and his sheer professionalism. He bought the *New York Times* style book and made people conform to that."

BENNETT SAMUELS: As the editor of *The Chatterbox* he did exposés, which got him in a lot of trouble. I remember one of them. One day, he had done an exposé of the general manager of a local TV station, and a young lady who was on another show over there. There weren't any punches thrown, but he was so angry that Jerry had written this hot story. His stories would also be on the front page of the Post, when he was still in high school. He had some people threaten him. But, he was fearless. He wasn't scared of them.

RABBI BARTON SHALLAT: He was an agent provocateur; he could get you red-faced and agitated immediately. That was his skill; he knew how to get his name in papers at all times, whether he was right-wing or left-wing or whatever he was doing.

A sign of what was to come was Jerry's provocative op-ed piece on frats. The high school had "social clubs," and he had succumbed to joining Sigma Delta Chi (the best Jewish fraternity on campus). Yet, he strongly opposed the concept and began to editorialize against it. He wrote, "Most of the clubs segregate and discriminate by race and religion. They teach their members to live only with the same general type of person. Through this type of discrimination, the social club becomes the breeding ground for prejudice and discrimination on a larger scale." In 1950s Middle America, this was controversial. He struck back with a second editorial. "The social club's traditions are not valuable but detrimental when they prohibit clear thinking and obstruct the establishment of new, constructive customs."

SHELDON "SHELLEY" GREENFIELD, HIGH SCHOOL FRIEND: Yeah, you know how high schools work. There were fraternities, and all the Jewish guys stuck together, and all that. And he wasn't really part of that . . . He wore a funny bowtie, because some columnist wore a bowtie.

FIRST ARTICLE

FIRST BY-LINE

And Jerry had sort of this hallmark bowtie that he wore all the time. Yet, nobody else wore a bowtie but him.

But Jerry was still light-years away from letting his freak flag fly. He struggled to fit in with the upper-class kids and his rebellion came in the form of an earnest belief in not only his abilities as a journalist, but the idea that what he was writing about was truly important. There lies a thread that continued throughout his entire life. Jerry was as dead serious in his disgust of the Vietnam War in 1968 as he was positively excited about pushing vitamin-infused drinks in the early 1990s. In all of his incarnations, he was too enthusiastic to be a charlatan. He must have been sincere: he just wasn't that good of an actor.

——————

Freshmen Defeat West Hi, 19-12

Bill Sprinkle, Al Wolf, and George Stivers exploded behind the crisp, vigorous blocking of Walnut Hills' resolute Frosh, for scores last Thursday, as the Eagles bounced back into the victory column by paddling the Big Maroons from Western Hills, 19-12.

After a fast exchange of punts, James Lloyd recovered a Western Hills fumble and carried it to the one yard stripe. From there Bill Sprinkle went over. The try for point was successful and the resolute Walnut Hills freshmen led 7-0.

Promptly after the second quarter was touched off the Big Maroons from Western Hills took possession on the 13 and a pass play from Smith to Moss netted the tally. The try for point was futile and the Eagles held grimly to a 7-6 lead.

The spark of the second Eagle score was ignited in the middle of the third period of play. Jim Dearworth intercepted a Maroon pass, returned it to the 22 where Al Wolf took advantage of his openings and plunged over. The point was not made and our Frosh now led 13-6.

Their third and last score was tallied by George Stivers, who reeled off ten yards to pay dirt. Two other scores by Al Wolf and Jim Lloyd were called back because of Eagle penalties. Westerns' final marker came via the pass route, Smith to Huff.

THE CHATTERBOX

Frosh Tie Purcell To Close Season

By Jerry Rubin

Lulled to sleep for three quarters by the freshman of Walnut Hills, mighty Purcell woke up in the nick of time last Thursday, as they struck from far midfield for a last-minute touchdown and changed almost-certain defeat into a 6-6 tie.

With only 30 seconds remaining, and an Eagle victory almost seemingly in the bag, Bob Meyer, hard running Cavalier back, spurned the Eagle's last hope for victory by churning seven yards around right end into touchdown territory.

Al Wolf Sparks Drive

This play climaxed a well-battled defensive game between two explosive lines. For Walnut Hills it was Al Wolf in the driver's seat, forever pecking away at Purcell's weak right side, while the ultimate star, Bob Meyer provided the chief means of offensive transportation for Purcell.

The Eagles drew first blood. About midway through the first period, Bill Sprinkle climaxed a 35 yard drive by plunging over from the two. The all-important point after touchdown was futile and the Eagle led 6-0.

Meyer Scores For Purcell

From there till the fatal fourth period it was a see-saw battle. At the start of the final quarter Walnut Hills developed a very bad case of "fumblitis" and the Cavaliers from Purcell took possession on the Eagle forty yard

5 in 55: Dad Runs for the Teamsters.

Meanwhile, a significant change in his father's career would inspire the future activist. Bob ran for Secretary-Treasurer of Teamsters Local 114, the Cincinnati Bakery Drivers union. When he returned home for school in the evening, Jerry would overhear cold calls: "Hello, I'm Bob Rubin. You don't know me, but I'd like you to vote for me." He even had a slogan, "5 in '55," which meant that in 1955, the following year, he was determined to reduce the driver's six-day workweek to five. His father's victory was not only a boost to family morale; Bob traded in a predawn workday and a driver's uniform for a suit and a tie, higher salary, a new car, and a 9 a.m. start time. Even at the height of his antiestablishment, Yippie phase, Jerry never thought that his father had succumbed to middle-class values; rather, he said he was "a real crusader, out there battling for the working man." (Subconsciously, Rubin also learned the effects of donning a suit—but that would come decades later.)

When Bob Rubin was still delivering bread, he'd get out of his truck and have a friendly word with his customers. When he became a union leader, he never thought he was any better than any of the drivers. Jerry felt that he inherited his father's gregarious nature and egalitarian principles.

Hoffa, Nixon, and Lenny Bruce: Jerry Seeks Out Fame.

RABBI BARTON SHALLAT: Bennett was driving. Jerry was in the middle. I was on Jerry's right. And suddenly, Jerry, as a joke, puts his foot on Bennett's gas pedal, so the car is now speeding, and then he said, "Oh, what if we died? Who would get the biggest eulogy?" He said, "Bennett, you're a country music singer, you'll get a little bit." He said to me, "Bart, you'll get nothing. But I will get the biggest obituary." I said, "Jerry, I don't care who gets the biggest. I just want to be the one reading it." He thought that was funny. The day he died in California, I got a call from Bennett and he said, "Well, I guess Jerry won. Jerry got the biggest."

Jerry's lifelong, minor obsession with famous people became evident when he was a teenager. Jerry was enamored with Lenny Bruce, a standup comedian known for his edgy sociopolitical material and for pushing against conventional boundaries. Heroin use resulted in his death in 1966 at age forty-one, after years of arrests for obscenity charges and police harassment. Jerry listened to Bruce during his Yippie years, to amp up before speaking to large crowds and to emulate his outrageousness.

Jerry Rubin Interviews Adlai; Story Circulates Nationally

Jerry Rubin, former CHAT-TERBOX editor, is shown interviewing Governor Robert Meyner who recently married Helen Stevenson, cousin of Adlai Stevenson.

by Burt Davis

Jerry Rubin, co-editor of the 1955-56 CHATTERBOX, and now a reporter for Oberlin College, recently secured an interview with Adlai Stevenson.

Mr. Stevenson was in Oberlin, Ohio to attend the marriage of his distant cousin, Miss Helen Stevenson, to Governor Robert B. Meyner of New Jersey.

When Mr. Stevenson arrived in Oberlin, Jerry requested an interview, and the former presidential candidate invited him to his apartment the next day. The

"Other reporters looked on shyly but Adlai didn't recognize them."

On another occasion Jerry discovered to his dismay that the world of journalism very often is more concerned with selling papers than quoting accurately.

When one of Jerry's statements was misconstrued by the United Press city editor, Jerry questioned him about it, only to receive the curt reply, "What do you care? You're the biggest writer in the country right now and we're selling papers!"

SHELDON GREENFIELD: He was always trying to convert me, to be more radical. That got worse, and we ended up having a split. But during that time, he had me go down to the Cincinnati Music Hall, when Jimmy Hoffa came. And his father was, you know, in the union. So, Jerry dragged me down there. One night, Jerry and I drove up to Dayton, Ohio, to see comedian Lenny Bruce. Lenny was heavily drugged that night, but anyway, we sat in the front row. Because Jerry had turned hard against the society that he grew up in as well as society in general. And of course, Lenny was part of that. He was part of that rebelliousness of social criticism.

In his book *Growing (Up) at 37*, Jerry Rubin wrote, "I fell in love with Lenny and went to see him again the following night. Someday, I told myself, I would be like Lenny Bruce, speaking out the truth about our society."

GIL RUBIN: I remember being inside Cincinnati Gardens with my brother, on the floor. And Nixon is walking down the center and we're on the aisle. And Jerry said, "Shake his hand! Shake his hand!" And this hand actually shook Richard Nixon's hand.

BENNETT SAMUELS: In the early '70s, I went to meet him at the Cincinnati airport, and just as we're walking into the terminal from the runway, the announcer said, "Mr. Jerry Rubin, pick up the red courtesy phone," or something like that. And I said, "what's going on?" Jerry says, "Wherever I go, I have myself paged, so they'll call out my name—that way everyone knows I'm in town!"

Jerry Lands *Cincinnati Post* Job: The Adlai Stevenson Years.

Just weeks after he graduated from high school, Rubin began working for the *Cincinnati Post* covering sporting events and running errands. When autumn came, he enrolled at Oberlin College. He remained at Oberlin for just one semester, transferring to the University of Cincinnati when the *Post* offered him a full-time reporting gig. In January 1957, just before Rubin left Oberlin, he cornered Adlai Stevenson in a hotel lobby, who was visiting the college town for a wedding. Stevenson invited Rubin to meet him for breakfast; Rubin had ambitiously prearranged to have the interview published in a Cleveland paper. Stevenson had captured his attention during his 1952 presidential campaign. Rubin said, "I just happened to turn on the TV and there was Adlai giving the introductory address to the Chicago convention. I don't think I even knew who he was then. He was a real dark horse and I was just fourteen years old. But, wow, I fell in love with him. He was so funny!" *[Author's Note: Jerry fails to mention that Stevenson was addressing the 1952 Democratic delegates in the same International Amphitheatre building that the 1968 events were held. Talk about foreshadowing.]*

This was the very beginning of a politically charged Jerry. Despite his love of baseball, he created a serious rift with his uncles when one afternoon, he switched the TV in the living room from a ball game to a Stevenson speech. Unwittingly, Jerry had just instigated his first protest riot regarding a Democratic presidential campaign. Years later, Jerry remembered, "I was a Stevenson fan, like I was a Cincinnati Reds fan. When I root for something, I'm always very dogmatic and very total about it."

The *Post* editors loved Jerry's zeal and writing style. Now back in his hometown, Jerry began socializing with the team's general manager's son; he learned that business decisions were the driving force behind the team, not the heroics of the ballplayers. Disillusioned, Rubin sought out other assignments at the paper.

His opportunity to move up (or least sideways) came with the offer to be the *Post's* youth editor. At the age of nineteen, he'd be part of the editorial staff—co-writing and managing a two-page section of the paper on Wednesdays. He also got his own Friday column,

> *I'd take guys and, with fancy paragraphs, I'd romanticize them out of all recognition. The kids used to call it "the Rubin treatment."*
> —JERRY RUBIN

"Campus Capers," in which he'd cover high school and college events, including his own. Jerry wrote profiles of local radio DJ's, puff pieces on recent high school grads, and even dating advice. Keep in mind that this was still fresh-faced 1950s "Leave it to Beaver" America; Jerry was not commenting on the nationwide school-integration debates concerning Little Rock, Arkansas for example.

Jerry was now a local celebrity, and his father was particularly proud of him. Most admirable was his work ethic; Jerry worked forty hours a week at the paper and carried a full class load at the college. He was Doing It! Several years before Marshall McLuhan coined the phrase, Jerry learned "the medium is the message"—as a journalist, he "learned that the guy who writes the story makes the story. The guy being interviewed is just a hapless subject. I'd take guys and with a fancy paragraph, I'd romanticize them out of all recognition. The kids used to call it 'the Rubin treatment.'" Later, as a political activist, he turned it around, using those "same tools to manipulate the media. I know what the media wants. I know the little things they need to blow something up all out of proportion."

Jerry realized that just about everyone else at the paper had long since burned out. Since he was living at home and could slide by, he let his paychecks stack up on the payroll desk for weeks on end—and delighted in the look of horror on some guy's face who noticed "this punk kid who's not doing it for the money." Jerry's roots were working class—he wasn't mocking his coworkers' need to pay the bills with that stunt, but it bothered him that they didn't share his sense of purpose. He noticed one lunch break that everyone seemed alive, only assuming a sullen, dead look when they returned to their desks.

It hit Jerry that they were simply hired help. He recalled in the book *Don't Shoot—We Are Your Children!*, "I didn't have to be Karl Marx to figure that out. If people feel part of something, if their ego's involved, then they'll really enjoy it. This really radicalized me. I can remember telling people it would be better if we all owned the paper, all shared in the money, and elected a city editor." His co-workers' response: "What are you? Some kind of Commie!?!"

DADDY AND GIL: DID YOU GET MY 3-LETTERS-IN-ONE? NOW RIDING BUS FOR AIRPORT TO PARIS: GETTING LAST LOOK AT SMALL HOUSES AND CROWDED LONDON STREETS WITH TWO-LANE SIDEWALKS— ONE FOR BIKES! YESTERDAY TOOK TOUR TO SEE CASTLES OF 18th-19th CENT. KINGS. STAY HERE VERY SUCCESSFUL, MADE GOOD FRIENDS OF SPANIARD AND ENGLISHMAN. EVERYONE ON THIS BUS IS SPEAKING FRENCH. DAD! THINKING OF HOME VERY MUCH, AND WAITING TO ARRIVE IN INDIA TO HEAR FROM YOU. JERRY

DADDY AND GIL RUDIN, 1816 CATALINA AVENUE, CINCINNATI 37, OHIO, U.S.A.

Orphaned in India: Jerry Loses His Parents.

In the spring of 1960, Jerry heard that UC Berkeley students were battling police over the actions of the House Un-American Activities Committee. HUAC was a congressional watchdog that routinely subpoenaed those across the nation who they deemed "Un-American." Although they normally operated out of the House of Representatives in Washington DC, they were then in the San Francisco Bay Area conducting hearings. Inspired by the rumblings of student protest, Jerry quit the paper, despite his promising career. He jumped into the summer program at the University of Cincinnati and kept the pace up when fall classes began.

In *Growing (Up) at 37*, Jerry wrote: "I was twenty-one, lost and confused, bored at being a newspaperman. There was a more direct way if you wanted to be near the news: Berkeley! It would take me five years to get there, but the minute I heard that radio report I decided I would go to Berkeley and help create events that would become radio headlines in between Chuck Berry and Elvis Presley, headlines that would inspire other people like me locked up in the prison of no choice."

Jerry on his way to India, 1962.

During this time, both of his grandparents passed away, followed by the death of his mother on August 3, 1960. She was in her early fifties. His brother Gil told me in 2014, "We think she had colon cancer that metastasized to the liver, but she was never told she had cancer as that was commonplace at the time. She thought she had hepatitis."

Many years later, Jerry wrote: "Every time I move into a yoga position, such as the shoulder stand, some part of my unconscious recalls the image of my mother dying of cancer at fifty-one. For two years, I went to the hospital every day and sat next to her bed, doing my college homework. To the end she believed she had hepatitis and would recover, even though she kept getting weaker and losing

"Our house in Jerusalem."

weight; pound by pound, death ate her up. Her pain was so great that I found myself praying for her die."

With his undergrad degree nearly completed, Jerry focused on his future. He considered going to grad school before settling on a scholarship to India, at the University of Lucknow, where he would focus on political science and writing. In June of '61, Jerry left for India, making stops in several European countries along the way. He got as far as a West Berlin youth hostel when he received a message from the American consulate to return home immediately. On July 2, 1961, his father, Robert, died due to coronary occlusion and coronary sclerosis. Jerry knew that his father had a heart condition, but his desire to make something of himself won out. "I had to lead my own life, I wasn't going to wait around until he died."

Jerry Fights for Custody of Gil. Thus began a family battle as to who would raise his brother Gil, who was a few months' shy of his fourteenth birthday. Although his uncles wanted him, Jerry wanted to keep Gil away from the anti-Rubin Katz family. Luckily there was some family money left in reserve. Jerry decided he'd try the political science graduate program at the University of Cincinnati, and enrolled Gil into his high school alma mater, Walnut Hills.

After his brief taste of Europe, Cincinnati felt incredibly provincial. It didn't help that he'd lost both parents within a year, and his grandparents just before that. Plus, there were now just two Rubins sequestered amongst all those Katzes. Another "Katz" (no relation) controlled his parent's trust; he gave Jerry grief about how to raise his younger brother. Jerry wanted to bring Gil to India, but attorney Al Katz wouldn't budge on paying out the money for that adventure.

GIL RUBIN: I'm sort of this green, moldable thing that now Jerry can test some of his ideas on. Wasn't there this educational thing called Summer Hill at that point? And so I heard my father die in his bedroom, I found him deceased, and so I'm telling Jerry that I'm having problems sleeping, because I hear noises coming from that bedroom, and so I'm then forced to sleep in that bed, in that bedroom. This was way before Dr. Phil. Jerry was always ahead of the curve, so he's Dr. Phil. That was Jerry's idea of me getting over this.

Jerry was determined to leave the country with his brother in tow. He finally settled on Israel, which he knew would fly with the Orthodox Jewish lawyer and some coaxing of his uncles. He and Gil left America in June 1962.

RABBI BARTON SHALLAT: The Katz family took Gil in after the funeral. And they said to Jerry, "We'll take care of your brother, but not you." They didn't want to do that. They said, "You're older. You can take care of yourself." So Jerry whisks his brother off—this is 1962—took his brother and went to Israel.

Jerry and Gil Go to Israel. In Israel, Jerry studied Hebrew with hopes of learning it well enough to understand university lectures. When he didn't fully grasp the language, he retreated to the library to read sociology books in English. Israel was not providing him with the stimulation he was hoping for.

MIMI LEONARD: He went to Israel to attend university there, and met Palestinians and understood their issues and I believe it actually caused a huge rift in his relationship with his high school friend and hero, Shelley. That was the beginning of his radicalization—realizing that the Palestinians had a point in that they should not have been thrown out of their homeland. And with his amazing courage and idealistic nature, he stood up to his friends and told them his opinions.

He shared an apartment with a man from Southern Rhodesia—the first black person that Jerry had ever spent time with—and developed a close friendship with an Israeli Communist, with whom he spent hours discussing politics. The first Marxist theorist Jerry had ever encountered was eye opening. After a year, both Jerry and Gil were ready to return to America. Despite his political awakening, Jerry "still saw himself as more of an academic than an activist and wanted next to study sociology at UC Berkeley." He wrote to a friend that it was time to "build a career." It would be different than what he imagined . . .`

patience for that. This community is so intellectually exciting, what with so many interesting students, speeches and courses at the university, that I could and should be very happy. One problem is I'm not certain that I want to become a professor so in a way it's contradictory to stay in a university setting. I realize, and admit to myself and my friends, that staying at the university is one form of escapism for me, as I don't know what else I could do. Yet I'm interested in human behavior and in politics and here I'm getting it in big, fast doses. That's good. Good chance next year I'll have a chance at teaching, and that should be fun. In the back of my mind is ~~getting~~ my doctorate, and running off to africa or somewhere to ~~get~~ and do research. If one spends too much time asking oneself what one isn't doing, that one spends too much time not doing well what he is doing. You can't win.

I hate writing hand-written letters. But my typewriter, and my books and clothes, won't be here at least until March. So —

I was very happy to hear that Bart & Jane did come to see me again after all. Unfortunately they wrote some nasty things about me to their (Bart's parents back in Cincy, and through the grapevine (not your mother) I heard them.

The Making of a Revolutionary

I arrived in Berkeley in January 1964, at the age of twenty-six, with short hair, a handlebar moustache, white shirts, and sport jackets with holes in the sleeves. Within two weeks I had met every radical in town. I ran from group to group asking a million questions about politics and the movement, putting it all down in my notebook. Some people thought I was a cop.

—*JERRY RUBIN IN* GROWING (UP) AT 37

The Draft.   On the fringes of American politics since 1956, Vietnam was a small conflict before John F. Kennedy was assassinated in November 1963; according to one White House aide, it was "no bigger than a man's fist on the horizon." That changed radically when Lyndon B. Johnson was sworn in over Kennedy's dead body on Air Force One. Johnson declared a "war against Communism" and sent more men into combat. As president, he controlled the Selective Service System—"the draft." All men between the ages of eighteen and twenty-five had to register, and could be conscripted into military service.

"Draft dodging" meant a prison sentence, so men sought exemptions by claiming they were homosexual, or dropped massive quantities of LSD to fail the physical, or ran off to Canada to live as a fugitive. Heavyweight boxing champion Muhammad Ali was stripped of his title when he refused to go, saying, "[The Vietcong] never called me nigger, they never lynched me, they didn't put no dogs on me, they didn't rob me of my nationality, rape and kill my mother and father."

As political activist Eldridge Cleaver pointed out in his book, *Soul On Ice*, the early 1960s civil rights protests by black students on southern college campuses had inspired northern white students to politicize themselves—including one Abbot "Abbie" Hoffman—and the draft fueled the antiwar movement. More than any other war in the history of the United States, Vietnam created a generation gap; postwar "baby boomers" outnumbered their parents and America shifted toward "youth culture."

Jerry Returns.   Jerry was disillusioned with Israel. He thought how they treated Palestinians was wrong—and he was at odds with their nationalism, declaring himself an "internationalist." He heard about the movement in the San Francisco Bay Area, and set his sights on UC Berkeley for his graduate work. As he was still his brother's guardian, he pulled Gil out of the kibbutz and they flew back to America. On the way home, they heard about the assassination of President Kennedy. The brothers drove out to California from Cincinnati, leaving their domineering relatives behind.

GIL RUBIN: We stayed in a small hotel on University Avenue, over flashing neon bulbs, and I enrolled in a high school.

In Berkeley, Rubin met his first girlfriend, Barbara Gullahorn, a political science major who thought about joining the Peace Corps after she graduated. Meeting Rubin altered her plans. The two young University of California, Berkeley students debated politics—Rubin as a pseudo-Marxist and Gullahorn as a Kennedy-loving liberal.

Soon after his arrival, Rubin picketed a grocery store that wouldn't hire black people. Fighting for causes he believed in energized him, and after just six weeks as a sociology grad student, he dropped out to become a full-time protester. Rubin was now walking in more picket lines than anyone else in Berkeley.

In a 1964 Letter to Bennett Samuels, childhood friend from Cincinnati. Jerry writes, "I don't know what else I could do. Yet I'm interested in human behavior and politics . . . "

THE MOST EXCITING STRUGGLE IN THE WORLD IS GOING ON IN NORTH AMERICA. YOU LIVE IN THE BELLY OF THE BEAST.

—Che Guevara to Jerry Rubin

Jerry Goes to Cuba. In June of '64, Jerry visited Cuba via the "Fair Play for Cuba Committee" based on the Berkeley campus. While there, he listened to speeches by Fidel Castro and met Che Guevara, who told him that he wished he could return to America with Jerry, because "the most exciting struggle in the world is going on in North America. You live in the belly of the beast."

Suze Rotolo, who was immortalized on the front cover of *The Freewheelin' Bob Dylan*, was part of the same entourage that Jerry was traveling with. In her 2008 memoir she remembered that, "at every factory, school or organization that we were taken to, Jerry asked very detailed questions." She described him as a "quiet and intense young man" who "was constantly writing in his notebook." Suze, and other members of the group, would groan whenever Jerry would make an inquiry. He asked "long and convoluted" questions that would require the translators to provide an equally "long and convoluted" response. She compared his later Yippie image to the earnest individual she met, an all-work, no-play, fact-gatherer. "He never seemed to enjoy himself." Suze wasn't the only musician's girlfriend to encounter Jerry during this period. The mother of Mick Jagger's first child and subject of the song "Brown Sugar"—Marsha Hunt—was a UC Berkeley student then and fondly remembers participating in Anti-Vietnam War marches led by Jerry.

The Free Speech Movement: You Got to Put Your Bodies Upon the Wheels.

The Free Speech Movement (FSM) was spearheaded by Mario Savio. Along with the assassination of JFK thirteen months earlier and the arrival of Beatlemania on American shores in February '64, the Free Speech Movement was another stepping stone of an ever-evolving mutation of the wholesome 1950s America into the turbulent, war-torn, drug-fueled, rock 'n' roll 1960s that Jerry Rubin became a poster child for. In 1970, Jerry noted that the Free Speech Movement directly inspired events like the takeover of Columbia and the protests at Kent State—because young teens around the country had watched the FSM events on television and then acted upon them years later, when they were of college age.

The FSM rebelled against the administration's policies limiting students' freedom of political expression. Savio stood on the steps of Sproul Hall on the UC Berkeley campus surrounded by thousands of students (and hordes of angry police) in early December 1964 and declared: "There's a time when the operation of the machine becomes so odious, makes you so sick at heart, that you can't take part! You can't even passively take part! And you've got to put your bodies upon the gears and upon the wheels . . . upon the levers, upon all the apparatus, and you've got to make it stop! And you've got to indicate to the people who run it, to the people who own it, that unless you're free, the machine will be prevented from working at all!"

MICHAEL LERNER, FSM & SDS ACTIVIST, RABBI: I met Jerry during the Free Speech Movement at Berkeley. I was on the executive committee of the FSM and we struck up a friendship. He was still a graduate student that first year in Sociology and we were both very proud to be involved in the FSM but also felt that there was something more than issues on the campus that interested us . . .

MARILYN MILLIGAN, FSM ACTIVIST: I got arrested in the Free Speech Movement and got radicalized by the difference between what was happening and what the newspapers at the time were saying, especially the *Oakland Tribune*.

Marilyn Milligan had come to Berkeley for postdoctoral work on animal behavior. She became enthralled with the FSM and participated in the demonstration of October 1, 1964. A former grad student, Jack Weinberg, was manning the Congress of Racial Equality (CORE) information table. The campus police asked for his identification card and Weinberg refused. He was arrested and put into a police car. Students surrounded the vehicle and refused to let it leave. For the next thirty-two hours, Weinberg remained inside while the car remained stationary. At the peak of the sit-in, there were approximately three-thousand students surrounding the car. The top became a podium for speakers, which lasted until the charges against Weinberg were dropped. Aside from Mario Savio's speech, it was the most iconic moment of the Free Speech Movement.

GIL RUBIN: I remember the Free Speech Movement thing in October '64 . . . and Jerry just fell for it hook, line, and sinker.

The FBI was paying attention. The birth of the Free Speech Movement at UC Berkeley not only politicized white, middle-class students; it provided an excuse for J. Edgar Hoover to launch attacks on the academic left-wingers that he'd despised for years. When the first reports of the protests at Berkeley crossed his desk, Hoover scribbled across the top page (and underlined it for effect), "This presents the bureau with an opportunity . . ."

Yours faithfully,

J. Edgar Hoover

Vietnam Day Teach-In.

After returning from Cuba, Jerry needed a place to stay. He managed to squeeze himself into the Gullahorn family home in Palo Alto, where he touted Fidel Castro and Che. While he was there, the Free Speech Movement exploded forty miles north and he missed much of the action.

> BARBARA GULLAHORN: Jerry went off to Cuba at some point and then I went off to stay with my mother, For Jerry and I, it was the first of our multiple semi-break-ups. I can remember looking out the window of my bedroom one day, and seeing this curly-headed mop go by the window. "Oh my God. That's Jerry!" He just somehow discovered us in the depths of suburbia. And my mother never liked him. She wouldn't let us sleep together in the house, so Jerry had to sleep in the garage.

Years later, Gullahorn recalled, "I don't think he ever forgave me for keeping him from the birth of the Free Speech Movement!" The couple eventually moved back to Berkeley and actively enrolled in FSM activities. According to Gullahorn, "Jerry and I sort of said, 'what can we do together?' and came up with the notion of having a teach-in." They called *San Francisco Chronicle* music journalist Ralph Gleason, a progressive thinker who would go on to cofound *Rolling Stone* magazine with Jann Wenner. Gleason said it sounded like a great idea and connected them to Bill Graham, Norman Mailer, and others. They needed at least one faculty member to use the campus facilities, so their next stop was the office of Professor Smale, with whom they'd marched with. He accepted.

Before There Was Abbie, There Was Stephen Smale.

Smale was a maverick mathematician who, in the late 1950s, had shaken the scientific world by proving it was theoretically possible to turn a sphere inside out. Later, he was awarded the most prestigious prize in mathematics, the Fields Medal, at a ceremony in Moscow. Despite his fame, few know that in 1965, he cofounded the Vietnam Day Committee (VDC) with Jerry and Gullahorn: a short-lived but important organization. Smale's first impression of Jerry was that he was "boisterous, imaginative, bold, very strong ideas— you know, qualities I like very much. We agreed very much on the political actions we needed to do for the antiwar movement." They become the organizers for the Vietnam Day Teach-In.

Decades later, Smale recalled to his biographer Steve Batterson, "We would sit around Jerry's apartment making suggestions for speakers. It was like a competition to see who could propose the biggest, most provocative names. There was practically no limit to our ambitions: Bertrand Russell, Fidel Castro, the ex-president of the Dominican Republic, Norman Mailer, US senators, Jean-Paul Sartre, and so on. Then we would call them up then and there, or send telegrams. And sometimes it worked and invitations were accepted."

It was at this event that Jerry first met Phil Ochs in person. They quickly became comrades. Ochs not only wrote topical protest songs: he lived them.

> MICHAEL OCHS, PHIL'S BROTHER AND MANAGER: They needed a singer, and Paul Krassner said to Jerry, "you oughta contact Phil Ochs." So he did, and that is how Jerry and Phil met.

> STEPHEN SMALE: We were doing very bold, theatrical-type things. We had press conferences a lot. We would make outrageous statements, things like that.

The concept of a twenty-four-hour event quickly expanded to a thirty-six-hour one. As more names signed on, Jerry and Gullahorn were concerned that the Berkeley administration might balk; Smale, as a tenured professor, was confident. The May 21, 1965 event was greenlit with an impressive and diverse collection of orators, including the following:

Stephen Smale in Berkeley, circa 1965.

• Dr. Benjamin Spock: A pediatrician whose 1945 *book Baby and Child Care* was a best seller. Its message to new mothers was, "you know more than you think you do." Spock was as an outspoken opponent of war. He also gave a speech at the 1967 Levitation of the Pentagon, and in 1968 he was indicted on federal charges of conspiring to counsel draft evasion.

• Senator Ernest Gruening: The first senator to represent Alaska, and one of only two senators to vote against the 1964 Gulf of Tonkin Resolution—which brought America full scale into the Vietnam conflict. Many contend that the attack on the destroyer USS *Maddox* by North Vietnamese torpedo boats never occurred, or least not in the way that LBJ claimed to Congress to rope America into an all-out war.

    [Author's Note: Admiral George Morrison was commander of the US naval forces in the Gulf of Tonkin during that August 1964 incident. He's also known as the father of the Doors' Jim Morrison.]

• I. F. Stone: An investigative journalist from the 1930s until the early '70s, Stone was associated at various times with the Socialist & Communist Parties. In 1964, Stone was the only American journalist to challenge LBJ's account of the Gulf of Tonkin incident.

• Dick Gregory started out as a standup comedian whose act consisted of making jokes about being black in America. He quickly emerged as an author and civil rights activist. Before the Teach-In, he'd published a book called *Nigger: An Autobiography*, and he used its title to playful effect at the event. "The book's dedicated to my mother . . . it says, 'Dear Mom, wherever you are, if you ever hear the word nigger again, remember they're just advertising my book!' Gregory claimed that he had sent the book to President Johnson. "I wasn't that stuck on him having my book. I was just determined to get me a Nigger in the White House!"

RON DAVIS, SAN FRANCISCO MIME TROUPE FOUNDER: I think the Teach-In was a very successful event, and it was a great one, because everybody needed to know what the freak was going on. Most people don't know what the fuck's going on. If you watch television and you eat hamburgers . . . If you just are surfing the pop culture, you can't figure out shit. You can't figure out anything. A teach-in says, "Okay, you're going to have to be able to listen to a bunch of people talking about a similar subject, from different points of view, and you might learn something."

Other speakers included novelist/political agitator Norman Mailer and future Yippie cofounder Paul Krassner (and editor of *The Realist*), as well as music performances by topical folksinger Phil Ochs. Over the course of the day and a half of nonstop, around-the-clock lectures, some twenty to thirty thousand people (both students and local residents) listened and engaged. Given the historic nature of the event, a double album titled *Berkeley Teach-In: Vietnam* was compiled from those thirty-six hours and released on Folkways Records. Strangely, Jerry is not mentioned anywhere within the detailed liner notes, nor do any of Ochs's songs appear.

The VDC Headquarters: Jerry Meets Stew.

MARILYN MILLIGAN: Jerry was a very forceful person, but he, like Mario Savio, didn't want to be the only leader. And so, meetings worked by consensus. Anybody could go to a meeting—the door was open at the Vietnam Day Committee—and he would always introduce the FBI. He would say, "and in the back of the room, standing in a particular position, that's our FBI agent for today." He once invited a [suspected FBI agent] to chair a meeting. They declined. They said, "thank you, no." They were pretty obvious, because they usually wore suits, and nobody was dressed like that.

The Students for a Democratic Society (SDS), an antiwar organization had got its start on the Ann Arbor campus of the University of Michigan in 1960, had formalized its political manifesto in 1962 through the mind of Tom Hayden, amongst others.

MARTIN KENNER, JERRY'S FRIEND AND BLACK PANTHER FUNDRAISER: Jerry's greatest accomplishments were in Berkeley . . . It was really the period where Jerry was a master of the mass demonstration. Later on, that got ceded to Tom Hayden and the irony is Tom Hayden was really against mass demonstrations for a long time. SDS was a latecomer to the anti-Vietnam protests. And Berkeley was really a leader, and Jerry was a leader in Berkeley.

Jerry was now a full-time activist, running the VDC Headquarters on Fulton Street in Berkeley.

MARILYN MILLIGAN: The first time I went to the office I met Jerry. At first, I thought he was kind of gruff. The more I got to know him, the

more I worked with him, the more I came to admire and love him. Jerry was somebody who I always felt to be totally non-sexist. Where some of the other men were kind of sexist—just prior to the feminist movement. Jerry really encouraged me to take leadership roles.

One morning Jerry arrived at the headquarters to discover a long-haired hippie sleeping on his office floor who would go on to become his right-hand man: Stew Albert. In his 2004 memoir, Stew recalled arriving in Berkeley with no place to crash, so he stumbled into the VDC's Victorian residential offices and made himself at home. As payback for stuffing envelopes, he felt entitled to a place on their friendly floor. He detailed his first exchange with Jerry:

> *I rolled over. I could tell it was morning because the office was bright with sun. Above me stood a short, angry-faced man with a thick mustache, crowned by medium-length dark, straggly hair. He was wearing a white, long-sleeved shirt and baggy woolen pants. He held a spiral notebook that he kept waving in my face.*
> *"I fell asleep."*
> *"Don't get smart. Just get out of here. Because of people like you, we can't get respectable folks to work here."*
> *I stood on my feet to meet this angry, accusatory face and gave my persecutor a focused, intense look of more than average duration and he seemed to calm down. "Look man, I was working here last night doing envelopes, and it was convenient for me to crash. I wasn't trying to screw things up."*
> *"We have a new rule. You should have gone to our last membership meeting. No sleeping in the office. You should go to the meetings."*

OPPOSITE: Jerry with Marilyn Milligan (to his right) at a VDC protest march.

ABOVE: Frank Bardacke stuffing envelopes at the VDC office.

Rennie Davis, Stew & Jerry. Photo © Leni Sinclair

WHO THE HELL IS STEW ALBERT!?!

IN 1998, WRITER RATSO SLOMAN compiled the definitive oral history of Abbie Hoffman, titled *Steal This Dream*. He was on *The Howard Stern Show* promoting his new tome when the host began ribbing him about the lack of compliments for the book. "Well, Stew Albert likes my book." Sloman countered. "Who the hell is Stew Albert!?!" Stern bellowed.

According to Albert's *New York Times* obit from 2006, "It was he who lectured the 82nd Airborne on the larger lessons of the Lone Ranger during the March on the Pentagon in 1967…[and] when it came to what were called New Left politics, Mr. Albert did not miss much. He participated in demonstrations for free speech at Berkeley; [pranked the] New York Stock Exchange to satirize capitalism; befriended Black Panthers; and was investigated in connection with bombing the United States Capitol but never charged with it."

TOM MILLER, ACTIVIST/JOURNALIST/TRAVEL WRITER: He was so far smarter than any of the rest of us. Somebody would make a comment about something in Algiers or some historical event in the history of the American Left and he would say, "Well, actually, it happened this way," and he would correct us. He wasn't admonishing anybody, but he was just so far smarter than the rest of us.

MARTIN KENNER: Well, Stew was political. He was in the Progressive Labor Party, or the Movement [which was the PLP's youth affiliate]. He was familiar with that kind of more traditional Left. And Judy Gumbo, of course, is a red diaper baby from a Commie family in Canada, I believe. So he brought the old Left, in the guise of the new Left and the Yippies, to Jerry. There's no question of doubt, Stew was a link between the old and the new.

Stew's life partner was Judy Gumbo, originally Judy Clavir. When Eldridge Cleaver met Judy, he was shocked that she hadn't taken Stew's last name. As historian W. J. Rorabaugh pointed out, "Cleaver was a militant, but no feminist." So he insisted on calling her "Mrs. Stew." When Judy protested, Cleaver began calling her "Mrs. Gumbo." No card-carrying Yippie was going to refuse an endearing name given by a Black Panther. Judy and Stew didn't actually get legally married until a decade later. Jerry was the best man with attorney Bill Kunstler as master of ceremonies!

BARBARA GULLAHORN: Stew was a real combination of political and brother. I see him and Jerry as brothers; after a while, one started seeing the two of them as two parts of a whole. I mean, they would complete each other's sentences. And Judy Gumbo was another lucky part of that. She fit the two of them just perfectly. I remember when she arrived, that was Jerry's family.

After the '60s, Stew and Judy lived off the grid, retreating to the woods of Upstate New York. And yet, they still were harassed. FBI agents watching Stew's cabin filed a report mistaking Jerry (who was there for Thanksgiving) for Abbie, who was in hiding. This unsung hero was, in many ways, more important in Rubin's Yippie career than Abbie.

JUDY GUMBO: Stew was Jerry's buddy, supportive. He really was the one that helped Jerry work through whatever particular political issue, or personal issue happened to be going on at that moment. That was one of Stew's skills, was to be able to mediate it. Sidekick! That was what people would call Stew, Jerry's sidekick—in the Yippie days.

ROBERT FRIEDMAN, JOURNALIST: I think, in many ways, Stew was the glue that kept Abbie and Jerry together. Because those were two pretty strong egos, who didn't always agree or get along with each other, and needed some kind of buffer. And I don't think [Paul] Krassner played that role.

I think Krassner was more of an excitable guy, goading from the corners, and maybe giving good advice, but not the mediator type.

JUDY GUMBO: You have to understand how fluid everything was. Right? So there was certainly the "Jerry-Stew-Abbie" dynamic, for fifteen minutes. And then there was the "Paul Krassner-Abbie, maybe Jerry's out with Stew" dynamic for fifteen minutes. I mean really . . .

STELLA RESNICK, JERRY'S FUTURE PARTNER: Stew gave Jerry great ideas. There were times I heard him quote Stew word for word. Stew was like Jerry's rabbi. He talked like a rabbi, and he was heartfelt and he also was brilliant and creative and Jerry was enthralled by him. Stew was more important, in that way, for Jerry than Abbie.

Stew shadowed Jerry during the Yuppie years. He continued to advise Jerry when Jerry donned a suit and tie, while Stew never deviated from his deviance, remaining an unwashed Yippie forever.

KATE COLEMAN, JOURNALIST: If anything, Stew was more like a troll under the bridge, because he had horrible personal habits. Jerry was clean; Stew was disgustingly filthy at certain times. And he had his hair in those blond dreadlocks, and finally they were so dirty, that he came to me, and I cut his hair for him. I had to cut the dreads out—I couldn't get them undone. He also had this big toenail that was blackened and like two inches long. It was just the grossest thing I'd ever seen. And I said, "You've got to clean up your act, honey." But I loved him.

TOM MILLER: Jerry would say, "Oh, I don't know if I want to do that," and he'd talk to Stew and Stew would say, "Well, here are your alternatives. You could do this, this, or this." I just don't think Jerry made any major decision without consulting Stew.

JACK KURZWEIL, FSM AND VDC ACTIVIST/PROFESSOR: Stew was incredibly serious, in addition to being incredibly amusing and funny. But he also had a sense of detachment and a sense of play and a sense of humor that Jerry never had. And he didn't take himself seriously, while being serious. Jerry, from his carrot juice diet, to stockbroker, to New Age

guru, to whatever he did, took himself immensely seriously. I remember once, asking Stew about one of Jerry's metamorphoses, "is he playing a game, or does he really believe this?" And Stew said, "he really believes it."

JUDY GUMBO: One of Stew's functions was to help Jerry realize his goals, and so Stew would come up with organizing strategies. Stew claims he was the one who came up with putting the new left and the counterculture together. Stew's brain was very syncretic—I think is the word—he could put things together really well. Whereas Jerry was a sort of a—I would call him an "ad man." He was a marketing man, he was able to take ideas and put them out in the world in a way that a lot of people could understand. That was really one of Jerry's strengths.

In 1969, Stew led the protests in support of the People's Park in Berkeley, which led to Marvin Gaye recording the seminal anthem, "What's Going On." Renaldo Benson of the Four Tops was on tour in the Bay Area when the events caught his eye; he was enraged by the police beating on the longhairs (coupled with the thought of all the young people being shipped off to Vietnam) and composed a skeletal theme, later sharing it with Gaye. The vacant city lot became a battleground between local residents who wanted the space as a public park and the police—acting on behalf of the University of Berkeley, who wanted it for an athletic field.

According to the *New York Times*, "In 1970, shortly after being released from the Alameda County jail in California, Mr. Albert campaigned to replace the sheriff who had supervised his incarceration. He lost, but got 65,000 votes, and carried the city of Berkeley."

MICHAEL LERNER, RABBI: The first thing is, Stew was very creative in his own right. He was somebody who a) had a deep understanding of progressive politics, b) he was somebody who had a deep commitment to challenging American society and doing it in a creative way. He always came up with creative ideas for how to move forward. So, sometimes the ideas that Jerry was promoting were ideas that Stew came up with and there wasn't very much recognition of that from Jerry. Stew also was much more of a "people person." He was like the "man of the people" kind of person for Jerry and he wasn't seeking any recognition himself, which meant that Jerry didn't feel the slightest bit threatened by him.

Much of Stew's 2004 autobiography *Who the Hell is Stew Albert?* is a tribute to his friend Jerry who died ten years earlier. The memories are fond and robust. He had spoken to Jerry the day before he died. "We were masters of the great phone conversation. It was a phone call that will last a lifetime."

Stew explained that he'd just gotten into town. Jerry called him "another drifter crashing on our floor." Albert defended himself. "I might stick around." "Sure you will," was the reply. When someone yelled "Jerry!" with the news that a *San Francisco Examiner* reporter was on the phone and wanted to speak to him, Jerry shot into the next room with supersonic rapidity. One of the few black volunteers approached Albert: "Jerry Rubin is a little like Stalin." "I guess you don't like Jerry?" Stew inquired. "Not true. He's just being authoritarian in his own way. I respect the guy. Rubin kind of started the VDC. He kept the faith in the Teach-In when the experts said it would flop. He's got drive, ambition, and he makes things happen."

In many ways, that exchange summarizes Jerry for the rest of his life: "drive, ambition, and he makes things happen." And coming from an African American activist in 1965, it foreshadows the relationships that both Rubin and Albert would forge with Eldridge Cleaver, Bobby Seale, and Huey Newton in the years to come. In his own words, Stew was "an almost-nice Jewish boy" who left his job as a welfare inspector in Brooklyn to explore life in California. Jerry quickly put him to work for the VDC manning the tables on the Berkeley campus, where Stew blossomed as an articulate mouthpiece for the movement. A friendship grew between the two with Stew playing the role of a behind-the-scenes lieutenant, whom Jerry would grill for insights throughout the rest of his life.

BARBARA GULLAHORN: Well, to an extent, it's a mystery to me, not because Stew isn't equally capable. But that he took it on himself to play this sort of secondary role. And Stew was capable of doing many things, and what he did was terribly important. It was like he was a constant sounding board for Jerry. Stew seemed to know just how to back off and push in the right ways. He came up with ideas of his own; I think he would push his ideas.

One of Stew's ideas would ultimately shape the Yippies: the combination of political protest with the counterculture. In his memoirs, he recalls: "My passionate post-Maoist idea was to politicize hippies . . . one day I took an acid trip and walked barefoot in a section of Telegraph Avenue that was thick with hippies. An emphatic command came to me from the depths of my 'inner voice': 'Talk to them about revolution.'"

LEFT: Stew Albert at the *Berkeley Barb*.
ABOVE: Barbara Gullahorn at UC Berkeley.

BOB DYLAN, ALLEN GINSBERG, AND THE HELLS ANGELS

IN DECEMBER 1965, Bob Dylan rolled into the San Francisco Bay Area for a series of concerts—and both Allen Ginsberg and Jerry Rubin wanted to engage him in their Vietnam Day Committee protest. The VDC had also caught the attention of the Hells Angels, led by Sonny Barger (who turned up at the end of the decade in the Rolling Stones movie *Gimme Shelter*). Barger's crew had threatened to attack the pacifists, but followed up with a press release that said it would "demean [them] to attack the filthy marchers." They "wouldn't touch 'em with a ten-foot pole: dirty communists." Simultaneously, they sent a telegram to LBJ's White House offering to "fight against the commies in Vietnam" and offering themselves as "G-O-R-I-L-L-A soldiers."

All of this was on Ginsberg's mind while Dylan was camped out in the Bay Area for several days. When he first arrived, there was a television press conference broadcast on KQED, in which Dylan was asked if he would be joining the Vietnam Day Committee demonstration in front of the Fairmont Hotel that evening. "No, I'll be busy tonight." When pushed further to take a stand on political protesting, Dylan gave one of his classic surrealistic answers of that era, describing a "demonstration where I make up the cards you know, they have—uh—they have a group of protesters here—uh—perhaps carrying cards with pictures of the Jack of Diamonds on them and the Ace of Spades on them. Pictures of mules, maybe words and—oh maybe about 25–30,000 of these things printed up and just picket, carry signs and picket in front of the post office."

Knowing full well that Dylan was elusive, Ginsberg was determined to bring together the Hells Angels, Jerry Rubin, and the folk-rock bard. Dylan had given Ginsberg some thirty free tickets for the opening night's show at the Berkeley Community Theater. The front rows were packed with (in Allen's words), "a fantastic assemblage" of Peter Orlovsky, Lawrence Ferlinghetti, Neal Cassady, Ken Kesey, and Michael McClure, plus a handful of Hells Angels led by Sonny Barger, a couple of Buddhist monks thrown in for good measure, and Jerry Rubin, accompanied by several other Vietnam Day Committee members.

After the show, Ginsberg orchestrated a meeting between Dylan and Barger, in which Dylan shut the Hells Angels down and up. Barger tried to initiate the discussion by offering Dylan "a joint out of a cellophane bag of forty"—but Dylan rebuffed him. He harangued the Angels in the same cocky-yet-informed manner he did to British journalists that same year in the movie *Don't Look Back*. "Look, you guys got something to say, don't you? You want to talk to the people, saying something to the nation? Well, what's your act? Why don't you come to New York and we'll put you on at Carnegie Hall? But you gotta get your show together, get your shit together. Do you have any songs? Can you recite poetry? Can you talk? If you want to extend yourselves, you can't make it by hanging around Oakland beating up on your own image."

Over the next few days, a dialogue between Ginsberg and Dylan continued—focusing on an upcoming VDC march planned for later that week. Ginsberg explained the where/what/why of the march while Dylan pondered the situation. Finally, Dylan revealed that Jerry Rubin had sent a message to him, would he "join the march, lead the march?" Rubin wanted Dylan—but the latter was also aware that the VDC were arguing amongst themselves as to what form the protest would take, with some organizers wanting "an angry chain march." Finally, (and surprisingly) Dylan capitulated. But it had to be done his way, and that included not confronting the troop trains running through Oakland.

Dylan told Ginsberg to pass on to Rubin, "We ought to have it in San Francisco right on Nob Hill where I have my concert [the Masonic Temple], and I'll get a whole bunch of trucks and picket signs—some of the signs will be bland and some of them have lemons painted on them and some of them are watermelon pictures, bananas, others will have the word Orange or Automobile or the words Venetian Blind." Dylan went on to say that he'd pay for the truck rental and organize the painting of the signs and that he'd actually attend, saying that the VDC was "too obvious" and too far out of touch with what the kids want. Dylan wanted something more Dada.

Jerry wasn't able to visualize what "was being offered them on a silver platter," in the words of Ginsberg. Rubin was still a couple of light-years away from the Levitation of the Pentagon. Arguably Dylan may not have gone through with it either, but according to Ginsberg, Dylan "was interested, he wanted to do something," but not with the traditional stance of a protest march. That was "too negative, not good enough theater, not even effective as propaganda." Dylan was ahead of the curve in knowing you needed to present something more dazzling "to the young kids who didn't want to get involved in a crazed anger march." Jerry wouldn't have that epiphany until later.

The movement is a school and its teachers are the Fugs, Dylan, Beatles, Ginsberg, mass media, hippies, students, fighting cops in Berkeley, blood on draft records, sit-ins, jail. —JERRY RUBIN

Stopping the Troop Trains in Oakland.

According to author Steve Batterson, "At the Teach-In, Yale historian Staughton Lynd had proposed massive nonviolent civil disobedience as the next step in opposing the War, citing the Oakland Army Terminal as a target." Rubin and Smale decided to close down the Oakland Army Terminal. The city of Berkeley neighbors the Port of Oakland, which was the depot shipping soldiers overseas to Vietnam. The VDC's activities ramped up, culminating in an October 1965 march from the Berkeley campus to the Oakland Army Terminal in an attempt to prevent war supplies from being sent to Vietnam. Police dogs and tear gas greeted the marchers.

In advance of the march, Jerry and Gullahorn went to the depot.

BARBARA GULLAHORN: I remember Jerry and I had somehow talked our way in to the terminal, and they said, "could you please drive this guy, he's too drunk to make his way home." And it turns out he was one of the people in charge of sending dead bodies back. And he was drunk because he couldn't stand it anymore; he'd been lying all the time. They were sending back a hundred dead bodies and reporting it as fifty.

As the demonstration neared, Rubin and Smale received telegrams from railroad management detailing the criminal laws and conspiracy statutes they'd be guilty of—neither was deterred. Some five hundred people gathered at the train station; many running right onto the tracks, narrowly escaping being run over as the troop trains barreled past them. Soldiers on the trains hung signs from their windows: "We don't want to go."

They also understood the power of the media. While the FSM leaders had an adversarial view of the press, Rubin and Smale wanted to engage with it. Smale understood the power of television and that images of protest could provoke positive response from Berkeley residents. Rubin had instincts about handling the press from his days as a cub reporter for the *Cincinnati Post*.

GIL RUBIN: My memory of the train thing down in Oakland was I walked into a room, and there was about six people. One was Stew; one was Steve Smale who was a mathematician at Berkeley. And Jerry said, "Listen to this; I've got a great idea. We're gonna march down to the Oakland thing, we're gonna get thousands of people, be on the news every night, it'll galvanize the country, this'll be the first thing . . ." And I remember saying to him, "Yeah, right." And I walked out, and you know, a couple weeks later . . . That pipe dream was on Walter Cronkite, it was incredible.

MARILYN MILLIGAN: On marches, Jerry was definitely the leader. He was always out in front; he never hesitated to be out in front. He never hesitated to start chants. He never hesitated to talk to the press. And he really believed that we should get the attention of the media, of course.

Nancy Kurshan, who was there as a protester, wrote, "The troop train became a symbol of the war machine in its refusal to halt. It seemed clear to us that those who controlled the troop trains and the war machine had little regard for human life."

Hells Angels were in the crowd, and the protestors mistakenly thought they were their allies. When they started to clash with the police, the Hells Angels jumped in and attacked the demonstrators instead of the cops. This then put the police in the ironic position of having to defend the demonstrators.

Jerry was determined to try again. Unfortunately, conservative Leftists in the VDC, worried about the risk of another confrontation, resisted the idea of a second march.

STEPHEN SMALE: After the troop train demonstrations, there was a huge march we planned, into Oakland. This would be the fall of '65. Then the Oakland Police were going to just block the border. By that time, we had a very big organization. And Jerry and I were beginning to be outvoted by less radical radicals.

It was the beat poet Allen Ginsberg who stepped into the fray, attempting to broker a peace between the demonstrators and the Hells Angels. Allen had been at the head of the last march, chanting "Hare Krishna" as the violence erupted all around him. While they considered him naive, VDC leaders listened to Ginsberg's vision of a surrealist demonstration that would sway their opponents. Ginsberg proposed things like handing out flowers to the Hells Angels and building floats with tableaux of Thoreau behind bars. Though his ideas weren't used, they influenced Jerry and would later see the light of day in the theatrics of the Pentagon protest.

Regarding Ginsburg, Jerry said, "[He] wrote a poem that he read to a VDC meeting that absolutely blew everybody's minds. It was brilliant because it exploded all the categories of what a demonstration was and what Allen was saying is a demonstration is a celebration . . . that poetic proposal . . . opened my head up to a whole new possibility of politics, and I think it's very possible that it was the first time I ever thought of politics being theatrical."

The second day, some twenty thousand people showed up. As they marched, the leaders received news the police were waiting for them at the Oakland Army Terminal with tear gas and attack dogs. In the middle of the march, the leaders voted to turn back, overruling Jerry and Stephen Smale. This would be the first of many conflicts Jerry would have with what he called the "Orthodox Left."

JACK KURZWEIL: [Jerry] wanted that confrontation, because of the spectacle. Jerry was into spectacle. Jerry was, on the one hand, a brilliant and charismatic organizer. And, on the other hand, could be remarkably irresponsible, and self-aggrandizing.

It was a probably a good thing that Jerry was overruled, as his zeal for publicity overrode other concerns. Jack Kurzweil recalls an incident during the first march.

JACK KURZWEIL: At times of these elemental upheavals, what happens is that you have some people who are so swept in the emotion of it, that they lose a sense of reality. And at these troop train demonstrations, there were a few young kids. And particularly one of them, who was so bound up in the passion and ecstasy of it that he was going to lie down on the tracks. These troop trains are like fifteen feet high, a locomotive, and they don't stop real easy. And this guy was lying down on the train tracks.

I was standing there with Jerry and Stew Albert, and other people. And my response was, "Jesus, we've got to drag this kid off the tracks!" And Jerry's response was, "Oh no, let him stay there. If he dies, it will be great publicity!" And I looked at him, and I didn't know the guy that I was looking at. And I just grabbed this kid off the tracks, and he was in a state of religious bliss. And that was a moment when, on a certain, basic level, I stopped trusting Jerry.

RUBIN'S FIRST ARREST

THE NEXT VDC PROTEST was a direct engagement with General Maxwell Taylor in San Francisco. Taylor had been the Chairman of the Joint Chiefs of Staff, the Ambassador to South Vietnam, and was currently an advisor to LBJ on Vietnam. When the general arrived at the Fairmont Hotel on August 24, 1965, there were a hundred people to greet him, including Rubin, Smale, and Gullahorn. Some of the VDC carried signs depicting Taylor as a Nazi war criminal. They surrounded his limo as he arrived and lay across the hood.

Hotel manager Dick Swig tried to help Taylor into the elevator to escort him to his room, but VDC protestors had filled up the elevator and the area surrounding it, forcing Taylor and Swig to head for the staircase. On the mezzanine level, the two men locked themselves into a hotel management office suite. About fifty of the VDC crew followed them and began chanting, "We Shall Not Be Moved."

BARBARA GULLAHORN: "The head of the Fairmont came over and pleaded with us all to leave . . . [Jerry] immediately sat down because he wanted to be arrested . . . And the police said, 'Now look, they've all gone.'" . . . I said, 'really, my boyfriend will be hysterical if I don't get arrested. So just arrest me.'"

Smale Leaves the VDC.

According to Smale's biographer Batterson, Smale was losing faith in the VDC, and went back to his previously scheduled life. Jerry felt betrayed. Smale had been both a mentor and a partner—and much like the relationship that Jerry would later enjoy with Abbie Hoffman, "each would have been less effective without the other." Over the next several months, various factions sprang up within the VDC accompanied by the power plays that invariably are part and parcel of the territory. Both "Rubin and Smale's influence diminished as the VDC expanded."

STEPHEN SMALE: We did the almost impossible, we got together different Left-wing groups, which never worked together before—they had always fought each other. They participated in our meetings and cooperated to make the big marches and the big Teach-In. So I think that was one of our big successes. And that's been very hard to duplicate, ever since.

Although Smale was involved in the movement for less than a year, the Vietnam Day Teach-In and the VDC were not only indispensable to Jerry's formative years, but essential components of the entire bloc of anti-Vietnam protest. It is fitting that the last interview Jerry ever did (in July 1994, a few months before he died), he paid tribute to the man who had instigated his activism: "In six months, Smale laid out the whole direction of the antiwar movement. He was almost like the Lone Ranger. He came in on his horse and gave us the message, and then dropped the silver bullet and went off. What happened in Berkeley with the Vietnam Day and with the troop train protests was the script for the whole decade. Stephan Smale wrote that script, and then he left the others of us to carry it out."

When Jerry Met Nancy.

Soon after the Oakland marches, Jerry would become friends with a newcomer from Madison, Wisconsin, named Nancy Kurshan. Nancy, a self-described "red diaper baby" (her family was part of the American Communist movement, prevalent during the '30s–'50s), had been politically active since her teenage years, participating in the civil rights movement as early as 1958. The assassination of Malcolm X struck Nancy hard. She'd seen him speak on the Madison campus and, in her own words, "had recognized his power and beauty." Dr. Mavis Hetherington (her only female teacher during four years as an undergrad at Madison) encouraged Nancy to go to UC Berkeley. Coupled with the fact that Berkeley was, as she described, a hotbed of "radical political engagement, " she decided to head there for the Psychology department's graduate program.

She arrived just in time to attend the second march on Oakland, and was immediately derailed from her PhD in Child Psychology by a "fairly clean cut" young man wearing "starched white shirts and slacks . . . He had a handlebar mustache and a swarthy appearance that gave him the look of a classic Italian anarchist." Enter Jerry Rubin.

NANCY KURSHAN: I actually don't remember where I met Jerry, but there was this big Vietnam Day Committee, and they were organizing all kinds of activities, and I went to every single thing I could possibly go to. So I encountered him immediately, and we became friends very quickly. He was cute. He had one of those handlebar moustaches, and I thought he looked kind of like an old-fashioned anarchist or something.

We got along well, and we used to hang out at Kip's, a hamburger joint, and The Mediterraneum, which is also on Telegraph Ave. He liked to just schmooze around there, and bump into various people. But then, he really wanted me to meet his friends, his good friends. . . He just really took me in, and I told him, because our romantic relationship came up, I told him, "I have this boyfriend, back in Wisconsin, and I'm not really looking for a relationship."

He said, "That's okay. Then we can just be friends."

But the two fell in love. Jerry told Nancy in a June 1966 letter:

My last three days in Berkeley were spent "with you." I talked with people we talked with, I sat in places we sat in (last booth in Kip's!), I talked incessantly and too much about you, I even slept in your bed. . . when we first met we both realized that we would become close quickly; it was something physical, something unconscious, something beyond reason . . . Please don't take anything in this letter as pressure on you. Whatever you do, I understand. Don't confuse my honesty with forms of pressure. I don't mean it that way. Good night!

Love, Jerry

Much like in his relationship with Barbara Gullahorn, Nancy became Jerry's partner in his political activities, playing a key role in some of the most significant events of the 1960s—from Jerry's appearance before HUAC, to the Levitation of the Pentagon, to the founding of the Yippies, and, finally, the Chicago 8 Trial. Making coffee and making bail, Nancy was the logistical underpinning of every move Rubin made during his radical years. Jerry has stated himself that without her, his ability to be a leader fell apart.

The Bombing of VDC Headquarters.

The following spring, just after midnight, in the early morning of April 9, 1966—the VDC headquarters in Berkeley was mysteriously blown up. Stew Albert was sitting at the Caffe Mediterraneum, on Telegraph Avenue, when he heard the blast and rushed out the door. In a memorable scene in *The Graduate* [filmed a year after the bombing], Dustin Hoffman is sitting in the Caffe staring blankly across the street at Moe's Books, another Berkeley landmark.

Years later, Stew recounted that explosive moment in his memoir. "I ran at double speed to the nearby Fulton Street address of [what was now at that moment] the former VDC building. 'The fascists were here!' [said a fellow VDC member] with a voice sad with resignation. I looked at the smoking ruins, the collapsed wall, and the sidewalk that was littered with leaflets. By some peculiar quirk of terrorist incompetence, nobody was dead, and the human injuries were of the minor type. The cops and firemen were leisurely in their arrival. I had time to poke my way through the charred debris. The explosion came from the back. The front rooms were damaged, but the rear was in shambles. The VDC toilet was blown into the front office. Fortunately, no one was sitting on it when the bomb exploded."

It did have the distinction of being "the first politically inspired bombing in Berkeley." According to Seth Rosenfeld's book *Subversives*: "The US Department of Justice instructed the [FBI] not to investigate the bombing"—although, also according to Rosenfeld, the bureau had been following VDC activities for a while, most notably when "They obtained the organization's bank records, without a subpoena, including lists of deposits and payees on each check. A bank employee tipped off Rubin, however, and he held a press conference." The FBI denied it. The bombing of the VDC headquarters rendered the entire building useless and signaled the end of the VDC.

In May of '66, there was a celebratory teach-in to mark the one-year anniversary of the previous year's historic event. With only a hundred people in attendance versus the tens of thousands that had shown up the first time (coupled with the complete destruction of the office) Rubin was forced to concede that the VDC "may have played itself out."

> ## "PEOPLE CALLED HIM THE P. T. BARNUM OF THE LEFT."
> —NANCY KURSHAN

HUAC Subpoena: Rubin Steps onto the National Stage.

"I wanted to do something before the committee that would grab the antiwar attention of the country."
—Jerry Rubin, *Growing (Up) at 37*

RON DAVIS: Jerry said he had the idea of wearing a three-cornered hat. And then I said, "Why don't you wear the whole uniform? A Revolutionary war uniform, a George Washington outfit, because you're a patriot, and you're opposed to the American Empire, etc. And you're as patriotic as they are, if not more so."

Jerry rented an American Revolutionary costume for $35 from a theatrical store. When he arrived at the Capitol, the federal marshals would not let him in the hearing room, despite the fact he had been subpoenaed. When he eventually got into the room, he handed out copies of the Declaration of Independence, explaining, "First, I want to introduce myself. My name is Jerry Rubin. I would like to make an explanation as to why I am wearing the uniform of the American Revolution of 1776." Congressman: "I don't care to hear that!" Jerry, unabated: "I am wearing it because America is degrading its 1776 ideals."

Jerry was ordered to sit down and was dismissed without ever giving testimony. He later recalled, "The press ate it up: it was on page one across the country. With that zap I had inspired rebellious people everywhere to be outrageous. I had used the media to spread my message."

JOHN SINCLAIR, WHITE PANTHER: That was a tremendous inspiration to me. First time I saw anybody on the left with a sense of humor.

A couple of days later, the committee canceled its hearings without ever allowing Rubin to testify. As he objected to not being called up to the stand, the Marshalls carried him out of the room as he screamed, "I want to testify!"

Statement to HUAC
by Jerry Rubin

I am wearing this uniform of the American Revolution of 1776 not because I take these hearings of the House Un-American Committee unseriously. I take these hearings deadly seriously. They are dangerous. Their purpose is to create a public atmosphere in which conformity is patriotism and dissent is treason. The goal of these hearings is to propagandize the idea that it is un-American to act on the basis of one's conscience in opposition to America's use of brute, ugly force in Vietnam. As these hearings proceed, American planes drop jellied gasoline on the villages of Vietnam, wreaking destruction on people who have neither invaded nor threatened the invasion of our land. The purpose of these hearings is to create a public atmosphere which will accept more destruction -- a ground invasion of North Vietnam and air attack on China.

I wear this uniform to symbolize the fact that America was born in revolution, but today America does violence to her own past by denying the right of others to revolution. Today America has become the policeman of the world, protecting narrow political, military, economic and ideological interests at the expense of millions of people who suffer from poverty, discrimination and indignity. These people need revolution to bring down the foreign-supported oligarchies which block non-violent change and material progress in their countries. How embarrassing it would be for Lyndon Johnson to have to explain to Jefferson and Paine the doctrines of American foreign policy in 1966: "Messrs. Jefferson and Paine," Johnson would have to say, "you must understand that internal revolution is external, Communist aggression. Protection of American property and military interests overseas is world freedom. All revolutions spring not out of people's legitimate needs, but out of a world conspiracy. And if people revolt, we will do to them what we are doing to the people of Vietnam -- for their own good." Jefferson and Paine would conclude: America has become the world's prosecutor, judge, jury, policeman and executioner. The present American government has become a traitor to the American Revolution of 1776.

All the arguments that are made against the revolution in South Vietnam could also have been made -- successfully -- against the American Revolution. Foreign troops? The French Navy played a more important role in the American Revolution than North Vietnamese troops have played in the South Vietnamese Revolution. Foreign supplies? Eighty per cent of the munitions used by the Continental Army in 1776-77 were supplied by the French. Foreign ideas? The ideology of the American Revolution was influenced by the European Enlightenment just as the ideology of the Vietnamese Revolution is influenced by Western Marxism. Limited popular support? It is generally estimated that 1/3 of the colonists opposed the American Revolution -- evidence is that there is less opposition in South Vietnam to the guerilla movement. Foreign cadres? What about Paine and Lafayette and the revolutionaries recruited from Europe? Terrorism? American revolutionaries certainly did not treat the loyalists non-violently. A contagious example? The American revolutionaries saw their revolution as a model for the world. They set an example even for Ho Chi Minh's 1945 Vietnamese Declaration of Independence which begins with a quote from the American Declaration of 1776. The Vietnamese people today are carrying out the ideal of the American Revolution -- the ideal of self-determination. I plan to give one copy of the Declaration of Independence of 1776 to each of the members of HUAC because this document is the best argument for the Vietnamese Revolution, for immediate American withdrawl from Vietnam.

What do we learn about popular support for the Vietnamese Revolution from our own governmental experts? The Pentagon tells us that it will take at least 750,000 Americans, even with the aid of air power, to have any chance of defeating 250,000 poorly-armed South Vietnamese. Or from Premier Ky's admission that it would take the USA 10-20 years to win in South Vietnam? Why has the bombing of North Vietnam not diminished resistance in the South one iota? Why do American estimates of 70,000 (at most) North Vietnamese soldiers in South Vietnam imply a North Vietnamese invasion of South Vietnam when America has 300,000 troops there and is constructing permanent military bases? Was there any single point in the history of the fighting when North Vietnamese troops in South Vietnam outnumbered American? Why do we support a military junta largely composed of Benedict Arnolds -- military men who fought for the French against the Vietminh? What is the significance of the fact that General Eisenhower wrote in his autobiography that if an election had taken place in

Vietnam in 1954 Ho Chi Minh would have gotten 80% of the vote? Why can't a Communist revolution be nationalistic, popular and indigenous? Why can't people choose Communism if they so desire? With what madness does America equate destruction of Vietnam with freedom and victory?

Gentlemen of the Pentagon, Messrs. Johnson, Rusk, McNamara and Humphrey -- today you need only push buttons and give orders and a massive military machine is placed into swift operation, at your wish. History is not so pliable or kind. History will condemn you. History will record that Vietnam has become America's Auschwitz, that the "Communist" dark-skinned Asian and Latin American peasant is today to America what the Jew was to Germany -- an alien, subhuman element to be exterminated. The unborn will judge America, and they will see in McNamara's cold statistics profound crimes against humanity.

American society brutalizes its black people and its poor people. American society builds its foreign policy on bogeyman notions of the world. American society conscripts its young men to become invaders of another land. American society uses inquisitorial committees to frighten opposition. American society defines its national interest as the interest of its leading corporations and the Pentagon. American prosperity lulls the American people into security.

Investigate the movement. Deny us elemental constitutional rights. Send us to jail. Blacklist us.

We shall never be silent. We shall always do our best to give aid and comfort to "the enemy" if by the enemy is meant the underprivileged of the world. We shall never accept our government's murders because of fear. You can silence us only by killing us.

As for you, gentlemen,

History will condemn you.

August 16, 1966.

NANCY KURSHAN: It was exciting. It was a little bit frightening; you don't know what's going to happen. Jerry, in those days, would meet an attack with a real pushback. And he was already into drama; I mean people called him the P. T. Barnum of the Left, which I think was a little disparaging, possibly. But he was really into theater and confrontation, largely because he had been a reporter and understood how the media works, already. And he knew that if there was political confrontation, it would probably be more likely to make it in to the media, and then people would know about it.

JACK KURZWEIL: It was the final round of breaking the spell of the terror of that committee. When people defied the committee, it lost a good deal of its potency. And Jerry, I think, helped put the final nails in the coffin by ridiculing it.

REX WEINER, SCREENWRITER/JOURNALIST: If you see the counterculture as part of a continuum of American History, in which the ideals of the founding fathers have been pursued intermittently, what I call the interrupted revolution. And the proof of that is Jerry Rubin's dressing up as a so-called revolutionary.

Black Power Day. On June 5, 1966, James Meredith started his "March Against Fear," a one-man walk from Memphis to Jackson. A sniper wounded him. After the shooting, Stokely Carmichael, Martin Luther King Jr., and others continued to march and they were arrested. Upon his release from jail, Carmichael gave this historic speech to a crowd of supporters: "This is the twenty-seventh time I have been arrested and I ain't going to jail no more! The only way we gonna stop them white men from whuppin' us is to take over. What we gonna start sayin' now is Black Power!"

Nancy Kurshan's archives contain a wealth of documents relating to the organization of Black Power Day. There's a two-page letter signed by Jerry Rubin (as the Berkeley Students for a Democratic Society a.k.a. "Campus SDS"), in which he outlines why it's important to support the concept of Black Power, how the mass media deliberately distorts the idea of Black Power, and how the event would be a strong follow up to the Teach-In of May 21, 1965.

There's a memorandum from the Assistant Dean of Students from October 12, 1966, outlining the rules and regulations of the event and the responsibilities that SDS must take on for the "proposed conference on Black Power" to be endorsed by UC Berkeley. Apparently SDS disagreed, as there's a memo boldly titled "NO AGREEMENT!" which reads, in part, "The 'guidelines' by the Administration for their granting of facilities for Black Power Day are neither within the framework of the traditions of free speech on this campus, nor are they compatible with the implementation of an effective conference on Black Power."

These earnest documents are naively charming—and the timing is significant. The phrase Black Power was just starting to emerge on the West Coast—as was the Black Panther Party, which coincidentally was founded just down the road (in West Oakland) during the exact same week these memos were going back and forth across the Berkeley campus. There had been no interaction between Jerry and Black Panther Party cofounders Huey Newton and Bobby Seale yet. On October 15, 1966 (just two weeks before Rubin's Black Power Day), they established the Black Panther Party for Self Defense by writing the "Ten Point Program" detailing and demanding, "What We Want, What We Believe."

BOBBY SEALE: The first time I saw Jerry—he was running for Mayor of Berkeley speaking at a rally.

Also in Kurshan's archives is a flyer that cries out, "Black Power Day Crisis!" telling the public that "we need $2700 by October 19th" to present the event. All expenses are listed, including flying Stokely Carmichael from Atlanta for $300, Floyd McKissick from New York for $300, Rennie Davis from Chicago for $200, and "four from Watts" for $100 total. Make checks payable to "S.D.S. Black Power Day," and send them to N. Kurshan at 2632 Regent Street in Berkeley. Another flyer says, "Come off it baby, ain't no white folks around, let's tell it like it is."

Jerry, Nancy, and Michael Lerner had decided to organize a Black Power Day event on the Berkeley campus. To do so, they joined forces with the SDS (Students for a Democratic Society) an organization that was often at odds with Jerry's political approach, favoring the more traditional door-to-door technique of grassroots campaigning. The three were ahead of the curve by organizing this event. Two year later, cries of "Black Power!" would be commonplace amongst white radicals, but not in 1966.

Although he was not yet Governor of California, future candidate Ronald Reagan was already publicly defaming the VDC and other student protest groups at speeches throughout the state. He made accusations that "[top members of some Democratic volunteer groups] are members of known Communistic front organizations." Over time, the FBI and Reagan would become close pals in fighting the Black Panthers and any other radicals that crossed their path. In fact, according to investigative journalist Seth Rosenfeld, the Hoover/Reagan axis had begun years earlier, when, as President of the Screen Actors Guild, Reagan would meet with FBI agents privately in the evenings and name names of supposed Commies in Hollywood.

Although both Reagan and current Governor Pat Brown were invited to speak, neither appeared, but Stokely Carmichael did, along with Ron Karenga—who would go on to start the Black Nationalist "US" Organization in Los Angeles (a group that would later be involved in the death of two Black Panthers on the University of California, Los Angeles campus). Rennie Davis led a lecture on "Organizing Whites." There was some six hours of speeches by both blacks and whites at UC Berkeley's outdoor Greek Theater on October 29, 1966. Some ten thousand people heard Carmichael finish the event with a speech that began with: "It's a privilege and an honor to be in the white intellectual ghetto of the West . . . We wanted to say that this is a student conference, as it should be, held on a campus, and that we're not ever to be caught up in the intellectual masturbation of the question of Black Power. That's a function of people who are advertisers that call themselves reporters." And ended an hour later, with: "We have been tired of trying to prove things to white people. We are tired of trying to explain to white people that we're not going to hurt them. We are concerned with getting the things we want, the things that we have to have to be able to function. The question is, can white people allow for that in this country? The question is, will white people overcome their racism and allow for that to happen in this country? If that does not happen, brothers and sisters, we have no choice but to say very clearly, 'Move over, or we're going to move on over you.' Thank you."

"Come off it baby, ain't no white folks around, let's tell it like it is."

White Kids and Black Power

For a long time one of the central slogans mouthed by the new radical student left has been that people should participate meaningfully in making the decisions that vitally affect their lives. Now that part of the negro movement has taken these slogans seriously - in terms of organization, action, and control of power in black communities the new radicals are challenged - just as the white middle class is challenged - to decide just where it stands. For example, does their "participatory democracy" go beyond mere introverted concern with internal problems to create a joint strategy and to build complementary white movements ? Moreover, how do these concepts of black community organization affect our priorities and our directions as white kids working in the movement ? To discuss these issues, Students for a Democratic Society is calling for a massive and crucial conference in Berkeley on Saturday, October 29th (hopefully on campus).   Major exponents and critics of "black power", revolutionaries and reformists, black and white have been invited to debate - "Black Power and its Challenges".

STOKELY CARMICHAEL
(National chairman of SNCC)

IVANHOE DONALDSON
(Harlem SNCC organizer)

RENNIE DAVIS
(Organizer of poor whites in Chicago)

Others to be invited include Martin Luther King, Dick Gregory, and members of the white establishment including Governor Brown and Ronald Reagan. Spokesmen from Negro "riot" areas will also be present.

GOAL: To raise the issues of "black power".
To collect thousands of dollars for the movement.

DATE: All day Saturday, October 29th.

PLACE: Since thousands of people are likely to attend the conference we requested Upper Sproul Plaza. This request was refused by the University. We now have to decide where the conference will take place.

COME TO THE NEXT SDS (Students for a Democratic Society) MEETING
THURSDAY, OCTOBER 6th at
Westminster Hall, 2700 Bancroft at 7.30 p.m.

HELP PLAN: BLACK POWER CONFERENCE
ANTI-WAR PROGRAM
ANTI-APARTHEID CAMPAIGN

HELP BUILD THE MOVEMENT ON CAMPUS AND IN THE COMMUNITY

BLACK POWER AND ITS CHALLENGES

SATURDAY
GREEK THEATER

9:15 - MIKE MILLER - "HISTORY OF BLACK POWER IN SNCC"

10:00 - IVANHOE DONALDSON (N.Y. Director of SNCC)

10:40 - "A STATEMENT FROM MARIO SAVIO"

11:00 - "The White Radical's Dilemma"
(a debate edited to the movement)

11:50 - CLAY CARSON (from Watts)

12:00 - ELIJAH TURNER (Oakland Black Organizer)

12:20 - "TWO VIEWS ON BLACK POWER" (with audience questions)
-- JAMES BEVEL (Southern Christian Leadership Conference)
-- IVANHOE DONALDSON (SNCC)

1:40 - RENNIE DAVIS (Chicago) "ORGANIZING WHITES"

2:10 - PANEL "BLACK POWER IN LOCAL COMMUNITIES"
-Watts: DANNY GREY
BROTHER LENNIE
- Richmond: KATHERINE HIMES
- Oakland: ELIJAH TURNER
- Moderator: MIKE MILLER

3:10 - "ORGANIZING STUDENTS"
--MIKE SMITH (SDS)
--MIKE PARKER (SDS)

3:50 - JAMES BEVEL (Southern Christian Leadership Conference)

4:30 - STOKELY CARMICHAEL (Chairman of SNCC)

Campus SDS

BLACK POWER DAY CRISIS!

Stokely Carmichael

BERKELEY CONFERENCE SDS
WE HAVE UNTIL OCT. 19 TO PRESENT "BLACK POWER DAY"

leading advocates of black power in from around the country and pay the airlines in advance. Quite frankly, S.D.S. is broke. Unless we raise $2,700 before Wednesday, Oct. 19, all of the negotiation with the administration will be academic. We just won't have the funds. This is a breakdown of what the money will go for:

1. Flying Stokely Charmichael from Atlanta $300
2. Flying Floyd McKissick from New York 300
3. Flying Rennie Davis from Chicago 200
4. Flying Ivanhoe Donaldson and probably two
   others from New York 900
5. Speaking fee to CORE for McKissick 500
6. Publicity, arrangements, etc. 400
7. Four from Watts 100
                                                  _____
                                                   $2,700

BLACK POWER DAY WILL NOT BE SUCCESSFUL
UNLESS S.D.S. CAN RAISE THIS MONEY BY OCT. 19

PLEASE HELP! Donate nickels, dimes, quarters, dollars or more to the S.D.S. barrels at the entrance to the campus. If everyone donates just 50¢, we will be able to meet our expenses. Any donation will be appreciated.

LOOK FOR OUR BARRELS

DONATE AS MUCH MONEY AS YOU CAN ---

make checks payable to --- S.D.S. BLACK POWER DAY ---
mail to --- S.D.S.
c/o N. Kurshan
2632 Regent St.
Berkeley, Calif.

THANK YOU

Campus S.D.S.

The Human Be-In—Jumpstarting the Summer of Love.

The Summer of Love got off to an early start in January 1967, when the "Human Be-In" was held in San Francisco's Golden Gate Park. The event included acid guru Timothy Leary, who encouraged the assembled masses to "turn on, tune in, drop out." Beat poet Allen Ginsberg chanted mantras and Jefferson Airplane and the Grateful Dead provided musical entertainment. Tens of thousands showed up and dropped LSD. Jerry was invited to speak on behalf of the Berkeley contingent of antiwar activists.

Ginsberg had chanted an optimistic mantra to the crowd: "Peace in America, Peace in Vietnam," and gotten a lukewarm response, while Jerry's confrontational antiwar rants alienated the crowd. Jerry Garcia said that Rubin's "angry tone" was scary and made him "sick to his stomach," while Paul Kantner claimed that the San Francisco scene "didn't give a shit about politics." According to Rubin's account in *DO iT!*, during an organizational meeting for the Human Be-In one San Francisco hippie got so turned off by the rhetoric of the Berkeley radicals that he proclaimed, "There's got to be more love in this room: roll some more joints!" While the Be-In became a significant landmark of the counterculture, foreshadowing Haight-Ashbury as the crown of creation for the summer of '67, Rubin's participation was just a footnote.

Jerry with the Grateful Dead at the Human Be-in, 1967.
Photo by Lisa Law © 2017

Ron Davis was with the San Francisco Mime Troupe who, along with the Diggers, led by Emmett Grogan, were early proponents of political satire; they would later inspire Rubin. The Troupe and the Diggers helped to organize the Be-In. It was Davis who had given Jerry the idea to dress up as a revolutionary war soldier for the HUAC hearing in 1966. Also worth noting is that the world's most notorious "dance hall keeper," Bill Graham (of the Fillmore East & West), made his first foray into the counterculture of the Bay Area by managing the Mime Troupe.

Davis gave me an eyewitness account of that January 14, 1967 spectacle:

> So Emmett Grogan exaggerated as much as Jerry, only in a kind of perfectly reasonable way, which you almost believed it. Grogan said it was two hundred thousand [people who attended the Human Be-In], I read that three times [in Grogan's memoir *Ringolevio*], and I said, "this guy's out of his mind." I was there, and maybe twenty thousand. Maybe. We're talking the polo grounds in Golden Gate Park.
>
> Okay, so the night before, we in the Mime Troupe and the Diggers, we put up a circular fence, like a chicken wire fence, and hung meat on it. Grogan stole these big slabs of meat that were the ribs of cows. And we hung it on this big circular thing to talk about the internment or hamlet camps that the US was putting up in the military in Vietnam. We put it up at night. In the morning, when the soccer players came, they took the thing down, because they thought it was a pain in the ass. We put it up so the Be-In would see it. They took it down because the soccer players had reserved the space [laughs], and they took the goddamn thing down.
>
> Up on the stage, three or four guys in white, and then Jerry Rubin. And what I thought was that Jerry Rubin had made

the step over to the Hippie movement. Which was a great idea. Which was fine, to bring in something besides Ginsberg's "yada-yada" and Leary's bullshit, and the other people's vagueness. I thought that Jerry's contribution was actually very good. Whether or not he could convince that crowd that there was a war going on [laughs], or that the big problem was that the military-industrial monstrosity was going to ruin their lives, not quite sure.

But I thought it was a very good move, as a matter of fact. And I thought it was courageous, because he was outnumbered by the guys on the platform. He didn't give a shit. I mean, that's fine. That's where a guy like him was very valuable, [although] Jerry's not the greatest speaker, if you want some kind of rationality. Also, if you're surrounded by hippiedom, and Ginsberg's "Om-ing" and all the vagueness of hippiedom, and all the chatter . . .

And did it affect everybody? The problem is that the San Francisco scene was dominated by the Hippies, and the Berkeley scene was dominated by the political people, but there was a very great mix. I think it was a good attempt by Jerry [to politicize the situation]. Not too many people would dare do that.

Tom Hayden couldn't make a step towards that. It would be impossible. There was a whole bunch of political people that couldn't do it. Robert Scheer could never sit there and start "Om-ing" with people. I mean, there were political sharpies in the FSM movement, who were around. But none of them could do it. I don't know how Jerry got there. How did Jerry get in there?

_____

Jerry Runs for Mayor.

After working on Bob Scheer's failed campaign for congress, Jerry decided to run himself—as mayor of Berkeley. Although he didn't have a name for them yet, his Yippie tactics were beginning to evolve. While he attempted to demean the office by claiming he'd resign if elected, Rubin ran a "serious campaign" with a pro-marijuana, anti-Vietnam platform. He had a team of campaign volunteers going door to door and wound up with twenty-two percent of the vote, coming in second out of four in the race.

NANCY KURSHAN: Stew and I were real active in Jerry's campaign for mayor. And in the beginning, we said to ourselves, "There's no way we're going to win this, but we're going to use it to educate." We spent a long time putting together a campaign platform, which had opinions on everything from the kitchen sink to what our opinion on China was. So very important for a mayor!

JACK KURZWEIL: The idea of Jerry running for mayor of Berkeley was utterly bizarre, and utterly Jerry. But, the campaign brochure that he put out was brilliant! It was a wonderful campaign brochure. And the thing about it that struck me is that he actually put forward a program. And it was good politics. You know, a little utopian, but what the hell? But it was a substantial discussion of a political vision.

NANCY KURSHAN: The problem was, the further we got into the campaign—the more Jerry really wanted to win. And he really thought he could. He drove us all crazy. He didn't win, though he got some nice votes. After that, things were kind of quiet, and we didn't know what to do next, we were trying to figure it out.

MICHAEL LERNER: What happened during that campaign was that, although he got a big percentage of the vote—I don't know the exact percentage. I mean, it was extraordinary given the radical nature of his platform. But a lot of the people on the left were denouncing him.

_____

The Old Left Criticizes Jerry.

MICHAEL LERNER: People kept saying he's just an egotist self-promoter looking for power for himself. So, here he was running for office, he had a platform, he was asking people to join with him, and a lot of people on the left, instead of joining with him, were denouncing him even though what he was saying was totally consistent with what they were saying.

NANCY KURSHAN: Some people liked Jerry, and some people didn't like Jerry. Some people really didn't like the theatrical, political confrontational style of things. Especially SDS, which was very "you have to go door to door in the neighborhoods," kind of thing. Jerry was skipping over the door-to-door, going right for the front page. Too bad they couldn't figure out how to work both ends, because it would have been effective. But Dave Dellinger, for some reason, he got it. And he wanted that energy.

An Invitation from Uncle Dave.
Frustrated with the lack of support from the conservative Left, and their criticism of him as an egotistical self-promoter, Jerry decided to accept Dave Dillinger's invitation to move to New York City and chair his upcoming planned march on the Pentagon. While Nancy stayed behind to settle their moving arrangements, Jerry went on ahead and met his future partner-in-crime, Abbie Hoffman.

NANCY KURSHAN: Dave Dellinger called from the East Coast, he was a leader of the National Mobilization Committee to End the War in Vietnam, and he invited Jerry to come East and be the project director for this big demonstration that was going to happen in the Fall in Washington, DC, against the war. He also offered Jerry the opportunity to bring several people with him, and they'd all be paid staff on the National Mobilization Committee. I got hired too and he brought us all East. So that was Uncle Dave.

MICHAEL LERNER: I see his egotism as an understandable reaction against the failure of the Liberal Movement to give adequate support and adequate caring to the people who were providing leadership. Jerry, after that, was so discouraged that he decided to move to the East Coast, and went there to Levitate the Pentagon in the big demonstrations of 1967.

OPPOSITE: Vote for Jerry Rubin for Berkeley Mayor, 1966, artist unknown. Collection of the Oakland Museum of California

---

To the people of Berkeley:

When I ran for mayor four years ago, the decisive issue was Fair Housing. I know that Jerry Rubin would never refuse to non-whites the rights he has always enjoyed as a white. The incumbent Mayor, on the other hand, was elected primarily because he refused to non-whites the same housing right he has enjoyed all his life because he is white.

Jerry Rubin would never refuse to the Vietnamese people the right of self-determination which our Revolutionary forefathers fought so hard to win for us. His opponent, Mr. Johnson, however, favors our intervention in Vietnam despite the fact that this denies self-determination to the Vietnamese people.

If you believe in equal rights for all Americans and in the American Revolutionary principle of self-determination for all peoples, I hope you will join me in voting for Jerry Rubin for Mayor of Berkeley.

Dr. Fred Stripp

❋ THE CAMPAIGN AT A GLANCE ❋

WITHDRAW TROOPS FROM VIETNAM	NO TUITION
FIGHT POVERTY	18 YEAR OLDS SHOULD VOTE
LOWER RENTS	LEGALIZE MARIJUANA
LOW COST PUBLIC HOUSING	TURN TELEGRAPH AVENUE INTO A MALL
CONTROL THE POLICE	PLANT TREES AND FLOWERS
OPPOSE CAPITAL PUNISHMENT	END TRACKING IN THE SCHOOLS
JOBS FOR THE UNEMPLOYED	

IF YOU HAVE NOT YET READ OUR BROCHURE, PLEASE CONTACT US FOR A COPY.

THE POST

Wednesday, March 22, 1967   CALIFORNIA'S LARGEST NEGRO—LATIN NEWSPAPER

Jerry Rubin Says Mayor Discriminates

Jerry Rubin, young man seeking to oust the present mayor of Berkeley in the April 4 election, gave clear-cut reasons why.

"This campaign," he said earnestly, "is an extension of the one four years ago, when Wallace Johnson ran on the platform of being against fair housing. He is not interested in the needs of minorities. I am."

One of Rubin's first acts as mayor would be the cancellation of Mayor Johnson's business license, because of what Rubin terms "racial discrimination at his factory." Johnson operates the Upright Scaffolding Co., 1013 Pardee St., in an area of Berkeley which "is about 90 per cent Negro, and with high unemployment."

Rubin contends that of the work force of 60 there, no Negroes hold "up front" or supervisory jobs, and only one holds a skilled "blue-collar" job. The three other Negro employees work in the "lowest paid, most difficult and dangerous jobs...in the foundry."

The articulate young man condemns the absence of progress in racial equality in the twenty-year-old factory as "appalling." He acknowledges that conditions there are no different from other private industries -- but this one is owned by the mayor of a supposedly progressive city, and this fact Rubin cannot reconcile with his own beliefs.

Rubin described BART as the biggest work project Berkeley is likely to see in years. "Berkeley also has many unemployed," he said. "Yet are the minorities working in

BART? No, trained white workers are being brought in."

Rubin said if elected mayor he will force BART to recruit and train local Negroes and other minorities for work on the project.

He also objected to the fact that rapid transit tracks would begin to surface south of Alcatraz St. as they joined the ground-level Oakland section, instead of at the border. He contended this would create a white-Negro barrier in the neighborhood.

Jerry Rubin
Instead of private ownership of the right-of-way above the

tracks, which he said Mayor Johnson is proposing, he stated emphatically that this newly created land should be city-owned and used for low-cost housing and recreation.

Jerry Rubin, who is 28, grew up in Cincinnati. His father was a bread driver and a business agent for the Bread Drivers' Union, a branch of the teamsters. Jerry graduated from the University of Cincinnati in 1961 with a B.A. degree in American history, then worked five years as a full-time reporter for the Cincinnati Post and Times-Star. He studied sociology in Israel, and came to Berkeley in 1964 for graduate work at U.C. Later he devoted full time to numerous anti-war efforts and political campaigning.

Jerry Rubin is a likable young man, with ideals he is eager to see realized. He is for more things than against, which indicates an open-minded, generous spirit. He is opposed to the Industrial Park as he believes it would displace the poor from their low-cost housing. But he is

for neighborhood health clinics, nursery schools, playgrounds, low-interest funds to develop a poor people's co-op, abolition of all property tax on small homes, but high taxes on speculative real estate belonging to the large property owner. If elected, he said he would serve the interests of the disadvantaged, poor, minority people and would work to make Berkeley a city without racial discrimination.

ELECT RUBIN MAYOR

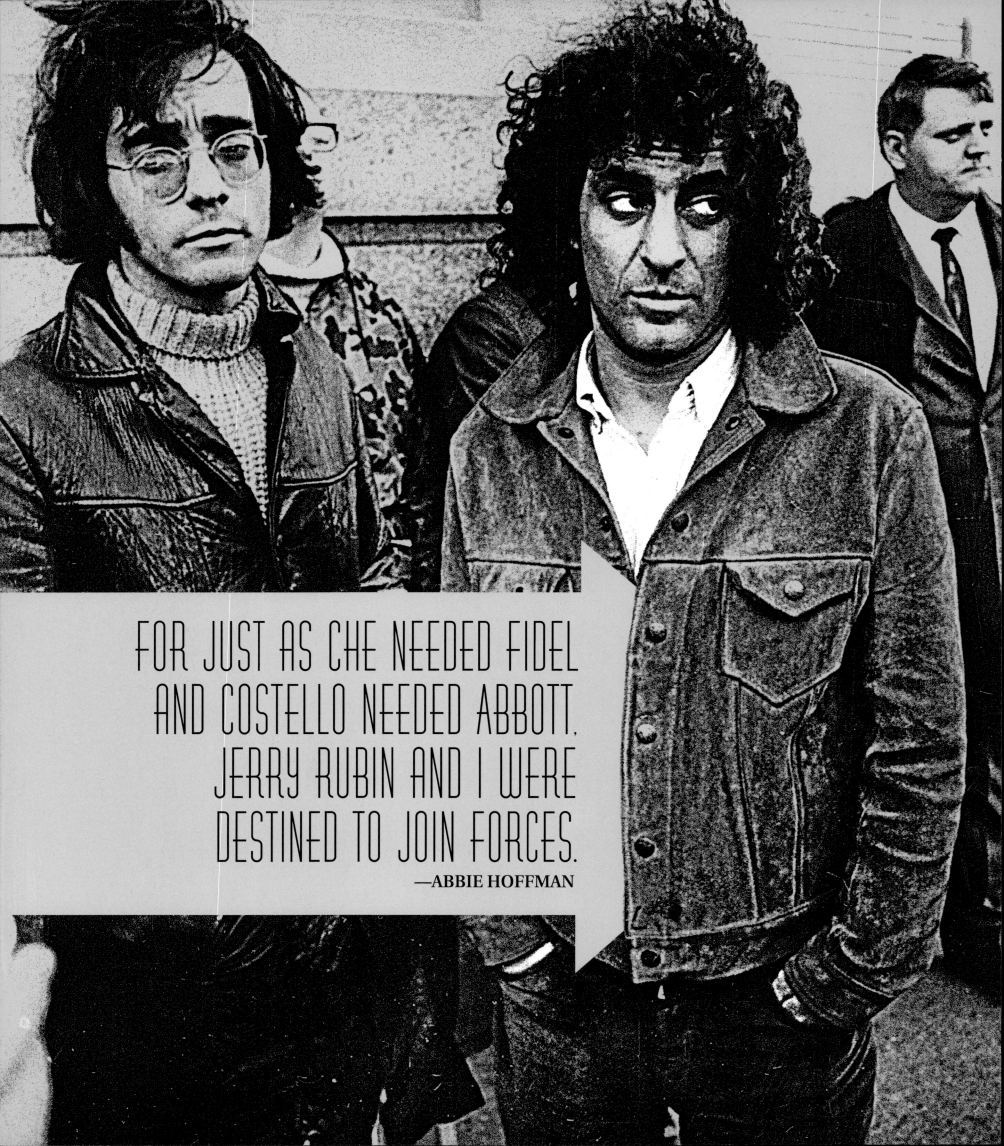

FOR JUST AS CHE NEEDED FIDEL
AND COSTELLO NEEDED ABBOTT,
JERRY RUBIN AND I WERE
DESTINED TO JOIN FORCES.
—ABBIE HOFFMAN

Abbie

of the Vietnam Day Committee followed the trucks transporting napalm in an old truck. Jerry had painted it battleship gray, and attached was a large yellow banner, warning "Danger! Napalm! Bombs Ahead." In March 1966, Jerry traveled to New York for an antiwar rally. His rhetoric echoed a bit of Allen Ginsberg's *Howl*-era poetry: "We are a dangerous country, a neurotic country possessing deadly power"; the "declared worldwide American policy [is] a symptom of our society's sickness."

> ## JERRY ROLLED INTO TOWN, AND I WAS LIKE, I GOTTA MEET THAT GUY.
>
> —ABBIE HOFFMAN

Most people don't realize that, when they met, Jerry was more famous than Abbie—Abbie was a fan of Jerry before Jerry even knew Abbie existed. According to Jonah Raskin's book *For the Hell of It: The Life and Times of Abbie Hoffman,* "He was impressed with Jerry's appearance at HUAC in 1966 and he admired Jerry's rhetorical skills so much that he called him 'the white Rap Brown.' Jerry didn't alter Abbie as intensely as Abbie altered Jerry, but Abbie needed him nonetheless as a comrade, business partner, and costar." When he met Abbie, Jerry had interacted with different factions of the antiwar movement, while Abbie had not.

MARTIN KENNER: I had to give a talk at the New School, and I couldn't go, and Abbie substituted for me. And people didn't know who Abbie was then. But when I met Jerry, I already felt like I was meeting a star.

NANCY KURSHAN: Abbie had been involved in the civil rights movement in the South, but he hadn't been involved in the antiwar movement at all yet.

DAVID SPANER, YIPPIE/FILM CRITIC: When Abbie and Jerry met, Jerry was more ideological and political than Abbie. He identified more with that kind of struggle going on around the world and in Berkeley, and in the stuff he was organizing. Where Abbie had come out of the civil rights movement, and was just getting into the counterculture of the Lower East Side. It's kind of interesting that Jerry was the more politicized when they initially met. But by the end, that had kind of flipped. Abbie was the leftist organizer now.

Although it's rarely mentioned, Abbie and Jerry nearly crossed paths in the early '60s. Abbie had completed his undergrad degree at Brandeis University in the spring of '59, and arrived that fall at UC Berkeley as a grad student studying psychology. A year later, Abbie begrudgingly left Berkeley to marry his first wife, Sheila (who was pregnant), in Massachusetts. In his book *Fug You,* Ed Sanders mentions that Abbie participated in at least one political act while in the Bay Area. On the evening of May 1, 1960, Abbie—along with many others, including Shirley MacLaine and Marlon Brando—stood outside of San Quentin Prison for an overnight vigil leading up the execution of celebrated *Cell 2455, Death Row* author Caryl Chessman.

Had Abbie stuck around, he may have bumped into Jerry, who arrived on campus at the beginning of '64 as a sociology grad student. Jerry didn't last long in the classroom either, leaving before he completed his first term. But he remained in Berkeley until mid-'67, doing other proto-Yippie stunts. Napalm was being manufactured in the Bay Area, and to raise awareness and incite outrage, members

OPPOSITE: Abbie with Abe Peck, Michigan Ave, October 1969.
Photo © Paul Sequeria

THE DAY I ARRIVED IN NEW YORK,
A FRIEND TOLD ME, "ABBIE HOFFMAN
THINKS IT'S MORE IMPORTANT TO BURN
DOLLAR BILLS THAN DRAFT CARDS."
—JERRY RUBIN, *GROWING (UP) AT 37*

Wall Street. Jim Fouratt was one of the first Yippies in 1967, and by '69 was an outspoken gay activist involved in the Stonewall Riots. He "divided his time between the glittering world of Broadway and the Bohemian hubs of the Village," and it was Fouratt who suggested the New York Stock Exchange prank to Abbie—where Abbie and Jerry would meet.

JIM FOURATT: We felt that we wanted to bring home the message that the war was really being fought at home. American soldiers were being killed, Vietnamese people were being killed; but where this was really being financed by was Wall Street, and they were completely detached from this sort of human tragedy of the war . . . We went and looked at the stock exchange and they had no glass up. You just got the balcony. And so, we decided we would go and shower money down on the floor, with the proper slogans about "Stop the War," "the War Lives Here," and all that.

LARRY "RATSO" SLOMAN, AUTHOR: We had to go upstairs at the Stock Exchange, to get to the gallery, and there was a guard there, and he said, "You can't come in." And Abbie said to him, "Oh, you're not gonna let us in because we're Jewish?" And the guy gets all flustered and goes, "All right." Didn't want to be accused of being anti-Semitic at the stock market. And then we go over to the balcony, and then Abbie and Jerry and everybody else is showering money. Dollar bills are cascading down, and literally, this is one of those things where time stops. All the din of the stock market stops, and they're looking up at us. And as they hit the ground, there's like a mad scramble, and everybody—all the traders—are going for the bills. And then, when there's no more bills, they started booing.

JIM FOURATT: We got hustled out quickly, and I was like the *New York Times* guy. I would talk in sentences, and Abbie was more like the [sound bite of] *Daily News* or the *New York Post*. So, I made up a story . . . And I'm dyslexic, so I can talk. Abbie's on speed, and I'm dyslexic. I very seriously told the *New York Times* reporter that I had raised the money principally from General Westmoreland's mother, because she was so beside herself that her son was really the principal in charge of the military. I did it dead-faced and that got in the news. All hell broke loose at that point . . .

LARRY "RATSO" SLOMAN: Then we went downstairs, and that's where the famous picture of Abbie and Jerry burning the five-dollar bill came from. When they did that, we heard police sirens; and Abbie grabbed me and the reporter from the *East Village Other*, hails a cab, and just leaves everybody to fend for themselves. And Abbie goes, "I can't wait to see this on the six o'clock news!" And that was one of the great protests of all time!

Jerry and Abbie burning dollar bills on Wall Street.

In *Growing (Up) at 37,* Jerry wrote: "Police grabbed the ten of us, dragged us down the stairs, and deposited us on Wall Street at high noon in front of astonished businessmen and hungry TV cameras. That night the attack by hippies on the Stock Exchange was told around the world—international publicity! The next week the New York Stock Exchange announced they were building a bulletproof window above the tourist section as a protection against future invasions. I fell in love with Abbie."

In Berkeley, Jerry and Stew Albert had discussed integrating hippies into the antiwar movement. After meeting Abbie, Jerry saw the possibility turn into a reality. Unlike confident Hoffman, who disdained the middle class, Jerry needed to prove himself to those who had snubbed him for his working-class roots. Jerry's lack of self-assurance drove him to succeed, which would pay off later. While Hoffman treated politics as a joke, Rubin took them seriously, like when he campaigned for Adlai Stevenson as a teen. Although Hoffman had a flair for humor, Rubin was willing to mold his persona to any situation that presented itself, street theater or otherwise.

In his memoirs, Stew Albert recalled, "I arrived in New York, went to see Jerry, and he says 'Look, we don't have time to talk, there's gonna be this great event at the Stock Exchange today.' We got stoned and went down there and Jerry introduced me to Abbie. It's a funny place to meet Abbie Hoffman—right on Wall Street. Abbie was really encouraging Jerry to get independent of MOBE [National Mobilization Committee to End the War in Vietnam]. He thought it was kind of a mistake for Jerry to be with them. He wanted Jerry to come and work with him . . . He was saying to Jerry, 'You ran for Mayor in Berkeley. You got this big vote.' That really impressed Abbie."

Jerry told Ratso Sloman, "I learned a lot from that Stock Exchange event, because Abbie was applying the whole role of myth; create one little event then all of sudden it gets talked about, it gets written about—it gets a whole story. The whole use of the mass media—it was awesome. Now that's taken for granted because everyone does it. Ronald Reagan perfected what we did. Little one-sentence stories that go Bop! And Pow!"

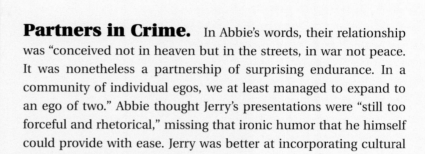

Partners in Crime.

In Abbie's words, their relationship was "conceived not in heaven but in the streets, in war not peace. It was nonetheless a partnership of surprising endurance. In a community of individual egos, we at least managed to expand to an ego of two." Abbie thought Jerry's presentations were "still too forceful and rhetorical," missing that ironic humor that he himself could provide with ease. Jerry was better at incorporating cultural revolution into the bigger picture.

Nevertheless, as Abbie points out in *Soon to be a Major Motion Picture,* "We were two people who sensed the opportunity of blending the political and cultural revolutions. Jerry's forte was political timing, mine dramatic. I trusted his political judgment more than anyone's . . . stubborn, attentive to the ways of power and the universe; Jerry had the drive and the political instincts to ride the movement waves."

RON DAVIS: I was trying to figure out, what is Rubin about? And without being negative here, but essentially being critical, he had a quarter of [Paul] Krassner, a quarter of the Diggers, one quarter Abbie, and one quarter himself, the advertising man, or the newspaper man.

The Diggers were a radical group from Haight-Ashbury led by the charismatic Emmett Grogan. One primary difference between the Diggers and the soon-to-be Yippies was that the Diggers preferred anonymity, while the Yippies loved celebrity—that's the primary reason why the Diggers are mostly unknown. They taught the Yippies many of the tricks of the trade—especially to Abbie, who gathered many of them in *Steal This Book*—which chagrined the Diggers, who wanted those "how to live on zero dollars a day" techniques to remain on the down low.

RON DAVIS: Peter Berg came out of the Mime Troupe [that I founded]. So did Grogan. I'm also the author of the 1965 article called "Guerilla Theater," which then sprung out and then did all sorts of things that I didn't agree with. I didn't agree with what the Yippies were doing. That was not Guerilla Theater, as far as I'm concerned. That's imagistic kind of stuff.

Levitating the Pentagon

WE ANNOUNCED THAT WE
WERE GOING TO CLOSE DOWN
THE PENTAGON, AND LYNDON
JOHNSON SAID ON TELEVISION,
"I WILL NOT ALLOW A SMALL
GROUP OF DISRUPTERS TO
CLOSE DOWN THE PENTAGON."
"THANK YOU, LBJ. YOU JUST
TOLD THREE MILLION PEOPLE
THAT WE ARE PROTESTING ON
OCTOBER TWENTY-FIRST."
—JERRY RUBIN

Jerry had initially come to New York to join the National Mobilization Committee to End the War in Vietnam (MOBE). As Jerry and Abbie started hanging out and smoking dope, Dave Dellinger began to regret his decision. MOBE had wanted, in the words of Rubin in *Steal This Dream*, "an orderly, peaceful, middle-class protest, and I brought in Abbie. It was a perfect partnership because Abbie added the theater, the humor, the sparkle; and I added the purpose." As Dellinger recalled in his memoir, *From Yale to Jail*:

> *I recruited Jerry Rubin to play a key role in organizing the Siege on the Pentagon. Jerry had flair, had helped organize activities on the West Coast that moved from mass rallies to civil disobedience and worked well with others at Berkeley's Vietnam Day. But this time, it didn't work as well. I kept getting complaints from other staff members that Jerry did no work. Surprised and puzzled, I investigated.*
>
> *The problem was that something else had come along that was far more exciting to him and that he thought would make a greater contribution to ending the war and to developing a new spirit in the country, particularly among the youth. Jerry was captivated by the action that Abbie Hoffman, Jim Fouratt, and other hippies had engaged in at the New York Stock Exchange.*
>
> *I don't know if Jerry, like the people who had stopped going to demonstrations, thought beforehand that he had grown tired of the same old routine, straight political actions, with or without civil disobedience. That didn't seem to be behind his decision to accept our invitation [to come from Berkeley to New York]. But that's how he felt after he participated in the Wall Street action and got to know Abbie, Paul Krassner, and others.*

In the oral history *From Camelot to Kent State*, Jerry recalled telling Dave Dellinger: "'You know, this march on Congress, Dave, doesn't really make sense to me. People don't see Congress as the enemy. They elect Congress. There's no point to be made by doing that. We should march on the Pentagon.' I saw things in media images, in terms of good versus evil, and the media image would be the Movement versus the Pentagon. That's all we had to. Nothing else. No words. You don't need words."

It's Not a Protest . . . It's an Exorcism.

With the change in venue, not only did the MOBE demonstration change its strategy, it changed its vision—a vision that verged on the surreal after Jerry invited Abbie, according to a 1980s interview with Joan and Robert Morrison. At the first meeting that Hoffman attended, he put forth the concept of exorcizing the Pentagon. By surrounding the five-sided building with a circle of hippies, "they would make the Pentagon rise from the ground a few inches. And all the evil was going to leave." In a "it could only happen in the 1960s" moment, the General Services Administration (which oversees the Pentagon) began to negotiate with Jerry. The government set limits on how close they could get to the building, how high the levitation could go, and so on. As Jerry later pointed out, "By LBJ saying that he wasn't going to allow us to close it down, he gave us the power to have that possibility. So in a way, just by announcing it, we created a victory."

Although Abbie is generally credited for coming up with the idea to levitate the Pentagon, there's some dispute. In *Arthur* magazine, *Realist* editor Paul Krassner said, "The idea for the exorcism originated with Allen Cohen, editor of the *Oracle,* and painter Michael Bowen, after they read, in *The City in History* by Lewis Mumford, about the Pentagon being a baroque symbol of evil and oppression." (Bowen was an organizer of the San Francisco Be-In and the first person to give Rubin LSD.)

In *Steal This Dream,* Allen Ginsberg said, "It was Gary Snyder who had conceived the notion of the levitation of the Pentagon." Gary Snyder's controversial poem "A Curse on the Men in Washington, Pentagon" was published in March 1967. Jerry admitted: "It could very well have been Gary Snyder's idea. I don't know. All I know is Abbie was the PR man for it. So Abbie's the one who made the exorcism real. I directed Abbie. Abbie was just doing these wild things in the streets of New York, which was a lot of fun, but I took the Abbie windup doll, I wound him up, and pointed him toward the Pentagon."

"I took the Abbie windup doll, I wound him up and pointed him toward the Pentagon."
—Jerry Rubin

The March Begins.

Decades later, Rubin felt the October 21, 1967 event was "probably the best demonstration in the '60s." Jerry didn't want to just change protest strategy; he wanted a new kind of protestor.

DANA BEAL, PROVOS & MARIJUANA ACTIVIST: "So we said we were going to have a smoke-in at the Levitation of the Pentagon. We got our hands on a few pounds of pot. We rolled up joints and gave them away. And at the time, a lot of kids were basically straight SDS kids, and they weren't smoking pot. Smoking pot went from a Lower East Side phenomenon to a national phenomenon."

The Provos were originally an anarchist movement in Holland, who took their name from a mid-'60s doctoral dissertation, which defined "young troublemakers" as "provos," a word derived from the Dutch word *provoceren* (to provoke). Rubin wrote, in *DO iT!*, "A new man was born smoking pot while besieging the Pentagon . . . he didn't feel at home in SDS . . . a stoned politico. A hybrid mixture of New Left and hippie coming out something different." Benjamin Spock and Norman Mailer led the march; the atmosphere was festive. More than fifty thousand people had descended on Washington, gathering at the reflecting pool at the Lincoln Memorial, the

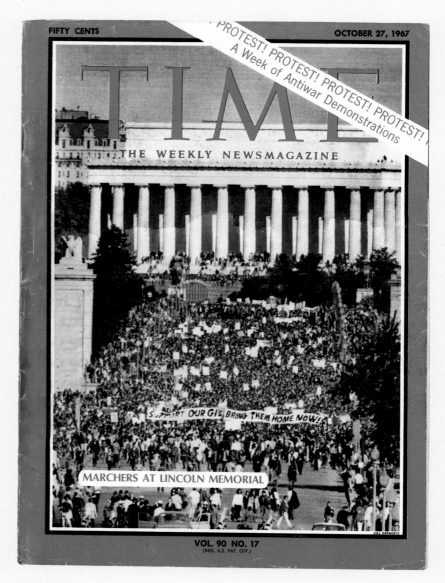

FIFTY CENTS

OCTOBER 27, 1967

PROTEST! PROTEST! PROTEST! PROTEST!
A Week of Antiwar Demonstrations

TIME

THE WEEKLY NEWSMAGAZINE

SUPPORT OUR GIS, BRING THEM HOME NOW!

MARCHERS AT LINCOLN MEMORIAL

VOL. 90 NO. 17
(REG. U.S. PAT. OFF.)

same location as Martin Luther King Jr.'s "I Have a Dream" speech. The march was thirty-five thousand strong (some stayed behind to take chartered buses home the same day), and so it took three hours to complete the journey to the Pentagon. One marcher known as Super-Joel yelled at Dr. Spock, "Hey! This march is going too slow for us speed freaks."

The protesters taunted the twenty-five hundred armed soldiers—many of whom were the same age—they met at the Pentagon with, "we have music, we have drugs, we have women" (Rubin is quick to add "we were sexists then"), and suggested that the young soldiers put down their guns and come join them. In *Steal This Dream,* Anita Hoffman, Abbie's wife, remembered, "I was wearing the Sgt. Pepper jacket. And we had Mr. and Mrs. America paper Uncle Sam hats."

The Exorcism. The cool October air carried the patchouli scent of the Summer of Love (which had peaked just months earlier in Haight-Ashbury). The Fugs, Norman Mailer, Allen Ginsberg, and thousands of others chanted "out, demons, out." Che Guevara had been murdered a few weeks prior, and his image was flying in the breeze, along with Vietcong flags. Phil Ochs performed on a make-shift stage, and filmmaker Kenneth Anger incanted underneath it. Norman Mailer, in his *The Armies of the Night,* described it as "ritual theater." Participants were "Revolutionary Alchemists."

ABE PECK, *CHICAGO SEED* NEWSPAPER / JOURNALISM PROFESSOR: I had gone to the Pentagon demonstration and the whole "levitate the Pentagon" thing had an appeal to me. The reason it had an appeal to me is because first of all, it was "far out," but also I liked the meta-jujitsu of the whole thing. The soldiers had the guns and we didn't want them, especially at that point. I was really a flower child. It wasn't even hippie militance but it was that Yippie blend of resistance and über-hipness.

One plan that never got off the ground was to have an airplane drop two hundred pounds of daisies. The flowers had been bought (by the owners of the Millbrook estate in upstate New York—where Timothy Leary conducted his LSD experiments) for Michael Bowen to distribute. Some FBI agents had responded to a want ad in the *East Village Other* asking for a pilot, and they undermined the plan by not showing up at the airport. Bowen trucked the daisies to the Pentagon and hand-distributed them. The upside was something more potent (than if the flower-bombing had occurred). The iconic image of a golden-haired boy (wearing a turtleneck sweater) putting daisies in the barrel of a soldier's gun circulated in newspapers and magazines around the globe—and still crops up in documentaries today.

Ratso Sloman talked to an activist known as Super-Joel, who said: "I just took the flowers and one by one, boom, boom, boom, put 'em in the gun barrels . . . Then that guy [Joe] Rosenthal, who took the Iwo Jima picture, took that famous picture of me." *[Author's Note: Whether or not it's Super-Joel is up for debate. Other sources say that it's Hibiscus, cofounder of the Cockettes—the "flamboyant, psychedel-ic gay-themed drag troupe"—who was, at the time, an aspiring New York actor named George Harris. It's been confirmed that the photog-rapher is Bernie Boston, who also photographed Martin Luther King Jr. and every president from Johnson to Clinton.]*

KATE COLEMAN: Abbie grabbed Anita and got in the face of the National Guard. I was young, but these guys looked like they were barely eighteen, you know. They looked like real rubes. He started dry-humping Anita, standing up with her legs around him like they were making love, as if to say "you poor slobs." I thought it was horrible. It was rude. They couldn't move from their positions, and he was just right under their noses.

Stew Albert, in his memoir, remembered it differently, with the protestors shoving and fist-fighting the soldiers. Standing three or four deep, the soldiers would rotate to keep up with the assaults, but the physical aggression petered out into small talk and jokes.

OPPOSITE: October, 1967: the Revolution is captured on the front cover of *Time.*

LEFT: Paul Krassner and Kate Coleman, circa 1967.

AUTHOR JONAH RASKIN ON MARCHING ON THE PENTAGON

"I REMEMBER GOING IN A BUS with lots of people, and it did seem bigger than any other demonstration that I'd ever been at before. It was really diverse and had all different aspects of people who were opposed to the war. Hippies, mobilization people, old lefties, Dr. Spock. I was a Dr. Spock baby; my mother read Dr. Spock and said, 'You can just blame it on Dr. Spock. You were raised to be a protester. You got it along with your breast milk and all that.'

"I do remember crossing a bridge, and there was a guy who was on the bridge who was holding a sign that said,

LBJ—PULL OUT NOW LIKE YOUR FATHER SHOULD'VE DONE.

I'd been at a lot of demonstrations but I never seen a sign that was so funny. We were all laughing hysterically, it was part of the way that politics had gotten sexualized by people bringing sexual metaphors into the political vocabulary. That was part of the youthful feeling of it, the subversive irreverence of the thing.

"When I first heard this notion of levitating the Pentagon, I thought, *'Well what the fuck is this? You can't levitate the Pentagon, it's this huge building!'*

But then I started to think this is absolutely brilliant. It was also kind of like when Allen Ginsberg would go around and say, 'I declare the end of war.' It's sort of like 'people power,' if you believe enough in something it will happen.

"Before I went to the Pentagon march, I went to a protest led by the Progressive Labor group, sort of an old-time protest; a small ideological group. After singing a few songs and standing around hearing some speakers, everyone went home. Well, at the Pentagon, nobody wanted to go home. I remember it got dark, and the protesters didn't want to go. They wanted to stay. People had sleeping bags and brought food. By that time, people started to get arrested. People were really being rowdy. So it was an embodiment of what it meant to go from the kind of safe rallies that I'd been to—to this real demonstration that had an edge to it. A protest where people were willing to put their bodies on the line and go to jail. I was a changed person after the Pentagon in 1967."

In 2015, Nancy Kurshan remembered that, although she, Jerry, Abbie, and Anita were in the front lines, they didn't lead the demonstration. In her unpublished memoir she wrote, "You might think that we had some kind of tactical leadership role to play, or at least Jerry would have. But that was not the case, as far as I can remember. As would happen many times in the future, we had helped to create the stage, had set up the situation as best we could, but had no clue as to how to influence the actual event. Inevitably there were others who would move in to fill that vacuum."

Time magazine reporters, going undercover as hippies, described Jerry as a twenty-nine-year-old, wild-haired "co-project director" of MOBE, and a "former Berkeley nonstudent leader [who] is an uncompromising radical." Jerry is quoted as saying, "We are now in the business of wholesale and widespread resistance and dislocation of American society." Jerry was the more famous one at the time. The reporter didn't even know Hoffman's full name, identifying him as "one New York hippie known as Abbie."

And it wasn't just the Pentagon that had inspired the *Time's* editors to make it the cover story—it was part of a weeklong series of protests that raged "from Berkeley to Brooklyn," which included a suburban LA housewife setting herself on fire on the steps of the Federal Building, burning to death like the Buddhist monks in Asia.

I DEMANDED THEY CHARGE ME WITH "URINATING ON THE PENTAGON," A POLITICAL-SEXUAL CRIME. INSTEAD THEY BOOKED ME FOR "LOITERING."
—JERRY RUBIN, *DO IT!*

White People's Arrest. The protest lasted two days, with some protestors only leaving when they were dragged off by the cops. Kurshan remembers getting arrested with Abbie, Anita, and Jerry, but because the police separated men and women, she doesn't know what Jerry went through during his detention.

NANCY KURSHAN: It was scary because we sat there through a night and a day, and the next night. And we were towards the front, and they would club people and drag them away, sometimes. So I wasn't too hot for getting clubbed, but luckily I didn't. But then, when we were arrested—I say in these interviews, lately, when people ask me how I got involved in prison reform, I say, "Well, I was arrested in '67 at the Pentagon, and I call it white people's arrest, and nobody ever thinks that's cute, so I have to stop saying that. But it was white people's arrest . . . because they arrested about a thousand people, segregated us by gender, and took hundreds of women and put us in some big schoolroom that they had commandeered for this purpose. And they had rows of cots lined up, and we all slept. And Anita Hoffman was with me, and we were next to each other. We just spent the night, like a big pajama party.

Aftermath.   The not-yet-named-as-such "Yippies" had garnered media attention; the event was a resounding success and they'd slapped the status quo around a bit.

> COUNTRY JOE MCDONALD, MUSICIAN: Jerry and Abbie both had a sense of confounding the enemy. Just fucking with their heads so much that they didn't know what to do.

Years later, Jerry reflected, "probably because of that event, [President] Johnson saw his power slipping and decided not to run again." Daniel Ellsberg confirmed in a 2015 phone call to me that he and Secretary of Defense Robert McNamara were standing side by side inside the Pentagon looking down at the protesters, debating their impact. The event did not inspire him to release the Pentagon Papers: the idea came a few years later.

Jerry said, "We hadn't physically levitated the Pentagon, but we had spiritually levitated it." Dave Dellinger remembers how "Abbie Hoffman used to tell people that they had 'only been partially successful. We raised it only ten feet.' Too bad!" After this highly publicized weirdness eroded the social conventions of America, Rubin, Hoffman and the others realized they didn't belong in the traditional protest movement. After the events of the Pentagon, there was no turning back.

> NANCY KURSHAN: We weren't so committed to working with the MOBE anymore. There were a lot of affinity groups developing. Like, in New York, there was the "Up Against the Wall Motherfuckers." We were really into collective, mass, civil disobedience. We wanted people who showed up in DC that day who hadn't planned on doing civil disobedience to come along with us.

After the Pentagon, Jerry and Nancy joined with thousands of others to shut down New York's Whitehall Street Army Induction Center—which, in his song "Alice's Restaurant," Arlo Guthrie would describe as "where . . . you get injected, inspected, detected, infected, neglected, and selected." Nancy remembered, "this was the first time that people on the East Coast had used the "mobile tactics" that had been developed in California during Stop the Draft Week." The concept was that small groups of people ran around chaotically, rather than marching. The police rode through the crowd with horses, and there were mass arrests.

Armies of the Night.   Inspired by Tom Wolfe's and Truman Capote's New Journalism, Norman Mailer recreated the Pentagon march in his Pulitzer Prize-winning novel, *The Armies of the Night*. Having been part of the Berkeley Teach-In and having co-led the march on the Pentagon, Mailer—then in his forties—liked these young revolutionaries.

> PAUL KRASSNER, *REALIST* EDITOR: Mailer knew I had interviewed George Lincoln Rockwell, head of the American Nazi party. The first thing Norman asked me about him: "And what was his style?" He was always interested in style. I said, "He's a Nazi! It's *probably* Nazi style." Mailer liked the style of the Yippies. He appreciated the style of the Yippies, as well as their purpose.

Soon after the Pentagon event, Mailer invited Jerry into his Brooklyn home for several weeks. He interviewed him, taking notes in longhand, and had Jerry review his first draft of *The Armies of the Night*. Jerry provided Mailer with typewritten "factual points," which Mailer incorporated. Mailer wrote, "Suddenly an entire generation of acidheads seemed to have said goodbye to easy visions of heaven . . . the hippies had gone from Tibet to Christ to the Middle Ages."

> J. MICHAEL LENNON, MAILER'S ARCHIVIST: I cataloged all Mailer's papers and I found, in looking at the stuff that Jerry made corrections to, that Mailer was interested in the nuances and the personalities, and Rubin was more interested in the actual structural elements of the event. There are a number of references to Rubin in those manuscripts basically saying that Rubin was critical to him in getting all the facts straight. This is especially important in the second half of *Armies of the Night* which is more of a historical overview of the whole event. One of Mailer's kids is writing a screenplay about *Armies of the Night*: John Buffalo Mailer, who is Norman's youngest son. I just read the screenplay and obviously Rubin is a key character.

NORMAN MAILER AND JERRY RUBIN

AS JUDY GUMBO AND STEW ALBERT NOTED in their anthology *The Sixties Papers,* in his 1957 essay, "The White Negro: Superficial Reflections on the Hipster," Norman Mailer predicted the 1960s. His essay "foresaw the imminence of black and [white] youth rebellion, male/female war, and a pervasive tendency for white middle-class intellectuals to adopt the hip style of the black lumpenproletari- at . . . out of the pain and psychic brutality of American life would come a generation of violent, angry, and potentially political rebels."

After convincing Mailer to participate in the two biggest political events of his life, there was no way Jerry wasn't going to rope Mailer in for a third. Mailer testified at the Chicago 8 trial:

> *Mr. Rubin said that he was working on plans to have a youth festival in Chicago in August when the Democratic Convention would take place, and it was his idea that the presence of a hun- dred thousand young people in Chicago at a festival with rock bands would so intimidate and terrify the establishment, that Lyndon Johnson would have to be nominated under armed guard. And I said, "Wow." I was overtaken with the audacity of the idea, and I said, "It's a beautiful and frightening idea."*
>
> *And Rubin said, "I think that the beauty of it is that the establishment is going to do it all themselves. We won't do a*

> *thing. We are just going to be there and they won't be able to take it. They will smash the city themselves. They will provoke all the violence."*

Mailer attended the Chicago convention as a journalist for *Harper's* magazine, spending time in the park and watching the demonstrations. Dave Dellinger chided Mailer for not speaking. Mailer told Dellinger that, "I did not want to get involved because if I did and got arrested, I would not be able to write my piece in time for the deadline." Mailer was feeling "ashamed" of himself that he hadn't spoken, so he stepped onto the platform in Grant Park one afternoon and told the crowd that he "thought they were possessed of beauty, and that I was not going to march with them because I had to write this piece." Hundreds of Yippies shouted back, "Write, Baby!" At two in the morning, the follow- ing day, Mailer told the crowd how "beautiful" they were.

When asked during the trial if Jerry meant to "intimidate" the es- tablishment, Mailer replied,

> *It would be impossible for me to begin to remember whether Mr. Rubin used the word "intimidate" or not. I suspect that he probably did not use it, because it is not his habitual style of speech. He would speak more of diverting, demoralizing the*

establishment, freaking them out, bending their mind, driving them out of their bird. I use the word "intimidate" because, possibly, since I am a bully by nature, I tend to think in terms of intimidation, but I don't think Mr. Rubin does. He thinks in terms of cataclysm, of having people reveal their own guilt, their own evil. His whole notion was that the innocent presence of one hundred thousand people in Chicago would be intolerable for a man as guilt-ridden as Lyndon Johnson.

> ## TO CALL ON RUBIN WAS IN EFFECT TO CALL UPON THE MOST MILITANT, UNPREDICTABLE, CREATIVE — THEREFORE DANGEROUS — HIPPIE-ORIENTED LEADER AVAILABLE ON THE NEW LEFT.
> —NORMAN MAILER,
> *THE ARMIES OF THE NIGHT*

Mailer wrote another successful nonfiction novel in just two weeks: *Miami and the Siege of Chicago*, which was subtitled *An Informal History of the Republican and Democratic Conventions of 1968*. It incorporated his reporting from the oft-forgotten Miami Convention that endorsed Richard Nixon. In his 1968 book review in the monthly *Commentary*, Peter Shaw wrote, "There is compassion here for the right wing of the Republicans, giving more evidence that Mailer's gift from the beginning has been to feel the emotions of the Right." And, "What happened to Mailer in Chicago, I believe, was that the hippies acted out the furthest extremes of his own imagination."

In 1969, Mailer decided to run for Mayor of New York City against incumbent John Lindsay. Mailer's running mate was fellow writer and Pulitzer Prize-winner Jimmy Breslin, who was aiming for City Council president. After Mailer's death, Breslin recalled him "arguing brilliantly at Brooklyn College that the minds of white and black children would grow best if they were together in the same classrooms." One student asked, "We had a lot of snow in Queens last year and it didn't get removed, what would you do about it?" Mailer replied, "I would melt the snow by urinating on it."

At the beginning of his campaign, Mailer assembled "emissaries from different ideological camps," including Jerry Rubin, Nancy Kurshan, Gloria Steinem, and Flo Kennedy, a black lawyer and the cofounder of the National Organization for Women (NOW). (She had also represented the woman who shot Andy Warhol, Valerie Solanas, in the courtroom.) Mailer received about forty-one thousand votes, but he never did secure the old-school Right.

In 1976, Jerry was writing his memoir about his time as a radical in *Growing (Up) at 37*, and hoped Mailer would endorse it with an introduction or a blurb. He recognized that Mailer would probably "disagree with a lot of it" since it reflected his new lifestyle, but that Mailer would "understand it better than anyone else." Mailer read two-thirds of the manuscript and sent Jerry a rejection letter. Mailer told him to "forget about it," go on to the next one. He encouraged Jerry to stay in touch.

At that point, Jerry had spent the previous summer traveling throughout China and India, taking extensive notes. (Richard Nixon—and Black Panther Huey Newton just before him—had opened the Western doors to China just three years earlier.) He wrote Mailer a letter about it: "China works; India doesn't. China is creating the new human being. It's the biggest story on the planet, and no American publisher or journalist seems interested." He suggested that they discuss it in detail. Whether they did or not is unknown. Among Jerry's personal belongings, I found the "China Diary," one hundred and forty-four handwritten, single-spaced pages. It would arguably make a great book of its own—if anyone could actually read it. It's a sprawling mess bordering on neurotic genius. In that pre-internet, pre-Beijing-Olympics world, China was, as Rubin noted on page one of his notebook: "Surreal" and "Impressionistic." His opinions are both insightful and entertaining: "Try explaining to the Chinese what is a hippie. They will not understand." And for reasons we'll never know, scribbled amongst Jerry's sociological thesis was singer Bonnie Raitt's home address and phone number.

Two decades later, in an interview with Peter Manso, Jerry said,

There was this father thing there; that we were the children of Norman Mailer's writings. In '65, the father figure had come out [to UC Berkeley] and said, "I approve of you." Then came [the Pentagon and] The Armies of the Night, and father says, "Hey, these people have something to say, they're going to influence the future of our country." And when he testified [in Chicago] he told the jury, in effect, "I may be crazy, but I'm a writer. These people are a little crazy too, but it's the crazy people who tell you where sanity lies. Listen to them; their craziness has the ring of truth."

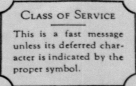

CLASS OF SERVICE

This is a fast message unless its deferred character is indicated by the proper symbol.

WESTERN

TELEGRA
W. P. MARSHALL, PRES.

The filing time shown in the date line on domestic telegrams is LOCAL TIME at point of

LL528 509P EST FEB 14 70 KQYLSYA812 KB4

K VEA518 SB PDF TDVE CHICAGO ILL 14 355

NORMAN MAILER

142 COLUMBIA HEIGHTS BROOKLYN NY

GOING TO JAIL TONIGHT CALL OFFICE

JOEY RUBIN

(400). Jerry

If there was one lesson learned at the Pentagon it is that young people didn't give a hang about political theories, ideologies, plans, organizations, meetings, or negotiations with the cops. The only vanguard is the vanguard in action. All those hundreds of hours of bullshit [planning] meetings were just that—bullshit. I support everything that puts people into action, which creates disruption and controversy, which creates chaos and rebirth.

—Jerry Rubin, "I AM the Walrus,"
Win, *circa 1968*

OPPOSITE: Brian Flanagan, Jerry, Phil Ochs, Stew.

The Birth of the Yippie

In *Steal This Dream,* Jerry said, "If you want to see the birth of Yippie, [it's when Allen] Ginsberg came out and gave a speech about how to march with the Hells Angels attacking." Ginsberg suggested incorporating sparklers, rubber swords, and colorful pinwheels into demonstrations.

Further proof that the Yippie aesthetic originated from Rubin's Berkeley days came from Abbie himself, who wrote in *Soon to Be a Major Motion Picture*, "I knew Rubin before he knew me . . . Jerry had defied the arch villain HUAC in a unique way. Dressed up as an American revolutionary (from the first revolution) Jerry successfully engaged the enemy in symbolic warfare . . . Jerry was a lovable, cunning bastard all right. I had begun to track his efforts . . . he organized political rallies emphasizing the cultural ingredient."

In a 1969 issue of the *East Village Other*, Jerry wrote, "The Pentagon demonstration in October '67—it might be described as a Yippie demonstration, because it combined theater, the mythic, drugged new culture consciousness with the direct attack on a physical institution—the Pentagon. The political and hippie worlds converged and they couldn't be separated."

The Birth of YIP. By the late 1960s, mainstream media was using the term "generation gap" to explain the growing sociopolitical divide between the emerging baby boomers and their parents. In *DO iT!*, Rubin wrote, "The 1950s were the turning point in the history of Amerika. Those who grew up before the 1950s live today in a mental world of Nazism, concentration camps, economic depression and Communist dreams Stalinized. A pre–1950s child who can still dream is very rare. Kids who grew up in the post–1950s live in a world of supermarkets, color TV commercials, guerrilla war, international media, psychedelics, rock 'n' roll, and moon walks. For us nothing is impossible. We can do anything. This generation gap is the widest in history. The pre–1950s generation has nothing to teach the post–1950s, and that's why the school system is falling apart. The pre–1950s generation grows more desperate. We dreamers disturb straight Amerika's dreamless sleep."

"THE SECRET TO THE YIPPIE MYTH IS THAT IT'S NONSENSE."
—JERRY RUBIN

The Realist, Dept. S
595 Broadway
New York, N.Y. 10012

Enclosed please find:

☐ $7 for a copy of *How a Satirical Editor Became a Yippie Conspirator in Ten Easy Years* by Paul Krassner

☐ $3 for a six-issue subscription to *The Realist* beginning with the long-awaited 13th Anniversary Issue

Name _____ Apt _____

Address _____

City _____ State _____ Zip _____

Gimme a "Y". In Ronald Sukenick's book *Down and In*, Don Katzman recounts a story. Hoffman, Allan Katzman, and Walter Bowart, cofounders of the *East Village Other*, held a meeting to decide what to call this new political party. Don Katzman: "Rubin and Abbie Hoffman came up with the idea of the Crazies . . . I said, 'If you wanted to have a reason for the cops to take a good shot at you, call yourself the Crazies. You got a perfect reason for them to take out their guns and shoot you.' . . . Abbie Hoffman was arguing for Crazies, but Jerry said, 'No, I think that Don is right. Let's not call ourselves the Crazies. We can't give 'em any more reasons for taking shots at us.'"

On the eve of 1968, not far from the Fillmore East, Rubin, Kurshan, the Hoffmans, and Paul Krassner realized that they'd changed protesting into an art form. It was a presidential year and the possibilities were endless, as they could sway public opinion through their carefully constructed antics. They needed a brand name. In his memoir, Krassner said he separated from the group and went into a bedroom:

I paced back and forth, juggling titles to see if I could come up with words that would make a good acronym. I tried Youth International Festival. YIF. Sounds like KIF. Kids International Festival? No, too contrived. Back to YIF. But what could make YIP? Now that would be ideal, because then the word Yippie could be derived organically from YIP. "Yippie" was a traditional shout of spontaneous joy. We could be the Yippies! It had just the right attitude . . . The Yippie logo was designed by Judy

Lampe, using a particular style of Japanese lithography she had studied.

PAUL KRASSNER: "Collectively they come up with Yippie!..." That's total bullshit. Ironically, when I came out of the bedroom and went back to the living room and described my brainstorm, Jerry was hesitant about it and Abbie had to persuade him. Others there were surprised about the myth of "collectively" that spread around because both Jerry and Abbie wanted to show that it was a group, not an individual, they told me."

In *DO iT!*, Rubin outlines their manifesto. "Yippie is the sound of surging through the streets. Yippies—the name of a non-organization, non-political party—the Youth International Party. Also the actor in the party: a Yippie! And the battle cry: 'YIPPIE!' Yippies were radical hippies who would join the Youth International Party. In Rubin's words, "The Marxist acidhead, the psychedelic Bolshevik." Rubin imagined teenagers across America dropping acid, growing their hair long, abandoning their conventional homes and repressive schools, and running off to join the cultural and political revolution.

MICHAEL LERNER: Now, that view was exactly what a huge number of people wanted to hear . . . They were in college and he picked the right moment to help those people formulate a vision of themselves, not as isolated individuals who wanted to rebel against their parents, but as a revolutionary force that could transform the whole society.

DAVID SPANER: I think the great contribution of Yippie is that historically the Left had organized around class. Yippie organized around culture, specifically youth culture.

Shoplifting for The Movement. One of John Lennon's first post-Beatles singles was "God Save Oz." (The B-side was "Do The Oz.") It was released in July 1971 in support of an obscenity/freedom of the press trial involving Richard Neville, the editor of the countercultural newspaper *OZ*. Along with the *International Times* (*IT*), *OZ* was one of the most important British-based papers during heyday of swinging London; it often covered Yippie activities. The magazine was known for its psychedelic graphics created by Martin Sharp, who became internationally recognized for his album cover for Cream's *Disraeli Gears*.

In his memoir *Hippie Hippie Shake*, Richard Neville wrote about his first encounter with Rubin in New York in the April of 1968. Neville attended a Yippie meeting in which "plans were being finalized for a Love-In at Central Park the following day." People were asked to donate food to a "build a mountain for Dr. King's poor people." King had just been murdered and, in attempt to keep things peaceful, the New York City authorities were encouraged to lift the ban on music in the park. "I've tested the flowers for the plane-drop by throwing them off the Empire State," one woman announced; then Neville caught sight of Rubin whom, he said, "radiated a brash and powerful energy." A form was passed around the room, "tick the square":

I Can Steal For Yippie:

☐ mimeo paper

☐ money

☐ records

☒ dope

☐ flowers

At the park the next day, he witnessed chants of "Get hip, give to Yip." He described it as "a pre-Woodstock overture of rock bands, babies at breasts, defiant spliffs, balloons, and poster giveaways."

A few days later, Neville attended a Yippie gathering in Union Square; the outrage over the Martin Luther King Jr. assassination was still in the air. Black people were handing out flyers, which read, "We'll write vengeance on the walls of the White House." From atop a soapbox, Rubin said: "It's our festival of youth. The Yippies are the children of the middle class and we refuse to grow up. We say, 'fuck you white America!'" Plans for disrupting the upcoming Democratic National Convention in Chicago were put forth:

- The underground press will come from all over the country and publish a daily paper that week, teaching people how to start their own
- Daily workshops on draft dodging
- Yippies dressed like the Vietcong, shaking hands with politicians
- Cars painted like taxicabs to collect delegates from O'Hare airport and drop them off in Wisconsin

One anonymous Yippie said, "For funds we'll loot Macy's. Twenty of us can hand the cashier a flower and head for the door. Thousands of us will burn draft cards at the same time and the paranoia and guilt of the government will force them to bring thousands of troops. Our long hair alone will freak them out and remember, the more troops, the better the theater." Neville described Jerry, at that moment, as "hoarse, short, and unstoppable . . . *Hair* was more than a musical, I realized. It was the symbol of a new world order—or disorder." As Neville points out, the British radicals didn't dare be so vocal in public; they wrote essays instead. "The Yippies seemed to speak for the entire counterculture, for the spirit of the changing times."

KEROUAC AND THE YIPPIES

IN A 1968 ESSAY, Jerry declared: "What's needed is a new generation of nuisances, who are freaky, crazy, irrational, sexy, angry, childish, and mad. People who burn draft cards; people who burn dollar bills; people who redefine reality, who redefine the norm; people who wear funny costumes. People who say 'fuck' on television."

Although Beat Generation icon Jack Kerouac would protest against the protestors until the day he died in October 1969, Rubin's words (above) parroted Kerouac's 1957 epic novel *On the Road*: "The only people for me are the mad ones, the ones who are mad to live, mad to talk, mad to be saved, desirous of everything at the same time, the ones who never yawn or say a commonplace thing, but burn, burn, burn like fabulous yellow Roman candles exploding like spiders across the stars."

Kerouac himself was capable of some Yippie-style rhetoric. In a September 1968 episode of the William F. Buckley television talk show *Firing Line*, Kerouac told Buckley, fellow guest Ed Sanders, and the audience, "I think the Vietnamese war is nothing but a plot between the North Vietnamese and the South Vietnamese, who are cousins, to get [American] jeeps into the country."

Every generation should look to the younger generation for leadership, because it is the younger generation which is the most directly and emotionally affected by society's repression. The younger you are, the clearer is your head.

—*JERRY RUBIN, 1968*

★

YIP Goes International. By the spring of '68, Jerry's idea of an international youth revolt was quickly becoming a reality. In May, Paris exploded with fifty thousand people marching down the Avenue des Champs-Élysées, carrying banners and singing the left-wing anthem, "L'Internationale." One Parisian student demanded "the right to piss wherever I please," which would have delighted the Yippies. Student protests erupted in early July at Belgrade University with a seven-day strike. The police responded with beatings. Protests at Warsaw University had occurred in March over the government banning the performance of a play that contained supposed anti-Soviet remarks. In August, Russian troops stormed through Czechoslovakia, crushing a several-months-long renaissance of political reforms that had allowed the Czech people some respite from Soviet dominance. The Tlatelolco massacre—in which several hundred students were murdered by military gunfire during a protest calling for social change—was just ten days before the start of the Olympic games in Mexico City. And that's just the short list.

DAVID SPANER: Whether they were Black Panthers, or Yippies, or White Panthers, or SDS, or whatever—people openly identified as revolutionaries all over the place. You could go to any newspaper, and all the people working there would identify as revolutionaries. It wasn't just an American thing. It existed in France, all over Western Europe, Canada. It existed lots of places, for example, in Paris in 1968. But there's a period there that's bracketed by the two political conventions, 1968 and 1972, which are both high points of Yippie activism.

In early '69, Richard Neville received a letter at his London office from Jerry. He printed it in *OZ*: "*1965 already seems like a childhood memory. Then we were going to conquer the world . . . [ending the war, wiping out racism, mobilizing the poor, taking over universities] . . . We're the most exciting energy force in the nation, stealing the kids out of schools . . . [And because of this, arrests and court appearances have] bottled up our resources, sapped our energy, and demoralized the spirit. Meanwhile, the cops are smiling.*"

The First Yippie Be-In.

As a warm-up for Chicago, there was a Yippie Be-In at Grand Central Station in Manhattan. Thanks to Bob Fass at WBAI spreading the word, three thousand freaks occupied the building, carrying in their own food and drink, guitars to play, and dope to smoke. Meanwhile, "straight people" were coming off the trains and trying to exit—but couldn't, because of the congestion. Although the vibe was festive, the cops were getting antsy and urging people to leave. When they were ignored, they poked and prodded at the Yippies, who would exit through one door and come back in through another. Finally, members of a radical fringe group—"Up Against the Wall Motherfuckers"—climbed up on the giant clock in the middle of the terminal and began shouting. "Time is meaningless." "Let's abolish time." It was playfully surreal, as opposed to shouting out something mundane like "let's take over"—however, the existentialist fun ended when they ripped the hands off the clock and the police moved in to bash skulls and break legs. The Yippies now understood that bloodshed would be part of future scenarios.

Several years before he met John & Yoko and recorded *The Pope Smokes Dope* for Apple Records, street musician David Peel was signed to Elektra. The title of Peel's 1968 debut album *Have a Marijuana* was taken from a *Time* magazine article about the Yip-In. Time's reporter on the scene misheard Peel singing "Mari-marijuana, mari-marijuana" as "have a marijuana." After Elektra A&R man Danny Fields read the statement "The Yippies stormed into Grand Central Station, singing 'Have a Marijuana,'" he declared, "*that* is the title!"

The Diggers and The Provos: Forefathers of YIP.

In Ratso Sloman's oral history of Abbie Hoffman, several folks point out the influence of the Diggers on the Yippies. Danny Schechter says, "Abbie was very inspired by . . . the whole spirit of the Diggers as a way of building community . . . it was the Digger notion that things should be free." Peter Coyote adds, "The free food was a theatrical event, it's just that there was no stage," and that, "Abbie was blown away by the free store, which was basically [Digger] Peter Berg's invention." Abbie quickly set up his own Free Store in New York, and began calling himself a "New York Digger." Despite this, there was animosity between the Diggers' leader Emmett Grogan and Abbie.

DANA BEAL: I was a New York Provo. And there was a thing called the Diggers. And I did not understand, until I read Paul Krassner's book, that there was tension between Emmett Grogan and Abbie, apparently there was a whole hassle involving a little unsolicited sex with Anita. But Emmett was really upset that Abbie glommed the Diggers. Which seems a little unfair, since Krassner did a whole issue of *The Realist* on the Diggers.

The Provos, from Amsterdam, were much more copacetic about us using their name. So we started something called New York Provo. Not to be confused with the Northern Irish Provisional Army, which was a different Provo. In 1966, the Dutch Provos led a series of provocative street demonstrations that forced the Mayor of Amsterdam out of office. In many ways, they were the forerunners of the French Student Revolt of 1968. The Provos were the first of a set of people that came up at that period in time. We saw them in *The Village Voice*, and we thought, "those guys are cool, let's do that here!"

Before I went underground and fled to Mexico, Abbie wanted me to join the Yippies. To bring the Provos into the Yippies, which was going to be a big thing, it was going to subsume the Provos and the New York Diggers, and we were going to go to Chicago. When I got to Mexico, I wrote a letter to Jerry but it turned out there was a different Jerry Rubin on East Third Street, and he never got it.

OPPOSITE: "A Meeting of the Yippies." Photo © Leni Sinclair

Black Panthers, White Panthers, SDS, and Weathermen.

A year before their renowned Woodstock performance, Santana played a benefit in Los Angeles to raise awareness for The Peace & Freedom Party. The PFP was a new organization that got off to an explosive start, by nominating Black Panther Minister of Information Eldridge Cleaver as president for the '68 national election. Cleaver chose Jerry as his vice presidential running mate.

On the November 5, 1968 ballot, Cleaver received more than thirty-six thousand votes nationwide. He conceded the election in favor of the Yippie candidate, Pigasus, declaring, "The pig is mightier than the Cleaver." Although the Peace & Freedom Party hadn't blessed the union, a Panther-Yippie alliance was hatched. Cleaver, Rubin and Stew Albert met in the Berkeley Hills, smoked a ton of weed, and cowrote the YIPANTHER PACT. Eldridge's part of the missive said,

Let us join together with all those souls in Babylon who are straining for the birth of a new day. A revolutionary generation is on the scene. Disenchanted, alienated white youth, the hippies, the Yippies, and all unnamed dropouts from the white man's burden, are our allies in this cause.

Later, the Black Panther newspaper would run an article: "The Hippies are not our Enemies." In November 1969, Cleaver would pen the introduction to *DO iT!*: "If everyone did what Jerry suggests in this book, if everyone carried out Jerry's program, there would be immediate peace in this world. Amerika, in particular, would cease to bleed." But Cleaver was nothing if not pragmatic when he added: "I do not believe that everybody is going to follow Jerry's program, which makes me sad, because that means we must think in terms of alternatives." The White Panthers (obviously inspired by the Black Panthers) were a group of freaks in Michigan who loved poetry, pot, jazz, and rock 'n' roll. The manager of the MC5, bard John Sinclair, organized them, and the team of merry outlaws were eager to align with the Yippies. White Panther Leni Sinclair told me, in 2014, "We

11:00 A.M.

Sisters and Brothers,

A year ago we blew away the Haymarket pig statue at the start of a youth riot in Chicago. The head of the Police Sergeant's Association called emotionally for all-out war between the pigs and us. We accepted. Last night we destroyed the pig again. This time it begins a fall offensive of youth resistance that will spread from Santa Barbara to Boston, back to Kent and Kansas. Now we are everywhere and next week families and tribes will attack the enemy around the country. It is our job to blast away the myths of the total superiority of the man.

We did not choose to live in a time of war. We choose only to become guerillas and to urge our people to prepare for war rather than become accomplices in the genocide of our sisters and brothers.

.... sisters .... high schools and campuses. But

Guard your planes, guard your colleges, guard your banks, guard your children, GUARD YOUR DOORS.

Bernardine Dohrn

Jeff Jones

Bill Ayers.

This is the fifth communication from the Weatherman underground.

---

became aware of the Yippies through the media like everybody else, watching their antics in New York at the Stock Exchange and so on. This was Guerilla Theater; we loved what they were doing. They were the closest in the movement to doing what we were doing, being hippies and freaks making a political statement but not in the traditional, political means." The White Panthers also wanted to change their name, especially after being mistaken for a white supremacist group.

LENI SINCLAIR: We knew we had to get rid of the name White Panther Party and we threw around suggestions like The Woodstock People's Party, and so on. Then we started talking about getting rid of the White Panther Party and forming a joint organization with the Yippies.

JOHN SINCLAIR: We realized the Yippies could organize a hell of a press conference or a demonstration. But we couldn't go to the Yippie headquarters—there wasn't one! There wasn't anybody there on the phone.

LENI SINCLAIR: We already printed stationery that said "Youth International Party." Then we had a meeting at our headquarters in Ann Arbor and Jerry Rubin was there, but Abbie wasn't. We had meetings during the day, and I remember that late at night after everything was said and done, we did our usual thing, blasting rock music and dancing. Somehow this was a little too much for Jerry and he just kind of withdrew into his own room and locked the door. I always thought Jerry must have been a little intimidated when kids started taking off their clothes and partying.

DANA BEAL: There was this meeting at Tom Forcade's loft, sponsored by the White Panthers, to set up an organization that would be called the Youth International Party, which would merge the White Panthers, the original Yippies, and various other groups to form this new thing that would replace SDS, which was becoming unraveled.

Of all the different factions, the SDS was still the most conventional, even after some members broke off and formed the Weather Underground.

Martin Kenner: SDS was a slightly constipated group. It was on campuses, but it took a long time for the activist faction, led by Mark Rudd [Weather Underground leader], to overcome this so-called "praxis-axis" of people reading books and deep study, and almost an anti-action. Actually, it was Rudd who jerked it out of that mode. One of his first acts was when the head of Selective Service came to Columbia he went up and threw a pie in his face.

"This is the fifth communication from the Weatherman Underground"—addressed to "Sisters and Brothers"—received at the YIP office; Tuesday October 6, 1970 at 11 a.m.

BEWARE THE CREEPING MEATBALL

FROM 1950 TO 1954, in Jerry's hometown of Cincinnati, radio raconteur Jean Shepherd spun records on WSAI and had a nightly comedy show on WLW. Starting in 1956 (and for the next twenty-one years), Shepherd beamed out across New York City via WOR with wacky tales, funny commentary, and silly songs. Marshall McLuhan declared Jean Shepherd "the first radio novelist" for his ability to spin a tale that kept the listener's attention for up to an hour, despite piles of diversions and digressions. The March 1957 issue of *Mad* magazine featured a Jean Shepherd essay made up of "off the cuff" remarks concerning the "Night People" vs. "Creeping Meatballism." It was a blend of text and seminal *Mad* graphic imagery:

The average person today thinks in certain prescribed patterns. People today have a genuine fear of stepping out and thinking on their own. "Creeping Meatballism" is this rejection of individuality. It's conformity . . . The guy who has been taken in by the "Meatball" philosophy is the guy who really believes that contemporary people are slim, and clean-limbed, and they're so much fun to be with . . . because they drink Pepsi-Cola. As long as he believes this, he's in the clutches of "Creeping Meatballism."

Shepard's satire cautions the reader of "a scourge then sweeping the nation"—a menace that was exposing Americans to the harms of commercialism—that could "transform America into a race of dimwitted robots who completely identified with The Pepsi Generation." In other words, *Creeping Meatballism* was "the acceptance by society of mediocrity as a virtue."

And that is the origin of the infamous Yippie slogan: "Rise Up and Abandon the Creeping Meatball!"

As Ethan Thompson points out in *Parody and Taste in Postwar American Television Culture*, "The Yippies' embrace of television on their own terms, using it for their own subversive ends, is analogous to *Mad's* parodic approach to media texts, finding pleasure and producing meaning through and against them [via satire]. There are, therefore, clear connections between the tactics of these political radicals and the content of *Mad*: the outlandish, crazy event or "story" that upsets "normal" or mainstream understandings of life and the critical embrace of television culture. In this sense, the Yippies and *Mad* both [made] cultural interventions—[by] creating counterculture."

(And for readers confused whether "Jean" was a man or a woman, Shepherd's name wasn't "Eugene," and because it was a French spelling he suffered from school classmates teasing throughout his youth, which he didn't appreciate. It did, however, inspire his friend Shel Silverstein to compose Johnny Cash's 1969 hit song, "A Boy Named Sue.")

The Weathermen, who took their name from Bob Dylan's "Subterranean Homesick Blues," were an SDS offshoot. They believed that the only way to end the Vietnam War was to bring the violence home. When a bomb they were building at a Manhattan townhouse blew up and killed several members, they decided to only destroy property and not people, going on to bomb institutions like banks and government buildings after hours. In the '70s, leaders Bernardine Dohrn, Bill Ayers, Mark Rudd, and others went underground, but all charges were dropped when they turned themselves in. The FBI was afraid of exposing too many of their own dirty tricks in a trial, such as plans to kidnap members' relatives and illegal wiretapping.

JOHN SINCLAIR: The Weathermen tried to follow the Yippies, but they didn't understand teenagers. They were middle-class white people who were going to be lawyers. They were barely aware of the Beatles as a revolutionary force. They didn't even get high! Fucking wasn't on their priority list. They were stiff. No, I'm serious. That's why the Yippies were so effective; because they knew where the kids were at. These kids were trying to bust out. They were our constituency. We didn't give a fuck about a college student. The SDS didn't have any bands. We *had* a rock 'n' roll band, man. The MC5!

JIM FOURATT: Coming back from "Back to the Drawing Boards," Bernardine, Bill, Abbie, Paul Krassner, and myself drove east and Abbie gave Bernardine and Bill their first tab of acid. That changed the way the SDS and the Weather Underground thought about their politics.

Convention of Death Meets Festival of Life.

While many of Jerry's "old school" Marxist friends in Berkeley figured that his new rhetoric was the result of too much LSD melting his brain cells, Jerry recalled decades later that Abbie had taught him how to talk "like a hippie" rather than like an East Bay politico. Jerry was now fully ensconced in New York and the humorless Berkeley contingent was no longer his concern. Jerry was increasingly concerned with the upcoming 1968 Presidential Democratic Convention to be held in Chicago in August.

In the final months of 1967, Jerry, Abbie, and other like-minds, such as political satire pioneer Paul Krassner and poet/songwriter Ed Sanders of the "original" freak-folk band the Fugs, tossed around ideas. During one meeting, Sanders pointed out to Rubin the successful sociopolitical intersection that occurred at the Monterey Pop Festival that summer. They discussed how incredible it was that so many popular rock bands (Jefferson Airplane, the Byrds, Buffalo Springfield, and many others) had performed for free for a gathering of the counterculture. Although the attendees paid to see the bands, all the revenue gathered went to charity. Sanders suggested they consider something similar for '68, a free festival featuring major bands.

At another meeting, Hoffman, Rubin, and Krassner decided they needed to make a stand against Johnson's Vietnam policies. Since

President Lyndon Johnson had yet to step down, they assumed he'd be the Democratic candidate at the National Convention. Jerry felt that a positive message needed to be conveyed to attract the burgeoning group of radicalized teens and college kids that were sprouting up across America. Rather than see the proposed gathering as a "Convention of Death," it needed to be a "Festival of Life," ideally held in a park. It was now time for the Yippies to announce themselves to the rest of the world with a press release. It declared:

An Announcement: Youth International Party (Or Yip!) Is Born

Join us in Chicago in August for an international festival of youth music and theatre. Rise up and abandon the creeping meatball! Come all you rebels, youth spirits, rock minstrels, truth seekers, peacock freaks, poets, barricade jumpers, dancers, lovers, and artists. It is summer. It is the last week of August and the NATIONAL DEATH PARTY meets to bless Johnson. We are there! There are 500,000 of us dancing naked in the streets, throbbing with amplifiers and harmony. We are making love in the parks. We are reading, singing, laughing, printing newspapers, groping and making a mock convention and celebrating the birth of FREE AMERICA in our own time . . . Everything will be free. Bring blankets, tents, draft cards, body paint, Mrs. Leary's cow, food to share, music, eager skin and happiness. The threats of LBJ, Major Daley, and J. Edgar Freako will not stop us . . . The life of the American spirit is being torn asunder by the forces of violence, decay, the napalm, cancer fiend. We demand the politics of ecstasy. We are the delicate spoors of the new fierceness that will change America. We will create our own reality. And we will not accept the false theatre of the Death Convention. We will be in Chicago. Begin preparations now! Chicago is yours! Do it!

The *New York Post* ran the press release on page five, and it slowly spread across the country after that. Jerry and his partner Nancy spent a lot of time with Abbie and Anita Hoffman, plotting the Chicago event. As Anita pointed out later, "Jerry understands power. Abbie was an artist." Stew Albert's view was that Abbie wanted to be the front man and expected Jerry to make it all happen behind the scenes. Because Jerry didn't want be a silent partner, Abbie felt that Jerry was stepping on his toes. Jerry later said, in *Steal This Dream*, "Abbie was very entertaining, but I'd say when does the entertainment end and the serious discussion begin? I saw all American youth waiting to be organized, from working class to hippie to children of the rich. We had this whole idea, we were gonna take the children away from the establishment, channel the working-class anger into politics, politicize the hippies. It'd totally isolate the government."

THE YIPPIES WERE BORN on New Year's Eve, right at the beginning of the most tumultuous year of the '60s; every month of 1968 had a milestone event.

January: The Northern army launched the Tet Offensive against the South, signifying the beginning of the end of the Vietnam War.

February: CBS reporter Walter Cronkite declared the war was unwinnable, causing President Johnson to announce his decision to not run for reelection.

April: Martin Luther King Jr. was gunned down in Memphis, causing riots across the nation.

May: The action switched to Paris, with mass student protests followed by a crippling nationwide workers strike for two weeks.

June saw the assassination of Presidential hopeful Robert Kennedy in Los Angeles.

August brought the Chicago riots during the Democratic Convention, riots that the Yippies would ultimately be put on trial for. At the same time, thousands of Soviet tanks rolled into Czechoslovakia to end "Prague Spring"—a period of freedom in the Communist country.

September: the Miss America Pageant spring boarded the Feminist Movement, when hundreds of woman threw high heels, girdles, and bras into the "Freedom Trash Can" on the boardwalk of Atlantic City.

October: During the Olympics held in Mexico City, two African American athletes did the "Black Power Salute" before millions of television viewers.

November: The Beatles released the *White Album*, which "spoke" to Charles Manson.

December brought the year to close with the Rolling Stones' *Beggars Banquet*, which contained the rallying anthem "Street Fighting Man" and a reflection of the times: "Sympathy for the Devil." When the Stones performed it at Altamont twelve months later, it became the soundtrack to the dying embers of the Peace and Love Generation.

Jerry's image, especially, was popular culture. I mean, it was sort of strong, militant, but he was all about the youth culture and "let's change the world." If you wanted to count numbers, I would say that the cultural side of things was a bigger number than the political, antiwar movement side. The culture thing was huge. And I was okay with it, but we were just pathetic compared to Jerry and Abbie. The Yippies would just go out there and light everybody's fire. Really, it was great. So the political scientists today need to go a little deeper, in terms of what made up the constituency, then. Go back

to Haight-Ashbury and then progress that forward, and there you have the representation of Jerry and Abbie, with that group of people.
—RENNIE DAVIS

Legacy of the Yippies.

JIM FOURATT: WikiLeaks are the Yippies of today. I see The Yes Men and "Anonymous" as the grandchildren of the Yippies. The outrageous sense of play The Yes Men have—that was the Yippie spirit. We weren't getting killed like the Panthers were. There was that white skin privilege.

NANCY KURSHAN: The legacy of the Yippies is that you can participate in social movements, using culture, humor, multimedia, and reach people in all those different ways, not just through the written or spoken word. Today, a lot of people are trying a lot of Yippie-type things. Certainly, Occupy did. But, I think it's much harder to break through the media right now.

The Yippies said, "Be creative. You don't have to just follow these molds." That you could be outside the box and do all kinds of things. People think of the Yippies as theater and costumes. But there's another level of the Yippies, and that was figuring out ways to really confront the powers that be.

DAVID SPANER: A lot of people in the straight left didn't like the Yippies, and didn't like the whole emphasis on counterculture. Yet, there was a certain irreverent attitude that a lot of people were drawn to. Jerry and Abbie used humor because it's a basic thing—it's hard to hate someone when you're laughing with them. It opens people up to your perspective. Some people look back on the Yippies as just a bunch of clowns, that's not what it was about. While it had that humorous aspect to it, there was also a dead serious revolutionary side to it. We wanted to overthrow capitalism and create a utopian anarchist society.

RENNIE DAVIS, SDS AND MOBE LEADER/CHICAGO 8 DEFENDENT: The view is that Jerry and Abbie sort of gave voice and became the archetype for the Cultural Revolution. And people like Tom Hayden and me were more into the politics of the antiwar movement. But I never saw it that way. I never saw any discrepancy between how Jerry thought about things and I did. I would say the Yippies were a handful, from my point of view. But, at the end of the day, let's just take Chicago for example—I mean, that's really where they emerged. Given Chicago, what was really going down, I was eternally grateful to Jerry and Abbie. I mean, to throw humor into this mix was the best possible thing. It needed to be done. Going in there with our big antiwar placards was really not going to make it. And the people that came to Chicago were more of that cultural side, anyway. They were young people who were fearless. And not so much in the militant sense, but just in the beautiful sense. So, Jerry and Abbie gave voice to that, to whatever that was—it was very hard to organize that—to whatever degree there could be some coherence. I counted them as allies. If Tom Hayden was sitting here, I would say, "Tom, you should get over it." [*Laughter.*] Jerry's fine. It's like a family feud or something, forty years later, you still can't let it go . . . it's like that.

Abbie and Jerry already were political. There wasn't any politicization that you needed with Jerry, or Abbie either. They were fine; they just had their side, their humor and everything. That's my point of view. I just see it as one big, happy family.

JIM FOURATT: There was civil disobedience in the Occupy Movement that really reminded me of the Yippies, but Occupy couldn't get people engaged. It was really awful. The first time I went to an Occupy meeting, it didn't remind me of the Yippies, it reminded me of the Gay Liberation Front. Because in the GLF, we used Native American principles. We'd go in this big circle and everyone would have to speak before anyone else could speak again.

Jerry and Abbie were not consensus people but the meetings were set up in a model of consensus. If they got what they wanted, then they were fine with the consensus. But if they didn't get what they wanted, then they didn't fucking care what the consensus was! There was a suspicion of leadership in the women's movement and in the Gay Liberation movement, but there was no suspicion of leadership in the Yippies.

FROM CANADIAN STALINIST
TO AMERICAN YIPPIE: JUDY GUMBO

ABOUT TEN MINUTES AFTER I first began researching this book, my phone rang. It was music scribe Michael Simmons. Through the years, he's rubbed shoulders with all sorts of Yippies, even attending Jerry's memorial. He quickly let me know what was up. "Word on the street is that you've just inked a deal to write Rubin's story. Congrats. Here's the deal: Gumbo and Nancy are gonna kick your ass if you become the next author to eliminate women from Yippie history."

Judy turned out to be a valuable resource. As a dedicated Yippie herself, and as the spouse of Jerry's lifelong best friend, Stew Albert, she provided an insider's perspective—given that Stew and Jerry weren't here to speak for themselves. Anita Hoffman said it best in an October 1974 letter to Abbie: "Did I tell you that I saw Judy Gumbo and Stew? She has a terrific mind. I wish I'd gotten to know her better back in the sixties; it's a shame so many of us then were unaware of the value of friendship, especially between women. I like learning about Marxism from her because she's not only smart, she's mellow."

Like her comrade Nancy Kurshan, Judy Clavir began life as a "red diaper baby"—with a twist. She was born and raised in Toronto. She wrote in her memoir, "My father was the first person the Soviets recruited to distribute Russian films on the North American continent. By the time I was six or seven, I'd perch on my grandmother's forest green sectional to preview classic Soviet films like *Potemkin* and *Ivan the Terrible* from the great Soviet director Sergei Eisenstein." A child of a Communist Party family, she "learned that communism meant I must work hard. Take things seriously. Be a force for good." When she encountered Stew Albert in '68, she became a Yippie, and the rules changed to "have fun. Take nothing seriously. Be a force for good."

Judy was so politically driven that even Stew Albert was intimated. Years later, he recalled that she made him feel like a "hippie lightweight." Stew was trying to get laid and induct her into the Yippies. Judy was "madly attracted to the Black Panther Party" and, lucky for Stew, he counted Cleaver as a close friend. He played the buddy card

to impress her. Stew and Judy socialized with Eldridge. Eldridge may have been a progressive politico, but as a man, he was old school. He insisted on calling Judy "Mrs. Stew," much to her chagrin. She protested that she wasn't just Stew's "old lady." Eldridge capitulated. "All right, then. I'll call you Gumbo." The name stuck. Judy Clavir become Judy Gumbo ever after. In 2015, Judy recalled, "Gumbo would give me the freedom to make myself into whatever kind of woman I wanted to become. Even though my name defined me as Stew's counterpart, I knew I could make Gumbo into a name of my own."

In Judy's memoir *Yippie Girl*, she recalls meeting Jerry and Nancy for the first time:

On my third day in New York City, I met Jerry and his girlfriend Nancy Kurshan. Like cousins in extended families, Nancy and Jerry lived across the street half a block down from Anita and Abbie. The location of their two apartments may have symbolized the Abbie/Jerry relationship: close but on opposite sides of the flower child/serious politico street.

As Stew and I trudged up the stairs, it smelt as if an air-freshener emitting cannabis had been installed on the building's topmost landing. At the far end of a fourth floor hallway stood a brown metal door marked #16. Stew knocked. A peephole unlocked. I glimpsed an eyeball. Bolts squeaked as an iron bar moved. The door opened. A bearded man with hair like a brown Brillo pad smiled at me. He wore a crew-necked, short-sleeved T-shirt in yellow and red stripes. What atrocious taste in clothes was my first, uncharitable thought on meeting Jerry Rubin.

Jerry slapped Stew on his back in the universal gesture of male bonding then beckoned us into the apartment. He jammed the door bolts into place. I found myself in a three-and-a-half room flat, with plaster walls and faded white wood sash windows open to the early summer air. The flat was crammed with hippies: hippies on the floor, hippies on the couch, hippies on the windowsill, hippies at the door. Male hippies, female hippies; long-haired, short-haired, no-haired hippies; hippies here, hippies there, hippies, hippies everywhere, as if the felines in Millions of Cats, *my favorite book of children's poetry, had shape shifted into human beings in 1968.*

In one corner of the room, the latest model RCA TV perched on Danish modern legs. Jerry noticed me looking and uttered offhandedly, "Every revolutionary needs a color TV. You know why? Because television creates myths that are bigger than reality."

Nancy claimed that Pigasus, the Yippie candidate for President, would steal the Democratic Party's thunder. Jerry jumped in with, "Why vote for half a pig when you can have the whole hog?"

At that moment I abandoned my Red Diaper heritage of being serious. To be a Yippie, all you had to do was act like one.

Then Jerry yelled—in what I'd come to recognize as Jerry's exaggeration-made-believable-by-enthusiasm voice—"The way to eliminate fear is to do what you're most afraid of! Rise up and abandon the creeping meatball!"

At that, the curiosity I've had my entire life won out. I took in a breath and, in a voice that sounded to me no louder than my heartbeat, but which I must have shouted, asked, "Jerry, what does abandon the creeping meatball mean?" "Whatever you want it to," Jerry replied.

At age 25, fear had never been a creeping meatball for me. My meatballs had been more mundane: [My first husband's] infidelity, my mother's vicious diatribes, and the Victorian limitations imposed on me in Toronto. I could rise up and abandon them if I chose to be a Yippie. As my favorite Canadian writer Margaret Atwood put it, I was surfacing.

Judy would accompany Stew and the others to Mayor Daley's amusement park that August, and help organize the "Free the Chicago 8" movement that was the result. While planning trial strategy, Gumbo had an epiphany: "I was swimming in a sea of freedom struggles: for sexual freedom, for Vietnamese independence, for liberation of African Americans and all people of color, for eight Chicago Conspiracy defendants, but not as yet for me."

As noted in Robin Morgan's "Goodbye to All That," in a post-Chicago landscape, women in the movement began to see things differently. They needed their own cause célèbre. For some, it meant leaving the antiwar movement to focus on women's issues. For others, it was a blend. In 1970, Genie Plamondon, wife of Pun, the White Panther's Minister of Information, joined Nancy Kurshan and Judy in Hanoi. It was a "women's only" delegation of three: a Midwest farm girl and the two high-energy East Coast Jews. They had their differences, but a bond developed. Nancy told me in 2013, "being in Vietnam, just the three women, was pretty liberating."

They witnessed firsthand the determination of the North Vietnamese. As they toured the country in a rusted-out bus, a hole in the floor gave them a glimpse of river water rushing underneath their feet. Their guide told them, "the North Vietnamese army moved war material by train, oxcart, bicycle, and foot across this bridge to the South. Every day this bridge is demolished [by American bombs], every night it is rebuilt. The courage of the peasants is a local legend." Along the journey, they experienced "the sound of falling bombs and heavy artillery fire." They met female artillery gunners wearing pitch helmets and black silk pants. Judy remembers posing for a photo with a massive antiaircraft weapon, the same type that got Jane Fonda branded as "Hanoi Jane" two years later when she visited. The North Vietnamese gunner said, "These are American friends, come to observe what we do to liberate our country . . . You, dear friends, inspire us. You help end war in your country."

In January 2013, Judy and Nancy toured Vietnam again along with Rennie Davis (of the Chicago 8) to help celebrate the fortieth anniversary of the Paris Peace Accords. Upon their return, both women blogged about the contrast between their 1970 and 2013 visits. In short, their second visit speaks volumes about their continuous commitment to social justice and ending war.

Judy and Stew remained lifelong partners as well as close friends with Jerry throughout his many permutations. In a 2012 article, Jonah Raskin described Judy as "a Yippie Girl, a college teacher, fundraiser for Planned Parenthood, antiwar organizer, writer, activist, wife, and mother. Along with Stew, she edited *The Sixties Papers* (in 1984), an anthology that contains essential writings that shaped her and Stew, and that they also played a part in shaping." Judy told me in 2015, "When I first heard Jerry Rubin's slogan 'Kill Your Parents,' the phrase appalled me. But Jerry wasn't saying you should guillotine your closest relatives. 'Kill Your Parents' turned out to be a metaphor for letting go."

OPPOSITE: Genie Plamondon, Nancy, Judy in Montreal via Vietnam, June 1970.

LEFT: Judy & Nancy at Moscow airport, en route to Vietnam, 1970.

YIP
32 Union Square East, Room 607
New York, N.Y. 10003

TO: Richard J. Daley, Mayor of Chicago
    William McFetridge, Park Commissioner of Chicago

Dear Sirs:

Thousands of young Americans, possibly upwards of 500,000, will be coming to
Chicago this summer from August 25 to August 30 for a national youth festival--
a celebration of life and an affirmation of man and community.

The festival will be held in Grant Park, and will last continuously for the week.
A major part of the festival will be an emphasis on music and theater, and for
this we will use amplified sound, which we will provide. More than 100
entertainers, including rock groups, have already agreed to participate and
we expect that this will be the nation's biggest music festival. The festival
will be entirely free.

Response to the festival of life, also called the Yippie festival, has been
overwhelming. Throughout the country groups and individuals are organizing
to come to Chicago. Articles have appeared in major newspapers and
magazines, on television and on radio.

Because of the other affair being held simultaneously with our festival, and
because of the enormous number of people expected, those attending the
festival will need to sleep in the park. We are urging them to bring sleeping
bags, blankets and tents.

We are asking the city to cooperate in providing portable sanitation units. In
addition, our emphasis will be on food sharing and we will ask the Health De-
paertment to cooperate with us in the setting up of kitchens in the park.

We look forward to your response.

For fun and freedom,

Paul Krassner   *Valerie L. Walker*   *James Neville Fawcett*

Jerry Rubin   *Abbie Hoffman*   *Bob Carol*

Lee Katz   *Steven Kravos*

Al Rosenfeld   *James V. Kato*

THE YIPPIES
March 26, 1968

Chicago '68

Vietnam was the first war to be brought right into the living rooms of America each evening and could be considered the first reality television show. Young people witnessed the carnage of both soldiers and civilians—including the burning of villages—and thought, "why would I want to go and join that war?" Unlike World War II, the threat to the American way of life seemed minimal. The draft heighted the tension. Every young male received a number and a draft card that identified them. That felt less like the American Dream and more like Nazi Germany. It even became a federal crime to burn a draft card.

Abe Peck wrote, in *Uncovering the Sixties*, "As the stage was being set for Chicago and the Democratic National Convention, Tom Hayden and SDS would advance the power of student revolt. Rennie Davis and Dave Dellinger would continue the broader-based National Mobilization Committee to End the War in Vietnam [MOBE] that had marched on the Pentagon. The McCarthy kids, 'Clean for Gene,' would back the Minnesota senator in his drive to liberalize

(but not radicalize) the presidency. But it would be the Yippies—the Youth International Party, most closely identified with Abbie Hoffman and Jerry Rubin—that would grab the spotlight, in large part because it chose to fight its battles on the field of media. The Yippies would capture and divide public imagination, test the ethics of organizing via media, end flower power as a factor in the papers, and fuel the most divisive debate in the history of the underground press."

Jerry saw the Chicago event as something in which just the presence of a massive amount of longhairs and freaks all enjoying themselves with free love and music would force the local authorities into a state of violent paranoia, in turn destroying their own city. He kept refining the concept over time, in which a like-minded group of people, inspired by political change, guerrilla theater, and rock music, would convene in the heart of Chicago. The plan was to arrive with the advance blessing of the city having already obtained permits to perform music, sleep in public parks, and hold rallies. The Yippies gave a list of demands to Mayor Daley's office.

JIM FOURATT: We went to Chicago in June to apply for a permit. I had wrapped it up in a *Playboy* centerfold thinking that's what Chicago's about [since *Playboy* was published there]. Did not go over well at all when we handed it in.

Daley's administration didn't respond, but the Yippies forged ahead. Jerry later recalled to Milton Viorst: "Abbie and I worked out of our homes, called each other in the morning and met in the office. It was like two energy centers. And we held insane meetings on Fourteenth Street, where there'd be a couple of hundred people, and they'd end up in fights and craziness and madness. Everybody was bursting out, whatever they wanted to be and whoever they were. Everybody was really asserting themselves. It was a wonderful, exciting, creative, weird and . . . dangerous period."

the ...ts of Chairman Jerry

proto-provocateur of America's Red Guard, aims to lead a charge of Yippie guerrillas from here to revolution

Deliciously

Wim
REUBEN S

a bed of sauerkraut
a Wimpy Hamburg
topped with grilled
served on a toaste

WORLD
wimp

Hell No, We Won't Go! Since Ed Sanders was in an established band, the Fugs, and was connected to other well-known musicians, he was asked to round up sympathetic performers. No surprise that protest singer Phil Ochs agreed, along with Country Joe McDonald (who would wow the Woodstock Festival in 1969 with his "F-U-C-K" cheer and "I Feel like I'm Fixin' to Die Rag"). Over time, everyone except the MC5 and Ochs pulled out—including Abbie Hoffman's pals Grace Slick and Paul Kantner of Jefferson Airplane—mainly due to the lack of permits and threat of police violence. The lack of bands was purposely kept secret for fear it would discourage kids from coming.

RON DAVIS: Jerry called me to go to Chicago; he wanted the Mime Troupe to do a show in Chicago. I said, "Jerry, if I do a show in Chicago, I want armed guards. I wouldn't do a show in Chicago, the cops are gonna beat the shit out of you." I told him over the phone, "We're not gonna go." Jerry replied, "Oh, but we're gonna have a festival there." I said, "Yeah, you could have a festival, but I wouldn't do anything except have a marching band, with everybody having a crutch as a sword. As a defense mechanism, so when the cops come with their billy clubs, you could at least have a weapon in your hand, so you could fend off the cops."

JIM FOURATT: When we were planning for Chicago, we'd have those weekly meetings at the loft on Fourteenth Street. Both Allen Ginsberg and I objected to the way it was being organized: as a "Festival of Life" and all that.

HISTORY HAS CHOSEN US, BORN WHITE IN MIDDLE-CLASS AMERICA, TO REVERSE CENTURIES OF AMERICA—TO VOMIT UP OUR INHERITANCE—OURS WILL BE A REVOLUTION AGAINST PRIVILEGE AND A REVOLUTION AGAINST THE BOREDOM OF STEEL, CONCRETE, PLASTIC. —JERRY RUBIN, 1968

Masters of Hype. As savvy as the slickest madmen in advertising, the Yippies tried to project universal messages. "Everyone is a leader." And, "the Festival is whatever you want it to be." As Jerry told Abe Peck in 1985, "It was mutual manipulation. To interest the media, I needed to express my politics frivolously—if I had given a sober lecture on the history of Vietnam, the media camera would have been turned off." Besides, the Yippies didn't have cash flow or political clout, so they had to use the currency of hype. They beefed up the numbers of people they expected (or did actually turn out) at every event. Why say one thousand people are expected, when five thousand sounds more exciting? Their tongue-in-cheek humor played into mass media. When they announced they'd dose the entire city of Chicago water supply with LSD, nobody in the media did the math to realize that it was impossible (according to author David Farber, the Chicago Public Works ascertained that it would take five tons of acid to effectively contaminate the water supply). Just the suggestion that public sex acts might occur would send the media into a tizzy. Jerry and Abbie played the reporters. They made up crazy shit and the newspapers regurgitated it every time.

SAM LEFF: Marshall McLuhan was an important part of the perspective that we all had: namely, creatively using the media. So far as this whole Yippie thing is concerned, there was a small group of people that were changing the world. One of the chants in Chicago '68 was "the whole world was watching" [on television], which was one of the reasons the Russians felt capable and had the guts to go into Prague during the week of the Democratic Convention, as the world was watching [and was distracted by] Chicago. The Yippies had signs saying, "Welcome to Prague," and "Czech-ago," and there was even a demonstration at the Russian consulate.

During the same week as the Chicago protests, thousands of Soviet tanks rolled into Czechoslovakia to eradicate the "Prague Spring"—a short-lived period of liberalization in the Communist-held country.

Paranoia was striking deep inside the average Chicago resident, thanks to rumors printed in the Sunday August 25, 1968 (the day before the Democratic Convention began) *Chicago American* daily paper:

Here's why an army of 20,000 police and soldiers is needed in Chicago this week. Every one of the following acts of sabotage has been threatened by black or white militants . . . Militants have said they will put agents into hotel or restaurant kitchens where food is being prepared for delegates and put drugs or poison into the food. The water supply has been threatened either by sabotage at pumping stations or dumping drugs in the lake near intake pipes. A mass stall-in of old jalopies on the expressways at a given time would stop traffic. . . Yippies said they would paint cars as independent taxicabs and take delegates away from the city. Yippies' girls would work as hookers and try to attract delegates and put LSD in their drinks . . . Threats to the Amphitheater include gas in their air conditioning system, shelling it with mortar from several miles away, storming it with a mob, cutting the power and phone lines. How many other sophisticated schemes of sabotage exist may only be imagined.

Jerry knew that the Yippies couldn't compete with the power of the war machine, so he and Abbie fought back with their own power source: communication. They learned how to manipulate journalists to create an interest in their message. Jerry knew that "one demonstrator could steal the national media any day with a bold act."

Yippies and the Underground Press.

The Yippies' relationship with the underground press was quite different than with the mainstream papers. Mainly, the underground media posed real and challenging questions. They wanted facts rather than hype. Were the Yippies staging a festival or a riot? Jerry recalled in 1985, "It was important to perpetuate myths in the underground press, so I have to say that I tried to manipulate it. [But] the underground press was easier and harder to manipulate than the mainstream press. Easier because some of them shared [our] vision, so you could say, 'Let's go further with this vision.' Harder to manipulate because they were more cynical. They were aware of the vision."

In *Uncovering the Sixties*, Abe Peck reflected, "Seated in my Chicago apartment . . . Rubin became Jerry as he talked quietly but enthusiastically about a festival of youth, music, and theater in Sweet Home Chicago! And if it just happened to coincide with the Democrats' Convention, well, as the press release had said, 'the two are, of course, entirely unrelated.' That night, Jerry described a nonprofit Woodstock, one year early. But if his confrontational fingers were crossed, my arm wasn't twisted when I said I'd be the Yippie's man in Chicago. Naive, flattered, I nevertheless hated the war, disdained straight society. The Yippies weren't some boring Leftist sect, but all-American rebels who, instead of arguing over slices of the pie, wanted a whole new menu. And the whole thing sounded so exciting! Hadn't the tail end of that press release said, "Chicago is yours! Do it!"

JANN WENNER WAS THE BENEDICT ARNOLD OF THE '60S.
—ABBIE HOFFMAN

Some papers put serious heat on the Yippies' Chicago plans. There was a particularly scathing piece in the May 11, 1968 issue of *Rolling Stone*, written by publisher Jann Wenner. He noted that politics served no purpose in music—and recommended that people not attend the upcoming Festival of Life planned in Chicago. Abbie Hoffman later put it brilliantly: "Jann Wenner was the Benedict Arnold of the '60s."

In Craig Pyes's 1972 essay, "*Rolling Stone* gathers no politix" [sic], he points out that while Wenner told his readership in '68 to boycott the Chicago Convention, he wasted no time in cashing in on the Conspiracy Trial later on. The trial had been such a pop culture media spectacle that Wenner needed to jump on the bandwagon. He commissioned a major feature article when the trial was done, and ran "full-page ads in many papers: 'Our Reporter Was There.'" There was a subscription form at the bottom of the advert. *Rolling Stone* ignored their previous stance against the Yippies. Now the idea was to exploit the "turned-on youth" culture to maximize the magazine's reach. Except there was just one little problem with the slogan "Our Reporter Was There"—the reporter in question, Gene Marine, had been sent to Chicago by *Ramparts* magazine, so, in theory, the ad should have read, "Their Reporter Was There."

In Robert Sam Anson's *Gone Crazy and Back Again: The Rise and Fall of the Rolling Stone Generation*, he describes Wenner's attitude toward political coverage:

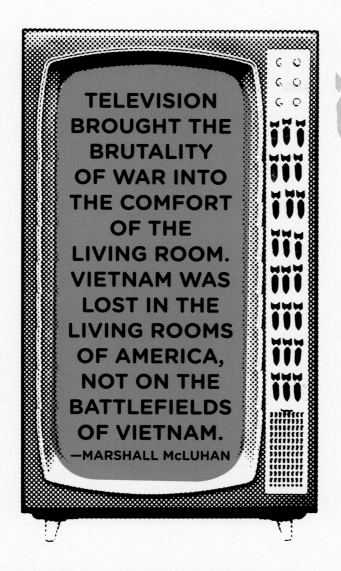

TELEVISION BROUGHT THE BRUTALITY OF WAR INTO THE COMFORT OF THE LIVING ROOM. VIETNAM WAS LOST IN THE LIVING ROOMS OF AMERICA, NOT ON THE BATTLEFIELDS OF VIETNAM.
—MARSHALL McLUHAN

Jann [was] meant to be with the heavies, not the Hoffmans and Rubins and Dellingers, but the people who practiced "politics politics"—the Kennedys and McGoverns, the real politicians, the grown-ups. Now it made sense . . . He was the man always searching after gods, the larger-than-life figures who got their names in the New York Times *and* Time *magazine. He liked being with them, sharing their company, basking in the attention they lavished on him, hoping the approval they received would, by his very proximity, rub off on him. "Wenner had been disparaging in print of the Yippie antics in Chicago in '68. "It looks like a shuck," he'd written. [Fast forward to] 1977, and Jimmy Carter had landed a spot in the White House, so Wenner threw a party to celebrate. Jerry Rubin, who had been "so excoriated" by* Rolling Stone *throughout the '60s, asked Wenner at the celebration why the magazine now embraced the political system. Wenner replied, "We're not going with losers anymore. We want winners."*

Others, such as Michael Rossman of the *Berkeley Barb*, provided a more studied-if-critical approach. Rossman published an "open letter" to Jerry. He felt the Yippies were being "totally irresponsible" by suggesting everyone come to Chicago to enjoy some good vibe music when the possibility for violence was strong. Dated March 16, 1968, the "Letter to Jerry Rubin" read:

Let me tell you what I see happening. A scant handful of guys— centering around you, Abbie, Krassner, etc.—are pouring charismatic energy into an unprecedented style of organizing. In the first stage you run up and down the coasts, turning on rock groups, head shops, happeners, underground mediamen: "Come to Chicago to do your thing, be the Festival of Life confronting the Convention of Death; and spread the word . . . However many go, the ground condition they will find there seems clear. There will likely be blood. The black thing there is near blowing, black radicals are warning white organizer friends, "Stay off the street. We won't be able to protect you." Chicago has more cops per capita than a nightmare; Daley's preparing the sewers for mass arrests. Chicago in August will harbor the nation's richest pool of uptight bad vibes, set to flash. Pack 200,000 kids in there, with where we are in America these days when not even our inner millennium has come, and it's sure to blow.

Afterward, Rossman pointed out, "What was acted out in Chicago had little to do with the Democratic Party or electoral politics. The conflict expressed was between the old order and its young."

Not all left-wing media was critical of the Yippies—one supporter was African American Julius Lester (who was one of the few blacks writing for the mostly white underground press). In the *Guardian*, he aptly pointed out that the Yippies "helped politicize the hippies (who, he agreed, may not have always been political), projected an alternative lifestyle, and did not engage in the nitpicking common on the Left."

Jerry Rubin in *The SEED*, 1968: "The Yippies are with the Vietnamese peasant guerillas wherever they are, and the black and other struggling people of America. [My vision of Chicago is] a kid turns on the television, and there is his choice. Does he want to be smoking pot, dancing, fucking, stopping traffic, and going to jail, or does he want to be in a blue uniform beating people up, or does he want to be in the convention with a tie strangling his throat— making ridiculous deals and nominating a murderer?"

The Six O' Clock News. Jerry's goal was to create enough of a stir that Walter Cronkite would have to announce on the evening news that Chicago had become a "police state." Jerry wanted to bring H. Rap Brown's statement that "violence is as American as cherry pie" to the media's attention. In *Steal This Dream*, Jerry wrote that he "wanted the inherent violence of America to be exposed. I felt America was a violent country, but the violence was being done to invisible people, browns, blacks. So I wanted the violence to be on TV, prime time, nonstop, boom! Smack right in your face. My plan in Chicago was we want good to be facing evil, we want young white kids beaten up by the cops."

Cronkite was the most popular and trusted newscaster, one in whom people of various political factions could depend on to tell the unbiased truth (within the confines of mainstream media). Even Jerry agreed. "Walter could announce the end of the world, and you'd believe it." When Cronkite denounced the war in Vietnam during his February 27, 1968 nightly newscast—"For it seems now more certain than ever that the bloody experience of Vietnam is to end in a stalemate . . . But it is increasingly clear to this reporter that the only rational way out then will be to negotiate, not as victors, but as an honorable people who lived up to their pledge to defend democracy, and did the best they could"—President Johnson saw that as his cue to not seek reelection. He is rumored to have said while watching the broadcast, "If I've lost Cronkite, I've lost Middle America." It's hard to imagine in the twenty-first century: one of the three national networks (CBS, NBC, and ABC) declaring a war unwinnable and the President stepping down in defeat.

About a year later, Rubin paid Cronkite a visit at his CBS news office in Manhattan. Cronkite was flattered by Rubin's enthusiasm to meet him. Rubin wanted to tell him, "We are going to let you announce the victory of the revolution." What Rubin did tell him was, "Watch out, Walter, Spiro [Agnew] is going to get you." Cronkite replied, "When the Nazis come to my door, I hope you guys are going to be outside on the barricades."

In *DO iT!*, Jerry said, "Walter Cronkite is SDS's best organizer. Uncle Walter brings out the map of the US with circles around the campuses that blew up today. Every kid out there is thinking, 'Wow! I wanna see my campus on that map!' Television proves the domino theory: one campus falls, and they all fall." In the book *Can't Find My Way Home*, Jerry told Martin Torgoff, "the real drug was Walter Cronkite—it's hard to describe how excited we were when we realized how easy it was to get on those sign-off pieces at the end of the evening news broadcasts . . . the more visual and surreal the stunts we could cook up, the easier it would be to get on the news, and the more weird and whimsical and provocative the theater, the better it would play." I would argue this is the primary reason that scholars like Todd Gitlan resent the Yippies to this day—they despise the inspired shortcuts the Yippies took to band together their followers, rather than using traditional methods like door-to-door campaigning and organizing disciplined student groups.

In 1994, just a week after Jerry's death, Gitlan saw fit to pen a negative letter to the *New York Times* in response to their positive obituary:

> *Your obituary of Jerry Rubin repeats the canard that the Yippies were the quintessential 1960s protest group. The Yippies were the brainchild of a stoned New Year's Eve party in 1967, at which fewer than a dozen people, including Jerry Rubin, decided to invent something the media would pay attention to . . . The media endlessly declared the Yippies and their stunts "quintessential." . . . The never-numerous Yippies did capture (indeed "inhaled") one of the spirits in the air of those days. But most of that decade's activists belonged to less photogenic civil rights, antiwar, and women's groups.*

I asked Gitlan in 2013 if he'd care to revise that statement. He responded:

> *I would add that the Yippies expressed quite widespread sentiments—insouciance, rambunctiousness, flamboyance, aggressiveness, bravado, boldness, etc. but as a group they were minor . . . and that [Jerry and Abbie] are not famous [in 2013] because they were leaders of a group but because they had various forms of genius in public performance via media.*

OPPOSITE: Inside the Chicago Democratic Convention, August '68.

Bobby Kennedy and The Revolution that Almost Got Canceled.

DANA BEAL: I didn't realize the extent to which the whole thing had been like a Robert Kennedy trip; the Yippies were going to have the protest because he wasn't running. Then he was running, so they were actually going to cancel the protest. They figured he's going to become the Presidential nominee, because everybody was moving in that direction. Because Hubert Humphrey, he didn't have the charisma. The Yippies were just about ready to cancel the protests in Chicago, and then RFK got shot.

With President Johnson now out of the race, and Robert Kennedy stepping into it (along with another antiwar candidate, Eugene McCarthy), the Yippies considered calling off their Chicago protest. Both Kennedy and McCarthy pledged to end the war, which swelled their campaigns with youth support. The protest in the park would now be marginalized with Kennedy and McCarthy duking it out in the Convention Hall. Meanwhile, the leaders of other antiwar groups that were planning on going to Chicago too, such as Tom Hayden and Rennie Davis, didn't want the Yippies to announce they weren't going, as it might discourage the SDS and MOBE followers from showing up.

While in San Francisco, Hayden bumped into Kennedy and reiterated, "I want to work with your people on demonstrations in Chicago against the war." Kennedy's reply was brief, but positive: "Good."

PAUL KRASSNER: In February of '68, the three of us went to a college paper editor's conference. Bobby Kennedy had not announced his run for President, at that point. So we got out of the train, in Washington, and we saw Bobby Kennedy there, with just two aides, no big entourage. And the three of us stood there, in our hippie clothes, looking like the hippie Three Stooges. We each had different reactions that were revealing about the three of us. Jerry said, "Wow, look how handsome Bobby is. He's so tan!" And added, "we've gotta do something, we can't miss this opportunity!" Whereas Abbie, without a moment's meditation, just yelled out, "Bobby!" You got no guts!" Kennedy just flinched a little bit. And I remember thinking that Abbie was the right lobe of the brain, which was doing something on impulse, spontaneity, whereas Jerry was the left lobe of the brain, all these details about the lists [he put together] indicate that Jerry would try to think things out, figuring out what to do.

ABOVE: Bobby Kennedy supporters mourning his assassination at the 1968 Democratic National Convention.

The Assassination of Bobby Kennedy.

The events leading up to Chicago were tumultuous: the assassination of Martin Luther King Jr., the abdication of Johnson, the rise and fall of Eugene "Gene" McCarthy. When Bobby Kennedy was shot, it was (from the Yippies point of view) both good and bad. While they would have preferred to see Kennedy become president, they saw Vietnam as a bigger concern—which in terms of loss of life, it was. Bobby was one man, while thousands were being killed in Vietnam. With Kennedy gone, the protest in Chicago for which they'd already invested months in planning (predating Kennedy's decision to run) was now back on track and likely to receive the media attention they craved.

The unexpected assassination of Kennedy on June 5th changed the landscape considerably for the radical Left. Jerry and Abbie were frustrated by the lack of cooperation they'd been getting from Mayor Daley's office to get permits for the use of the parks. They debated whether they should cancel. Meanwhile, the more "straight-friendly" Tom Hayden had penetrated Bobby Kennedy's inner circle during the campaign, who were considering Hayden's plea to lobby Mayor Daley's office to give "the protestors" their desired permits.

The night of the California primary, Hayden, like so many others, was watching the returns and was pleased by the results—until the bullets struck. Hayden recalled in his book, *The Whole World Was Watching*, that, "Sometime in the night, Jerry Rubin called in hysteria, saying he believed Sirhan did it 'because he's an Arab.'" Later, some would be offended by Rubin's offhanded statement "Sirhan Sirhan is a Yippie." They didn't realize that Jerry was sarcastically lamenting that with Kennedy out of the race, that the doors had been blown wide open for full-scale revolution on the streets of Chicago. It was now not only desirable, but quite necessary.

Hardly anyone on the left would have cheered the death of Kennedy. One poignant, yet playful, story of Kennedy on the campaign trail comes from Tom Hayden by way of Jack Newfield of the *Village Voice*. Hayden recalled, "Newfield showed me a napkin bearing Kennedy's scribbled signature. Late one night at a restaurant, the candidate had mischievously asked Jack what he wanted from an RFK presidency. "Only two things," Jack immediately replied, "get out of Vietnam and make 'This Land Is Your Land' the national anthem. Kennedy, laughing, signed his agreement on the wrinkled napkin."

The evening of his murder, the last thing Bobby Kennedy said to both the hundreds gathered around him, as well as the television audience, was, "On to Chicago!" For Rubin, Hayden, and others, amped up for what lay ahead, that phrase had a whole new meaning.

Getting Permits from Mayor Daley.

In the weeks leading up to the protests, Hoffman, Rubin, and Krassner kept meeting with Mayor Daley's people, trying to secure permits to gather in Lincoln Park. They tried a number of tactics: they threatened to dose the entire water supply of Chicago with LSD, and half-jokingly told the Mayor's office that, for $100,000, they wouldn't show up at all. In the days just before the Convention, Hoffman was at his most manic. He wasn't sleeping—just talking nonstop to the press every chance he could. Jerry was feeling pushed out of the way, as Hoffman's rhetoric focused mainly on himself. There was history being made and Hoffman seemed determined that it would be his. It reached a point where Jerry and Abbie were no longer speaking and operated independently of each other.

Pigasus and the Rivalry between Jerry & Abbie.

There was a discussion of getting a pig and bringing it to the park, so they could announce that the Yippies were supporting "a pig for president!" Hoffman chose one that Jerry felt was too cute, so Jerry got another one that was not as friendly looking. At one point, Jerry and Stew Albert presented "Pigasus" in downtown Chicago while singing the "The Star-Spangled Banner." Despite the anticipated press coverage (*Time* magazine reported it), Hoffman sat it out, which was both a reflection of the growing divide between the two men and the fact that Hoffman didn't think Jerry was capable of pulling it off by himself.

On the morning that Jerry, Phil Ochs, Stew Albert, and other Yippies unleashed Pigasus (who weighed in at around two hundred pounds) to a group of admirers and news reporters, the police were waiting in ambush. Just minutes before Jerry and his posse arrived, a "straight-looking man" approached a longhaired Yippie girl and asked her if Rubin had arrived yet. When she replied "No," he said, "Can you give Jerry this?"—and handed her a paper bag. She opened it up and saw it was stuffed with weed and hash; she threw the bag down and ran. The police arrived at the exact moment as Jerry did. The cops began shouting at each other, "Get Rubin, make sure we get Rubin." The Yippies (and their pig) were arrested for disturbing the peace.

Hoffman had not attended the Pigasus event due to not only his disagreement on what the pig looked like, but, more importantly, his disagreement with Jerry's strategies. Jerry felt that neither he nor Hoffman should attempt to lead the Yippies, but rather they should allow themselves to fade into the masses, thereby preventing the media from focusing on any individuals. This would also allow the masses to operate collectively. Hoffman was of the mind that his persona—as well as Rubin's—were their primary tools of protest and an integral part of Yippie street theatrics. According to David Farber's book *Chicago '68*, Hoffman saw it as "irresponsible to simply fade away into the crowds." Furthermore, according to Farber, "Rubin accused Hoffman of letting Yippie become a personality cult, [while] Hoffman belittled Rubin's 'Marxist approach.'" Name-calling ensued, and later, cooler heads prevailed with an agreement: "to divide responsibilities and keep their distance in Chicago."

NANCY KURSHAN: Abbie chose this really cute pig, and Jerry was really upset with him. He wanted this angrier pig. And I think that was a true dichotomy . . . Jerry was more hardcore political, confrontational, militant in that sense. And Abbie was always using humor to be more acceptable to people. But there was that dichotomy between them, which the pigs maybe represented.

JAMES LATO, OWNER OF HEADLAND PSYCHEDELIC SHOP: I had a head shop in Chicago. And Phil Ochs had a concert that week in town, so he walked into my shop, and said, "Could you hang onto my guitar?" It was a beautiful, beat-up, vintage '30s Martin Guitar . . . it was like three days later he shows up and gets his guitar. And it turned out he had been hanging out with Jerry in town.

We were at someone's apartment, and we were talking about the convention coming up, and how the Democrats had a donkey for a mascot, and the Republicans an elephant, and the Yippies should have something. And someone said, "Well, it should be a pig, that would be appropriate." So, we said, "Where do we get a pig?" I said, "Well, there's farms north of Chicago, here." So it was a Sunday morning that Jerry showed up, and Phil was with him. And I had an old Fiat 600, so we hopped in.

We pulled into the first farm, and there was a family, late Sunday morning. They were sitting on the porch, Mom, Dad, kids, and there was a border collie and a bunch of puppies there. We asked them if they had a pig for sale, and they were a little disconcerted at that request. "We're having a play in Chicago, and we need a pig for this play. It's gonna be out in the street." So that relaxed them enough to tell us about a neighbor who was selling hogs.

So then we go and find this old German farmer. And he had a pen, maybe fifty or sixty sows in there. And there was this one that a gnarly face and a big torn ear, and all three of us, at one time, said, "that one!" And the farmer looked at me, looked at all of us, and looked at the pig. "Twenty cents a pound," he said.

It was a hot August day, so, we put a big tub in the back with some water and ice in it, to keep the pig cool, and a couple ropes. We drive it back into the city. And it's about one o'clock now, it's getting even hotter. As we're pulling onto the expressway, Jerry says, "Man, this pig looks awfully hot." And he slides his window forward, and I slide mine backward, and we gave about a three-foot berth there, and this pig takes one look at the open window, and tries to dive out of the jeep.

We both had ropes; Jerry was on one side of him, with me on the other. And the pig pulling both of us out the window. The three faces, the pig's, Jerry's, and mine, hanging out the window. And we're looking out at all this traffic, looking back at us. And the looks on people's face, this was everything they ever thought about dirty, filthy, Commie hippies, was absolutely true!

We finally got her in the jeep, and we pull over to the Civic Center. Jerry got out the front, and handed it off to him and this young kind of black hippie kid. And they took it about ten feet from the jeep, and within seconds, about fifteen cops were all over those guys.

The Festival of Life.

Jerry Rubin, I believe, said it would be a good idea to call it the Festival of Life in contrast to the Convention of Death, and to have it in some kind of public area, like a park or something in Chicago. "Do it!" was a slogan like "Yippie." We use that a lot and it meant that each person that came should take on the responsibility for being his own leader—that we should, in fact, have a leaderless society.

—ABBIE HOFFMAN, DECEMBER 29, 1969
TESTIMONY AT THE CHICAGO TRIAL

Sunday, August 25. Thanks to the editorial in the *Chicago American* that morning, which claimed the Yippies were insanely out of control, Sunday's activities in Lincoln Park, the first day of "The Festival of Life," were fractured. By the time of the park's 11 p.m. curfew, a couple of thousand protesters had vacated the grounds in anticipation of the police sweep. Those that remained were invited to leave by police clubs beating down on them. The only band crazy enough to play the "Festival of Life" was the infamous Motor City Madmen. The MC5 began playing around 4:30 p.m. Ed Sanders read some poetry first, and then WBAI's Bob Fass introduced the band.

The police forbade the Yippies from using a flatbed truck as a stage, so the MC5 were forced to perform on the grass. The band hadn't played for more than a half hour or so when the plug was pulled on the amps. While the electricity was being restored, Abbie decided to instigate a power play of his own. He was determined to bring a flatbed truck into the park and put the MC5 on its bed. Super-Joel, with Hoffman's urging, drove a truck into the park and toward the band. The police and the Yippies began to clash. When Super-Joel was arrested at a quarter past five, the proverbial shit hit the fan, with verbal abuse, bottles, rocks, and batons flying in all directions. Stew Albert got clobbered on the back of the head, and by that point Hoffman's announcement that "the music festival was over, stopped by the police" seemed superfluous.

In 2002, a documentary titled *MC5: A True Testimonial* featured film clips originally shot by the FBI of the band's Chicago "performance": perhaps the most "rock 'n' roll" government surveillance footage ever captured.

LENI SINCLAIR: Because I came in a separate car, I never got to see the MC5. Because when I pulled into the parking lot of the hotel where the Yippies had their headquarters, where I was supposed to meet my husband John, a car pulled up right next to me, the trunk opened and the driver pulled out a couple of rifles. I didn't have any idea about what was going on and I just kind of . . . I just turned right around and went back to Detroit.

Monday, August 26. On the first day of the Convention, Mayor Daley welcomed the delegates with a speech. Meanwhile, marches and protests sprung up around the city, culminating with the building of a barricade in Lincoln Park. When the police moved in for their ritual 11 p.m. curfew beatings, at least a thousand kids remained in the park to protest. Tear gas and violence ensued, which spread to the neighborhoods surrounding the park. Even local residents were getting pulled off their porches by cops and clubbed. That night, the police took special care to beat as many journalists as they could.

Tuesday, August 27. A diverse cast of luminaries—including Black Panther Bobby Seale, writers William Burroughs and Terry Southern, French novelist Jean Genet, Dick Gregory, Phil Ochs, and Allen Ginsberg—made speeches. Events were scattered around the city, including Lincoln Park and the Coliseum. Some four thousand demonstrators gathered in Grant Park to hear African American activist Julian Bond, along with Rennie Davis and Tom Hayden. The peaceful rally was within earshot of the Hilton Hotel, where many delegates and television crews were staying. While the Grant Park gathering was allowed to remain all night, the police performed their 11 p.m. beatings like clockwork upon two thousand kids camped out in Lincoln Park.

OPPOSITE: "The Whole World is Watching." Photo © Paul Sequeira

Wednesday, August 28. Another banner day for speeches, with more than ten thousand people arriving in Grant Park to hear author Norman Mailer and protest organizers, including Rubin, Dave Dellinger, and Tom Hayden. They focused specifically on the war, while the delegates inside the Convention Amphitheatre were voting down a platform of peace. The Democratic Party had decided to officially support the Vietnam War! As word spread around Grant Park that the Democrats preferred war to peace, fighting erupted between the crowd and the police and Rennie Davis was beaten unconscious. When the rally drew to a close, Dave Dellinger suggested marching to the Convention. Some six thousand people marched towards the Amphitheatre, but the police stopped them. Thousands of protesters dispersed into the streets and were greeted with mace and beatings, followed by arrest. Many of them fought back, which caused the melee to escalate. For nearly twenty minutes, television crews stationed at the Hilton Hotel filmed this bloodbath, and when the protesters began chanting, "The whole world is watching. The whole world is watching," the TV crews sent a live feed to television sets across America. Rubin had gotten his wish. Middle-class Americans were witnessing "good facing evil" as they watched the police beat their sons and daughters. The entire nation was entranced as newscaster Walter Cronkite spoke over the footage. "The kids, my God, look what they're doing to the kids."

News began flowing in the other direction, as the delegates caught wind of the violence occurring outside. When Senator Abraham Ribicoff spoke to the entire convention, he denounced the "Gestapo tactics on the streets of Chicago." Mayor Daley can be seen on television screaming, "Fuck you, you Jew son of a bitch. You lousy motherfucker! Go home." This was the Democratic Party at its finest, and there would not be another Democratic president from January 1969 until January 1977. The Yippies had successfully ousted the Democrats out of the White House—the party that perpetrated the war in Vietnam. Decades later, Jerry recalled that particular Wednesday as a "great day."

ALL PHOTOS © DAVID FENTON

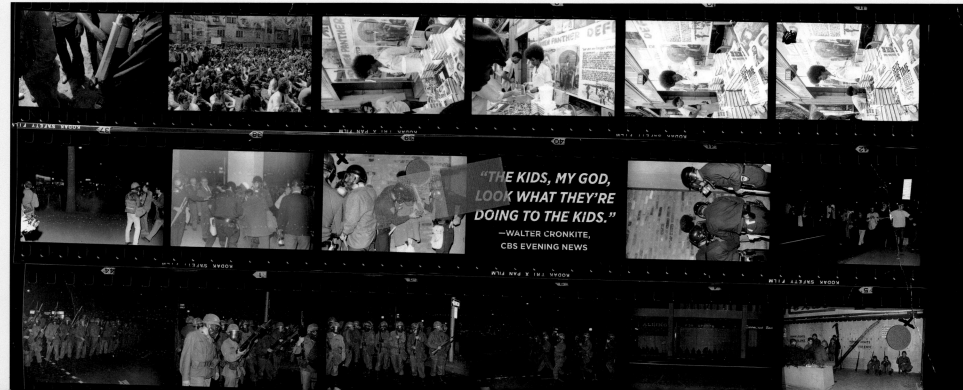

"THE KIDS, MY GOD, LOOK WHAT THEY'RE DOING TO THE KIDS."
—WALTER CRONKITE, CBS EVENING NEWS

Thursday, August 29. On Thursday, August 29, the antiwar presidential candidate Senator Eugene McCarthy spoke to some five thousand people assembled in Grant Park. After his speech, many protesters, led by convention delegates, attempted to march to the Amphitheatre but were kept away with tear gas. Around midnight, the 1968 Democratic Convention adjourned. Between Sunday and Thursday of that week, 668 people had been arrested, while numerous people had been injured. Local hospitals had seen 111 people; however, street teams of technicians on behalf of the Medical Committee for Human Rights had treated upward of one thousand demonstrators. The police claimed 192 of their officers were injured. Forty-nine sought doctor's treatment. During that week over in Vietnam, 308 American soldiers had been killed and 1,144 injured. And while the Yippies felt victorious in having embarrassed and upset the Democratic Party, it paved the way for Republican Candidate Richard Nixon to secure the national election in November. In spite

of the fact that they had actually helped him win by default, Nixon had decided that the Yippies would suffer his wrath.

On November 8, 1968, three days after Nixon won the presidency, Henry Kissinger visited the RAND Corporation in Santa Monica and told Daniel Ellsberg that, "Richard Nixon is not fit to be president." However, that sentiment didn't stop Kissinger from immediately accepting Nixon's invitation to be National Security Advisor. During that same visit, Kissinger told a RAND audience: "I have learned more from Dan Ellsberg than any other person [about our situation in] Vietnam." Later, when Ellsberg leaked the Pentagon Papers, Kissinger said to Nixon, "he is a despicable bastard," and that "son of a bitch has more information that he's saving for the trial—examples of American war crimes." Gordon Liddy and Howard Hunt were dispatched to find enough dirt on Ellsberg to inspire him to commit suicide—the same ineffective technique that J. Edgar Hoover fantasized about doing to Martin Luther King Jr.

EVERYONE WAS JUST "DEMONSTRATORS" IN CHICAGO, ACCORDING TO
THE PRESS. I DIDN'T GO THERE TO DEMONSTRATE—EXCEPT TO DEMONSTRATE
THE EXISTENCE AND BEAUTY OF THE ALTERNATIVE CULTURE, THE LIFE CULTURE.
I THINK THAT'S WHY ABBIE AND JERRY WERE IN CHICAGO, ALSO. I WOULDN'T
WALK ACROSS THE STREET TO DEMONSTRATE AGAINST THE DEMOCRATS.
FUCK THE DEMOCRATS!

—JOHN SINCLAIR, CIRCA 1970, IN THE EAST VILLAGE OTHER

OPPOSITE: Grant Park '68. Photo © Paul Sequeira

LEFT: After the Deluge, Chicago '68.

The struggle between the protesters and the police at the Chicago '68 Democratic Convention is symbolic of the sociopolitical makeup of the '60s. The generation gap was fought in the streets and parks of the "Windy City," while for the kids and parents at home watching on TV, the battles took place in the living room and around the dinner table each night. Chicago marked a turning point, in which many realized that perhaps the status quo was not right and maybe these kids had a point after all. "The whole world is watching," indeed. It was actually a global conflict with similar events that year in Paris, Prague, Mexico City, and other cities—in each circumstance every participant had their own reality, each party felt that their actions were justified. Nobody's right if everybody's wrong.

The band Chicago included on their debut album, *Chicago Transit Authority*, a suite of songs inspired by the August '68 protests. One track, titled "Prologue, August 29, 1968," contained recordings of the demonstrations, mainly the chant of "The Whole World is Watching." (Which actually occurred on the 28th, not 29th.)

Beat Generation Surrealist William Burroughs came to Chicago on behalf of *Esquire* magazine to cover the protests. His essay in their November '68 issue was partially a journal of observations. He remembered spending the morning of Monday the 26th of August in Lincoln Park with Jean Genet, chatting with various Yippies. Genet sweetly told them, "I can't wait for this city to rot. I can't wait to see weeds growing through empty streets." Burroughs figured the way things were going, they may not have to wait long. Several cops told him that "[if you're] talking about brutality, [you] haven't seen anything yet." That evening he witnessed "cops impartially clubbing Yippies, newsmen, and bystanders. After all, there are no innocent bystanders. What are they doing here in the first place? The worst sin of man is to be born." On Tuesday the 27th, he felt "The Yippies are stealing the show. I've had about enough of the convention farce without humor barbed wire and cops around a lot of nothing."

Although the exact numbers are unknown, most guesstimates come in at ten thousand protestors, including Yippies, hippies, MOBE, SDS, and various local teens. On the other side, the numbers

THE HELLS ANGELS AND JERRY'S UNDERCOVER BIKER BODYGUARD

DURING HIS VIETNAM DAY COMMITTEE DAYS, Rubin and other protestors had battled the Hells Angels over the war (which the Angels supported). Yes, the Angels and other biker gangs were nonconformists, like the Yippies and the Vietnam Day Committee, but as Hunter S. Thompson pointed out, "[The Angels'] political views are limited to the same kind of retrograde patriotism that motivates the John Birch Society, the Ku Klux Klan, and the American Nazi Party." In an interview with the *San Francisco Chronicle*, one Angel, known as "Louie," told the paper, "I got a lot of respect for Uncle Sam and for my mother and my brothers and sisters and even for my own two little kids. If I ever catch my two little kids marching [against the war], I'll break their heads in."

Despite this, when the Yippies first gathered in Chicago's Lincoln Park, they were greeted by a large pack of motorcyclists. These were mainly white, working-class toughs that shared little of the Yippies' ideals other than being social rejects and fellow authority haters. For Jerry, seeing the motorcyclists was both scary and exhilarating. Bikers had always held a fascination for members of the counterculture, beginning with a namecheck in Ginsberg's epic *Howl* in 1956, and infamously culminating with the death of Meredith Hunter at the Rolling Stones' Altamont concert in December '69.

When a biker offered to be Rubin's personal bodyguard for the rest of the Convention, Jerry was quick to accept. The biker was an undercover cop but played his role well, getting involved in much of the hand-to-hand combat between the Yippies and police in the first few days of the protests. Later, the biker turned up as policeman Bob Pierson at the Chicago 8 Trial, testifying against Jerry for (amongst other things) trying to incite a riot by throwing his sweater at a cop!

In 1971, Jerry wrote, "So when I said to Pierson one morning in an offhand way, 'It's amazing with all the violence here that no one kills a cop,' it was turned by Pierson on the witness stand to, 'We should isolate and kill a cop.'"

Jerry later recalled to Milton Viorst, "Abbie and I had this crazy idea that the white working class would join us, and when this guy volunteered to be my bodyguard, I thought, 'Damn, I've got a genuine biker who's been radicalized.' I took it as a real compliment. It didn't even dawn on me that he was a cop. We were seduced by our own macho fantasies."

totaled around twelve thousand of Chicago's finest, accompanied by a combination of twelve thousand regular Army and Illinois National Guardsmen. On average, there were twice as many "pigs" as there were "outside agitators."

Mayor Daley's henchmen were also openly hostile to the media. Dan Rather was punched on live TV while reporting. Rather kept on talking, saying to an entire nation of viewers, "This is the kind of thing going on outside the hall. This is the first time we've had it happen inside the hall. I'm sorry to be out of breath, but somebody belted me in the stomach." Walter Cronkite chimed in: "I think we've got a bunch of thugs here, Dan." On another occasion, Mike Wallace was forcibly removed from the convention floor. Various reporters were beaten with clubs while watching the comings and goings of protestors and cops in the streets and parks.

And yet, all of this bloodshed on the streets of Chicago (courtesy of Mayor Daley) could have been a giant "What If?" According to Tom Hayden's book *The Whole World Was Watching*, Mayor Richard Daley's son (another Chicago Mayor named Richard Daley!) told Hayden in 1996 that, "My father told LBJ in 1966 that he had to get out of Vietnam, just get out. He said, 'appoint a commission of five, with at least three to tell you to get out. Put Father Hesburgh [President of Notre Dame] on it. Have Bobby Kennedy included, and take their advice.'"

On a September 1968 episode of the William F. Buckley talk show *Firing Line*, Buckley's remarked idiotically that "if only the Yippies and the Democratic Convention could have been more separated, maybe the cops would not have resorted to violence."

Ed Sanders replied, "They were very clearly separated. There were two movements operating in Chicago. The Yippies wanted Lincoln Park, which is many miles from the Amphitheater [where the convention was held] and is many miles away from the Hilton [where the delegates stayed]. We wanted to have a Festival of Life with rock music in the park, theater classes, with Guerilla Theater, with various poets and people coming together for a Festival of Life."

William Burroughs, Terry Southern, Allen Ginsberg, Jean Genet in Chicago.

PHIL OCHS AIN'T MARCHING ANYMORE . . .

AFTER LBJ WAS ELECTED PRESIDENT in his own right in 1964, the war in Vietnam (and the protests at home) escalated. Singer/songwriter Phil Ochs began to obsess about Southeast Asia, attending lectures on the topic at the Free University in NYC. It was there that he first met (future Yippies) Stew Albert and Paul Krassner—editor of the political satire magazine *The Realist*. Both Stew and Krassner would become key figures in Phil and Jerry Rubin's life. Stew was about to move to Berkeley and become Rubin's lifelong comrade in arms, while Krassner, along with Jerry, Abbie Hoffman, Nancy Kurshan, and Anita Hoffman, would cofound the Yippies as 1967 came to a close.

Jerry was still in Berkeley, leading demonstrations as part of the Vietnam Day Committee. Rubin, along with UC Berkeley math professor Stephen Smale, was in the midst of planning a thirty-six-hour Teach-In on the campus with lectures by Norman Mailer, Mario Savio, Dick Gregory, Dr. Benjamin Spock, and others. Which, between May 21 and 22, 1965, attracted tens of thousands, the largest of event of its kind of that era.

Krassner (who was also invited to speak at the Teach-In) suggested Phil Ochs (whom Jerry had never met nor heard of) to be part of the entertainment. The idea was that Phil would perform a song or two intermittently during the two days to break up the monotony of continuous speeches. Most of the speeches were quite dynamic, and led to a two LP set of highlights released by Folkways Records, titled *Berkeley Teach-in: Vietnam*. Strangely, neither Rubin nor Ochs appear anywhere on the vinyl souvenir of the event.

Despite the captivating orators, Ochs's stirring song "I Ain't Marching Anymore" could entertain and educate even the most rapt politico. When prompted by Jerry, Phil would sing between speakers. He had canceled several paid concerts to attend the Teach-In, and the whole event was a revelation for him. It cemented a passion to perform for as many students as possible, wherever he could—and for the remainder of the decade, Phil was more likely to perform for free at a demonstration than to get paid for a concert hall gig. Krassner recalled to Michael Schumacher that Phil said, "A demonstration should turn you on, not turn you off."

Jerry told Ochs biographer Marc Eliot, "I remember taking him on a tour of the campus the day before the Teach-In began, and genuinely liking him. He was totally unpretentious. He listened as much as he talked. He was really there, he was fascinated by the Berkeley campus, the students, the political activists, the Free Speech Movement." A bond was established between Jerry and Phil that would find them crossing paths countless times until Phil's suicide in 1976.

PHIL HAD THESE TERRIFIC CONFLICTS BETWEEN WHAT WAS GOOD FOR HIS CAREER AND WHAT WAS GOOD FOR HIS CONSCIENCE—WITH MOST ARTISTS IN AMERICA—THIS CONFLICT GETS EASILY SOLVED VERY EARLY BY AGENTS, MANAGERS AND PRODUCERS AND SYCOPHANTS. AND EVERYBODY GOES FOR THE BUCKS, AND IF PHIL WANTED TO TAKE THAT ROUTE, THERE'S NO DOUBT IN MY MIND, THAT HE HAD THE TALENT TO PULL IN MILLIONS OF DOLLARS, BUT HIS CONSCIENCE ALWAYS THREW HIM BACK TO THE STREETS.
—ABBIE HOFFMAN

PHOTO © ALICE OCHS, 1969

On October 1, 1967, Phil played at Carnegie Hall. The concert featured his sociopolitical songs, as well as the debut of a more introspective style he had developed for his forthcoming *Pleasures of the Harbor* album. As an encore, he brought out Jerry and Abbie to announce their plans for a gathering in Chicago the following summer. Jerry was just beginning to fill the audience in when Abbie grabbed the mic and declared, "Fuck Lyndon Johnson, Fuck Robert Kennedy, and fuck you if you don't like it!"

Neither the audience nor the Carnegie Hall management was amused. However, this did not deter Ochs from supporting the Yippies whenever he could. He participated in the Levitation of the Pentagon three weeks later.

On January 28, 1968, Carnegie Hall hosted a tribute to Woody Guthrie that became best known as Bob Dylan's (with the Band) return to the stage after eighteen months of seclusion. Other performers included Guthrie's son Arlo, Pete Seeger, and Jack Elliot. Strangely, Ochs—who, other than Dylan himself, was the natural heir to Guthrie's political songwriting legacy—was not invited to perform. He watched from the audience. Not for the first time, Ochs felt upstaged by Dylan, and he decided it was time to leave New York and move to LA. Phil sublet his Village apartment on Prince Street to Jerry. They made an arrangement that Phil could always use it a crash pad whenever he was in town, and that if Jerry vacated it for any reason, Jerry needed to maintain the sublease. After Nixon was reelected in November '72, Rubin (despondent because McGovern lost) relocated to San Francisco, but continued to send checks to Phil for several more years to cover the rent.

As 1968 continued on toward the August Democratic National Convention, Jerry and Ochs publicly debated (via the underground press) their opinions about the presidential candidates. Phil liked Kennedy and supported McCarthy, while Rubin felt that all were morally corrupt and mourned the chance to mock LBJ after he'd dropped out of the race. In October '67, Bobby Kennedy had given his first speech on the Senate floor against the Vietnam War—a moving denunciation of the policy that his brother John supported during his presidency. Phil was there and happened to grab the same plane back to New York as RFK. On that flight, without a guitar in hand, Phil sang his song "Crucifixion" to Kennedy. Midway through, Bobby realized the song was about his brother, John. Bobby Kennedy was "absolutely wiped out" by that, according to Jack Newfield of the *Village Voice*, who witnessed it.

Despite minor political squabbles, Jerry and Phil remained tight, and on the weekend of July 26, 1968, Jerry invited Phil to accompany him and his girlfriend Nancy to the Newport Folk Festival to see Joan Baez, Tim Buckley, and Joni Mitchell. Phil resisted, because he hadn't been invited to perform. Jerry quickly overcame Phil's insecurity by saying, "I'm inviting you!" Phil quickly capitulated and joined the couple. In classic Yippie fashion, the trio entered the grounds by displaying phony press credentials. Jerry and Nancy handed out copies of the *Yipster Times* that included this charming pronouncement:

Who says that rich White America can tell the Chinese what is best? How dare you tell the poor that their poverty is deserved?

Fuck nuns; laugh at professors; disobey your parents; burn your money; you know life is a dream and all of our institutions are man-made illusions effective because YOU take the dream for reality.

According to Ochs biographer Marc Eliot, "Someone recognized Rubin and he was immediately ejected from the festival grounds." Eliot goes on to describe encountering Phil, Jerry, and Nancy later that evening, drinking in a local bar, when Phil spotted William F. Buckley. Phil engaged Buckley in a conversation about Gene McCarthy's bid for president now that Robert was dead. The trio was later kicked out of a party hosted by Newport Festival organizer George Wein. With the Chicago protests exactly a month away, Rubin declared, "Don't worry, Phil—the real party is just beginning."

During much of his career Phil was blacklisted from radio and television. This understandably bothered him and compounded those weird situations when he got left out of the Woody Guthrie tribute and the Newport Festival. Phil did indeed join the Yippies in Chicago. The catchphrase of that year was "Pig." The Black Panthers shouted, "Off the Pigs!" (meaning kill racist cops), and the Yippies and other demonstrators also embraced the phrase "Pig" to describe policemen. Jerry took it a step further in Chicago, and announced to the media:

The Republican Party has nominated a pig for President and pig for Vice President. The Democratic Party is going to nominate a pig for President and a pig for Vice President. And our campaign slogan is, "Why take half a hog when you can have the whole hog." And so we're nominating a pig for President. We're requesting Secret Service protection. Our pig promises to run on the following principles, the same principle this country has always been governed on—garbage.

Phil and James Lato (who ran a local head shop back then) accompanied Jerry in the search for the perfect pig in the rural outskirts of Chicago. When the pig was unleashed into the streets by Jerry, Ochs, and Stew Albert a sea of policemen stormed the area, arresting the Yippies and capturing "Pigasus" in the process. Phil was amongst the ones rounded up, and, according to Michael Schumacher's Ochs biography,

Phil drew howls of laughter by loudly protesting that the police were being too rough on the pig and therefore guilty of police brutality. Stew Albert was also arrested and put in the same paddy wagon as the others. He recounted to Schumacher, "Jerry Rubin was concerned that they might get rough with us, but I told him I didn't think so, that it was just too public. We were held in one big jail cell, and at one point a cop came to our cell and said, "Boys, I have bad news for you. The pig squealed."

As the week wore on, protestors burned their draft cards while Phil sang. Ochs was in heaven. Sadly, the euphoria went to his head and Phil become convinced that he could inspire the National

Guard to drop their guns and join the protest. He tried addressing large groups of guardsmen with a bullhorn, as well as approaching them one at time. A soldier told him that he used to enjoy Phil's songs but now would never play his music again. Phil was genuinely hurt. When the majority of the Democratic delegates voted against ending the war effort, Phil was devastated.

A decade after Phil's death, Jerry remembered that Phil was a little to the right of what the Yippies believed in: "I remember at one demonstration, Phil ended a song by saying, 'When you protest today, be sure to protest with dignity.' I remember getting upset about that, because what right does Phil have to preach to us about dignity when the United States is undignified about dropping bombs on the Vietnamese and anyway is dignity really gonna end the war? What's gonna end the war is total outrageousness—and that was kinda my difference with Phil. He believed in reason. He thought that reason would finally end the war . . . but at the same time, he liked the Yippie sense of theater. For example, he was arrested as part of our Pigasus demonstration in Chicago."

Upon his return to New York in early September 1968, Phil explained the events in Chicago to Izzy Young:

The Chicagoans were unable to recognize that this was a national convention. They literally, psychologically couldn't. They kept thinking, "This is our city, our convention." I'm really beginning to question the basic sanity of the American public. I think more and more politicians are really becoming pathological liars, and I think many members of the public are. I think the Daily News, Tribune *poisoning that comes out is literally creating—and television, all the media are creating a really mentally ill, unbalanced public. And it's significant. I think what happened in Chicago was the final death of democracy in America as we know it: the total, final takeover of the fascist military state—in one city, at least."*

Phil's next album was titled *Rehearsals for Retirement*, and the front cover featured a photograph of a tombstone that read:

Phil Ochs
(American)
Born: El Paso, Texas 1940
Died: Chicago, Illinois 1968

"Pretty Smart On My Part" was the opening track on *Rehearsals for Retirement*, and the Feds were irked by its imagery about wanting to "assassinate the president and take over the government." Ironically, those lyrics were couched in pacifist satire against doing such things, while also mentioning hunting, misogyny, and S&M.

To say that Phil's emotional state never fully recovered after Chicago would be an understatement. He sunk into a deep depression, cut back on performing, and focused on self-loathing, rage against the government, and the feeling that the Yippies were incapable of provoking any kind of change in the status quo. But his hijinks with Rubin and Stew Albert weren't over just yet; there were expeditions to the UK and South America in the future. Another

fallout from Chicago was that Phil now had J. Edgar Hoover following him. Hoover considered white radicals just as dangerous as Black Panthers, and Ochs was added to Hoover's personal "asshole" list. His topical protest songs had been on Hoover's radar for years, branded as "subversive" and "potentially dangerous."

Now Hoover was ramping it up, as detailed in the Ochs biography by Michael Schumacher. The FBI boss's missive stated: "Ochs is considered one of the principle subjects involved in demonstrations at the Democratic National Convention. Our investigation is aimed at establishing possible violation of Federal antiriot law." He asked his G-men in San Francisco "to conduct an active investigation in an effort to locate subjects for interview. Do not rely solely on efforts being made by sources. This phase of the investigation must receive continued vigorous attention."

Phil was placed on a list by the United States Attorney's office that stated, "there does not appear to be a basis for prosecution in this matter. However, due to the apparent association with Jerry Rubin and others, [we] may consider Ochs as a witness and issue a subpoena for this appearance before the Grand Jury in Chicago." Ochs would appear on the stand, but as part of the defense for his comrades in the Chicago 8 trial.

In December 1969, Ochs was in the courtroom being examined by defense attorney William Kunstler. The angle was that Americans had a legal right to sing and celebrate in public parks and on the streets. There was a talk of having Phil play a song in the courtroom as an example of his participation in the August 1968 events. Ultimately, Ochs did not sing, but he did give respectful responses to both Kunstler's friendly fire and the aggressive prodding from the prosecution's lawyer, Richard Schultz. Bill Kunstler asked, "Can you indicate to the Court and jury what Yippie was going to be, what its purpose was for its formation?"

Ochs replied, "The idea of Yippie was to be a form of theater politics, theatrically dealing with what seemed to be an increasingly absurd world and trying to deal with it in other than just on a straight moral level. They wanted to be able to act out fantasies in the street to communicate their feelings to the public."

Kunstler asked, "Now, Mr. Ochs, do you know what guerrilla theater is?" Ochs: "Guerrilla theater creates theatrical metaphors for what is going on in the world outside. For example, a guerrilla theater might do, let us say, a skit on the Vietcong, it might act out a scene on a public street or in a public park where some actually play the Vietcong, some actually play American soldiers, and they will dramatize an event, basically create a metaphor, an image, usually involving humor, usually involving a dramatic scene, and usually very short. This isn't a play with the theme built up. It's just short skits, essentially."

When the prosecution took over the Q&A, Richard Schultz posed questions such as: "In your discussions with either Rubin or Hoffman, did you plan for public fornication in the park?" During the events in the park, Ochs had sung from time to time, including his trademark song "I Ain't Marching Anymore," at the request of Jerry. When Kunstler submitted Ochs'

guitar to the court as evidence and asked him to sing "that song so the jury can hear the song that the audience heard that day," Schultz protested, "This is a trial in the Federal District Court. It is not a theater. We don't have to sit and listen to the witness sing a song. Let's get on with the trial. I object." Judge Julius Hoffman barked out, "I sustain the objection. I am not prepared to listen, Mr. Kunstler."

Judy Collins had also testified at the trial and said she'd been shut down for attempting to sing an a cappella version of "Where Have All the Flowers Gone?" When Fugs songsmith Ed Sanders was on the stand, he playfully threated to yodel—and was rebuked by the prosecution. Arlo Guthrie did manage to recite the chorus of "Alice's Restaurant" in the courtroom as part of his testimony. "You can get anything you want at Alice's Restaurant/ Walk right in, it's around the back/ Just a half a mile from the railroad track."

Arlo stated, "Abbie asked me if I had any song or kind of theme song for the festival, and I said yes, 'Alice's Restaurant,' and Jerry said, 'What's that?' He had never heard it, and I proceeded to tell him about 'Alice's Restaurant.'" A few months later, Jerry and Abbie asked Arlo to come to Chicago and perform the song at their Festival of Life—but Arlo declined due to lack of permits and fear of police violence. The March 14, 1970 issue of *Cashbox* carried a small news item that "Phil Ochs is trying to work out a multi-label [album] project so that the witnesses at the Chicago 7 trial can project their feelings musically. Participants could include Arlo Guthrie, Judy Collins, and the Fugs."

In October 1970, Phil did accompany Jerry and Stew Albert to England for their infamous appearance on the *David Frost Show*. Ochs decided to not appear on the show, as he didn't want embarrass Frost with any Yippie shenanigans. Phil was also low-key when the ensemble traveled to Paris, sitting out a Yippie television appearance there as well. Phil was still suffering from Post-Chicago-Traumatic-Stress-Disorder, and while the European jaunt lifted his spirits somewhat, he was generally avoiding the press and live performances, even for political causes. By 1971, Phil felt that the movement had "dwindled out" due to a "lack of a real ideology and a lack of a party structure." He blamed the government for

OPPOSITE: Phil, unknown, Nancy, Jerry.

88

the infiltration of drugs into the movement and the death of four students at Kent State, which he believed had sent a message to white middle-class kids across America "that the government was prepared to blow your head away" with a rifle.

A tape has circulated of Phil and Jerry at John Lennon's apartment in 1972. The tape begins as Phil finishes performing a song, and he asks Lennon, "Could you follow the words?" Lennon replies he didn't pay attention to the lyrics, because he loved the melody so much, wanting to know its origins. Phil informs him that it's a public domain tune that has been rewritten many times; Woody Guthrie used it for the song "Tom Joad." Lennon answers, "[in that case], I'll have it!" Jerry suggests that Phil sing "Chords of Fame"—Phil begins to play it, telling Lennon, "This is a song about the dangers of fame, okay?" Lennon wonders what key it's in, then picks up a Dobro guitar and plays a tasteful, restrained lead to accompany Phil's passionate rendition of his composition, which first appeared on the 1970 album titled (tongue-in-cheek) *Phil Ochs Greatest Hits*.

Phil did eventually find a cause he was passionate about: the new Communist government in Chile, led by Salvador Allende, who was becoming the next Fidel Castro poster boy for the remains of the American radical Left. Allende had achieved the impossible, becoming the first Marxist revolutionary leader "to rise to power through free, democratic elections." Phil wanted a taste of this energy firsthand, and asked Jerry to join him. Jerry suggested that Stew join them as well. Although Phil liked Stew, he was disappointed for the duo to become a threesome, as he was hoping to use this trip as an opportunity to reconnect with Jerry on a personal level after the Chicago experience. With Stew along, the dynamic would be different. Years later, Stew told Ochs biographer Michael Schumacher that he could feel the tension immediately when they met up with Phil in Chile. The trio traveled throughout the country enjoying cheap-but-delicious steaks and wine, with an occasional Cuban cigar. While walking the sunny streets of Santiago, they encountered "a handsome young Chilean with curly black hair, holding a guitar." Through broken English on the Chilean's part and nearly non-existent Spanish on Ochs' (and Jerry and Stew's part)—the Yippie delegation had accidently met Ochs' Chilean counterpart, Victor Jara!

Although the revolutionary folk singer was a household name in Chile, Jara was unknown to the American trio, and vice versa. But they wasted little time getting acquainted, accompanying Jara to meet a group of copper miners that would be engaging a local college basketball team in a scrimmage game. Jara was to be the halftime entertainment, and he invited Ochs to play as well. Phil later called it "the best serendipity of the trip," which was an understatement. Not only were the two folksingers politically simpatico, Jara was living the dream in Chile that Ochs tried to create for himself in America. Jara had helped peacefully overthrow an oppressive government by tactics such as appearances on national television. Phil still hadn't

performed on network TV in America. Over the following weeks, Jara was generous with his time: sharing a television show with Ochs at one point, and introducing Ochs to students and workers eager for political debate.

Meanwhile, Jerry was getting on Phil's nerves with complaints about real or imagined health issues. To be fair, Rubin had contracted some kind of upper-respiratory infection that he couldn't shake off, but refused to let a local doctor look at it, as he was concerned about the quality of care. David Ifshin, a fellow young, free-thinking American that the trio happened to meet in Chile, recalled in the book *There But for Fortune: The Life of Phil Ochs*, that "Phil was just disgusted" by Jerry's attitude toward the native doctors. Phil bitched "about how Mr. Revolutionary—Che Guevara with war paint—gets a cold and thinks he's dying and wants to Medevac back to the [United] States." Ifshin suggested a Yippie-style prank: "We ought to find somebody to dress up like one of those witch doctors and send him up there with a big jar of leeches." That idea came to naught,

but the writing was on the wall. Jerry and Phil needed to part ways. Jerry and Stew split for Peru, while Phil moved on to Buenos Aires, carrying a case of gonorrhea he'd picked up at a Santiago brothel.

In 1973, less than two years after Phil and Jerry left South America, there was a coup in Chile. Victor Jara was brutally murdered by General Augusto Pinochet's troops (supported by the CIA) while they toppled the government of the beloved president, Salvador Allende. The death of Jara shook Ochs to the core. Victor Jara was the "sailor from the sea" that Ochs had envisioned years earlier, in the song "Tape from California." Phil had seen himself tortured and murdered in his 1968 lyrics: "Peace has turned to poison/ The flag has blown a fuse/ Even courage is confused/ And now all the brave are in the grave"—and now that had happened to his new hero, Jara. Witnesses say that soldiers cut off Jara's hands and commanded him to "try to sing and play the guitar." When he carried on singing, they knocked out all of his teeth and said "try singing now." Eventually they shot him. This tragedy compounded the despair that had plagued Ochs since the horrible shit that went down at the '68 Democratic Convention.

Ochs then traveled to Africa (without Jerry) in an attempt to recharge his batteries and get some rest. His plan was to take in some of the political transitions occurring in Africa while traveling with David Ifshin, whom he'd met in South America. Strangely, Phil's idea of relaxation included a pipe dream to meet Ugandan dictator Idi Amin to confront him about his human rights atrocities. He also planned to explore some ethnic music in Nairobi, where he recorded a single for A&M Records sung in Swahili and Congolese. Only released in Africa, the rare seven-inch single did get mentioned in an October 1973 issue of *Billboard*.

One evening in Tanzania, as Phil walked alone on the beach, he was mugged by a gang that beat him, nearly strangling him to death. His vocal chords were permanently damaged: the sweeter qualities and upper range was now gone. While it was probably a random act, Phil wondered if the FBI or CIA had finally got their revenge on his subversive activities. Phil's spirit was now broken for good, pushing him even deeper into depression. Jerry and Phil remained friends right up until the end.

During the 1970s, Phil suffered from intense bipolar episodes and Jerry helped him seek medical attention. Even when Phil lashed out angrily, alienating most of those around him, Jerry remained loyal, checking in on Phil on a regular basis. When Dylan shunned Ochs from participating in the legendary Rolling Thunder Revue tour that included mutual friends Joan Baez and Allen Ginsberg, that shattered Ochs emotionally, so he visited Rubin who welcomed him with open arms. The last time that Jerry socialized with Phil was in his own apartment, not long before Phil's death. Phil half-jokingly pretended to jump out the window, even sticking a leg out. They left the apartment accompanied by their friend Ron Cobb to eat at Katz's Deli on the Lower East Side. As they parted ways on the subway platform, Phil mentioned jumping onto the electric third rail. Jerry never saw Ochs again.

Often dismissed by some as a polemical protest singer, Ochs's lyrics actually had a fiercely humorous, yet self-deprecating wit unlike anyone else's, save Tom Lehrer; as well as metaphysical imagery and transcendent melancholy more akin to Tim Buckley than most topical troubadours. His deep affiliation with the humbled and suffering was reflected early on in Beat Generation-inspired, early works such as "Morning"; and he would go on to work with producers and arrangers like Larry Marks and Van Dyke Parks on a quartet of art-pop albums that have inspired generations (*Pleasures of the Harbor, Tape from California, Rehearsals for Retirement, and Greatest Hits*). To some, his intensity and freewheeling wordplay invites extreme devotion; to those who don't get it, he comes off as corny.

In early 1974, Phil released his final recording. It was a seven-inch single titled, "Here's to the State of Richard Nixon"—a snarky rewrite of his civil rights-era classic, "Here's to the State of Mississippi."

Jim Carroll dedicated his poetry book *Living at the Movies*, and Ratso Sloman dedicated his *On the Road with Bob Dylan*, specifically to Phil Ochs. Patti Smith and others shaping the next round of youth culture keenly noticed the fierce personal energy of Ochs; it's hard to imagine The Clash recording *Sandinista!* without owing a debt to Ochs's revolutionary zeal (especially in the title track, which references Victor Jara). In the decades after his death, Ochs inspired many others, including Billy Bragg and Jello Biafra. During his lifetime, his songs were recorded by a range of personalities, from liberal icon Joan Baez to poster girl for the conservatives, Anita Bryant!

In the book *Down and In: Life in the Underground*, his brother Michael tells Ronald Sukenick that Phil's suicide occurred because "he felt like he had been a shaper of society and couldn't figure out how to keep doing that." In the excellent 2010 documentary *Phil Ochs: There but for Fortune*, there is one glaring omission: Jerry Rubin. Jerry's wife Mimi and their son Adam attended a showing of the film, as Mimi wanted Adam (who was only five when Jerry died) to get a glimpse of his father on the big screen and see the relationship between the two men defined. Mimi was surprised to see several references to Abbie (who wasn't nearly as close to Phil as Jerry was), yet Jerry written out of the story. It was (before I even met Mimi) one of the reasons I felt compelled to write this book. For a documentary about Phil Ochs that captures his friendship with Jerry, track down the 1984 doc *Chords of Fame* directed by Michael Korolenko, which has several onscreen interviews with Rubin. The connections between the two are more numerous than I've detailed here. For example, original copies of the infamous *at Carnegie Hall* album include a reprint of a 1970 *New York Times* review of Phil's scandalous performance in a gold lamé suit, performing Buddy Holly and Elvis tunes. Rubin was dutifully in attendance and gets mentioned for accompanying Phil to the Carnegie Tavern for drinks between performances.

WHAT MAKES YOU ANGRY ABOUT PHIL'S DEATH . . . HERE'S THIS NONVIOLENT PERSON, WHO SANG ABOUT NONVIOLENCE, HIS LIFE WAS A STATEMENT FOR NONVIOLENCE, WHO DIES BY HANGING HIMSELF, IT DOESN'T MAKE ANY SENSE.
—JERRY RUBIN

Dear Phil: You did it again--you brought us all together but with one
person missing. YOU.

Phil, the happiest and fullest moments in my life I spent with you from
Berkely to Chicago 68 to deportation from England and Ireland in 197o
to Chile in 1971 to countless meals and movies and adventures and good-
byes and reunions. It terrifies me to realize that I will never again
pick up the phone and hear your voice say "hey man, Ochs here, what's
happening?"

I first met you May 1965, when a group of searching college students
were just beginning to question our country's war and we were organizing a big teach-in about Vietnam, and we needed a folk singer to charm
the people and spice up the speaking monotony and everybody else was
busy and you cancelled a commercial engagement to fly to Berkely. You
arrived, one man and a guitar, new songs scrawled on pieces of paper
falling out of your pockets. And you had one quality which immediately
excited me-- your curiosity. I have memories of you in navy pea coat
and English cap carrying three newspapers and two magazines and hurry-
ing home through the Village to catch the evening news. You wanted to
know the details of everything. And when you felt good you kept these
innunerable small notebooks in which you recorded what you learned every
day. You were a student of life. You taught me to look at all life as
a movie and every incident as a scene. You loved being part of history,
part of your time.

Phil, because of the pressures of the competitive and capitalistic rat-race
of artistic "success" and "failure" in America, you punished yourself for
not being a production machine of non-stop creativity. But it will be a
hell of a long time before I grow tired of listening to the songs you

created. I understand the pain you were going through the past few years.

You felt you had lost your health. I remember a cold rainy winter day a

year ago when your family persuaded you to fly from New York to California

for a long rest. You felt that you were dying. You spent the day looking

for your friends to say goodbye to them. You drove an hour to Queens to

find me because the day before I had blown up in anger at you, because of

your poor health discipline. And you wanted to say something to me for the

last time. You said, "Jerry, I'm never going to see you again, promise me

that you won't be angry with me. See you in the next life." We hugged

and I could feel your body shaking with fear. You were convinced that we

would never see each other again. Well, Phil, I'm not angry at you. I

miss our companionship and your soft soul, your constant support and encour-

agement, your truth telling whatever the cost, your constant presence. I

miss the sheepish grin, the allowing manner, your sweetness. I know that you

went to your death a fulfilled man, because you lived, you travelled, you

felt, you wrote, you loved, you sure crammed a lot of life into those 35

years. I was privileged to know you for 11 years, and I hope that you

knew how much I loved you.

Fortunately, we all have Phil Ochs inside of us.

Thank you Phil for your sensitivity, your intelligence, your honesty, your

joy, your excitement at being alive. Goodbye Phil.

                                              -Jerry Rubin

PHOTO © NACIO JAN BROWN

**CONSPIRACY?
HELL, WE COULDN'T AGREE
ON LUNCH!**
—ABBIE HOFFMAN

The Trial

We wanted exactly what happened. We wanted to create a situation in which the Chicago police and the Daley administration and the federal government and the United States would self-destruct. We wanted to show that America wasn't a democracy, that the convention wasn't politics. The message of the week was of an America ruled by force.

Everything was by accident. Nothing happened as we planned. But it was all planned. Everybody played out their karma. It was perfect. After the convention was over—the question was not what had gone on inside, but why did the Chicago police go crazy. What's wrong with America?

—Jerry Rubin

On March 20, 1969, exactly two months after Nixon's inauguration, Rennie Davis, Dave Dellinger, John Froines, Tom Hayden, Abbie Hoffman, Jerry Rubin, Bobby Seale, and Lee Weiner were indicted by the federal government on charges of conspiracy, crossing state lines "with the intent to incite, organize, promote, encourage, participate in, and carry out a riot." "The Chicago 8" were charged under the new Anti-Riot Amendment (known amongst *the outlaws in the eyes of America* as "The Rap Brown Act") for crossing state lines with the intent to riot. The first and only people ever indicted under this law would be the Chicago 8.

Was it coincidence that the eight were a blend of Yippies, SDS, MOBE, Black Panthers, and academics? No. J. Edgar Hoover and Richard Nixon considered all of these groups enemies of the state. They were as carefully selected as the four Justices that Nixon nominated for the United States Supreme Court during his tenure as president. In October 1968, Hoover had circulated an internal memo that read, "A successful prosecution of this type would be a unique achievement of the Bureau and should seriously disrupt and curtail the activities of the New Left."

The Yippie protests in Chicago were more successful than the Yippies could ever have imagined, because they proved to most of America "that the establishment was just as sterile and violent" as they had said all along. Jerry Rubin wrote in the *East Village Other*:

What I would like to see is that we use the conspiracy indictment to build a REAL conspiracy. These indictments have brought together all kinds of different forces and styles that were really not together before Chicago. In Chicago, they were together in action but haven't been together since.

Now the indictments give us once again the handle to get all kinds of people moving again and thus bring much energy

back to the Movement. I think that by the fall there will be mass conspiracy demonstrations all over the country over issues such as Dope, the Blacks, Jail, Chicago, and Nixon. All through that will be the trial in Chicago.

Chicago was a great victory that cannot be reversed in the courtroom. On the contrary, it is going to be continued right in that courtroom and that is why we are so happy about the indictments.

Nixon was putting the '60s on trial, and the stakes were high. If the group lost, they faced serious prison time. Putting them behind bars would be a major coup for the Nixon White House. Yet, not every member of the Chicago 8 had actively planned or led a protest. Bobby Seale had flown into Chicago at the last minute (substituting for Eldridge Cleaver, who had been invited months earlier but had since fled the country) to give a speech to the assembled masses and quickly left. His actual "crime" was being the spokesman for the Black Panthers. Later, it would be the sight of him, bound and gagged by the bailiffs, that would help sway the conservative jury. Historians still wonder what wrong thing John Froines did, other than being an outspoken academic. The government indictments created a virtual all-star roadshow of '60s radicalism. Every important faction was represented: MOBE, SDS, the Black Panthers, college professors, and of course, the Yippies.

RON DAVIS: Some of the guys had no reason to be in the conspiracy, because they weren't . . . The government had formed this group; it wasn't necessarily a group before they got there. The government put them together.

MICHAEL OCHS: The funny thing was the quest for fame. When they started indicting people, Phil [Ochs] was terrified he was going to get indicted. He was scared shitless. Then, when they didn't indict him, he was furious that they didn't.

JAMES LATO: About a week after the convention was over, I got a call from the FBI. They came to my house—a local agent and one from Washington. They come in my house, and he opens up this book of photographs; Jerry, Abbie, Lee, Bobby Seale, and lays it on my kitchen table. "Do you know any of these people?" I said, "Yeah, who doesn't? They're in the papers all the time." And he said, "Do you know if they're Communists?" I said, 'I've never asked them." He said, "Well, did they come to town with a lot of money?" I said, "No." He said, "How do you know that?" I said, "I was the only one that had twenty bucks for the pig." He writes all this down.

"SANTA CLAUS IS THE ONLY COMMUNIST. HE WEARS RED AND GIVES EVERYTHING AWAY FOR FREE."

—ABBIE HOFFMAN

Jerry Appears Before HUAC Again. Jerry was now scheduled to appear in front of HUAC (the House Un-American Activities Committee) during the first week of October 1968. This time it was for alleged links between international Communism and the antiwar protests led by Rubin, Hoffman, Dave Dellinger, Rennie Davis, and Tom Hayden. With nearly the same cast of characters, one might confuse this with the Chicago 8 trial that began in September 1969, but this trip to HUAC was a separate ass-kicking from the Feds to the Chicago organizers.

As mentioned earlier, Jerry had been subpoenaed to HUAC (for his anti-Vietnam protests in the Bay Area) in 1966 and arrived in a 1776–era American Revolutionary War outfit. The HUAC congressmen were so shocked they canceled the hearings and tossed Jerry out of the building. The relatively unknown (at that time) Rubin got his photo in *Time, Newsweek,* and in newspapers across the country, catching the attention of future comrade-in-arms Hoffman, while inventing the Yippie street theater aesthetic before it was named as such.

Jerry was excited to repeat his performance with HUAC but he needed to make a more provocative statement this time around. 1968 had been a particularly bloodstained year, with the assassinations of Robert Kennedy and Martin Luther King Jr. (and the nationwide riots that followed). There were violent protests around the world, in cities like Mexico City, Paris, and Prague, while The Tet Offensive revealed that Americans were vulnerable to attacks from the North Vietnamese. To reflect the global conflict, Jerry dressed as a modern revolutionary. He sported a beret on his head, was bare-chested with sundry items draped around his neck, wore a pair of pants from the Vietcong Army, and wielded a (plastic) M-16 American Military rifle. Anita Hoffman and Nancy Kurshan were dressed as witches, carrying brooms and swept the floor of the HUAC room while burning incense and moaning. Photographs of Jerry brandishing his toy gun in front of Congressmen are priceless! Jerry was even called back to HUAC a third time in December '68 and came dressed appropriately as Santa Claus.

Abbie Does HUAC Too.

In the book *On the Ground*, Harvey Wasserman of the Liberation News Service recalls, "People were terrified of the House Un-American Activities Committee, and when Jerry and Abbie were dragged in front of HUAC, what did they do? They showed up in costume and did a comedy routine, and the whole committee collapsed. After terrifying people for decades, it took these two twenty-something guys to come in there shirtless, screaming and yelling to turn the committee to dust."

GERARD LEFCOURT, LAWYER: There was a competitive spirit between Jerry and Abbie as to who could outdo each other. And so there were meetings around HUAC, and what we were gonna do, and of course Jerry had previously been subpoenaed to HUAC. And that guided the thinking. Because Jerry really had done something—it was one of the most important things he had ever done. Which was to mock this devastatingly right-wing road show that went around the country, suppressing and intimidating. So, in preparing for the House Un-American Activities Committee, Abbie was trying to come up with what he would do, not only to mock the committee, but to also compete with what Jerry was doing. The government had just signed into law a new flag desecration statute.

So, Abbie got a flag shirt, and he wore that flag into the House Un-American Activities Committee. I spent lots of time trying to talk him out of it; that he was gonna get arrested under that Federal Flag Desecration statute. And on his way in, he got arrested. They literally ripped it off his back. And I'm screaming, "Let my client appear! He wants to appear!" And this went on, and they finally let him come in, and he blew the place apart.

Must Be the Season of the Witch.

When five out of the (future) Chicago 8 were called before HUAC in October, 1968, several female Yippies felt left out of the "fun" as only men had been subpoenaed. In 1966, when HUAC singled out Jerry for his Berkeley train troop activities and Stew Albert (disappointingly) wasn't, Jerry coined the phrase "subpoenas envy." But Nancy, Roz Payne, Sharon Krebs, and Robin Morgan were not to be outdone for the October hearing. Feeling ignored by not just the government, but also their male comrades, they organized W.I.T.C.H. (Women's International Terrorist Conspiracy from Hell) and donned black outfits complete with hats and brooms. Nancy and Sharon "dressed in [their] pointed witches' hats and clothes and armed with [their] brooms, walked up and down the aisles burning stick incense and casting evil hexes on HUAC."

(In a later chapter, feminist Robin Morgan's controversial—yet highly influential—1970 essay "Goodbye To All That" is discussed in detail as part of the decline of the radical Left's influence on people's lives as the 1970s pushed them in more introspective directions.)

The members of W.I.T.C.H. employed all the tactics of Yippie theater in the service of the women's liberation movement (a movement still in its infancy), pulling stunts like putting a hex on the New York Stock Exchange, and setting a hundred mice loose at a bridal fair. The W.I.T.C.H. acronym would change frequently, infusing humor and absurdity into the women's movement. The acronym was frequently swapped out: "Women Infuriated at Taking Care of Hoodlums," or "Women Indentured to Traveler's Corporate Hell" (as a protest against boring corporate office jobs).

ABE PECK: I was thinking about "Goodbye to All That," the manifesto that Robin Morgan wrote. Nancy is mentioned in there in a very kind of dismissive quote about Jerry, which is "The power behind the clown." Look, we were all guilty of ignoring the feminist movement.

Judy and Nancy and a couple of others were doing W.I.T.C.H., which in some ways were a kind of bizarre Ladies Auxiliary. But when the women went to Atlantic City (to protest the Miss America Pageant) Jerry was quoted somewhere as saying, "What are you doing that for? You gotta go to Chicago!" and I think that kind of sealed it for Robin and other women.

My memory of Jerry is not that of a macho pig. I couldn't remember one example of him saying anything like the old SDS line—"the only position for women in the movement is prone"—but it certainly was a male movement and he was probably guilty, as many of us were, of the implicit assumption of straight, white maleness.

Anita & Nancy in Chicago, February 1970.

Yippies and Women's Liberation.

In 1970, a British female reporter asked Jerry if there was anything he regretted about his recently published book *DO iT!* Jerry replied, "Yeah—the sexism." A year later, his next volume, *We Are Everywhere*, carried declarations such as this:

> *Women's liberation sprung up partly because veteran movement women discovered that they were prisoners to their babies, homes, and kitchens, while their men were still running around as free spirits giving speeches and fucking any women they could. The sickness of the Amerikan family was repeated in the movement. In addition, the sexual competitiveness of Amerikan society had women competing against each other for men. Women hated other women. Women began to realize that they had more in common with other oppressed women than they did with their own "men," who did not experience or share their problems. Women began to talk with other women.*

Women's liberation will save the movement, forcing men and women to recreate their relationships on a more human basis. Yippie in the summer of 1970 was taken over by Yippie women who confronted directly the male chauvinism of hippie-Yippie culture. Women took over national Yippie mythmaking, with Yippies Nancy Kurshan and Judy Gumbo and White Panther sister Genie Plamondon going on a trip to North Vietnam.

NANCY KURSHAN: Anita (Abbie Hoffman's wife) and I would never talk to each other, because we were each "stand by our man." We did later in life, but not back then. I think it depends what vulnerabilities you're talking about. Like you and I talked about sex, we did not talk about that with each other. I was twenty-three; I don't think I could have.

Yippie Women: Anita, Nancy, and Judy

NANCY KURSHAN: I think when Jerry and Abbie went to jail after they were convicted, that freed me up again in a lot of ways. Like when Anita and I did the burning of the robes together. And then she and I organized a big demonstration in response to the convictions. I also got a chance to travel around the country with Bill Kunstler and speak about the trial. Later Judy and I traveled to Stockholm, Algeria, and Vietnam. We were organizing this conference of fifty musicians and artists across the globe. But it wasn't a festival, it was a meeting, and it was going to be in Cuba, and we were organizing lists of who we were going to have go. But it got called off, so Judy and I went to Vietnam and Cuba instead. When I was with Jerry, I had a lot to do, honestly. I cooked, I shopped, I cleaned, and I worked a day job, which brought in a steady income.

In January 2006, Judy Gumbo explained the dynamic to interviewer Michael Simmons in film footage from *YIPPIE!* [an unfinished documentary by Michael Simmons and Tyler Hubby].

Perhaps the best way to talk about the Yippies and gender relations, is first you have to understand the context of the times. It was a male-dominated culture, a male-dominated society, and certainly that leached down and was part of the social protest movements. It was a very rare woman in 1967 or '68 who was singled out as a leader in a situation where men were also involved, so the media would go to Jerry, to Abbie, to Phil, to Eldridge. Now, were they talented? Yes. Did they have something to say? Yes.

Did Abbie then turn and say, "Now talk to Anita?"

Occasionally—pretty rarely. Did Jerry say the same thing about Nancy or Stew the same about me? Pretty rarely. So, men were dominant and that's who the media focused on, but what you have to look at, when you're talking about sexism and gender relations in Yippies, is you have to look at, "What did the women contribute?" What was our role, and what happened to us as a result of being a part of that? That's where it gets pretty complicated because what our role was, if you look at it from one point of view, it was to help the men out.

Did we do that? Yes. Did we bring coffee? Occasionally. Did that piss us off? Enormously, because the women's movement was coming along, so there was always this tension as to what the women did and what the men did. While the men were going off and being media celebrities, we were not simply sitting back and passively taking it. I mean, I certainly remember that we were the ones that got things done, which, of course, is typical gender relations, right? The men are out there shooting their mouths off and the women are the ones who are getting things done.

Who do you think organized the actual demonstrations? It was us! The men made the media call but we were ones that made sure the paints were there and the signs were there and the food was there, the medical stuff was there. We were the organizers. They could not have happened without us; without what we did. If you take a look behind the scenes, you will see that Anita and her influence on Abbie was huge, my influence on Stew was huge, Nancy's influence on Jerry was huge, and they were pretty dependent on us to keep things moving. From our point of view—and this is where Robin Morgan and I have had our historical difference for practically generations by now, and in a way it doesn't matter because it's so far in the past—but for me, it was a situation where I personally learned and grew an enormous amount.

OPPOSITE: Nancy Kurshan speaks to the press during the Chicago Trial, on her left: Anita Hoffman, on her right: Susan Schultz. Back row: Ann Froines, Tasha Dellinger, Sharon Avery.

LEFT: Abbie, Jerry, Tom. Photo © Nacio Jan Brown

Jerry Gets Kidnapped in Jail.

Jerry was in the middle of serving a month-long sentence for blocking troop trains going through the Bay Area. While in a California jail, the Federal authorities secretly brought him into custody and escorted him to Chicago without warning. For a few days, nobody knew where he was.

NANCY KURSHAN: Jerry was in prison in California for some antiwar thing. So he was already in jail when the Chicago trial was supposed to open. I say they kidnapped him, because one day we went to visit, and he wasn't there! What happened was they put him in a transport across country, shackled to this other prisoner— to bring him to Chicago. But the other prisoner wanted to escape. Jerry was in fear of his life the whole time, thinking this guy, who he was shackled to, was gonna run—and they'd both be shot. So I think it was really a harrowing trip.

The Trial.

After the adrenaline rush of the Chicago protests— which turned the Yippies into a nationwide phenomenon—Jerry and Abbie were a bit depressed while they wondered what to do next. In Jerry's words, "the government came through with a nice project: the indictments." They were back in the spotlight, and they relished the opportunity to spar with the Federal government. Despite their tomfoolery, the Yippies sincerely believed the war in Vietnam was wrong and that it was their First Amendment right to protest it.

Ramsey Clark was the Attorney General under Johnson's administration. In the months between the August '68 Democratic Convention and the January '69 inauguration of Republican President Nixon, Clark had investigated the Chicago riots, and felt that if anyone deserved punishment it was Chicago PD, not the Yippies. He was shocked when his successor, Nixon's Attorney General John Mitchell, handed out indictments. It was obviously a "show trial," with the eight defendants picked to represent the counterculture that Nixon and J. Edgar Hoover despised. Dave Dellinger represented the old-school pacifists; Rennie Davis and Tom Hayden stood in for the student-based SDS; John Froines and Lee Weiner gave the proceedings a local angle as Chicago-based academics. The crème de la crème was Jerry Rubin and Abbie

PHOTO © NACIO JAN BROWN

"THE DAY WE WERE INDICTED WE HAD A CHAMPAGNE AND GRASS PARTY. WE WERE THRILLED. IT WAS LIKE RECEIVING THE ACADEMY AWARD OF PROTEST."
JERRY RUBIN

Hoffman of the Yippies, and a member of the organization Hoover had declared Public Enemy #1: the Black Panthers. Although Bobby Seale did not take part in any of the marches—he was merely one of hundreds of people that spoke up in Grant or Lincoln Park that week—including priests, congressmen, delegates, Jesus freaks, Vietnam vets, parents, and civil rights activists—just the fact that Bobby Seale had been in Chicago gave the Feds a reason to continue their full-time job of dismantling the Panthers.

Abbie was already scheming. His plan was to "act crazy." He added that, once the cameras rolled, Rubin wouldn't be able to stay away, and that they would be "disrupting the legitimacy of the courtroom," forcing the police to intervene. Hoffman predicted that the court would be racist and mess with Bobby Seale. Jerry expanded on Abbie's philosophy in *Steal This Dream*: "We saw the vision. The courtroom would become a theater, good and evil, reduced to a cartoon. The judge would be evil. He'd represent parental authority, university authority, state authority, the United States government, the troops in Vietnam, the Pentagon. We would be seen as underdogs, as American revolutionaries, David versus Goliath. The media would be the window to the world. Having a drama of good and evil set in the middle of the country would absolutely make protest hip. The plan was to steal the youth away from the rich, to actually subvert the government by taking away their kids."

A week before the Chicago 8 trial, a pamphlet hit the streets.

The Conspiracy in the streets needs: freedom, actors, peace, turf, money, sunshine, musicians, instruments, people, props, cars, air, water, costumes, sound equipment, love, guns, freaks, friends, anarchy, Huey [P. Newton] free, a truck, airplanes, power, glory, old clothes, space, truth, Nero, paint, help, rope, swimming hole, ice cream, dope, nookie, moonship, Om, lords, health, no hassles, land, pigs, time, patriots, spacesuits, a Buick, people's justice, Eldridge, lumber, panthers, real things, good times.

IMAGES COURTESY OF ETHAN PERSOFF

Dave, who hails from Wakefield, Massachusetts, and has a lovely wife, Betty, and five beautiful children, "that I can lead our team to victory."

Glenn Thureson
15 DAVE DELLINGER, QUARTER-BACK At 54 he may have most of his future behind him, but there's no doubt that personable Dave Dellinger was—and is—"one of the great ones." "You can't have an anti-war movement without a pacifist," a sage observer once said, and "Old-Reliable" Dave has been the *quod erat faciendum* of pacificism ever since he varsity-lettered at the Union Theological Seminary in 1939.

A stalwart through the years for such international powerhouses as the Paris Peace Feelers, sandy-haired Dave's record is all the more impressive when you consider that he was out of action during the 1940, '43 and '44 seasons when he refused to sign a contract after being picked by Army in the annual free-agent draft.

Although never a big threat offensively, the 5'10" Dellinger has almost always succeeded in making a winning strategy out of being hit by pitched balls. When the Selection Committee chose the members of the Conspiracy team last September, the crafty old veteran seemed an almost automatic choice for captain: hence the oft-used monicker "Dellinger Et Al-Stars." "I'm confident," says

Nacio Jan Brown
1 RENNIE DAVIS, QUARTER-BACK Constantly improving Rennie Davis had his best season last campaign when he shared the National Mobes' quarterbacking duties with teammate Tom Hayden. Rennie packs less than 160 lbs. (soaking wet) on his 5'10" frame—that's extremely light for a frontline Conspirator in this dreadnaught era—but his deceptive speed, fine moves, and keen intuitive sense have helped this former all-American from Oberlin overcome his lack of size and heft. "Rennie's mild-mannered," confides one of his Dellinger Et Al-Star teammates, "but if you turn your back he'll kill you, or at least someone on his staff will."

Davis came on strong in 1969 pre-season play, and by the time July was in the history books he had already escorted three POW's home from Hanoi. Opines the young (29) quarterback from Lansing, Michigan: "I'm confident that with a little help from Tom Hayden, I can lead the Albatrosses on to victory."

Charles Pasternack
42 BOBBY SEALE, QUARTER-BACK The Conspiracy's heaviest slugger, the ever-dangerous Bobby Seale was a last-minute arrival for the '68 Lincoln Park tilt against the Chicago Clubs, and some considered him a surprise addition to the '69 edition of the Et Al-Stars.

But if there are any doubts about his eligibility for the Albatrosses, there can be none about his talent. A former stickout performer with the L.A. RAMs, where he was a leading exponent of the Statue of Liberty Play, Bobby thrilled Bay Area fans in 1966 by co-founding a new team, the Oakland Panthers, with whom he still remains as player-coach.

But just when Super-Stardom seemed within the grasp of this 33-year-old Merritt College product out of Dallas, the sophomore jinx lunged out of the shadows in the form of a kidnapping and murder indictment which, unfortunately for Bobby and the Conspiracy alike, is currently confining him to the San Francisco City Jail. But Bobby, who has a lovely wife named Monique and a darling little boy named Artie, is confident he'll be in Chicago in time for the '69 classic. "There's always

4

Vanessa Redgrave & Tariq Ali at London Protest '68

THE '68 CHICAGO DEMOCRATIC CONVENTION was held at the International Amphitheatre. That's where Hubert Humphrey, Mayor Daley, and thousands of delegates gathered. The Chicago 8 Trial had begun on September 24, 1969. The Rolling Stones tour, documented in the infamous *Gimme Shelter* film, stopped in Chicago (sans film crew) on November 16, in, of all places, the International Amphitheatre!

It was a Sunday night. Abbie had the "day off," so he and his wife Anita made their way backstage to greet Mick Jagger and see if the "Street Fighting Man" wanted to make a donation to the cause. After all, "Street Fighting Man" had been released as a 45 rpm single on August 31, 1968, just forty-eight hours after the rioting in Chicago calmed down. Jagger had been inspired by a large demonstration in London's Grosvenor Square, which he had witnessed firsthand. The event caused quite a stir in Britain. It featured speeches by actress Vanessa Redgrave and Tariq Ali, an outspoken antiwar activist in the UK. Coincidently, the Beatles released their high-energy version of John Lennon's "Revolution" as a single on August 26, 1968, some forty-eight hours before violence erupted in Chicago (a more laid-back version appeared on the *White Album* released later that year).

Abbie and Anita ran into the Stones' road manager/pianist Ian Stewart, and inquired about meeting Mick. Stewart had no idea who they were, so he asked journalist Stanley Booth if he knew "someone named Abbie Hoffman?"

According to Booth's exposé *Dance with the Devil: The Rolling Stones and their Times*, he thought to himself, "Not really, but close enough." He took the "bushy-haired, jovial, intense . . . nonleader of a nonpolitical party, the Yippies . . . and his pretty, dark haired wife,

ABBIE AND THE ROLLING STONES

Anita" backstage. Abbie said to Mick, "We're in the same business. Your thing is sex. Mine's violence." "Yeah, I love a good fight," Mick answered. Abbie continued, "Say, do you know where you are? What happened here, the demonstration . . ." Mick cut him off mid-sentence: "Sure, I know." Abbie asked, "Why don't you give us some bread?" Mick laughed, "For what?" "The trial," Abbie countered, "The Chicago Eight." Mick responded, "I've got to pay for my own trials."

At that point, tour manager Sam Cutler kicked everyone but the band out of the dressing room. Cutler's introduction, "Ladies and Gentlemen, the Greatest Rock and Roll Band in the World . . . the Rolling Stones!" famously kicks off the *Get Yer Ya-Ya's Out!* album recorded during this same '69 tour.

Stanley Booth, Abbie, and Anita exited the room together and headed toward the performance area. Abbie explained to Stanley, "I've been trying to talk to him all day. I even called the Ambassador East hotel and told them I was Elvis Presley." In his best Elvis voice, Abbie continued, "'Jus' wanna see how ole Mick is a-gittin' along.'" Abbie told Booth, "I may come to California for the free concert." That free concert became infamously known as Altamont.

Hoffman remembered, in 1971, that as he and Anita left the Stones's "sacred chamber," "a stocky-built man, about 48 years old, in a chauffeur's suit stopped us and smiled. 'Abbie, I'm Mick's private chauffeur. My name's Al.' We chatted trial-gossip for a while, waiting for the performance to begin, and then Al dropped the clunker: 'It's really a small world. You know who I chauffeur during the day?!?' He paused to suck me in real good, and lowered the boom. 'Judge Julius Hoffman!' *That chauffeur in Chicago probably knew more than Buddha.*"

In 1972, when the Stones' traveling circus pulled into Madison Square Garden for a series of gigs in mid–July, the enterprising Jerry Rubin called asking for tickets. Jo Bergman (the Stones's office manager) answered the phone. She yelled out to band manager Peter Rudge, "It's Jerry Rubin! He's on the phone and wants tickets for tonight's show. What should I tell him?" "Tell him to steal them," replied Rudge without missing a beat.

Guerilla Theater in the Court Room.

The most effective person in the courtroom *was Dave Dellinger, and the most effective people in the* pressroom *were Jerry and Abbie. So the boring person is Tom Hayden. He's a Democratic Party hack and a peacenik. If you read the SDS charter, Port Huron statement, it's all about making democracy work without mentioning capitalism. You can't do it, as far as I'm concerned. I think that anyone who has any idea what Marxism is about would say, "How are you gonna have democracy in a capitalist society?" Tom Hayden's the square in the group . . . the event in Chicago, well . . . Hayden was also for busting into the Democratic Party, or influencing the Democratic Party.* —RON DAVIS

In 1971, Jerry beefed: "Tom Hayden was the only one of us really pissed off at the indictment. It took him away from organizing in Berkeley. From the moment of the indictments Tom's position was consistent, however reprehensible I found it: most important thing is to win the case with the jury. Hayden's facial expressions killed many an idea and turned our meetings from 'turn-on' sessions, which they should have been, to bickering, useless personality conflicts, wrangling. Tom felt the Conspiracy trial was not that important an event, and that we should not try to build it into either a national myth or organization. Tom argued we should concentrate on winning over the jury through rational arguments and good behavior."

Julie's Judicial Robes.

In his book *We Are Everywhere*, Rubin details one of the hilarious stunts that he and Abbie pulled during the trial:

One night we got stoned and the battle of psychological war versus Julie [Judge Julius Hoffman] and the courtroom hit a new high. Wouldn't you love to see the expression on Julie's face if Abbie and Jerry walked into the courtroom wearing judge's robes! Wow! We both fell on the floor laughing so hard our insides hurt! He might have heart failure right then and there. But what could Julie do? It wasn't illegal.

We wore our winter coats into the courtroom so that marshals wouldn't stop us, then stripped them off and revealed to the full courtroom our flowing sacred robes. Julie's jaw dropped and his face reddened and his eyes glared and he froze. With his eyes stonily fixed on our smiling, joyous bodies, he stated: "Let the record show that the defendants Hoffman and Rubin entered the courtroom at 10:23 wearing collegiate robes."

"Judge's robes, Your Honor," I said. Muffled laughter filled the courtroom. "Black robes of death," someone uttered from the defense table. Exasperated, Julie turned his death stare to Kunstler. "Is this another one of your bright ideas, Mr. Kunstler?" Bill, suppressing a king-size belly laugh, said, "No, Your Honor, I'm sorry, I can't take credit for this one."

A few minutes later Abbie took off his judge's robes and underneath he wore the blue-and-white shirt of a Chicago policeman. A moment of absolute truth descended over the courtroom.

The trial turned out to be everything that Jerry and Abbie hoped it would be. They mocked the American justice system as they outraged the judge and Middle America with their guerilla theater tactics—while the media covered their every move. They averaged about seven minutes of coverage every night on the three national networks, ABC, NBC, and CBS. Each day after the trial, Jerry and Abbie would run back to their apartment so they could watch TV and bask in the glory.

NANCY KURSHAN: Jerry and Abbie loved watching themselves on the news. I think they were nuts about it. The whole fame thing was crazy.

Jerry and Abbie were mavericks in the courtroom, boldly going where no defendants had gone before in terms of comic relief and mayhem. Jerry put his feet up on the defense table and ate candy. Abbie perfected a technique to create pandemonium whenever it appeared that a prosecution witness was swaying the jury: he'd simply stand up and clap his hands! The network evening news would report on their antics rather than what the witnesses had said.

RIGHT: The inside of a holiday card sent out to supporters of the Chicago 7, this one includes personal notes from Jerry and Nancy to Barbara Gullahorn.

BELOW: Jerry holding his "Long-Hair" wig with Dave Dellinger, John Froines, Abbie

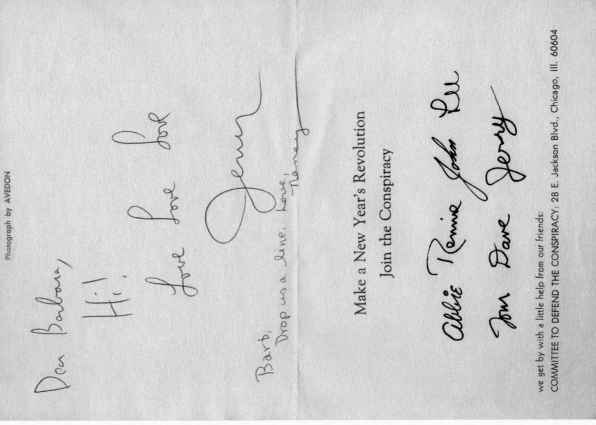

Photograph by AVEDON

Dear Barbara,

Hi!

love love love

Jerry

Bart,
Drop us a line. Love,
Nancy

Make a New Year's Revolution
Join the Conspiracy

Abbie Rennie John Lee
Tom Dave Jerry

we get by with a little help from our friends:
COMMITTEE TO DEFEND THE CONSPIRACY: 28 E. Jackson Blvd., Chicago, Ill. 60604

Send Jerry Your Hair Campaign. Jerry's hair had been buzzed into a crewcut while he was incarcerated, so he issued a statement asking longhairs to send in locks from which he would fashion a wig to wear in court (as well as one for the judge, who was bald). Dozens of envelopes began arriving each day from the around the country, filled with hair: pubic, underarm, head hair, leg hair, whatever you can imagine, people sent it in to the courtroom. Nancy Kurshan spread giant envelopes full of hair onto a table for the media's benefit. Jerry began wearing a wig in the courtroom.

NANCY KURSHAN: When Jerry got to Cook County Prison they shaved his head. So I started this campaign, where we ask people around the country to send him locks of their hair at the Federal courthouse. We would get mail, and we'd cart the mail out on the table. Sometimes people sent in marijuana.

During his trial testimony, Abbie praised Kurshan:

Nancy said that fun was an integral ingredient, that Americans, because they were being programed like IBM cards, weren't having enough fun in life and that if you watched television, the only people that you saw having any fun were people who were buying lousy junk on television commercials, and that [fun] would be a whole new attitude [in the movement] because you would see people having fun while they were protesting the system, and that young people all around this country would be turned on by that kind of attitude.

On weekends and during extended court recesses, the defendants would speak at college campuses around the country, raising money and awareness. They were treated like rock stars while the FBI watched and hoped they'd do something illegal, so they could revoke bail. At one point, Jerry and Abbie traveled to Washington as a publicity stunt. They stood on the steps of the Justice Department wearing boxing gloves, demanding that Attorney General John Mitchell come out and put up a fair fight.

CHICAGO BLACK PANTHER FRED HAMPTON AT THE TRIAL

JUST BEFORE THE TRIAL BEGAN in September '69, all of the Chicago 8 defendants and their lawyers met with Black Panthers Fred Hampton and Bobby Rush to discuss violent protesting. The Panthers were against the angry street violence being suggested by the all-white Weathermen. The Chicago Panthers wanted "a disciplined and orderly show of support for their chairman, Bobby Seale." Fred asked, "Who were these white kids anyway?" and hadn't they already learned enough about the brutality of the Chicago police force? Fred became a reassuring and calm fixture in the courtroom in support of Seale.

In his 1971 collection of free thought, *We Are Everywhere*, Rubin captured the essence of Fred Hampton:

I remember an automobile ride from O'Hare Airport to a hotel where The Conspiracy defendants and lawyers were going to meet for the first time the day before our arraignment. I'll never forget it. I arrived in Chicago by plane from New York about the same time Bobby Seale and Charles Garry arrived from San Francisco, so I waited to get a lift from them into the Loop. Fred Hampton met Bobby at the airport and on the way in by car we laughed and told stories and discussed the trial.

My attention focused on the driver of the car, Fred Hampton. I was wildly impressed by him, only twenty years old! It was the first time Fred met Bobby. Fred ran down to Bobby the state of the Illinois party, all the beefs on his head. "I got ten years! For stealing eighty-nine ice cream bars and giving them out free to the kids in the neighborhood!"

The next day at a rally I saw Fred speak and he electrified the crowd with his energy and passion: "I AM A REVOLUTIONARY!" he had the crowd chanting.

Hampton was the kind of leader whose self-confidence and drive would inspire other young blacks to join the party. When I saw him I thought of Huey, Eldridge, Bobby. Isn't there something ominous about Hampton? A cloud of death hung over his head.

He told us how the pigs were after him. "We don't have much time."

CONTINUED ☞

106   October 22 was Seale's birthday and Jerry brought a birthday cake into the courtroom that (written in icing) said, "Free Huey. Free Bobby." Judge Hoffman started to admonish Jerry: "I won't even let anyone bring me a birthday cake; I don't have food in my chambers. This is a courthouse and we conduct trials here. I'm sorry." A marshal began to wrestle the cake from Rubin. "That's a cake-napping," Abbie declared.

Rennie Davis said to Seale, "Hey Bobby, they arrested your cake." Seale told the courtroom, "They've arrested a cake, but they can't arrest a revolution." "Right on!" Fred Hampton and other Panthers cried out, raising their fists in the air.

On October 29, Seale told Judge Hoffman, "You are a rotten racist pig, fascist liar, that's what you are. You're a rotten liar." Seale was bound and gagged for the first time that day and for several days after.

On November 5, the judge informed Seale that "A mistrial has been declared with respect to you, sir. Your trial will be conducted [in April 1970]." Almost one month later to the day, on December 4, 1969, the Chicago police, in cooperation with the FBI, assassinated Fred Hampton.

The raid on Hampton's home was more of a "shoot in" than a "shoot out"—nearly a hundred bullets came in the house, while at most, one vertical shot was fired back. Hampton was asleep at 4 a.m. and never got a chance to respond to the assault. The police entered his bedroom and shot him dead at point blank range. He never awoke, as he'd been drugged ahead of time by an FBI infiltrator who'd slipped barbiturates into his drink earlier that night. Was it a coincidence that the Black Panthers were now completely neutralized in connection to the highly publicized Chicago trial?

SO YOUR BROTHER'S BOUND AND GAGGED AND THEY'VE CHAINED HIM TO A CHAIR, WON'T YOU PLEASE COME TO CHICAGO JUST TO SING.
- GRAHAM NASH

Shander for the Goyim.

NANCY KURSHAN: Abbie, Anita, Jerry and I hung out together during the trial. We went to the Museum of Science & Industry on LSD. And the four of us were walking around, having a good old time. And who should we bump into but the Assistant Prosecuting Attorney, Richard Schultz. He's there with his wife and two kids and he's Jewish, too. Everybody's shocked to see each other, and Abbie calls out, "you're a Shander for the Goyim!" Do you know what that means? It's like you're a front man for the white power structure. It's a shameful thing that you're doing. I thought that was pretty bold.

Young people around the country loved the descriptions of Abbie blowing kisses to the jury, Jerry arriving in court dressed up in judicial robes, and most famously, Bobby Seale telling the judge he was "a rotten racist pig" and a "fascist." Judge Julius Hoffman responded in kind by ordering that Seale be bound and gagged. The courtroom drawings of Seale tied up (no cameras were allowed in the courtroom) were reproduced around the world, and, nearly fifty years later they remain as one of the most indelible images of America during the '60s.

BOBBY SEALE: *All Power to the People!* and I really meant that from the heart; Blacks, Asians, Latinos, everybody—guys like Jerry Rubin really believed in that shit.

While the trial was still in progress, comedian Dick Gregory observed:

*Bobby Seale, trying to defend himself, ended up shackled to the chair, hands cuffed, mouth taped. In a courtroom where the worldwide press is watching. You dig? . . . If a man trying to defend himself in a courtroom where the world wide press is watching ends up getting shackled to the chair, hands cuffed, mouth taped, what do you think is happening in these courtrooms in America where there ain't nobody looking?"

In the mid-'80s, Jerry Rubin told Abe Peck, "Bobby Seale wanted to be gagged. He was being railroaded, and the only way to stop the railroad was to make Judge Hoffman so outrageous that the whole country would say, 'Stop oppressing Bobby Seale.' We were saying, 'Bobby, the judge is right there on the edge with you, and all you have to do is keep being provocative and do something really outrageous.' We didn't know what it was, but whatever it was, it going to be hot. They had already gagged him, but it wasn't a mouth gag—it was procedural gag. Finally, Bobby got up, and Julius played right into our hands by gagging him."

GERALD LEFCOURT: Charlie Garry [the Black Panthers lawyer] had come in the summer, made a motion to adjourn the trial. He had a gall-bladder operation he had to have. But, Judge Hoffman turned him down, kept the trial for September. The indictment had just been returned in April, making it one of the quickest trials in American history. Federal criminal trials with that much discovery involving eight defendants who are from different walks of life, from all around the country. It was bizarre. So you know, the Feds were on a mission. Therefore, Bobby Seale showed up without a lawyer. The judge tried to push one of us onto him, but he wouldn't have it. Because I refused to represent Seale—as did Michael Kennedy and Michael Tigar—we were held in contempt.

So, we're all there in the cell together with Seale. Jerry's serving thirty days. Michael and I have been held in contempt. It's now lunchtime, and the government has just opened. And I say to Seale, "What are you gonna do? I mean, you don't want us to represent you, you gonna represent yourself?" He said, "Yeah, I'm gonna represent myself." And I'll never forget this. I said, "I think it's your turn to open." He said, "What do you mean?" I said, "Well, the government opened. It's your turn to speak to the jury."

After lunch, he came out and tried to give an opening statement. And that's what ultimately led to the chaining and gagging of Bobby to a chair. Jerry was in the cell when this happened, Michael and Bobby, the four of us. So it was like very serious on the one hand, but there was also joking; they served some kind of food. Because it was a Friday, it was smelly fish. And I said, "I can't eat that shit." I asked Jerry if I could borrow his dessert, so I'll have two desserts. Bobby Seale said, "Lefcourt, there's no menu." [*Laughter.*] Jerry and Bobby got over on me, and we sang, "You get a little drunk. You land in jail." It was really one of the most incredible times of my life.

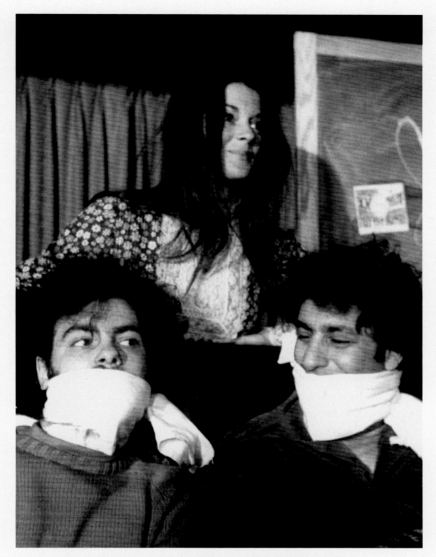

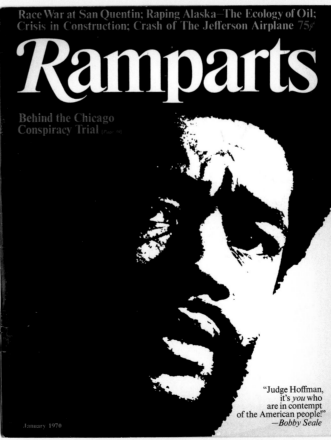

TOP: Jerry, Abbie, Rosemary Leary, 1970. BOTTOM: *Ramparts* documented the political turmoil of the era like no other magazine.

Graham Nash. "Chicago" by Graham Nash (on his solo album *Songs for Beginners*) is a pop song about the injustices inflicted on Bobby Seale. The song became even more popular when Nash included a version on Crosby, Stills, Nash, & Young's album *4 Way Street*, recorded live in Chicago on July 5, 1970.

CSN&Y had been invited to perform a benefit in Chicago for the trial's defense fund by the beloved Wavy Gravy (he emceed Woodstock, as seen in the movie). Apparently, Stills and Young were apathetic, and this song—written in dismay—was Nash pleading with the group to participate. Nash told author Dave Zimmer:

> *I saw Bobby Seale get chained and gagged and bound and put on the witness stand. And everyone goes, "Here, now we're going to have a fair trial." That was total bullshit and that's where [the song] "Chicago" came from, which I actually wrote to Stephen [Stills] and Neil [Young] . . . "Won't you please come to Chicago, just to sing?"*

Although CSN&Y didn't play that concert, Nash's song "Chicago" drew more attention to Bobby Seale's circumstances than if they'd played that benefit.

Murder in my Heart for the Judge. Judge Julius Hoffman (no relation to Abbie) was like a cartoon character; his thin, weedy voice was the perfect parody of evil. Later, it was discovered that Hoover and Nixon instructed him to rule against the defense at every opportunity, so the Yippies weren't the only ones using this as a show trial. The court transcripts are filled with Judge Hoffman citing the defendants (and even their lawyers, who were following the protocol of the legal system) for contempt of court, as well as interrupting witnesses for the defense countless times.

Although Julius Hoffman was the epitome of evil, the old buzzard wasn't always that bad. In 1960, he ruled in favor of *Big Table* magazine—the Chicago post office had seized four hundred copies on obscenity charges—because it contained an excerpt from William Burroughs' *Naked Lunch*. The judge ruled that Burroughs' novel was intended "to shock the contemporary society, in order perhaps to better point out its flaws and weaknesses." He also expressed admiration for a Jack Kerouac essay describing it as a "wild prose picnic." He cited the *Ulysses* ruling, "Art certainly cannot advance under compulsion to traditional forms, and nothing in such a field is more stifling to progress than limitation of the right to experiment with a new technique." Little did Judge Hoffman know that nine years later, he would be condemning eight defendants who were the cultural children of Burroughs and Kerouac, and that their mutual friend Allen Ginsberg would make a personal appearance in his courtroom.

Politically, Kerouac was a right-winger and didn't approve of the actions in Chicago. He declared, "Those Jews Ginsberg, Hoffman, and Rubin, all they're doing [in Chicago] is finding new reasons for spitefulness." That didn't stop Abbie from appearing at a July 1982 conference celebrating *On the Road* with Ginsberg, Burroughs, and Lawrence Ferlinghetti. Hoffman said, "We couldn't have had the '60s, the decade of social revolution, without the '50s. The Beats gave us a choice, showed us we could let our emotions hang out, we could fight City Hall, The Beats are alive today."

The '60s Take the Stand.

RON DAVIS: The defense brought dozens of witnesses on: Ginsberg, Krassner, and other people—the straight liberals and the radicals. They put them on the stand, because they wanted that testimony to be there.

With some twenty-two thousand pages of trial transcripts, it's difficult to summarize all the key events that occurred between the opening day on September 24, 1969, and the closing on February 18, 1970. The testimony for the defense included Phil Ochs, Dick Gregory, Timothy Leary, Ed Sanders, Arlo Guthrie, Paul Krassner, Judy Collins, Reverend Jesse Jackson, and Norman Mailer—the list is a cross section of the '60s, with musicians, folksingers, poets, comedians, activists, novelists, an LSD-guru, and a civil rights leader.

The Yippies' lawyer, William Kunstler, had even gotten Ramsey Clark, the Attorney General under President Lyndon Johnson, to speak on behalf of the defense; he was banned from speaking by Judge Hoffman. Just a few months previously, he had been the highest-ranking law enforcement official in America, and now he wasn't allowed to talk in a federal courtroom!

In Peter Manso's Norman Mailer oral history, Jerry said, "In January 1970, Norman testified at the trial—mainly, I think, for Abbie and me . . . Norman was on the stand maybe three hours, and like everything else with him, you put something in, it always comes out

KIDS WHO GREW UP IN THE POST–1950s LIVE IN A WORLD OF SUPERMARKETS, COLOR TV COMMERCIALS, GUERILLA WAR, INTERNATIONAL MEDIA, PSYCHEDELICS, ROCK 'N' ROLL, AND MOON WALKS. FOR US, NOTHING IS IMPOSSIBLE. WE CAN DO ANYTHING.

JERRY — RUBIN — 1970

better. He described us as satirists of society, that what we were doing was theater of the absurd. He said, 'They're not criminals, they're not irrational, they're good people who believe in America and who think America's gone wrong and want to alert people.' Every sentence was quotable. Like *The Armies of the Night*, it was a statement of what the Movement was all about. He sanitized us, which was exactly what our lawyers wanted. He presented us as theorists, people with a philosophy."

My Job Was to Sing "Fixin to Die Rag."

COUNTRY JOE MCDONALD: Because my father was hauled in front of a governmental committee, I wasn't happy about doing it and I knew things could go wrong, but they just asked me to do my job. I had a job; my job was to try to sing "Fixin' to Die Rag," and to stall and to make it as oblique and crazy as possible—and that's what I did. I flew into Chicago, they told me what to do, I went up there on the witness stand, I did it, and I got out of town!

Free John Sinclair. Pete Townshend infamously kicked Abbie off stage during The Who's performance at Woodstock, while Hoffman cried out for justice for John Sinclair. When I asked Nancy Kurshan why Jerry wasn't at the iconic music festival, she said that they were under deadline to turn in the manuscript for *DO iT!*

John Sinclair: I was in prison. I was supposed to be the first witness, but the court wouldn't allow it. They tried to get me to be the first witness, so they could get me out of prison for a couple weeks, you know? I went to prison a month before Woodstock.

Testimony on LSD.

RON DAVIS: Paul Krassner dropped acid before he testified, and he didn't say anything that made any sense, as far as I understand. I didn't read his testimony, but he disappointed the Yippies.

PAUL KRASSNER: When the trial was going on, Abbie said to me, we don't really need you to testify here, but you've been mentioned in so many other testimonies that it would be appropriate to have me testify. It turned out that a lot of them had been asked, "Who was at this first Yippie meeting?" and they named Abbie, Anita, and me. It was at their home, this was on the afternoon of December 31, 1967. Nancy was in Chicago at the time but they had all testified that she was at that meeting too, so I had to lie under oath and mention her. They said, "Who was there? Would you point them out?" and I pointed out Nancy, I pointed out Anita, and they waved to me. After that afternoon meeting, then it was New Year's Eve and we were off to a party. I remember there was snow on the ground and Jerry missed Nancy not being there and I got some snow and rubbed it on his head and sang the song from Wildroot Cream Oil Hair Tonic, because he had this really bushy hair. It became a factoid that Nancy was at that December '67 meeting—but she was not there because she was in Chicago at the time.

Robert Pierson, an undercover cop who had spent the week of the protests shadowing Jerry as his personal bodyguard, testified during the trial that when some Yippies placed flags on the equestrian General John Logan statue (positioned on top of the hill in Grant Park) that Jerry had called out, "Better than Iwo Jima!" Jerry didn't actually say that, but felt that was too provocative of a remark not to claim it as his own.

Trial Closing Statements. The lead prosecuting

attorney Tom Foran announced after the trial, "Our kids don't understand that we don't mean anything when we use the word 'nigger.' They just look at us like we're bunch of dinosaurs—we've lost our kids to the freaking fag revolution." Like any high-profile trial, it brought with it an air of celebrity. It solidified Jerry and Abbie as pop culture stars. They become college campus icons and not long after the trial ended, they (especially Jerry) formed a close relationship with the world's foremost rockstar couple, John & Yoko. Tom Hayden married Jane Fonda and Bobby Seale become a household name, even in Middle America. Only Angela Davis surpassed him as the embodiment of the Black Power Movement. Defense attorney William "Bill" Kunstler was involved in other watershed events for the era: the Battle at Wounded Knee and the Attica State Prison Riots. During the trial, Dustin Hoffman came around to meet fellow Hoffman, Abbie. Less than a month after the Chicago trial concluded, Diana Oughton and two other Weathermen infamously blew themselves up inside of a Manhattan townhouse. Through a hole torn into the building next door was furniture that had visibly shifted during the blast. Coincidentally, it belonged to Dustin Hoffman, who lived next to their hideout.

Even Charles "Charlie" Manson got into the act. He was eager to meet Jerry Rubin, who traveled to Los Angeles with Phil Ochs to greet the newly arrested, not-yet-convicted "cult hero." Manson asked Rubin for tips on how to conduct himself as defiantly in court as the Chicago 8 had. This was during a brief period when many thought there was no way in hell that the Manson Family could have done those hideous crimes, that they were railroaded for being hippies. Manson told him, "Rubin, I am not of your world—I've spent all of my life in prison. When I was a child I was an orphan and too ugly to be adopted. Now I am too beautiful to be let free." After their visit, Jerry and Phil agreed that Manson was "one of the most poetic and intense people we ever met, and he spoke from a world of experience we could not even imagine."

There was talk amongst Jerry, Abbie, and Rennie Davis to start a permanent national organization in a post-trial climate, ideally with Tom Hayden and Dave Dellinger as well.

ANNE WEILLS, ATTORNEY/UNION ORGANIZER: Right after the Chicago trial, all the men, except for Bobby Seale, talked about having a national organization called The Conspiracy. They put out communiqués—we didn't have email then—about how they wanted us to support it. I can remember Tom Hayden and I having a huge argument about it because they, all seven or whatever, were going to be the leaders of it. So here you're creating an organization flowing from the trial, and it's all men who are in leadership! I remember writing a letter to the *Berkeley Barb*, [saying]: How clueless. All these white males thinking they could just announce this organization and somehow all these radical women, of which I was one, were going to jump on the bandwagon? I couldn't believe it when he said it. I was like, "What?! Are you guys so clueless?"

Not entirely coincidently, Rubin's defining statement as an author, *DO iT!* (Subtitled: *Scenarios of the Revolution*), was published just as the trial came to a close. In fact, Jerry held up a copy of the book on the last day and proclaimed, "Judge, I used to look like this." (Inside, was a photo of a clean-cut Rubin during his days as a cub reporter.) "Most everyone around this table once looked like this, and we all believed in the American system—I'm being sentenced to five years, not for what I did in Chicago, but because some of us don't want to have a piece of the pie. You are sentencing us for being ourselves. Because we don't look like this anymore. That's our crime."

Jerry then handed Judge Hoffman a copy of *DO iT!*, in which he'd inscribed, "Julius, you radicalized more young people than we ever could. You're the country's top YIPPIE!"

OPPOSITE: Paul Krassner and Jerry share a joint.

ABOVE: Jerry with Defense Attorney Leonard Weinglass.

Acquittal. Bobby Seale was removed from the Chicago 8 trial and began serving a four-year sentence. In 1970, he was lumped in with the New Haven Black Panther trial and charged with murder; he was in jail until proven innocent in 1972. The jury acquitted the rest of the now-Chicago 7 defendants of conspiracy charges (although five of them did get convicted of "crossing state lines to incite violence" with a five-year prison term). The judge sentenced the Chicago 7 (including their lawyers) from anywhere to two months to four years for contempt of court. 1972 was filled with hearings and appeals and by 1973, the government was bored with the case and dropped it.

***

DO iT! Although he had started it before the trial, Jerry took advantage of his "enforced time off" to complete his version of the Yippie manifesto: "*DO iT!*" Instead of sitting down at a typewriter, Jerry spoke his thoughts into a tape recorder, resulting in hours of recordings that his girlfriend Nancy dutifully transcribed. The original manuscript weighed in at over seven hundred pages. (In interviews for this book, Nancy mentioned that she and Jerry missed the Woodstock Festival, because they were too busy working on *DO iT!*) Given that Jerry was on Ritalin during this time period, his ideas spewed forth in all directions, resulting in a crazy, speed-fueled narrative made even more frenetic by the contributions of his friends.

> JIM RETHERFORD, EDITOR: I wasn't around for the tape recording but my understanding was that Jerry and Abbie and Stew and Paul, and even Phil Ochs, did it at different times, and who knows what kind of drugs were involved in it? It was really rambling stuff, but there was a lot of brainstorming that was going on. That's where these ideas came from.

The design of *DO iT!* was the work of Quentin Fiore, who had collaborated with Marshall McLuhan, media perception scholar, on the influential book and record *The Medium is the Massage* in 1967. (The book was supposed to be called *The Medium is the Message*, but was misprinted and McLuhan loved the pun.) Both *Medium* and *DO iT!* share a "collision of verbal and visual information," which ignites the reader's imagination. Foire's style is a blend of images and text (in various fonts and sizes), resulting in a dynamic visual that captured "the tumultuous spirit of the time." McLuhan was certainly ahead of his time; he claimed in his 1964 book *Understanding Media* that the electronic image had already supplanted the written word. He died in 1980, just before computers began to emerge into the mainstream.

Reading *DO iT!* was like drinking from a fire hose, and the publisher insisted that Jerry cut it down by half. As a result, several people edited and shaped the book. Some quit, some didn't get paid, and only a few received credit. The first would-be editor was Tom Miller. Like the other editors that followed, Tom's payment consisted of a cot to sleep on in Jerry's apartment and access to a big bowl of joints.

TOM MILLER, AUTHOR/ACTIVIST: I was basically sleeping on a cot up in the corner. I did my best to stay out of everyone's way, although it's hard to do that, but people were coming and going all the time. It isn't like there was just Jerry and Nancy and me. There were housewives from Long Island calling, saying, "Who do we make a check out to?" We had people calling from other countries and there was that point where—if you do a parallel of who's doing what, when, and where, Eldridge Cleaver is about to pop up in Algiers. Tim Leary is lurking in the background, too. So, these calls would come and go all the time. People would say, "Well, what time is it in Algiers? Well, it's noon. They're probably awake now, should we try calling?" It was quite surreal. I enjoyed every minute of it, I must say.

In spite of this treatment, Tom Miller went on to work on Jerry's next book, *We Are Everywhere*. The next editor after him for *DO iT!* was Mark Kramer, a journalist for the underground press.

MARK KRAMER: In the early spring of '69, I had just stepped away from the *Liberation News Service*, and was mostly floating on couches. I met Jerry and he was absolutely eager and hungry. I was shortly installed upstairs in the apartment on St. Mark's and presented with a huge mess of a manuscript. Jerry and I, over a peace pipe, agreed to a deal. And the deal was that I would try and cut it in half, and make it more continual and coherent and he would pay me twelve dollars an hour.

The manuscript that I was presented with was about seven hundred pages. I set to work and trimmed down the first two or three hundred pages of it, and meanwhile, found Jerry fairly inattentive, abusive, disengaged. Finally, I got exasperated with him. The final thing that made me decide to stop was I said, "I've been working for you for x length of time, put in so many hours, could you pay me please, because I need the money, and we made an agreement." And he said to me, "You smoked my dope, you fucked my women, contracts are what we're fighting against, man."

At that point, I was still so committed to the general idea of fighting the man, that even offended and unpaid, I didn't simply quit the project. I called Jim Retherford in Indiana, and I said, "I'm bailing on an interesting project that I'm in the middle of, because it's not right for me, but it might be for you." He showed up a few days later.

Picking up where Mark left off, Jim Retherford took one look at the bloated manuscript and decided to go in a completely different direction.

JIM RETHERFORD: Nancy had transcribed everything. Which I believe was 900,000 pages! I mean, it was a big stack of stuff, I looked at that and realized I didn't want to go there. Mark had been going through that and breaking it down into a chronology and he had been editing it like a traditional editor. And it wasn't very interesting.

I recall very quickly coming up with a concept—*it was a lightning bolt moment*. Which was to do a visual book, that had a very free-flowing, almost stream-of-consciousness narrative style. And instead of being a story of Jerry's life, it was a myth-making history of a Yippie hero. And I wanted it to visually work like the six o'clock news. I was, at that point, and still am, a big fan of the collaboration between Quentin Fiore and Marshall McLuhan, I really liked *The Medium is the Massage*, the way the images bent around pages. And I really wanted to get Quentin Fiore aboard to do it, but nobody knew how to get in touch with him. Finally, I found someone who knew Quentin and talked to him for us, and he ended up working on the book. Quentin goes back to the New York Dada days, the Art Students League in the forties. He went to jail as a conscientious objector in World War II.

DO iT! was on the *New York Times* best-seller list for about six months. I remember that it had been translated into eight languages; there was even a theatrical musical of *DO iT!* just a few years ago.

In the end, *DO iT!* became a classic political manifesto that stands shoulder to shoulder with Abbie's *Steal This Book*. As Jerry said on the *Phil Donahue Show*, "*DO iT!* is like a Molotov cocktail in your very hands."

SAM LEFF: It's ironic that Jerry's longest lasting legacy is that the big shoe company co-opted his slogan. Nike has *Just Do It* in all of their ad campaigns.

In 2001, Randy Anderson wrote and produced a play titled *DO iT!* based on the book. It's been performed on and off since then, with Anderson updating the script every so often. He told Stagebuzz.com in 2011, "I found the book at a used bookstore in college and the second I started flipping through it, I knew it would make a great play. There are pictures, poetry, sex, drugs, and hysterical hijinks. Not to mention some fantastic 'scenarios' that lent themselves perfectly to my newly emerging aesthetic."

Over time, Randy changed the title of the play to *Yippie!* and it's still occasionally performed. He describes it as looking back on the life of Jerry and his various transformations from "laid-back 1960s activist, to super left-wing radical anarchist, to hardcore political subversive who would stop at nothing to overthrow the government." He adds, "*Yippie!* explores this period [from the point of view of] Yuppie Jerry Rubin [who] contemplates his past actions in the face of the new youth movement's demise."

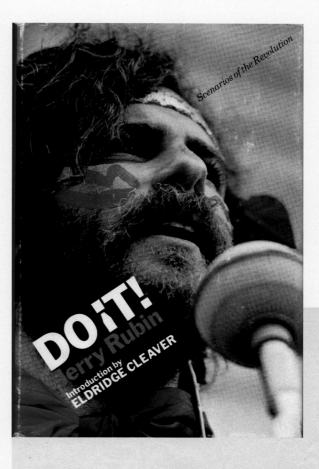

```
                                        Eldridge
                                        Alger
                                        Algeria
                                        Africa
                                        At Large
                                        Off The Pigs

                   September 6, 1969

Stew & Gumbo
Gumbo Stew
Jerry & Crew

Power To The Wrecking Crew!

    Sorry not to have responded to your kite sooner,
but so much shit to deal with.  How is Stew making it
in the can?  (Down With Jails & Jailers & and going
into them!)
    I would be honored to write the piece for Jerry's book!
Let's get our shit across!
    One hangup:  by the time you receive this kite, I &
crew will be in Korea (North) or on the way.  When I get
back to Algeria I can write the thing.
    So, Gumbo, plan like that and come on over heah!

                   Power To The Wrecking Crew!

                        Eldridge
                        Kathleen

            MADEO
```

FUG YOU!

IN 1970, GROVE PRESS PUBLISHED *Shards of God: A Novel of the Yippies* by Ed Sanders. The inner flap reads,

> *In this totally outrageous and insane novel, Ed Sanders, one of the non-leaders of the gang of subversives loosely grouped under the title "The Underground," has recorded for unwitting posterity the truth, the whole truth, and nothing but the truth about the depraved and degenerate street filth known as the Yippies.* Shards of God *is, indeed, a history of the Yippies, their passions, loves, foibles, weaknesses, and flights of nobility. The novel traces the growth of the Yippie conspiracy from its early inner-treason cell days up to its position as an international cartel of chromosome-damaged diplomats, Swedish generals, pentagon luminaries, war correspondents, bank presidents, nuns, poets, street fornicators, and peace apes—not to mention television personalities, rock stars, and Communist dupes.*

For those familiar with Sanders' love of the absurd, it will come as no surprise that one reviewer described it "as a put-on and put-down of Yippie detractors and their hysterical assumptions." As Sanders points out in the introduction, "the characters are real," and lists Rubin, Hoffman, Krassner, Ginsberg, et al. But that's just about where reality ends.

Jerry (much more than Abbie) seems to be the target of a number of (perhaps humorous at the time) fictional sequences. Rubin's apartment is described as a cave, with Jerry "attired in an otter fur groin sheath and stilts." An initiation ceremony is described with Jerry singing hymns in A minor and Abbie in E minor. Ritual sex acts are described while listing the first names of "the beautiful Yippie ladies"—"Anita, Nancy, Kate"—and others. The fantasy sequence quickly moves from somewhat humorous to fairly disgusting. Other instances of "humor": "There is divided opinion in the ranks of Yippie concerning the origin of Jerry Rubin. What is Jerry Rubin? A question buddy, that long caused trouble in my psyche I can tell you. For, if Jerry Rubin is a god, was he able to see me fuck his wife while he was recently in jail in Pleasanton, California? Or is he an example of the much-gossiped-about Metal Mammal?"

The next paragraph declares that Jerry has been "fantastically useful to planet Earth" by spreading consciousness of the Divine Waffle, "developing Computer Worship," and dosing high school girls with LSD. It goes on and on in this style, but I must credit Sanders with foreseeing that Jerry would be amongst the first in the 1980s to embrace computers!

There's an Egyptian-themed wedding between Jerry and Nancy that includes a mummified Pharaoh Akhnaton coming back after four thousand years to participate—with a date of June 15, 1968 given for the event. Sanders knew they had never formally wed, but that Jerry sometimes referred to Nancy as his wife (as did others

Shards of God a novel of the Yippies by Ed Sanders

at the time); a pagan ceremony of some sort didn't seem out of the question in the flower-power era. Nancy Kurshan confirmed that no such event ever took place; it was all pure fantasy on Sanders's part.

I tried several times over a period of two years to get Sanders to make a comment or two about the book. Sanders was (with me) a man of very few words, but he finally offered this up when I asked, "Why is Jerry the protagonist in *Shards of God?*" Ed's written reply was, "It was a SATIRE! I was poking fun and mirth at the whole recent history of the Youth International Party, and Rubin and Hoffman."

Not entirely satisfied by that response, I went digging into Sanders' own scrolls and found this in his '60s memoirs, *Fug You.* He wrote, "Like Phil Ochs, I had been wounded by the Chicago police riots and the thug-like conduct of the Democratic Convention, so I decided to set aside *The Hairy Table* ["a very fictionalized semiautobiographical account of my operation of the Peace Eye Bookstore and the adventures of the Fugs"] and with my oodles of free time (now that the Fugs were disbanded) to concentrate on a satiric novel [*Shards of God*] set inside the Chicago riots and the partisans of the Yippies. I added a sci-fi theme, the I-mouthed saucer people and their visits to Earth."

I also found out when Sanders decided to write his exposé on the Charles Manson clan, *The Family*, it was Jerry who recommended his book agent Carl Brandt to Sanders, who got him a deal with publishing house E. P. Dutton. Which made Sanders's response to my first inquiry about Rubin quite bemusing: "I didn't have much to do with him."

I interviewed more than seventy-five people over the course of three years; there were only two key players who were reluctant to speak. One was Sanders. The other was Tom Hayden. To be fair, Hayden responded to numerous emails trying to persuade him. His reluctance was that he had nothing good to say, and didn't want to present a negative view. I then suggested an "off-the-record," no-tape-recorder, conversation. That wasn't acceptable. Finally, I played the last card that I had. In the late '80s, when Hayden had written his memoir of the '60s, Jerry had willingly participated. I asked if Hayden could now return the favor on behalf of Jerry's family (who had wholeheartedly endorsed this project). His reply, in so many words, was "I could care less."

There was only one other refusal, but it was a dandy. Not a person of note, simply someone who had known Jerry during his social networking days and had done business with him. I reached out through a friend. The response was, "The idea of a Jerry Rubin book makes me want to puke." I replied, "I think you're holding back. why not do an interview and tell me how you really feel?"

ANNE WEILLS: Tom Hayden chafed at all the comical stuff, all the Yippie performing and behavior was not attractive at all. It was not consistent with the idea that "We were at war. This country is an empire!" There were these really clear ideological, political differences that always come out when you're talking about strategy or how to deal with the media. That's where a lot of the sharp contradictions developed between Tom and particularly Jerry, because "are you're going to have a press conference and make very serious statements or are you going to have a whole Yippie guerilla theater performance?"

There was a lot of criticism of Jerry's superficiality. A lot of it was that he was seen as a very egotistical person. In terms of the white male leaders of the movement at that point, it's not just unique to him, but [there was] a lot of "Me! Me! Me!" like a little kid who always gets in the middle of the photograph. But then again, there was a lot of major egos in that group! [*Laughs.*]

In *Fug You*, Ed Sanders writes, "To my disappointment, Judge Hoffman refused to allow into evidence a large Yippie flag I had brought to court with the inscription, 'Abandon the Creeping Meatball.' This referred to a song I had written back in early '68 to celebrate the birth of Yippie. The tune's opening lines were 'Rise up and abandon the Creeping Meatball in Nixon's land. We're going to

sing and dance in Chicago for the Festival of Life.'

Here's part of Ed's sworn court testimony from the Chicago 8 Trial, detailing his relationship with Jerry:

DEFENSE ATTORNEY LEONARD WEINGLASS: Now, directing your attention to the latter part of November in the year of 1967, did you have occasion to meet with any of the defendants seated here at the counsel table?

ED SANDERS: I met with Jerry Rubin. There was a conference at the Church Center for the UN in New York City.

WEINGLASS: Now, directing your attention to the evening of January 4, 1968, do you recall where you were on that evening?

SANDERS: Yes. I went to Jerry Rubin's house in New York City to get briefed on a meeting that had taken place.

WEINGLASS: What took place at that meeting you had with Jerry Rubin?

SANDERS: Well, first we had a period of meditation in front of his picture of Che on the wall for a half hour.

WEINGLASS: Picture of whom?

SANDERS: Che. Che Guevara. Che, the great revolutionary leader. Then we practiced for about a half hour toughening up our feet walking around in baggies full of ice, and then Jerry informed me about the circumstances of the meeting that had taken place, forming the Youth International Party, and that it was decided to hold a free rock festival in Chicago during the time of the Democratic National Convention, and that the convening would be a convening of all people interested in the new politics, guerilla theater, rock and roll, the convening of the hemp horde from all over the various tribes in the United States. I was asked by Jerry if I would help coordinate, since I knew the major rock groups in the United States, if I would contact them and ask them if they would play. I said I would be happy to and that I would proceed forthwith in contacting these major rock groups, and that I did.

Kudos to Sanders for that *Shards of God* level of satire under the pressure of a courtroom!

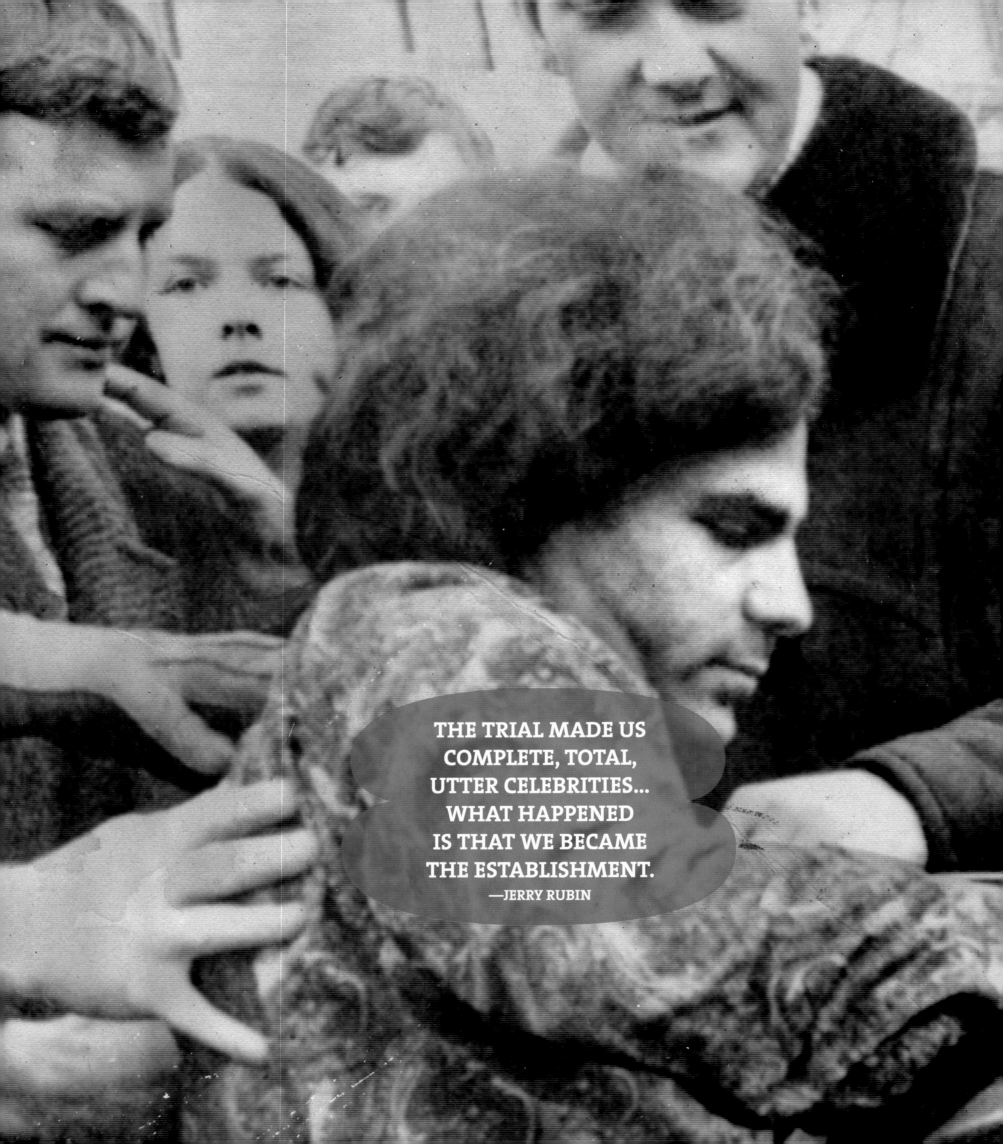

THE TRIAL MADE US
COMPLETE, TOTAL,
UTTER CELEBRITIES...
WHAT HAPPENED
IS THAT WE BECAME
THE ESTABLISHMENT.
—JERRY RUBIN

Fat Radicals Living Off the System

OPPOSITE: Jerry being escorted into a police car in Belfast, after the David Frost show appearance forced him and Stew Albert to be deported from the UK.

Supposing one day, trucks traveled through the city, announcing, "The war in Vietnam is over! The war is over! Turn on your radio for further information." Within two minutes, everybody would be calling their mothers. "Hey, Mom! The war's over!" Nixon would have to go on TV to reassure the American people that the war was still on.

—*Jerry Rubin, 1970*

DURING THE TRIAL, Jerry and Abbie hit the college lecture circuit, using their status as revolutionaries to become overnight celebrities. This soon gave way to a backlash as the Yippies became household names, as Jerry recounted years later to Ratso Sloman. "Abbie's plan at that point was to go out and lead millions of people: a total cultural revolution. What happened instead is that we became the establishment. The media builds you up and then tears you down. So the destruction of our myths began as soon as the trial ended. Dave Dellinger, Abbie, and I were a plane coming back from jail when the first *Newsweek* article came out saying how much we'd profited from the trial. The fat radicals living off the system. Book contracts, $2,000 speaking gigs. Of course, it was 100 percent true."

Jerry and Abbie were now effectively pop stars. This was an era in which musicians (John Lennon, Bob Dylan) were seen as revolutionaries, and revolutionaries (Jerry and Abbie, Bobby Seale, Eldridge Cleaver, Angela Davis) had their images hanging on college dorm room walls alongside posters of rock bands. Rubin and Hoffman (separately) began a series of successful speaking tours, drawing large crowds on college campuses across America. The size of these events cannot be underestimated. While a radical political speaker in the twenty-first century might draw a few hundred people, an appearance by Jerry in 1970 was good for a couple of thousand, depending on the campus.

UNITED STATES DEPARTMENT OF JUSTICE

FEDERAL BUREAU OF INVESTIGATION
New York, New York
February 25, 1969

*In Reply, Please Refer to
File No.*

Mailing of Large Volume of
"Valentine Greetings" Enclosing
Marijuana Cigarette in New York
City Area, February 13, 1969

The Valentine's Day Marijuana Massacre.

One classic Yippie prank after the Chicago Trial was the mass mailing of thousands of rolled joints to a random list of New York City residents, culled from the telephone directory. This was an era when most people still listed their home address with their phone number. On Valentine's Day 1969, some thirty thousand residents of Manhattan received a special treat in their mailbox. Surrounded by heart-shaped images, with a joint contained in each letter, it read: "Yippie! You are one of 30,000 lucky persons being sent this freshly rolled marijuana cigarette. We are doing this in order to clear the garbage from the air."

This letter proceeded to debunk many of the myths surrounding pot smoking; namely, that it's more dangerous than alcohol and leads to severe addiction. Jimi Hendrix gave Abbie and Anita a thousand dollars in cash to buy pot. On the evening of February 14, a newscaster read the letter and displayed the joint—he even called the narcotics squad during the broadcast. While he was still on the air, the police arrived and took the joint from him. They spoke directly to the television audience, telling them to call the cops if they received such a package: "Marijuana is a dangerous drug that can drive people insane."

Kill Your Parents/Kent State.

Rubin spoke at Kent State on April 10, just weeks before the tragic killing of four students in the May of 1970 (immortalized in Crosby, Stills, Nash & Young's song "Ohio"). Reportedly, he made this statement: "Unless you're prepared to kill your parents, you're not ready to change this country. Our parents are our first oppressors."

The statement was shortened to "Yippie leader Rubin encourages students to 'Kill your parents,'" and circulated amongst the media—including sensationalist newspapers, like the *National Enquirer*—and further widened the "Generation Gap." Jerry later explained to Milton Viorst "that he meant the statement metaphorically, to urge students to free themselves from parental domination." After the May 4 shootings, the university's president was drowned in letters, blaming him for allowing Jerry to speak on campus not long before.

In his own autobiography, *Growing (Up) at 37*, Jerry graphically describes purging his parents from his system (during a therapy session) by eating chocolate cake and drinking salt water and then forcing his fingers down his throat "to vomit the salt and brown shit—vomiting [his parents] out of his system once and for all," metaphorically speaking, as part of his early '70s journey to finding himself.

Not long after, at a $500 dollar-a-plate fundraiser in Texas, Spiro Agnew said that Rubin's speech incited the Kent State protests. Former Vice President Hubert Humphrey then compared Agnew to Joseph McCarthy, the Commie-baiting senator. Abbie raised the ante by announcing to the press, "I fucked Kim Agnew"—Spiro's teenage daughter.

When Nixon ordered American soldiers to invade Cambodia in April 1970, college campuses flared up in anger. He expanded the Vietnam conflict geographically, despite his public declaration just weeks earlier announcing a reduction in troops. That invasion was the cause of student unrest at Kent State, not Jerry's provocation.

IF YOU'RE STILL IN
COLLEGE TODAY,
YOU HAVEN'T
DONE ENOUGH.
BECAUSE IF YOU HAD,
YOU'D HAVE BEEN
THROWN OUT BY NOW.

—Jerry Rubin addressing 4,000 students
at the University of Washington, 1970.

Around the World in Eighty Days Freak Show.

After the Chicago Trial wound down, Richard Neville (editor of the British counterculture magazine *OZ*) paid a visit to Jerry in New York. "Rubin's comic audacity, which had so impressed me on first sighting, had a patina of surliness. For all the jokes in the transcripts, the Chicago Trial seemed to be grinding him down." After a discussion about Jerry's UK publisher for his book *DO iT!*, in which Jerry stated, "I don't care about the publisher's politics, I want a hip capitalist—easier to deal with," Neville suggested a charter flight, worldwide, of popular radicals: "Your trial as airborne theater, without the judge, plus rock groups, clowns, et al." They discussed the pros and cons of taking the show on the road, including stops in Sydney, Calcutta, Havana, Algiers, and Mozambique. Neville hoped for a couple more Chicago defendants besides Rubin, who said, "A couple? All of us will come!"

Who knows how much dope was smoked conjuring up this pipe dream, but Jerry did inscribe a copy of *DO iT!* "To Richard: until our freak circus conquers the planet. Let's turn on the Third World. Brothers across the water—death to the Queen!" The Around the World in Eighty Days Freak Show never got off the ground, but Jerry and Stew made their way to London for some hell-raising adventures, some of which Neville talks about in *Hippie Hippie Shake*. In November 1970, Jerry and Stew arrived at Neville's London apartment; he had left them a note: "Stuck at a family wedding. Make yourself at home." Rubin and company must have seen the invitation, because they crashed the nuptials. As Jerry came through the door, a guest remarked, "Good Lord, it's the Drugs Squad." Jerry and Stew were in full-on revolutionary personae, crassly commenting, "Who are all these pigs? We got a revolution to fight." The guests were equally candid: "Who's this mean-eyed little shit?" The UK's *Private Eye* magazine subsequently reported undercover agents from the Drugs Squad—with fake American accents—had raided the wedding.

Stew Albert had recently been in Algiers, where Timothy Leary was holed up inside of Eldridge Cleaver's compound. He told Jerry that Leary and Eldridge had toured Palestinian guerilla camps while Weather Underground women had arrived for weapons training.

The Revolution was certainly brewing on the southern Mediterranean coastline. Meanwhile, all sorts of British journalists were camped out at Neville's London pad, taking turns interviewing the co-leader of the Yippies. Jerry quickly made himself at home, holding court and occupying the phone line. According to Neville, one reporter, a woman, asked Rubin if there was anything in the recently published *DO iT!* that he regretted: "'Yeah—the sexism,' he said, updating his street-credo with enviable speed."

Neville complains in his memoir *Hippie Hippie Shake* that Jerry wasn't the most courteous of houseguests, and expected his hosts to "clear away the beer bottles and the pizza crusts." He reflects, "I was torn by his presence. Rubin was a street-smart prankster, whose war-painted pantomimes had knocked the stuffing out of the HUAC, the McCarthy-immortalized House Un-American Activities Committee." Rubin had won the "Academy Award of Protest" by being indicted for the events in Chicago. He "delighted in taunting authority wherever he went," as well as basking in the glory of the entire Chicago experience. "Becoming a revolutionary," he told Neville, was "like falling in love." Neville's partner Louise added the punch line: "with yourself." Jerry's Yippie-era partner Nancy Kurshan told me in 2013 that the post-Chicago era was Jerry at his most egotistical. She bailed on their relationship soon after.

Neville was witness to the planning and execution of Jerry's most notorious media stunt to take place outside of the contiguous forty-eight states. Jerry was invited to appear on the prestigious *David Frost Show*. (In September '68, the Beatles had performed "Hey Jude" live on the *Frost Show*, which has been rebroadcast countless times since.) This was a live television broadcast with the focus on Jerry! Not just a quick sound bite, but a chance to express himself for more than a moment or two. According to Neville's *Hippie Hippie Shake*, it played out as follows:

> Jerry: We can use TV to destroy TV.
> Neville's partner, Louise: Why?
> Jerry: My generation was reared
>   on hamburgers and Walter
>   Cronkite, so I know what a fucking
>   powerful mother's tit it is.
> Neville: Right on.
> Jerry: We need to take the TV away
>   from the control freaks to humiliate
>   the front-men, but we mustn't
>   become bastards of the media.

As the conversation was coming to a close, a friend of Neville's stopped by and congratulated Jerry on the recent UK publication of *DO iT!*. He snapped, "It's too individualist and chauvinist. I can't look at it anymore."

On the day of the broadcast, November 7, 1970, Neville's apartment was filled with a cross section of the London counterculture. They discussed how they'd torpedo David Frost's show that evening. Jerry began by telling the assembled team about Abbie's recent appearance on *The Merv Griffin Show*. Hoffman appeared wearing a shirt tailored out of an American flag. (This act violated some laws that were apparently selective, as, throughout the late '60s, Roy Rogers and Dale Evans often appeared in dog food commercials wearing similar flag apparel!) The CBS network chose to "black out" Abbie's body, so viewers saw Griffin conversing with an ominously half-black TV screen. Jerry declared, "The pigs censored his body, man. It was electronic fascism."

When they arrived at the TV studio, Jerry was given a dozen audience tickets, and he let even more freaks sneak in through the guest entrance. Backstage, Mick Farren of the Deviants was holding a smoke bomb; poet Felix Dennis (and future publisher of popular magazines *PC World*, *MacUser*, and *Maxim*) was wielding a squirt gun; and Warren Hague, an outspoken gay activist from Canada, planned to "out" himself to unsuspecting viewers for shock value. Jerry lectured them, "The media deadens our consciousness, tonight's our chance to shock the sleeping viewers into attention." "Yeah—how?" "By doing anything we feel like doing. We can be obnoxious, obscene, violent, horrible, immoral, contemptible . . .TV turns everything into a mashed potato, including slogans of revolution." Chants of "Fuck celebrity guests, we're taking over the show," "Let's have a party," "Far out," circled the room. Jerry added, "Right on. This is Chicago energy."

David Frost began the show by asking, "Jerry, you asked if you could be joined up here by two of your colleagues. Would you like to introduce them for us?" Stew Albert and another Yippie were sitting to the left. Jerry replied, "Because this whole thing is not me as an individual, we're involved in a massive revolution of young people." The signal for the rest of the posse (about a dozen total) to erupt was for Jerry to light up a joint and hand it to Frost. Jerry kept trying to get Frost to take the joint, saying, "it's an experience. Try it, it's an experience." Frost politely said, "No thank you." Jerry laughed, "he's nervous." Then the rest of the miscreants invaded the stage (they'd been sitting in the audience) shouting, swearing, and effectively bringing the show to a standstill. Frost stepped down from the platform and the Yippies began taunting him, visibly enthralled. Farren said to Frost, "The DDT content inside you is toxic."

As Frost began to back away toward the audience, the Yippies cheered louder. Farren said, decades later, "It was no big revolutionary protest. It was more like, let's have some fun on a Saturday night. *It was all television*, and I think if anybody understood that, it should be David Frost and I think he probably did." The show closed with a very agitated Frost scolding the outlaws, leaning into them like a schoolmarm: "It's so pathetic, so childish, and so pointless. *And we'll be right back!*"

THE Sun

RD WITH THE PEOPLE   6d. Saturday, November 14, 1970

IT'S PARTY TIME IN THE SUN NEXT WEEK
(WHAT A WEEK IT'S GOING TO BE!)
See Page Three

YIPPEE! THEY'VE GOT THE BOOT

...efiant. . . . Rubin giving a clenched-fist salute as he was arrested yesterday.

The Sun says: Good riddance

Page One Comment

YIPPIE LEADER Jerry Rubin and his chief lieutenant Stew Albert were under arrest in Belfast last night awaiting deportation back to America.

Long-suffering Britons who have been amazed at the antics of Rubin and his foul-mouthed "revolutionaries," will join The Sun in saying: GOOD RIDDANCE!

The Home Secretary, Mr Reginald Maudling, ordered the deportation of the two Yippies "because their continued presence is not conducive to the public good."

There can be no quarrel at all with that.

The pity is that Rubin and his cronies were allowed to stay even for a week.

We have enough problems of our own without importing them in the shape of Rubin and his Yippie yobboes.

Under arrest . . . Stew Albert

RUBIN FLIES TO THE U.S. TODAY

JERRY RUBIN and Stew Albert, the controversial Yippie leaders, decided last night not to fight the deportation moves.

They are now expected to be flown to London today and put on a New York-bound airliner.

The two Yippies—heads of the Youth International Party—were arrested by Special Branch detectives.

Maudling was frightened to death because he had gone to Belfast — "England's Vietnam."

GEORGE GORDON

Yippie! Britain chucks out Rubin

YIPPIE leader Jerry Rubin is to obey a Government demand that he leaves Britain.

The Home Office said last night that Rubin and another yippie, Stew Albert, had decided not to appeal against deportation orders.

They were arrested and jailed in Belfast yesterday.

PRISON

Earlier they said they would stay in Ulster "until the pigs act like pigs and try to throw us out."

Then it was announced that they planned to leave, and a "supervised departure" was being arranged.

It is believed that Rubin and Albert will be kept in Belfast prison until today, when they will leave for New York via London.

Both men took part in a yippie takeover of the David Frost TV show.

They fled to Belfast when their visas were due to expire on midnight on Thursday.

BEADS

Yesterday the Yippies were arrested and served with an order under the Aliens Act by a group of detectives as they stepped from a student's flat.

Rubin, wearing beads and a floral shirt yelled: "You have no authority to arrest me—this is Ireland, not England. This is an insult to Ireland. Free Ireland!"

And he told a Press conference earlier: "This is the battleground, Belfast and Ireland is England's Vietnam."

Mr. Richard Neville spreading the gospel of the Youth International Party (yippies) in London yesterday. Sitting on his left is Mr. Jerry Rubin, wearing beads, a leader of the movement.

Yippies form chapter in Britain

By Geoffrey Wansell

The foundation of a British chapter of the Youth International Party (yippies) in London yesterday.

tries throughout Europe and Africa.

The first public act of the British chapter was the disruption of the David Frost TV programme on independent television last Saturday, Mr. Richard Neville, author and former editor of the British underground magazine Oz, and an Australian, said yesterday.

Mr. Stew Albert, an American and one of a group of four

thers in America and the Irish Republican Army.

Mr. Stan Demidjk, a member of the British chapter, said British young people were frustrated at organized politics.

Mr. Mick Farren, another member of the British collective, said thousands of peaceful and sociable young people were in danger of taking drastic action against the state unless they were treated more reasonably

cated to the destruction of capitalism and imperialism."

He refused to say how long he and his supporters from America intend to stay here. He did not respect bureaucratic rules.

Mr. Albert said: "We are going to make them regret letting us in. I think we already have."

A delegation of 15 members of the party is travelling round the world forming what Mr. Rubin

Frost show shambles.

against the state unless they were treated more reasonably.

"We are a minority group, but we must be respected", he said. Young people were starving in the streets of London.

Mr. Rubin said that there were plans to attack newspapers in the same way as they had disrupted

world fo
called "
for the m
An Am
fighting i
Albert ac
intended
Republica
help its fi

Yippie in TV storm will launch a British party

By MIRROR REPORTERS

YIPPIE leader Jerry Rubin is planning to launch a British yippie party.

Rubin, centre of a row over Saturday's invasion of the David Frost television show, is co-founder of the revolutionary American yippie party.

He is expected to give details of plans for a British party at a Press conference in London today. Yesterday, Rubin called at the London School of Economics to chat with student sympathisers.

He would not discuss suggestions that David Frost set up the yipple invasion which disrupted his show.

But London Weekend Television, who produce the programme, again denied that there had been any advance warning of the disturbance.

Retreated

They admitted, however, that they took precautions in case of trouble.

A stand-by studio — the one Frost retreated to when the yippies got out of hand—was made ready in advance.

Clean-up TV campaigner Mrs. Mary Whitehouse, who demanded an inquiry after the disturbance, was invited yesterday to appear in a debate with the

Jerry Rubin . . . centre of the row over the yippie TV invasion.

gramme. Rubin demanded £200—double the normal fee. Frost offered him £100, which he accepted.

How did the other Yippies get into the studio on Saturday?

Said producer Geoffrey Hughes: "We restricted Mr. Rubin to seven tickets. I don't know where the rest came from.

"Perhaps our security at the studio is not very good."

Opinion: Page 8

By GEORGE WEBBER and MARTIN JACKSON

THE Home Office has been asked to investigate Saturday night's oath-filled invasion of the David Frost show and the alleged hooliganism during the show.

And a probe has also been ordered by Lord Aylestone, chairman of the Independent Television Authority. Protests poured in from viewers after the incidents.

NO CUTS

But despite all the objections a recorded version of the programme went out uncut last night —four-letter words and all—on eight ITV stations from Scotland to the South of England.

These stations always show the programme on a Sunday. It is

Yippies Show probe

Whitehouse, the National Viewers and Listeners' Association, said last night: "I'm not falling for that, one. I think all they want is more Saturday publicity for their case."

Yippy invasion said Mr. John Hopkins, who claimed he took part in the invasion, telephoned the invitation to her. She added: "He obviously only came to my programme

screened live on Saturdays to viewers of London Weekend, Midland, Channel, and Westward.

The I.T.A. gave the Sunday show stations a free hand in their treatment of the programme. A typical attitude was that of Granada, where an official said: "It was difficult to cut so we decided to put it out uncensored."

But last night's recording *was* preceded—at the request of the I.T.A.—by a warning telling people exactly what to expect.

THE PROGRAMME was a Frost interview with American Jerry Rubin, leader of the Youth Independence Party (Yippies) and one of the defendants in this year's Chicago riots trial.

During the interview about 30 long-haired Yippies invaded the Wembley studio. Three admitted they smoked pot and one offered Frost a smoke from a hand-rolled cigarette.

During the commercial break Frost and another guest had to move to another studio before order was restored and the programme could continue.

PROTESTS

HUNDREDS of viewers phoned in to protest. And Mr. Harold Soref, Tory M.P. for Ormskirk, has written to Home Secretary Mr. Reginald Maudling.

Said Mr. Soref last night: "It is monstrous that while the police and the authorities are doing their best to stamp out the evils of drugs, television should be allowed to display encouragement and exhibitions of public depravity.

"I am asking Mr. Maudling why these people were allowed into the country from Algeria, where they admit they have set up a revolutionary council. Why were they not deported?"

Rubin was given an air ticket from Paris to London by Jonathon Cape, the publishers of his book "Do It."

When he was asked to appear on the Frost programme, Rubin demanded £200—double the normal fee, Frost offered him £100, which he accepted.

How did the other Yippies get into the studio?

Rubin [standing, far left], followers, and Frost

THE DAVID FROST DEBACLE

IN MARCH 2008 FILM FOOTAGE from *YIPPIE!*, an unfinished documentary by Michael Simmons and Tyler Hubby, Mick Farren told interviewer Michael Simmons about the Frost debacle:

To be quite honest, there was some degree of it being a put-up job anyway; Jerry was promoting his book Do iT!, *Frost needed ratings, and I just went along for the fun of it. Disrupting a primetime TV show was something I'd never done before. I didn't think it was a great political statement, because there were too many of us and no great political statement was ever going to be made . . .*

Basically all went to according to our plan. We disrupted a primetime TV show, Frost had another hot studio the second half of the show, where he [was able] able to talk about what scum we were. And, it all got blown very much out of proportion. It was on the front page of the newspapers the next day, which happened to be Sunday, a slow news day. We were all over all the tabloids: "Hippie Scum Disrupts TV News Station." It was like The Johnny Carson Show, *for Christ's sake. People say, "Well, why didn't you make your political points?" and I said, "We weren't there to make a political point, it was a prank! It was fun!" Jerry and Stew were immediately deported.*

Actually, they went to Northern Ireland, which might have been a bit of a shock to them because there it was a little more real, with soldiers, armed cars, and explosions. They met with Bernadette Devlin and then were arrested and deported. This is in the aftermath of Yippie and flower power. Remember, this is almost two years after Chicago. This was a year after Woodstock. It was a bit of humor for the troops, and we weren't attempting to convert anybody. We weren't trying to make any philosophical points. What we were trying to do was just to do something nobody had done before, which was to turn a major TV show on its head.

It was insomuch that for this prank we called ourselves Yippies, and I think that's the one time there was a chapter of the British Youth International Party. I think we had a press conference or something, but there were massive amounts of alcohol involved in all of it.

A postscript for those who cite Bill Grundy's '76 interview of the Sex Pistols as the first example of extreme, foul-mouthed television appearances. The Yippies on *Frost* not only predates the Pistols by six years, Felix Dennis was the first person to say the word "cunt" on live British television. Before things got totally out of hand, Frost referred to Rubin as a "reasonable man." Dennis, still in the audience, barked out, in jest, that Rubin was "the most unreasonable cunt I've ever known in my life." A year or so later, when John & Yoko first met Rubin in New York they remarked how they'd been fascinated by Rubin's disruption of the *Frost Show*.

It was headline news in papers across Britain. Besides the usual cries of moral outrage (letters from shocked housewives, the whole bit), there was also an investigation called for by the ITA (Independent Television Authority), the British version of the FCC. The Yippies put their spin on it, suggesting that David Frost's producers staged the whole thing, while members of Parliament called for the Yippies to be deported.

Meanwhile, Jerry and Stew had scurried off to Belfast. Newspapers reported that he was in Ireland, but his exact location was unknown. He told the media, "I have to come to Ireland to foment a socialist revolution with my brothers and sisters." He supposedly met with the IRA and publicly challenged the commander of British troops in Northern Ireland to a television debate. The Royal Ulster Constabulary (the police) was told to track Rubin down and shut him up. Eventually, Jerry was arrested and flown to New York. When he arrived, he thanked Reginald Maudling, the British Home Secretary ("The butcher of Belfast") for the free plane ticket home. Neville told the British publisher of *DO iT!*, "Now that's what I call a book launch!"

15.11.70

Safety Frost Times

THE Frost Programme, which normally goes out live on London Weekend TV, was pre-recorded yesterday because, as David Frost put it " of information received." Last week's programme was disrupted by yippies led by Jerry Rubin and Stewart Albert, who flew out of Britain yesterday after being arrested in Belfast on Friday.

NANCY KURSHAN PAID THE PRICE, BUT LOOK HOW MUCH SHE GAINED

NOW IN HER SEVENTY-SECOND YEAR, Nancy Kurshan has been actively defending civil liberties since she was barely a teenager. Although sometimes referred to as Jerry's wife, that was just a front so that she'd have access to him in jail. This is *her* story, told for the first time.

Nancy was Jerry's partner from 1965 to 1970, participating in the VDC marches in Berkeley, the founding of the Yippies, the Levitation of the Pentagon, the Chicago Democratic Convention, and the infamous trial. She also helped compile the book *DO iT!*, traveled to North Vietnam in 1970, and conspired with Roz Payne, Sharon Krebs, and Robin Morgan to start W.I.T.C.H. (Women's International Terrorist Conspiracy from Hell). Like Jerry's best comrade, Stew Albert, Nancy is an unsung hero in the Yippie legacy.

Born February 4, 1944, Nancy was a "Red Diaper baby." As she notes in her unpublished memoir, "It's hard to really know what exactly my family's involvement with Communism entailed because, by the time I was old enough to understand anything about these matters, the country was shrouded in the McCarthy era and all kinds of people were trying to hide all kinds of things." She notes that her mother Charlotte was a "Communist Party cell leader, and was arrested raising money on the boardwalk in Coney Island." She collected contributions for the World Youth Conference of the American Youth Movement, "endorsed by none other than Eleanor Roosevelt."

Nancy's biological father Robert Kahn was a Communist; he went off to fight in World War II and her parents divorced when it was over. When Nancy was three, her mom married Norman Kurshan, and he adopted her. Her biological dad visited occasionally. Norman was also involved with "progressive political movements." Nancy recalls, "as a family, we were very emotionally involved in the fight to save Julius and Ethel Rosenberg from being executed as Soviet spies."

As a teenager, Nancy was empathetic to the plight of African Americans, and in the fall of 1958, she traveled to Washington, DC as part of the Youth March for Integrated Schools. She was one of ten thousand teens assembled at the Lincoln Memorial to hear Harry Belafonte, Jackie Robinson, and Coretta Scott King speak. After high school, she attended the University of Wisconsin–Madison. It was a politically charged campus; students protested the ROTC and Senator Joseph McCarthy.

It was now 1965 and Vietnam was heating up, with increased media coverage and burgeoning student revolt. Nancy was attracted to the Free Speech Movement protests on the UC Berkeley campus. She arrived in Berkeley that autumn and was immediately derailed from her PhD in Child Psychology by a political activist sporting "a handlebar mustache . . . that gave him the look of a classic Italian anarchist." Jerry and Nancy began spending time at the Mediterranean Café on Telegraph Avenue, "eating and drinking coffee, and arguing about politics."

> Nancy's really a long-distance runner, and that's what we all need to learn how to be.
> —ROBIN MORGAN

NANCY KURSHAN: Jerry kind of introduced me to those kinds of places in Berkeley, because he liked to just schmooze around, and bump into various people. He wrote me a letter about how when you meet someone and you just gel, just sync, he said that was happening with us, and he wanted me to meet Moe Hirsch and Steve Smale who were also on the steering committee for the Vietnam Day Committee, or VDC, as we called it. I thought Jerry was kind and giving to his friends, the people that he really cared about. I liked him.

Nancy was an active member of SDS, and felt pulled between their "model of grassroots organizing, going door-to-door, speaking one on one and trying to build organization in a slow, deliberate process." Yet, she was enamored of the VDC's style "of educating huge numbers of people and agitating and providing outlets for action."

When Jerry decided to run for Mayor of Berkeley, Nancy helped organized his campaign (initially just to educate the public on issues), but soon realized that Jerry was serious and it was distracting her from her graduate program studies. Dave Dellinger invited Jerry and Nancy to come help organize a march on Washington, DC on behalf of (MOBE) the National Mobilization to End the War in Vietnam. Nancy had just completed two years of her graduate program and was in good standing. She quit school right there and then.

NANCY KURSHAN: For the next five years we were inseparable and went through extraordinary times. Sometimes it felt like we were in control, changing the world according to our dreams. At other times, we were on a speeding train, way beyond our control.

Jerry went to New York first while Nancy stayed in Berkeley closing up shop. Not long after he got there, she received an excited late night call. Jerry had met a dozen freaks that convinced him to join their prank of dropping hundreds of dollar bills onto the floor of the Stock Exchange. When Nancy asked whom this new friend was, Jerry replied, "Abbie Hoffman." Years later, Nancy wrote, "From that moment on, life changed."

When Nancy arrived in Manhattan, she fell into a social circle with Abbie and Anita Hoffman, along with Paul Krassner and Phil Ochs. She remembers that everyone would "smoke some weed and talk, talk, talk." In 2013, Nancy told me that whenever Jerry and Abbie weren't getting along, "Anita and I would never talk candidly, because we each had to stand by our man. Later in life, we did talk. But not back then."

I asked Nancy to detail her daily activities in the Yippies:

Once I dropped out of the MOBE, I started working with Abbie on the Lower East Side. There was a free store and a free clinic. Really, I didn't know what I was doing, there was a doctor that saw people for free, and he would call me. One time somebody was having a bad trip, and I had to take her to the hospital, which was on the other end of the city. I did a lot of random things. We had an office. I was in charge of the literature, the buttons, and all the nuts and bolts of it. When the YIP-In happened, and everyone was

arrested, I was in charge of bailing everyone out. You know, I think in some ways I wasn't . . . although I agreed with all the Yippie stuff, I don't think I was a natural Yippie, performer kind of person. So I did everything else that wasn't flashy.

The movement and their relationship peaked in the late '60s. Nancy and Jerry took up the causes of black Americans and the Vietcong. Although nonviolent, they supported "selective violence" and shared "the feelings of extremist revolutionaries" (although neither fired a gun or planted a bomb).

Portrait of Nancy by underground cartoonist Spain Rodriguez. ©1970

They were committed to being "morally right." In their youth, they "had been taught that the Good Germans who did nothing to stop Hitler were also morally responsible for his crimes. They felt anger at the gap between America's ideals and the cold reality of its power system." Nancy says, "during those years Jerry and I beat with the same heart, politically at least." Yet, the media attention surrounding the Chicago Trial was part of their undoing as a couple.

NANCY KURSHAN: Well, I think the further we got into all this, and the further his fame grew, the crazier it got. I don't know what fame is like for other people, but I don't think it did him any good. He was nervous about his speaking abilities, even though he was a good speaker. He probably tried too hard . . . For a long time, it was not the greatest situation, and he was getting more and more famous, more and more crazed about being famous. And I wasn't

having such a good time. But, at the same time, he kept going to jail. I felt like I couldn't just leave. And I didn't really have anybody to talk to about it, hardly at all.

PAT THOMAS: Like you said, it wasn't like you were going to go to Anita, or somebody else, and say, "This is what I'm mulling over. What do you think?"

NANCY KURSHAN: Nope, because the lines of communication were not open between us. So that was what was so nice later about the women's movement. Then, being in Vietnam, just us three women [Nancy, Judy Gumbo, and Genie Plamondon of the White Panthers visited North Vietnam in 1970] was pretty liberating, seeing women in Vietnam in all walks of life—mayors of villages, women doctors, woman in the military. I was really ready for a change.

Nancy's Post-Yippie Adventures.

After Nancy and Jerry split up, she headed for Kent State—it was fall 1970. She connected with an old boyfriend who was involved with the Weathermen. They published an underground paper titled *Dragon Fire* while Nancy led a women's group for students. The campus was still recovering from the trauma of the shootings, so Nancy focused on helping undergrads cope with "whatever fears would exist for them, in terms of still wanting to participate in the antiwar movement."

When the United States supported a South Vietnamese invasion of Laos in the spring of 1971, Nancy spray-painted a slogan across the side of a college building, and a few months later she was busted on felony charge for her artistic statement. Emotions were still running high against the movement in Kent and she received death threats and obscene phone calls. When the local D.A. offered to reduce the charge to a misdemeanor if she left town, she headed for Cleveland.

In Cleveland, she and Howie, her boyfriend, identified as "Weather Yippies," in tribute to their Yippie-Weatherman consummation. The couple produced two offspring, Michael and Rosa. Nancy focused her attention on Ruchell Magee's defense committee. (Magee was implicated in the August 1970 Marin County courthouse shootout, in which Jonathan Jackson stormed the courthouse with guns. He was trying to free his brother, George.)

Meanwhile, Howie bumped into Weather Underground leader Bernardine Dohrn at a local flea market one day, and so he and Nancy officially joined the team as "above ground" members. Nancy spent a lot of time at San Quentin aiding black prisoners, as well as serving on Black Panther Geronimo Pratt's defense committee. As a Weatherman, she helped build an "above ground" organization called the Prairie Fire Organizing Committee, and they published *Prairie Fire*, the book that the Weather Underground wrote.

NANCY KURSHAN: I spent many years in the San Francisco Bay Area and then here in Chicago, doing all kinds of political work, but the central organizing fact was that I was in this cadre organization that sent people all over. But the Weather Underground fell apart, that's a long story . . . I wasn't even in Weather Underground until very late, when they had changed a lot. I actually went to their War Council in Flint, when I was in Chicago for the Eight Trial. Then I left, I thought, this is not for me, right now. But later, in 1974, I joined them.

I spent three days at Nancy's home with her husband Steve Whitman. Both are committed activists. When I asked how they met some years ago, they said they met when one bailed the other out of jail after protesting outside of a local Army base. Although Whitman didn't know Nancy during her Yippie years, he was eager to fill in the past few decades for me.

STEVE WHITMAN: I would say that the thing that characterizes Nancy most is a constant overarching pursuit of social justice. It's really burned into her heart and soul. As we get older, the number of people who were politically active, but who have stopped, some of whom have even stopped believing what they used to believe, is painfully large. And the number who have continued on, are few.

Nancy is one of the most remarkable people I've ever encountered in that way. Nowadays, it's complicated to figure out what's an optimal thing to do, what's a good strategy. Or whether we should drag our seventy-year-old bones out to a demonstration when it's zero degrees out. But the notion of the value of the demonstration, our desire to see the demonstration succeed, is unquestioned to Nancy. And I've never seen anyone persevere that much, in pursuit of social justice. She just truly and sincerely and passionately believes in the rights of the oppressed, and puts her body and her mind on the line for that, every day.

Nancy now is about seventy years old, and I would say she's been doing this since she's ten. So for sixty years, in different ways, she's been fighting like this. Robin Morgan wrote this famous essay in the '60s, called "Goodbye to All That." And at the end of the essay, there's a paragraph that says, "Free Robin Morgan." And the "All That" was sexism in the movement. "Free Kathleen Cleaver," and so on. And one of the names is "Free Nancy Kurshan." Several years ago, we saw that Robin was going to be keynoting a NOW convention at a Hyatt in the suburbs.

So I said to Nancy, "Why don't you go and say hello to Robin?" Because they were good friends back in the day, and Nancy said, "I don't want to bother her." And so I said, "Nancy, it's just the most ridiculous thing in the world, why don't you just take the subway, it's a buck-fifty, and if it's not good, come back." So she did. Halfway through her talk, Robin looked up and saw Nancy in the room, and she said, "I just have to stop for a minute, and introduce you to somebody. Because if you really want to know what we all need to do in order to succeed, it's that we need to be like Nancy Kurshan." Robin said, "Nancy's really a long-distance runner, and that's what we all need to learn how to be." She just stopped her entire keynote address to introduce Nancy. I don't know anybody who knows Nancy, politically, who doesn't feel that way about her.

Nancy and Steve dragged her children along to every political function. Prison reform became Nancy's strongest passion, and in 2013 she wrote a book, *Out of Control: A Fifteen Year Battle Against Control Unit Prisons,* that chronicles her work of organizing hundreds of educational programs and demonstrations fighting against the prison industrial complex. Nancy, Steve, and the children spent innumerable hours visiting prisoners. Because the drive could take hours, they would often stay from noon till eight at night. Whenever they could, they'd share a sandwich with an inmate. One time, the four of them were driving home after a long day of visitation, and her son Michael blurted, "the only time we ever sit down and eat dinner together as a family is when we're in a prison."

Minutes before I was due to leave, they dug out videotape from the 1980s. It had that warped look of being recorded "off the air" from the local news. Uniformed Neo-Nazis and skinheads are marching through the Chicago streets. Nancy and others are leading a "Stamp Out Racist Graffiti" counter-demonstration. Both sides are yelling back and forth when a huge fight breaks out. Nancy gets hit in the face, just below her eye. Bleeding profusely, the first thing she does (before seeking safety or medical attention) was to find the television crew covering the riot and yell into the camera, "We must get these Fascists out of Chicago!"

CONTACT SHEET © JOHN JEKABSON

The year is 1970. It's morning, and just like all the other housewives in the neighborhood, your kids are at school, you've got a pile of ironing to do, and you're bored—so you turn on the television. Maybe they'll have on Steve and Eydie, or The Galloping Gourmet. Instead, you turn the dial and this is what you get...

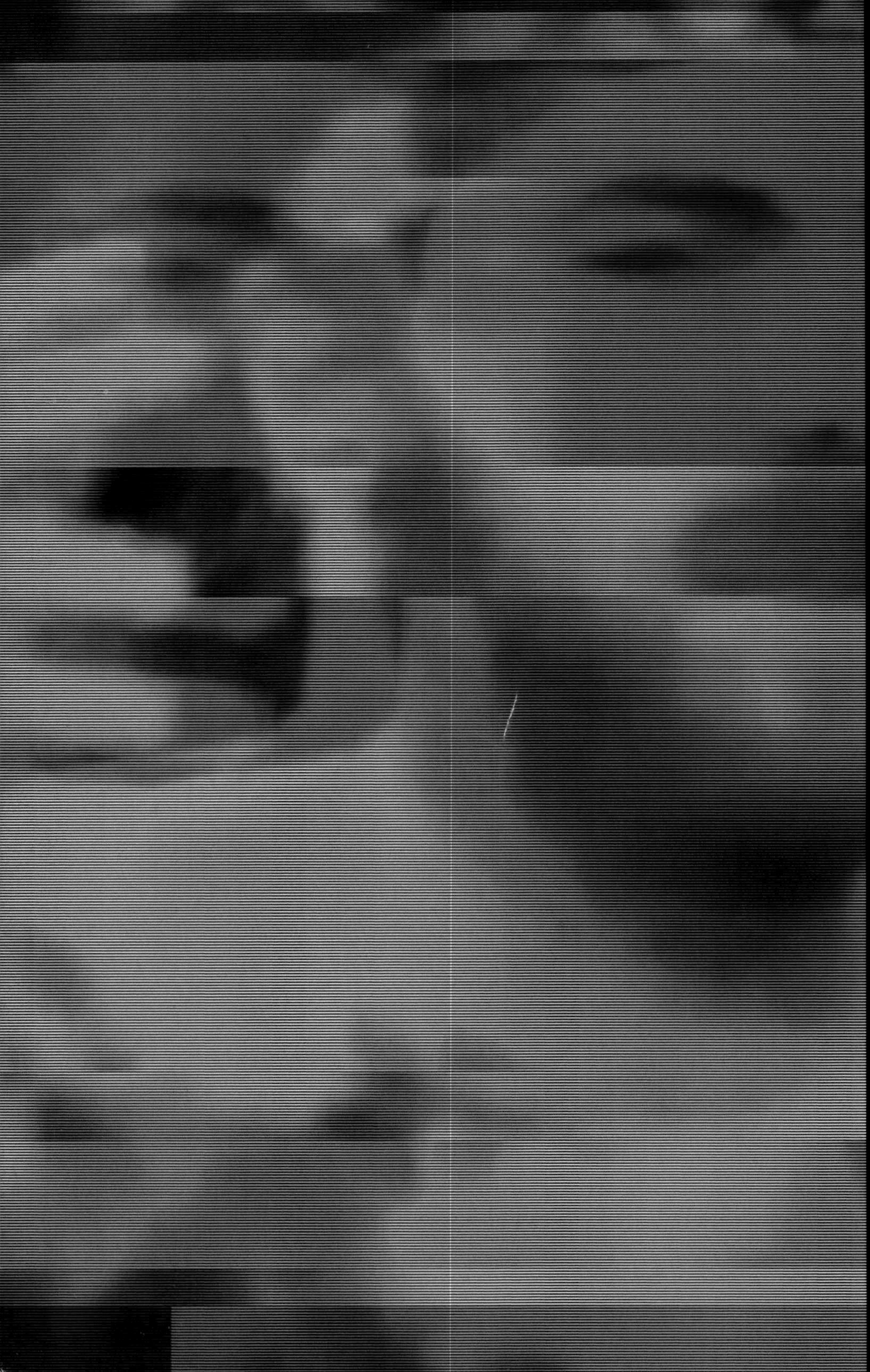

JERRY RUBIN: I'm giving you the answer that's in my head. Nixon doesn't think black people exist. Nixon doesn't think young people exist. Nixon's only concerned about the middle, Silent Majority, which we don't have to worry about 'cause it's silent. Young people are the only people in this whole country that are saving the soul of America by protesting the crimes committed in Vietnam and at home in the courts and in jails, etc.

PHIL DONAHUE: See, already I'm concerned about, see, I—

Mister Sincerity here.

I get the feeling you're giving me answer 23B, so you wanna—

No, it's 27A!

Well, you know what I mean, don't you?

No, I don't.

Well, I'm disappointed that you don't seem to able to converse with me. I ask you a question—you start waving your arms, looking at those people—why don't you look at me. And, uh, I'll ask you a question, because it's sincerely asked—

Didn't I just see you? I met you before . . .

I wanna know—

I met you before. Didn't we meet, 5th Street in New York—you sold me that dope?

(Short, embarrassed laugh.)

What are you? What are you doing? On the side, you're a TV personality—and you're one of the biggest dope dealers in New York City. And he comes on this show, real sincere, with "I wanna sincerely . . ." Tell the people about your real activities, man!

That's cute.

You got the best LSD and best pot in town. No wonder you know the air schedules so well; you're flying to NY and making deals on 5th Street, 6th Street, 7th Street. He comes on here real serious now. "Do you think it might prolong . . ."

You can understand that I would question the sincerity of your convictions about the war in Vietnam, when you come on here and tell funny stories about me selling dope. That's wasting time, here.

My wife is right now in Sweden, meeting with the Vietcong . . .

Now that's your wife. Let's talk about Jerry. Now here we are. You've got thousands of people out there who are listening to you now—mad at me because I put you on. All right. Here's an opportunity . . .

TAKE DOPE!
SMOKE DOPE!

(Jerry waves at the audience.)

Um . . .

The American army is falling apart 'cause of all the [po]t smoking. You dig that, don't you? You know how [t]he war on Vietnam is gonna end? The war in Vietnam [is] gonna end . . .

This is gonna be another cute story—

The war in Vietnam is gonna end when the Ameri-[c]an army puts down its guns or turns them around and [ai]ms them at the head of the generals. And marijuana [s]moking right now is so prevalent in the army. People [ju]st wanna get high. They don't wanna go out and fight [an]d die. You dig it?

You understand what bothers me?

No, 'cause you got a psychological problem and I'm [n]ot your psychiatrist.

(Donahue looks down.)

Look, young people know that this government has [n]o morality . . .

You speak for young people?

I'm speaking for myself, and I'm speaking for a truth [I] feel in the streets, and if you don't feel it, you're blind. [C]ause young people know the people that have power [i]n this country have no soul, no morality, and no ears!

(Audience applauds.)

. . . Absolutely none! And we know that this war is [n]ot gonna be ended by writing a letter to President Dick [N]ixon, 'cause Dick Nixon is a criminal. He's war crimi-[n]al. We know the only way to change this country is by [o]verthrowing the government.

(Cutting in.)

Wait! I can only get two sentences out and you act [li]ke you're on the toilet . . . UH UH UH UH! You're so con-[s]tipated! Why don't you shut up and let me talk? Keep [q]uiet—maybe the punch line will contain your answer.

I'm disappointed that you . . .

I'm sorry that you're disappointed. It won't be the [l]ast time. I'm sure you're disappointed in the young [p]eople that burned down the Bank of America. You see, [A]merica only responds to fire. They only recognized

poverty when the ghettos burned. These liberal [politi-cians] only spoke up after the crazies, the freaks, went into the streets.

We're talking with RUBIN (to the camera).

We're talking with PHIL DONAHUE!

We'll be back in just a moment—

AND SMOKE DOPE!

[THE DONAHUE SHOW, CBS TELEVISION, 1970]

YOKO ONO TOLD ME AND ABBIE THAT THEY CONSIDERED US TO BE GREAT ARTIST
ABBIE REPLIED, "THAT'S FUNNY. WE ALWAYS THOUGHT OF YOU AS GREAT POLITICI
—JERRY RUBIN

Christ, You Know It Ain't Easy:
The Ballad Of John & Yoko, Rubin & Sinclair & Peel & Weberman & Dylan

OPPOSITE: Jerry, Yoko, John, Abbie in NYC. Photo by Anita Hoffman, courtesy of Truusje Kushner

BY AUTUMN 1971, Bob Dylan had come under heat from the radical left because he hadn't recorded any political songs in years. They wanted something along the lines of "The Death of Emmett Till" rather than "Like a Rolling Stone" or "If Not For You." Dylan had returned to the Village after sitting out the last part of the '60s in Woodstock. He was now wandering the streets of Manhattan and trying to avoid A. J. Weberman, who stalked Dylan, pawed through his garbage, and accused him of nefarious deeds in the underground press. To this day, Weberman continues to hound Dylan on YouTube.

Dylan ultimately decided to collaborate with Allen Ginsberg on some political recordings. On November 17, 1971, with lyricist Ginsberg as the primary vocalist and Dylan on guitar (along with musicians like David Amram, Happy Traum and poet/vocalist Anne Waldman), they recorded the topical song "Going to San Diego." (It had just been announced that the 1972 Republican Convention would be held in Southern California.) On November 4, Dylan recorded the protest song "George Jackson," which paid tribute to the black political prisoner who'd been murdered by prison guards in early August. It became a classic.

John & Yoko were now living in Manhattan and hanging with Jerry Rubin, who was energized to knock Nixon out of the White House during his '72 bid for reelection. Lennon liked the politics that Jerry was feeding him and was impressed by where Dylan was headed musically, as it echoed his own "Power to the People," as well as anticipated the yet-to-be-recorded *Some Time in New York City* album. Lennon hoped Dylan would join him in a cross-country jamboree that would blend music and protest to help sway the presidential race. Lennon and Ono had moved to America around the time of the Attica Prison Riot in September, and were more interested in political action than musical recordings. As Jerry told Lennon biographer, Jon Wiener, in the early '80s:

> *We had all been talking to Dylan because Dylan had been hanging around a little bit those days. Dylan was being hounded by A. J. Weberman and he was really upset. This was also a time when a lot of class conflicts among the counterculture were real disturbing to a lot of folks.*
>
> *I forced A. J. to apologize publicly to Dylan in the* Village Voice, *in order to get Dylan to really go with us on the tour. That was my purpose. I thought if I could get A. J. to apologize to Dylan, destroy A. J.'s credibility, therefore Dylan would be free of A. J. and Dylan would be so appreciative that he would then say "yes" to me and John & Yoko—and then we would all tour the country raising money for prison causes, poor people causes, to feed poor people, whatever was necessary.*

All of this was under the auspices of Rock Liberation Front—led by A. J. Weberman—and endorsed by Lennon and Rubin, even though John & Yoko had yet to meet the notorious A. J., while Weberman and Rubin considered each other frenemies.

A. J. WEBERMAN: I went to Jerry's Prince Street apartment once. I took a firecracker, got some latex, put a cigarette fuse on it—not a firecracker, an ashcan—put it on the window and blew that window up at Jerry's apartment. That was a bomb. If you alter a firecracker, it's a bomb. That gives you an idea of what was going on. It was crazy versus crazy, like "Spy vs. Spy" in *Mad* magazine.

Lennon enjoyed how Weberman was hassling Dylan to get political—A. J. gave out badges that touted "Free Bob Dylan"—and with the release of "George Jackson," they all embraced Dylan's return to activism. The problem was, Lennon needed to throw A. J. *under* the bus so that Dylan might consider getting *on* the bus. David Peel was also part of the Rock Liberation Front.

RIGHT: A. J. Weberman takes a hatchet to his favorite Bob Dylan album. Photo courtesy of A. J. Weberman

DAVID PEEL: I met John Lennon on St. Marks Place in 1971, and from there I invited him to see—when I say John & Yoko, we thought of them as one, so when I say one of their names, it means both of them. John would never separate from Yoko, even for an hour. So he came to Washington Square Park to see me on Sunday, sometime in '71, with Jerry Rubin as their guide in the city of New York. Jerry was being like a clerical department, or an assistant for John & Yoko, in the Village.

From that point on, Jerry Rubin, myself, John & Yoko, became part of my and A. J. Weberman's organization. We had Rock Liberation Front, an activist organization to speak out about particular rights in America, anything from the civil disobedience to the war in Vietnam. And for anything else that was controversial, that we felt that the government were controlling like the NSA does today. We didn't have computers, but we had mouthpieces.

As the Rock Liberation Front, Peel, Rubin, Ono, and Lennon signed an open letter. They wanted "Weberman to publicly apologize to Bob Dylan for leading a public campaign of lies and malicious slander against Dylan in the past year." But the pronouncement gets embarrassing . . . and then insane: "Dylan is more than a myth—he is a human being, like you and me. He has feelings and sensitivities like you and me. Who is there among us who has not had his consciousness shaped by the words and music of Bob Dylan? . . . Weberman is to Dylan as Manson is to the Beatles—and Weberman uses what he interprets in Dylan's music to try and kill Dylan and build his own fame." Weberman capitulated. He wrote an open apology, which he signed as Minister of Defence [sic], Rock Liberation Front. A decade later, Jon Wiener asked Jerry how far discussions went with Dylan, and if he indicated interest. Jerry replied,

No, he gave no indication. It was just that he came to visit me a couple times and we just hung out and then hung with John & Yoko a few times. It was a dream that Dylan would do it; there was no hard evidence that he ever would . . . I was actually hoping that John and Dylan would form a new band. I thought we could make musical history as well as political history. I thought it was going to revive the '60s, that was my plan. This was at a time when the '60s were ending but no one really wanted to admit they were ending and it was a time when the leaders were blaming themselves, like I was blaming myself. I was thinking, "If only I was a better leader, if only I came up with more courageous or imaginative ideas."

DAVID PEEL: I met Bob Dylan at a café on 9th Street and then we walked through Washington Square Park. We're chitchatting, and I say, "By the way, Bob, Jerry Rubin lives on Prince Street. Why don't we go check him out? He's only about two blocks away." Jerry's shocked like hell I'm bringing Dylan to him. So there's some general conversation, gossip, and nothing really offensive. Dylan was always an honest guy. He didn't like A. J. Weberman and A. J. Weberman didn't like Jerry Rubin.

David Peel and Dylan knocked on Jerry's door, catching him and new girlfriend, Kathy Streem, as they were heading out to breakfast. She recalls:

Jerry was dying to meet Bob Dylan. He was going through all of Dylan's friends, anybody who might know him. They were all the wrong people. So, one time, we had just woken up, and were going out to eat breakfast, I had my coat on. And he wouldn't get off the phone, because he wanted to find Dylan. And then, finally he got off the phone and the doorbell rang—this is like one of those weird coincidences. And I look through the peephole, and its David Peel and Bob Dylan! And so, they walked in, and David Peel said that he was walking through the Village, and he ran into Bob. And oh, I'm going over to Jerry Rubin's house, and that Bob said, "*Oh, I've always wanted to meet him.*" So when Jerry heard that, he went, "*You did?! You wanted to meet me?!*"

David Peel introduced us and says, "this is Jerry, and this is Nancy." Because I was short and had dark hair, the Jewish look—Peel thought I was Jerry's previous girlfriend, Nancy Kurshan. And I didn't correct him. I just said hi. So he introduced us—me wrong—and then Dylan said, "*Oh, is this a bad time? I see you've got your coat on.*" And Jerry slaps my coat off of me, and says, "*Oh no, we just got back from breakfast. She just hasn't taken her coat off yet.*' [Laughs.] And so I didn't get to eat for a while.

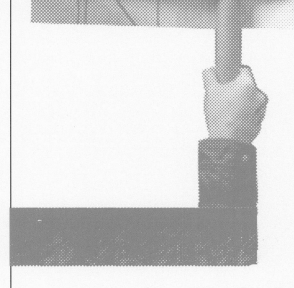

Jerry began showing Dylan some photographs, from Harvard and demonstrations and stuff like that. Jerry said, "*These are protesters and they're not happy anymore . . .. look at the energy back in 1969. Look at all the excitement, you don't see that happening anymore.*" And Dylan, who's very quiet—he's barely said a word—said, "*Well, the only people I'm exposed to are in the record industry, and those people are doing great. They're real happy.*" That was a very interesting conversation. [Laughs.]

Jerry would cross paths with Dylan again, during the Rolling Thunder Revue, when Ratso Sloman (with Dylan's blessing) invited Jerry to attend a performance. During the show's after-party, Rubin spoke with Digger Emmett Grogan, but unfortunately that conversation wasn't jotted down in Sloman's notebook. Another connection in the Rubin-Dylan axis is that Jacques Levy, who co-authored the lyrics on Dylan's album *Desire*, testified at the Chicago 8 trial. (At that time, he was the director of the off-Broadway production *Oh! Calcutta!*, in which the cast got naked.) Levy had also given Jerry and Abbie advice about staging events at their "Festival of Life."

Little did Lennon and Jerry know, but the Senate Internal Security Subcommittee submitted a memo to Senator Strom Thurmond in January 1972, stating that both men were "strong advocates of a program to dump Nixon." They suggested terminating Lennon's visa as a countermeasure.

JOHN & JERRY & DAVID & JOHN & LENI & YOKO

BY STU WERBIN

NEW YORK — John sat propped up on *the* bed next to Yoko who was wailing away on her tom-tom. John's rimmed eyelids and the neck of his new fiberglass Mitchell Special along with the steel soundbox stared directly into the mouth of Muhammad Ali, brought into their new West Village flat and the foot of *the* bed through the courtesy of New York's public tube facility, channel 13. Muhammad's mouth was moving, obviously he was saying something, but it could not be heard over the piercing scare-the-devil screams of Bible Belt crusader Dr. Jack Van Impe, recorded live at Landmark Baptist Temple, Royal Oak, Michigan.

"Nineteen Hundred and Seventy Four is the year they are planning for sex *on the streets* in every major city from Coast to Coast. And get ready for a shocker. The music they are planning to use to crumble the morals of America is the rotten, filthy, dirty, lewd, lascivious *junk* called *rock and roll*. God help you compromising preachers who allow this rock beat into your pulpits on Sunday just because it has 'Jesus Saves' tied to it. *It isn't just the words, it's the beat.*

"Four hundred girls in the Detroit area interviewed as to why they had illegitimate babies said it was not just the words but the beat. The fertility rights of the jungle are the same beats recorded into the modern rock to stir them up."

Dr. Jack used a portion of his speech to re-acquaint John and Yoko with the lives and writings of another couple, also seated in the flesh around *the* bed.

"You say I don't know what I'm talking about? The White Panthers leader Sinclair is now in prison for selling marijuana, he was the leader of Michigan's biggest rock and roll group, the MC 5. This is a revolutionary group. You're not hearing from a preacher now, you're hearing from the White Panther leader planning a revolution, a sex revolution by 1974 and all through rock music. Don't you dare defend it. In my city-wide crusade I preach against immorality, sex, liquor, I can preach against tobacco, name it, they take it. But I've had two churches pull out of my crusade because I hit on rock music. Brother, if it makes the Devil that mad there has to be something wrong with it."

John Sinclair, at the edge of *the* bed, laughed so hard that his huge abdomen heaved up and down like a whale break-
—Continued on Page 6

On February 17, *Rolling Stone* ran the article "John & Jerry & David & John & Leni & Yoko," detailing how Lennon wrote the song "John Sinclair" without having met the White Panther leader. He was inspired by Jerry's details about Sinclair's marijuana prison sentence. Jerry then called Leni Sinclair at 3 a.m. and recited the words to Lennon's new tune. A week later, John & Yoko appeared at the John Sinclair Freedom Rally. "Jerry was very persistent about the need for us to play in Ann Arbor," said Yoko. Lennon added, "Yeah, if wasn't for Jerry, we wouldn't have gone. But now we have the taste of playing again and we can't wait to do more. We want to go around from town to town, doing a concert every other night for a month." Lennon said, "We'll leave our share of the money in the town where it can do the most good . . . We want to raise some consciousness."

The voting age had been reduced from twenty-one to eighteen. There would be eleven million young people eligible to vote in the presidential election, so they planned to have a voter registration drive at each stop on the Lennon/Rubin musical protest tour. Out of jail and hanging at Lennon's apartment, Sinclair was quoted in the article as saying, "There's gonna be lots of resistance [from the establishment]." Lennon snapped that manager "[Allen] Klein will take care of that." The reporter described Sinclair visibly shaking at the thought of dragging the non-political, capitalist manager into the game. Jerry said, "We're trying to change the [music] business." Sinclair looked unconvinced.

In 2013, during a phone call, Sinclair told me, while smoking weed and listening to a Detroit Tigers game on the radio:

Jerry brought all those characters together—John and Jerry were pals. And Yoko approved of Jerry, because Jerry and Abbie were at the top of the fucking class, you know? They were the guys. John & Yoko wanted to do something interesting in the United States. So they hooked up with Jerry as their conduit, the one to actualize their ideas. He was key to the whole politicization of John Lennon, in the United States. And Yoko engineered it with Jerry Rubin.

I was friends with Jerry, and I was really good friends with Ed Sanders. Ed wrote a poem, in his inimitable style, in which he stated my case, and called for my freedom. Jerry took this to John and Yoko, because he was hanging with them. Jerry was a key figure. In my view, without Jerry, no benefit for my release from prison.

With Sinclair free, everyone wanted to focus on a tour that would radicalize the nation against Nixon while feeding the poor at each tour stop. Jerry told Jon Wiener in the early '80s:

We sat down and planned, wrote out cities, and it was going to be called the Yes Tour. John and Yoko always said you should never say no, everybody should only say yes. The band was going to be called the Yes Band and the tour was going to be called the Yes tour because we're saying "yes" to peace. "Yes" to the end of poverty, "yes" to happiness, "yes" to truth, "yes" to honesty. In every city—and this was Yoko's idea, really—in every city we would, in the local area, work with the local communities.

ABOVE: In 1970, Jerry wrote a letter to Ralph Gleason complaining that he couldn't get any coverage in *Rolling Stone*—when Rubin hooked up with John & Yoko two years later, they were eager to cover that!

The Plastic Ono Band briefly mutated into David Peel's Lower East Side Band, with Jerry as a drummer. The lineup nearly included Allen Ginsberg, an idea Jerry squashed.

DAVID PEEL: I wrote a song called "The Ballad of New York City," and what happened was Jerry told John & Yoko to go to 105 Bank Street to hear my song. I did the song "The Ballad of New York City" with John & Yoko participating and Jerry liked it, so very much. So later on, Jerry invited us to play on the streets. Me, John & Yoko, and Jerry Rubin came together to hit the streets with "The Pope Smokes Dope" right near the Fillmore East. Jerry and I started getting more close. Before that we had played at the John Sinclair Benefit in Ann Arbor. Jerry was my hand drummer, the percussionist in the band. What you don't know is that I tried to get Allen Ginsberg into the groove to be in the Lower East Side Ono band, so it'd be like the David Peel and the Lower East Side jam band, along with me and Jerry. I tried to get Allen Ginsberg to be part of the band and Jerry would have nothing to do with that. It was perpetual jealousy or personal differences.

Wiener asked Jerry why Lennon was attracted to Peel's music.

Because the Beatles cut him off so much from street music, where he originally came from. He said, "We'd done concerts and we didn't even have to sing, because the crowd was cheering so loud it overcame our voices. It was a joke. It was a farce." He said the whole of the Beatles era was one big farce, like he was a victim. He said it was almost too bad he was a Beatle. I'm sure he changed his mind in later years. This was also a rebellion against the '60s and that was part of it for him. David Peel was like discovering a street musician that he could support.

Jerry, Lennon, and many others were burnt out from the 1960s. Some had created great art; others had protested tirelessly against the war; and, in the case of John & Yoko, they'd attempted both with their Bed-In for Peace campaign. and the anthem "Give Peace a Chance." Jerry told journalist Stuart Werbin, in 1971, that he had been "very depressed and confused" the previous year, because "everyone in the Movement was condemning everything" from May Day to the Chicago 8 trial. His spirits lifted when he heard the songs "Working-Class Hero" and "Hold On John"—which he saw as a universal message. "Hold On John" could be "Hold On Jerry" or "Hold On Anybody," for that matter. He said that "Working-Class Hero" was like therapy. He hoped connecting to Lennon would reenergize both himself and the Movement.

Meanwhile, Lennon had gone through a horrible breakup with the Beatles, fueled by disagreements with Paul McCartney, which were a byproduct of his intimacy with Yoko, and his expansion from music into social commentary. He'd been mocked by the media for the couple's stunts: the *Two Virgins* album cover, Bagism, and the Bed-Ins. Lennon was a rock star, but that meant little to him when he arrived in Manhattan. He was eager to reinvent himself as a political spokesman. Jerry Rubin told Jon Wiener, "John was very bitter!

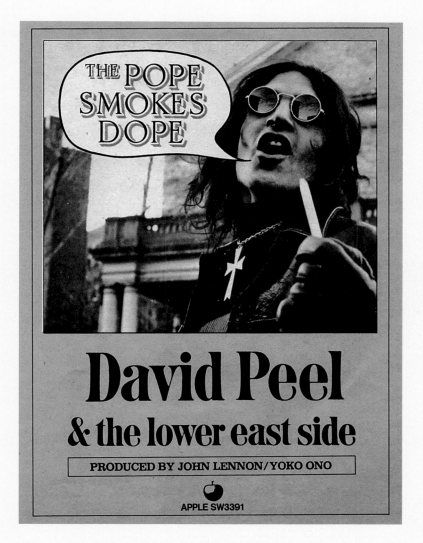

This is a bitter period! He ranted and raved about Paul McCartney. Ranted and raved about Allen Klein. Ranted and raved about the police. Ranted and raved about the misery of being a celebrity. Just to walk down the street, people would climb all over him and stand around him. It was horrible; he must've hated it."

Critics have long denounced the period that Lennon and Rubin worked together, questioning Lennon's motives and demeaning Rubin in the process. Yet, few have connected the dots. The Bed-Peace protests, sending out acorns to heads of state, hiding in a bag at public events, were all a mash-up of revolutionary Marxism, Marcel Duchamp surrealism, and Marshall McLuhan's media manipulation—exactly what Rubin and the Yippies were doing.

CRAIG PYES, JOURNALIST: John & Yoko were artists. Politics (to them) was just another form of art and art (to them) was just another form of politics.

DAVID PEEL
and the lower east side
with
JOHN & YOKO

Apple Records - 1700 Broadway, New York, N.Y.

Jerry Rubin recalled, "I introduced John & Yoko to a series of radical people: Huey Newton, Bobby Seale, Rennie Davis, Stew Albert, and my view was that there would be a whole kaleidoscope of people involved in this nationwide tour. I don't know about Bobby and Huey going on the tour full time, but they would've appeared sometimes. We were trying to get Stevie Wonder in this. It would be like a circus going around the country and end in San Diego and gathering steam as it went along. I guess it's naive to think that the government would allow it, huh?"

The chance to torpedo Nixon's reelection energized the streets of New York. It was a combination of Dylan being back in the Village, the mania of David Peel and his street band, the radical chic of Huey Newton and Bobby Seale, members of the Chicago 8 wanting to collaborate—all funneled through Jerry's infectious enthusiasm and driven by the star power John & Yoko could provide. At that moment, who wouldn't want to give that '60s dream just one more try?

Jerry explained, "What happened is that we brought Rennie Davis into the picture, and Rennie's an organizer. He said, "Well, I'll bring my washed-out operation here and we'll move into John & Yoko's basement and we'll mobilize the whole thing." He started moving his operation to New York City. It was just around that time [early 1972] that immigration went after John. The moment *that* happened, *boy*, the door shut, obviously."

ABOVE: Note Jerry behind Lennon on conga drum.
Photo courtesy of David Peel

Jerry suffered envious attacks in the media (by those enamored with the Beatles legacy) for grabbing onto Lennon's aura. Who among them could honestly say, "Nah, I don't want to be friends with John & Yoko, I'll just admire them from afar"?

JOHN SINCLAIR: Jerry Rubin was instrumental. John & Yoko were exhilarated at the outcome of the freedom rally. Even before I was released, they were exhilarated, because it was such a smash. It did everything that it hoped to do. It packed the place and raised money. It was a big hit in the media, it was broadcast live on FM radio, public TV stations showed the whole thing. It was a smash. No one expected my release. Most of all, me.

Jerry and John already had the idea of having some sort of Left-Wing tour, in conjunction with the Nixon reelection campaign. The idea was to dog Nixon around the country, with a series of concerts like my freedom rally. With a wide range of artists, local bands, local speakers, and us. We could do that in St. Louis, Chicago, Denver, and Boston, what have you. So we became an integral part of the planning team, because we knew how to make the thing happen in reality. Lennon would get his friends to play, and we would line up the other people and produce the shows. So that was the concept. And Jerry would stir up the education part, and so on.

And that's when they came after Lennon, you know what I mean? *The Department of Immigration.*

The end result was that the Federal Government crushed all this political-musical fraternizing. Their tactics included an outrageous plan to kidnap Jerry and Abbie and secretly hold them in a Mexican prison until the election was over. If that seems too weird to believe, follow the paper trail of the Committee to Re-Elect the President (accurately known as CREEP) led by G. Gordon Liddy and Howard Hunt. Kidnapping was too extreme for Attorney General John Mitchell, so he endorsed plans to take down McGovern and Lennon instead. The Watergate scandal and Lennon's deportation proceedings were linked by one common goal: "*keep Nixon in office by any means necessary.*"

The White House's desire to eliminate Yippies was proven real, when a taped discussion from August 1972 between Nixon and his top aide John Ehrlichman was released. The two men are discussing George McGovern's supporters and how they must be taken down. Nixon remarks that the only one they've went after so far is Jerry Rubin (followed by laughter) and the comment, "there must be others."

Amazingly, for the 1972 presidential campaign, the Republican Party borrowed Rubin's "Do It" slogan and distributed a psychedelic poster – using that phrase in large letters intertwined with images of hippies – and a declaration that strolling through a park, eating a hamburger, swimming outdoors and "facefuls of peace, not masks of war" would improve because "The Republican Party is doing it better for all folks."

Lennon sang "the dream is over" in his song "God," which summarized the end the '60s. Now it really was. John & Yoko dropped their political shenanigans and spent their energy on keeping Lennon from deportation. Fame and wealth helped. They had solid legal counsel and strong public support. Meanwhile, Nixon got reelected and Jerry hightailed it to San Francisco, dropping out of politics and engaging with the self-realization movement.

The INS (Immigration and Naturalization Service) wasn't the only branch of the Federal Government the White House pressured to go after political undesirables during the Nixon administration. One of Nixon's favorite ways to fuck with people was demanding the IRS audit their taxes. One IRS official told Rubin that he was ordered to find something "wrong" with Rubin's taxes, even if nothing illegal was identified. When Andy Warhol did a portrait of Nixon to be sold at a fundraiser for George McGovern in the '72 Presidential race, Warhol was audited for years afterward.

GARY VAN SCYOC, OF THE BAND ELEPHANT'S MEMORY: Nixon's reelection was so deflating. It was so intense, and then it was just like the air went out, you know? It affected the *Some Time in New York City* album, so that was not good. John was bummed. Everything went crazy at that point.

MAX'S KANSAS CITY AND ELEPHANT'S MEMORY

In his book *Down and In: Life in the Underground*, Ronald Sukenick recalls the scene at Max's Kansas City in its heyday. "Max's was like Alice's Restaurant, where you can get anything you want as long as you're an artist and a friend of Mickey's. In fact, Alice was a friend of Mickey's, and the two were involved for a while in a hip country scene in the Berkshires, where Alice's Restaurant was located. You had the feeling that anything could happen in Max's because of the synergy of the mix. It was a place where the attitudes of Abbie Hoffman and Jerry Rubin met the media knowhow of Madison Avenue."

In the book *High on Rebellion*, actor Marshall Efron remembered, "I was home when President Johnson came on and said he was not going to run for President. So I called Bob Fass at WBAI and said, 'I'll meet you at Max's.' Then we met Abbie Hoffman, Jerry Rubin, and Paul Krassner, and we all sat at Max's celebrating the fact that Johnson, the war president, was no longer going to be our president."

Elephant's Memory, best known as the backing band on John & Yoko's *Some Time in New York City* album, was, for a while, the house band at Max's. Jerry was both a fan and a friend, and introduced them to John & Yoko. Lennon's song "New York City" from that LP name-checks Jerry in the first verse. The second verse completes the story. "Well, we went to Max's Kansas City/ Got down the nitty gritty/ With the Elephant's Memory band laid something down."

In 2013, Elephant's Memory bassist Gary Van Scyoc discussed Jerry's connection to Max's and the band.

GARY VAN SCYOC: Max's Kansas City was where Jerry used to come and jam with us, every once in a while with a talking drum, or sometimes the bongos, whatever was lying around. Jerry was thrilled to just take part. *[Author's note: This is despite Jerry not having any real musical talent.]* And, of course, we shared the same politics at the time. But Jerry loved the music thing. He was totally into music, and anything that we would have recorded or something, he'd always ask for live copies of our live gigs, or any demos that we had. Very much into the music scene, and that's how we eventually connected with John Lennon, was Jerry just happened to have one of the tapes that we had made on a radio station in Long Island, called WLIR, still around. We did this recording of a live broadcast of our set, and I think Billy Joel was actually our opening act, at the time. So anyway, he took the tape, and I didn't realize he had befriended John and Yoko, but apparently he had, and he slipped them the tape, and that's how we got with John and Yoko.

THE NEW YORK TIMES, MO

Bob Gruen

John Lennon

Lennon the Chameleon

Eight years ago, when **John Lennon** and his wife, **Yoko Ono**, were facing deportation from the United States over his marijuana conviction, a friend of the couple publicly accused the Government of pressing the issue because of their radical image, notably "their antiwar stand" and "support of unpopular beliefs."

Now, Mr. Lennon, in a lengthy interview in Newsweek, has set out to slightly revise that 1970's image.

"That radicalism was phony, really," Mr. Lennon said, "because it was out of guilt. I'd always felt guilty that I made money, so I had to give it away or lose it.

"Being a chameleon, I became whoever I was with," he said, and he went on to reassess another leading light of the period, one of the personalities he presumably reflected.

"When you stop and think," he said, "what the hell was I doing fighting the American Government just because **Jerry Rubin** couldn't get what he always wanted—a nice, cushy job?" Mr. Rubin, once a leader of the Yippies, recently announced he had taken a position with a Wall Street brokerage firm.

Judith C

September 22, 1980

JERRY RUBIN

300 East 74th Street   New York, New York 10021   (212) 532-2925

Newsweek "Letters" Department For Publication.

An Open Letter To John Lennon:

Dear John,

Your "cheap shot" at me in your Newsweek interview----
"What the hell was I doing fighting the American government just because Jerry Rubin couldn't get what he always wanted--a nice, cushy job?"----provokes the following responses:

(1) John, you know from our close association in the early 1970s that your comment is a blatant falsehood. You know how committed I was to political and social change (and still am); (2) I am appalled that you give me responsibility for political decisions and actions that you made as an adult;

(3) I do not have a "nice, cushy job." I am working hard as a Venture Banker at the investment house of John Muir & Co. struggling through 18-hour days to apply my commitment to the financial world, working to help finance companies of the future;
(4) I wonder how you condemn me with the word "cushy" without any self-examination; (5) You are the only one of my friends who has criticized me in print for my new position and challenge;
(6) Despite yourself, I still love and respect you and Yoko, and value our friendship. I wish you great success with your new record.

Jerry Rubin

Jerry Rubin
New York City

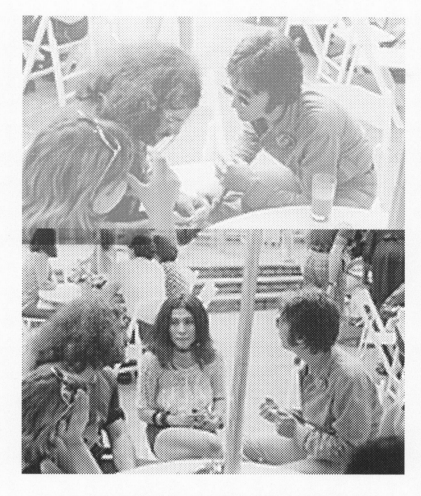

Nobody Told Me There'd Be Days Like These.

At the '70s progressed, Lennon disassociated himself from Jerry. In a 1975 interview with Pete Hamill, Lennon says that Rubin hijacked his musical direction the moment he arrived in New York. He blames Jerry for nearly ruining his songwriting, because "it became journalism, and not poetry." But Lennon doesn't mention his own interest in activism; he implied that Jerry hoodwinked him into writing protest songs. Yet, the last song Lennon recorded before meeting Jerry was "Power to The People." In another interview, Lennon declared, "the trouble with Rubin and Hoffman was that they never wanted laughter—they wanted violence." That seems odd, given the Yippies had made their name staging humorous pranks.

Numerous biographies have chronicled Lennon's temper, giving credibility to Jerry's 1980s recollection:

I used to go to their house. They would stay in bed all day, and I'd sit on their bed with the TV on. John was a non-stop genius talker on almost every subject—meditation, yoga, and politics. He was very radical in this period. He was into killing. He used to joke about their earlier peace and love period. He said, "Yoko, she's the peace and love one." You know, a drunken cop killed his mother, so he's angry. He's one of the angriest people I've ever met in my life. I mean, real anger. He wasn't political in the sense that I was political. I was a "planner." He was emotionally political . . . [on the night of the '72 election], he came into my apartment screaming . . . pushing people around and said, "You're not strong, you can't beat Nixon!"

And yet, John and Jerry socialized privately after the 1972 election. Stella Resnick—Jerry's partner during those years—recalled in 2013:

STELLA RESNICK: When we got to New York, Jerry called Yoko, and they had a nice rapprochement on the phone, and Jerry made a plan for us to get together. So that was the beginning of a number of visits to the Dakota, where they had a beautiful, sprawling apartment, half of which was not furnished. When they stayed at the Beverly Hills Hotel, they had a bungalow, and they invited Jerry and I to come visit. We specifically came down from San Francisco to hang out with them for an afternoon, which we did.

So, at times, it would be Yoko and me talking and it would be John and Jerry. I remember at one point, I said something very cheeky to John. I said to him, "So here you are. You're no longer part of the Beatles, and you're writing music and making your own albums, and at one time you had  all this acclaim and all your albums went platinum. Now, you're not getting that kind of reception, how does that feel to you?" Therapist that I am. And he looked at me and he said—I'll never forget it—he said, "One does what one can." A great answer.

Jerry told Jon Wiener, "I stayed friends with John & Yoko after San Diego, when the tour was canceled and all that; I still hung out with them. And I was spending time with Yoko when they were separated. I took Yoko to est; I took her under the name of Daphne. She thought it was like Japanese Zen. She liked it." When *Double Fantasy* was released, Lennon resurfaced. In a September 1980 issue of *Newsweek*, Lennon took no responsibility for his '71–'72 political declarations. "That radicalism was phony, really . . . being a chameleon, I became whoever I was with . . . when you stop and think, what the hell was I doing fighting the American government just because Jerry Rubin couldn't get what he always wanted—a nice cushy job?"

Jerry sent "An Open Letter to John Lennon" to *Newsweek*. "I am appalled that you give me responsibility for political decisions and actions that you made as an adult." Jerry was incensed that Lennon called his eighteen-hour workdays "cushy," and reminded Lennon "how committed I [am and] was to political and social change."

LEFT: Jerry, John & Yoko at Lennon's 31st birthday party in Syracuse, NY. Photos by Howard Smith © courtesy of the Smith tapes

jerry, this is a note that I"ve passed to John because my voice doesn't carry. and we both think that maybe we should pass it on to you, too. no hard feelings. but we have to know what we are doing because, from here on especially, people's fate is in our hands.

Though I love Jerry - the fact that Jerry is violent - basically longing for confrontation: the kind that happened in Chicago, is because his daddy and mommy diedand he has the pain of losing them twice - first he was never close to them - second he lost them anyway.

We can't sacrifice legs, arms and lives of our youth because of his personal pain that he is not aware of. We have to do it the hard way - which is patience and love - even for the ignorant pigs.

The fact that Jerry can't love the pigs - is a serious misgiving for the movement. The fact that Jerry did agitate the situation with Barbara, was not an outcome of courage but a consequence of his shallow understanding of the whole situation and indulgence in his emotion.

I have to confront Jerry with this because he will keep on with his emotionalism and fuck up somewhere - because he <u>wants to</u>.

But the people should not get the consequences of Jerry's emotionalism - that is unfair to them. Jerry must be more aware of where his pain is rooted in - and not mistake his emotion and think that his anger is a patriotic one, and therefore justified.

I just copied it by typ:ing it up. I'm sending this to you because I trust that you would not misunderstand my intension. We both love you very much and think of you as a very important person for the future of the people.

                              love,

                              Yoko

"[John] was extremely radical at this period. I think it was a delayed radicalism. I don't think he was radical in the '60s, but I think in the early '70s that happened to a lot of people, that kind of delayed radicalism. Even though there was no movement out there, it came out. Like one day, a Sunday morning, I remember I was home on Prince Street where I lived and Yoko sent me over a letter, giving me sort of a lecture on peace and nonviolence—but John was not nonviolent."

                              —Jerry Rubin, talking to Jon Wiener

Dakota Daze. While much has been said about Jerry supposedly selling out, little has been written about Lennon abandoning the movement.

PAUL KRASSNER: When I first met Lennon years ago, I asked him, "How do you get along with Jerry?" Lennon said, "Well, he has some great pot.'"

A. J. WEBERMAN: [Right up until his death], Lennon didn't want to bring any heat on himself. He was heavy into junk, and he was paying off the cops, buying them [bulletproof] vests. After he left Bank Street [in 1973] the heroin just destroyed him. When you see the last pictures of him when he's naked [on the cover of *Rolling Stone*], he's skinny. Emaciated. I saw him naked all the time when I came over to Bank Street and I know what he looked like. He looked healthy-like, and muscular, like a soccer fan from Liverpool.

In a series of essays, published posthumously as *Skywriting by Word of Mouth*, Lennon wrote, "the biggest mistake Yoko and I made in that period was allowing ourselves to become influenced by the male-macho 'serious revolutionaries.'" He blasts away about how Jerry didn't introduce him to any female revolutionaries. In the '80s, when asked about Yoko's feminism, Jerry replied, "Well . . . yes, but she's more of a *Yokoist*. What is she feminist about?"

Lennon was complex. Jerry described him as "a genius, an enormous energy"—which tempers some of Lennon's hypocrisy. During my research, someone gave me a tape of an uncirculated 1980s Rubin interview. Jerry tells an anecdote from 1971: "I was in a Jewish deli in the Lower East Side and a kid came over and gave John a picture of Meher Baba, and the kid went back and sat down. John took a pen and gave Meher Baba a Hitler mustache and as he walked out he put it back on the kid's table. John was against gurus. Especially religious gurus."

I then stumbled upon a different version of the same story recounted (just days after Lennon's death) by a longtime journalist friend of his. He'd been invited by Jerry and John to join them at the deli, and recalled, "A beatific, long-haired young man approached our table and wordlessly handed John a card inscribed with a pithy saying of the inscrutable Meher Baba. Rubin drew a swastika on the back of the card, got up and gave it back to the man. When he returned, John admonished him gently, saying that wasn't the way to change someone's consciousness. Acerbic and skeptical as he could often be, John Lennon never lost his sense of compassion."

Jerry was rarely a cynic, while Lennon nearly always was—so I tend to believe Jerry's version. When it came (competing with Lennon) to media manipulation—Jerry was out of his league. There was no way for him to spin the perception in his favor once he was attached to Lennon's legacy. Nearly everyone in the Western Hemisphere had awaited Lennon's comeback. The former Beatles' final months were spent recording new music and *playing the media* better than Jerry could. Just like Rubin however, Lennon "believed" whatever he was saying "at that moment" was the *truth*. John called himself a chameleon as an excuse for befriending Jerry in 1971.

But the main trait that separated Jerry from Lennon was that Jerry remained loyal to his former Yippie buddies. He never denounced them, but merely disagreed with how they should proceed in the present. Despite the Nixon administration crumbling years earlier, and Lennon's Green Card, Lennon put Jerry down. Privately, the story was a bit different. Jerry told Jon Wiener:

I saw Yoko about six months before John died. She called me up one morning. She said that she wanted to see me, so I went over there and she said that John was so difficult and his temper was so ferocious. We talked for a couple hours and John called when we were there. She said, "Wait a minute, I'll put somebody on," and we hadn't talked in a couple years. And Yoko said to me, "Have John try to guess who you are." I said, "Hi John," and John said, "Who is this? Let me guess . . . Klein? No, no, your voice is too warm for Klein. Let me think . . . keep talking." Then he said "God, Jerry Rubin? You mean Yoko's going to see you? Well if Yoko's going to see you then I'm going to see you." Then he talked about his son Sean and we had a conversation for a couple minutes, and then I left.

Just Gimme Some Truth. The release of the 2006 documentary *The U.S. vs. John Lennon* focused on "the outspoken artist and activist" who "in the midst of one of the tumultuous times in American history, stood his ground, refusing to be silenced." Jerry gets acknowledged but with no emphasis on his influence, despite interviews with Stew Albert and Paul Krassner. Yoko never mentions Jerry by name: only John Sinclair does.

Most wrongs were righted in the 2010 doc *LENNONYC*. Yoko praises Jerry and Abbie's tactics in Chicago. Tom Hayden mentions the Yippies had mastered Marshall McLuhan's media manipulation techniques, wisely asking Lennon to join them. Yoko credits Jerry for the introduction to Elephant's Memory. Both documentaries draw from the unreleased 1971 movie *Ten for Two* that documents Jerry, Rennie Davis, Bobby Seale, David Peel, and John & Yoko on stage at the John Sinclair Freedom Rally in Ann Arbor.

Perhaps Jerry should have heeded Stew Albert's warning to him in 1971: "Watch out, because if you get too associated with John and Yoko then you're going to be seen as celebrities, and you can't be a celebrity leader at this time."

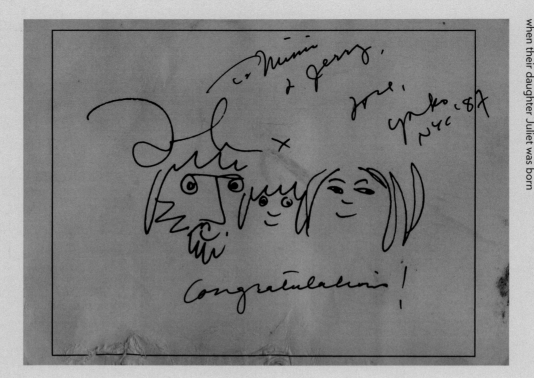

Delightful postcard sent to Jerry & Mimi from Yoko when their daughter Juliet was born

JERRY & JOHN & YOKO

Jerry as Drummer for John & Yoko. Jerry Rubin not only has the distinction of being name-checked on two different songs on the *Some Time in New York City* album; he also performed as a "musician" with John & Yoko several times during that period. Yet, he couldn't even play an instrument!

The John Lennon song "New York City" that closes side one of the *Some Time in New York City* album states, "Standing on the corner, just me and Yoko Ono—we was waiting for Jerry to land." On the home demo version (in the *John Lennon Anthology* box set), Lennon sang, "I was standing on the corner, just me and Yoko Ono—we was holding Jerry Rubin by the hand." The lyrics on Yoko's song "We're All Water" (which ends Side Two) has verses that pair together an odd cast of characters, including Chairman Mao & Nixon, Marilyn Monroe & Lenny Bruce, Eldridge Cleaver & the Queen of England, and this wishful couple: "There may not be much difference between Raquel Welch and Jerry Rubin, if we hear their heartbeat."

Jerry's first stage appearance with John & Yoko occurred at the December 10, 1971, John Sinclair Freedom Rally in Ann Arbor. John & Yoko were accompanied by three acoustic guitar players, David Peel on a washtub bass, and two percussionists, plus Leslie Bacon on backing vocals, and Jerry beating a conga drum.

Lennon starts the set by announcing to the fifteen thousand people assembled, "This song is called 'Attica State.' It was conceived on my birthday, October 9. It was ad-libbed, then we finished it off." Indeed, Lennon had made it up on the spot during his thirty-first birthday party, held in a Syracuse, New York hotel room, following an exhibition event held at the Everson Museum of Art for Yoko's visual artwork. Amongst the revelers were Phil Spector, Ringo Starr, and Allen Ginsberg, performing the old standard "Goodnight Irene."

At the Sinclair rally, the ragtag group also performed "The Luck of The Irish" and Ono's "Sisters O Sisters." Then Lennon said, "We came here not only to help John [Sinclair] and to spotlight what's going on, but also to show and to say to all of you that apathy isn't it, and we can do something." Lennon continues, "Okay, so flower power didn't work, so what? We start again." And they launched into "John Sinclair."

Two of the performances with Jerry appear on the *Lennon Anthology* box set: "Luck of the Irish" and "John Sinclair." A third ("Attica State") is included on the soundtrack to the movie *The U.S. vs. John Lennon*. None of the individual musicians are credited.

Jerry Returns to the *David Frost Show*. Jerry told author Jon Wiener that, when he first met John & Yoko in New York in 1971, they mentioned how much they had enjoyed watching Jerry and Stew disrupt the *David Frost Show* in London the previous year. Jerry told Wiener, "They thought the whole stunt was 'funny.'" Starting in the late '60s and throughout the '70s, David Frost was the consummate talk show host on both sides of the Atlantic. The British television journalist garnered a following in his home country covering the 1969 Apollo 11 moonwalk. He presented the Beatles on various stages, including their TV performance of "Hey Jude" in 1968, which is a fan favorite. In the '70s, he reigned on American television and was the only Brit with a regular, prime-time show. In 1977, Frost made history with a series of Richard Nixon interviews, focusing on the decline of his presidency.

On December 16, just days after the Sinclair rally, John & Yoko—along with David Peel and friends (including Jerry)—taped several songs for the *David Frost Show* in New York, which broadcast January 13, 1972. Peel and the Lower East Side band performed "The Ballad of New York City" with Lennon on washtub bass and Ono on a hand drum, sans Rubin. Not to be confused with Lennon's similarly titled song, Peel's song pays tribute to the couple by repeating over and over, "John Lennon & Yoko Ono—New York City are your people, John Lennon & Yoko Ono—New York City is your friend."

A bit later in the broadcast, John & Yoko—minus Peel, but now with Jerry on thumb piano, plus two acoustic guitarists—perform "Attica State." Jerry wears a T-shirt that said "This Is Not Here," which was the name of Yoko's art show in Syracuse. While they sing, a freak sits behind them, folding paper airplanes and making them fly over the performers' heads, toward the audience. Classic Ono-driven performance art.

Some of the studio audience are very upset that "Attica State" glorifies prisoners (in their opinion), and an intense debate ensues. Lennon stresses that the song is paying tribute to all the people that died, including the prison guards. Frustrated, Lennon declares, "We're like newspapermen, only we sing about what's going on instead of writing about it." This takes on a new meaning, since Mark David Chapman was incarcerated at the Attica Correctional Facility after murdering Lennon in 1980. Chillingly, an audience member asks John & Yoko how'd they'd feel if a prisoner did something to their family.

In 2013, Elephant's Memory bass player Gary Van Scyoc echoed Lennon's statement that they were like journalists: "Those records were turned out in a day. We'd go in at seven o'clock, and by seven the next morning, there would be a finished track. Not going back to replay it or mix it, none of that stuff. John used to talk about, 'we got an early press.' In other words, we gotta get this out in the morning. That's how the concept for the newspaper [artwork] came up. Because we felt like we were turning out stories that that had a deadline. Things were changing fast."

During the debate with the audience, Frost asks Lennon to sing a snippet of "The Luck of the Irish," which he does with approving noises from the spectators. Lennon mentions that they will be performing at the Apollo the following night as part of an Attica State benefit. The debate rages on while Jerry remains uncharacteristically quiet throughout. Frost must have demanded in advance that Jerry remain silent, given his disruptive behavior on his show a year earlier.

Next, Ono discusses the struggle of women's liberation, and then earnestly performs "Sisters O Sisters." Jerry makes a valid attempt to look like he knows what he's doing with that thumb piano (he's not mic'd). John, Jerry, and the others perform "John Sinclair." The aforementioned *John Lennon Anthology* doesn't contain this particular performance, but it does include Lennon's short preamble about how Sinclair was released on the Monday following the rally.

The show concludes with a performance by David Peel and the Lower East Side Band, with Yoko on hand drums and John on washtub bass. Lennon compares Lonnie Donegan's skiffle music and Peel's band. Although he wasn't on stage with Peel's group earlier, Jerry is now poised center stage with thumb piano in hand.

They close with Peel's "(I'm proud to be) A New York City Hippie." As the song and show come to a close, Frost steps on stage and begins to greet the band. Jerry attempts to shake Frost's hand, but Frost ignores him. In fact, Frost never acknowledges Jerry at all during the entire hour-long episode.

In 2014, David Peel shared his unique perspective on Jerry's appearance on *The David Frost Show*.

DAVID PEEL: To make a long story short, he was playing the thumb piano, which makes you look like an imbecile. At least when he was playing with me, he was playing the drums, but when he went with John and Yoko they gave him a little thumb piano, and he looked like an idiot. It put him back to nothing. Jerry Rubin knew nothing about music, and if you're gonna play music what could be worse than having that? It's like playing the kazoo. It's on the same level, maybe a little bit higher.

SOMETIME IN NEW YORK CITY
John Lennon/Yoko Ono
Plastic Ono Band with Elephant's Memory
● Apple-SVBB 3392
Produced by John, Yoko & Phil Spector

FREE—LIVE JAM LP
John & Yoko
and star studded cast of thousands
An additional 12" long player included inside
this album is yours at no extra cost when you
purchase Sometime in New York City. (Mfr.
sug. list price $6.98)

REGISTER TO VOTE / THE WORLD DEPENDS ON YOU

Live at the Apollo. The following evening, December 17, found John & Yoko with Jerry on shakers (plus the two acoustic guitarists from the *Frost Show*) on stage at the Apollo Theater! The legendary African American venue was staging a fundraiser, headlined by Aretha Franklin, for the victims of the Attica State Prison riots. Lennon said, "Hello, hello? I'd just like to say it's an honor and a pleasure to be here at the Apollo, and for the reasons we're all here. This song Yoko and I wrote is called 'Attica State.'"

And for the finale: "Thank you. Some of you might wonder what I'm doing here with no drummers and no nothing like that. Well, you might know I lost my old band, or I left it. I'm putting an electric band together; it's not ready yet. Things like this keep coming up so, I just have to busk it. So I'm gonna sing you a song now you might know. It's called 'Imagine.'"

Two of the songs from that evening appear on the *Anthology* box set. On "Attica State," none of the side players are identified. It simply credits the Plastic Ono Band. On "Imagine," only Lennon is credited as playing, despite footage on YouTube showing two other guitarists, plus Jerry and Yoko doing their thing. One thing is certain: Jerry's shakers are audible! Also notable is that one lyric in "Attica State"—"Free the prisoners, jail the judges"—was lifted directly from the title of a chapter in Rubin's book *DO iT!*

In the early '80s, Jerry told Jon Wiener:

> John and Yoko used to say to me, "We want to go to Harlem at noon and shake hands with the people." And I said that's naive to go to Harlem. First of all, you're rich celebrities, you're white coming out of a limousine to shake hands. I mean, they were really gutsy people.

The Mike Douglas Show. The *Mike Douglas Show* beamed across the country each weekday for ninety minutes, starting at 4:30 p.m. The core audience was housewives, switching it on for light entertainment. When Dad and the kids came home, they'd catch part of the show as well. Douglas's harmless blend of performing a few easy-listening vocal numbers, some chitchat with Hollywood celebrities (John Wayne, Sammy Davis Jr., Angie Dickinson), an occasional pop music group (Sonny & Cher, Beach Boys) and a cooking demonstration kept *The Mike Douglas Show* on air from 1965 to 1982, beloved by America's homemakers.

In 1972, for the week of February 14–18, John & Yoko co-hosted with Mike Douglas. They did most of the talking, and preselected the guests, including Jerry Rubin, Ralph Nader, Chuck Berry, George Carlin, and Bobby Seale. Elephant's Memory were on hand to play selections from the forthcoming *Some Time in New York City* album,

plus jam with Chuck Berry on "Memphis" and "Johnny B. Goode."

On the 15th, Jerry alienated *The Mike Douglas Show's* viewership when he called for voter registration drives (the voting age had recently been reduced from twenty-one to eighteen) to help ensure that Richard Nixon would not be reelected in November. Although Jerry kept his usual, sarcastic Yippie rhetoric to a minimum, he succinctly blamed Nixon for thousands of deaths in Vietnam, the tragedy at Attica State, and the four students killed at Kent State. "I think the system, in essence, is corrupt," Jerry added. Douglas was so upset he didn't notice that Rubin concluded on an upbeat note: "I think what's beautiful about [this nation] is that the children of America want to change the country and are going to change it. That's what's beautiful."

FBI agents watched the broadcast, and submitted a memo calling Rubin "an extremist" and Lennon an "SMNL: Security Matter, New Left." It was used to help rile up Washington bureaucrats so they would deport Lennon. Mike Douglas wrote about the incident in his memoir, *I'll Be Right Back*: "John's first request was Chuck Berry . . . Yoko's top draft choice was Jerry Rubin. Jerry was well known as an unrepentant anarchist and antagonist and I advised against inviting him, but John—and especially Yoko—wanted him badly. They mentioned that he had recently come out strongly against drugs and I could emphasize that."

Douglas figured "maybe it wouldn't be so bad," but the affable talk show host got more than he bargained for. After Jerry's anti-Nixon rant, Douglas tried to divert the conversation with some "just say no to drugs" talk. Rubin clarified that he wasn't anti-drug in general, just specifically anti-heroin, "because [it] is a tool used by the Gestapo police of this country to subjugate the black man."

Jerry became one of Douglas's all-time-least-favorite guests, part of a select few that got on the easygoing host's nerves. Douglas had been even more nervous about Bobby Seale's appearance scheduled two days later, but recalled in his memoir, "All I can say is, God Bless Bobby Seale. There was no trace of the rancor I anticipated. He didn't want to talk about 'pigs' or that 'up against the wall' stuff." Douglas was impressed with Seale's sincere speech about "shoes for the needy" and "breakfast for inner-city kids." These were issues that even he could identify with.

At a press conference held after the week of broadcasts, John & Yoko detailed their struggles with the show's format and booking policies, but patted themselves on the back for coping with it.

Yoko praised Jerry for his performance. When asked by a random reporter what she learned from Jerry's media tactics, she replied, "Well, he's an artist. When I came back to New York [from London], I met many artists who looked so commercial, like Madison Avenue-type people. And then I met Jerry and he looked like an artist. And then he said that we were the politicians . . . our awareness level is the same, and we just feel close to Jerry and Abbie."

Jerry weighed in as well, pointing out how great it was for all of them to reach millions of people, since usually "The only chance we have to get on television is on the Walter Cronkite show when we make the news." He added that this time they got to express themselves in their own words.

During the weeklong broadcast, John & Yoko (backed by Elephant's Memory) performed much of their forthcoming album together, including "Woman Is the Nigger of the World," "The Luck of The Irish," "Attica State," and "Sisters O Sisters." They also played "Imagine" and "It's So Hard," and Yoko performed a Japanese folk song, "Sakura."

But the most surreal moment of the week was not John & Yoko randomly phoning strangers to say, "We love you. Pass it on." (Remarkably, the couple remained undeterred despite most recipients of the call suggesting they do something to themselves which was physically impossible.) It was the Lennon and Chuck Berry jam, accompanied by Yoko, Jerry, and Elephant's Memory. "Johnny B. Goode" was uneventful, but "Memphis" was a freak show to the nth degree. Berry visibly grimaces when Yoko unexpectedly goes into her trademark vocal shrieking, while a beatific Jerry Rubin gleefully beats a drum. He's so pleased to be there he couldn't care less if he's playing in time or not.

From the tail end of 1971 through the beginning of '72, Jerry Rubin was *the* rock 'n' roll Zelig. He participated in four different John & Yoko performances, including the oft-cited John Sinclair Freedom Rally, the somewhat-forgotten-but-historic performance at the Apollo Theater, and two nationwide television broadcasts. Given their brief arc as live performers, Rubin arguably played more John Lennon Plastic Ono Band shows as a percussionist than any real drummer ever did!

John & Yoko with Jerry playing percussion onstage at the Apollo Theater (with guitarists Chris Osborne & Eddie Mottau)—note Aretha Franklin's band equipment in background. Photo © Bob Gruen

"BY 1972, I WAS A
BATTERED SOLDIER WHO
HATED HIS EGO, FEARED
HIS POWER, AND WAS
CONTEMPTUOUS OF HIS
NAME. PAIN HAD BECOME
MY TEACHER. I MOVED
FROM NEW YORK TO SAN
FRANCISCO IN NOVEMBER.
NEW YORK IS A CITY FOR
THE EGO. "WHAT DO YOU
DO?" THAT SAME QUESTION
IS AN INSULT IN THE BAY
AREA, WHERE NOBODY
DOES ANYTHING...

"INSTEAD
THE QUESTION IS,
"WHAT ARE YOU INTO?"
—JERRY RUBIN

The Dream Is Over:

The End Of the Movement

OPPOSITE: Jerry, Ed Sanders, Abbie 1972.

THE SPIRIT OF A DECADE generally doesn't change right when the clock strikes midnight on New Year's Eve. What we consider "The '60s" didn't begin on January 1, 1960, nor end on December 31, 1969. In 1960, the country was still very much in the conservative, *Leave It to Beaver*, all-American family mode with World War II hero Dwight D. Eisenhower as president. On the other end of the decade, the Vietnam War was still in full flight, the Chicago 8 Trial had a month and a half to go before its conclusion, and the Beatles hadn't announced their breakup yet.

If "The '60s" were defined by politics and violence (and they were), then the decade really kicked off with the assassination of John F. Kennedy on November 22, 1963, and ended with the signing of the Paris Peace Accords on January 27, 1973, which was the end of conflict in Vietnam. The first couple of years of "the '70s" still had the spirit of the previous decade, but when Nixon got reelected, the cultural landscape shifted from public protests to personal insights (via meditation, est, yoga, et al.), and the music shifted from the angry sounds of the MC5 to the mellow vibe of Carole King. It was time for Americans to recover from the tumultuous experience of three major assassinations (JFK, MLK, and RFK) and murders at home (the Manson Family) and abroad (Vietnam). There had been occasional triumphs along the way—the successful Moon landing, and three days of Peace, Love, and Music at the Woodstock Festival, to name but two.

But when the '70s came along, it seemed as if the revolution ended abruptly, as if it fell off the edge of the cliff. For such a passionate group of people to collectively throw up their hands and say "I quit," prompts those of us looking back at those times to ask, "What happened?"

For some, it was the loss of innocence—watching students get slaughtered at Kent State (expressively chronicled in Crosby, Stills, Nash & Young's song "Ohio"). For others, it was Nixon's reelection by a landslide. It was also the rise of women's lib, causing many key women in the movement (like Judy Gumbo, Nancy Kurshan, and Robin Morgan) to leave their male counterparts, which stripped the radical left of its backbone. The FBI's Counter Intelligence Program (COINTELPRO) was fueling paranoia amongst the ranks. And, last but not least, key leaders went underground to escape incarceration, such as Huey Newton (Black Panthers), Abbie Hoffman (Yippies), and Bernardine Dohrn (Weathermen). In the '70s, being a revolutionary wasn't fun anymore—*it was bad for your health.*

Tom Forcade, Dana Beal, and the Zippies.

In June 1970, President Nixon begrudgingly signed an extension of the 1965 Voting Rights Act, lowering the legal voting age from twenty-one to eighteen. He remarked, "Despite my misgivings about the constitutionality of this one provision, I have signed the bill." In the summer of '71, it became the Twenty-Sixth Amendment to the Constitution. Finally, eighteen-year-olds sent off to die in Vietnam could vote before they left!

In May of '72, the Black Panther Party campaigned for Bobby Seale for mayor and Elaine Brown for city council in Oakland, and registered several thousand voters. By the time of the 1972 Democratic Convention in Miami, the Yippies wanted to be known as the Youth International Party (YIP). Like the Panthers, the Yippies had decided to try to work within the system. Jerry and Abbie endorsed George McGovern for President, and actively encouraged all eighteen- to twenty-year-olds to vote.

Dylan's garbage collector A. J. Weberman, Tom Forcade (founder of *High Times* magazine), Dana Beal, and Aron Kay—a.k.a. "The Pieman"—decided to form a counter-Yippie organization called the "Zippies," claiming YIP had sold out by stumping for McGovern. Forcade also had a personal beef with Hoffman—he claimed that Hoffman owed him money for editing *Steal This Book*. Some felt "that the Zips were paid provocateurs," whose main purpose was "to discredit the youth movement." With Jerry and Abbie in their mid-thirties, the Zippies claimed the Yippies were too old to be relevant, and declared they would "Put the Zip back into Yip."

Although Jerry did not coin the phrase "Never trust anyone over thirty," he popularized it and is often credited for its origin. Jerry had picked it up from Jack Weinberger, a member of the Berkeley Free Speech Movement, who first used it in 1964. Wisely, Jerry kept it a secret that he had turned thirty about a month before the '68 Chicago Democratic Convention. But when Jerry turned 34 during the '72 Democratic Convention in Miami, the Zippies presented him with a "retirement cake." Later, in New York, they also beat him up and smashed his car windows. They held a "People's Tribunal" for Hoffman, with Forcade acting as prosecutor and Rex Weiner and A. J. Weberman as the jury; they found him "guilty." Forcade declared the Yippie "dynamic duo" as "nothing more than a glorified left-wing lobby of the Democratic Party" when they endorsed McGovern for President.

Just like they had done with the Black Panthers, the FBI's COINTELPRO squad hoped to divide the Yippies with anonymously mailed letters—such as the handwritten note they sent to various recipients in December 1970. It read, "Abbie Oink Hoffman, wanted for ripping off the street people, for pissing on the revolution, for fucking Jerry Rubin and YIP—looks like a comic book prince (fag), talks with a forked tongue (snake), favorite words: bread, cash, gold, me." I asked Zippie sympathizer Rex Weiner to give me some background:

REX WEINER: The idea that there was something called the Youth International Party was almost like an art concept rather than a program. There was great support for the Panthers, Young Lords, all of these groups that had their political programs well-articulated. The Yippies really didn't have any. There were the books that Jerry and Abbie wrote; *Revolution for the Hell of It* is the clearest declaration of purpose. Dada, surrealist, these things were closer to the Yippie intellect and aesthetic than an actual political program.

So, along comes Dana Beal from the Midwest, a very obsessed, articulate, self-defined revolutionary pot dealer. Dana was a Yippie theorist, if such a thing exists, and he would write manifestos, like Dostoevsky. Young, troubled, obsessed, fists knotted up and waving in the air, talking a mile a minute.

I never took him all that seriously, but Tom Forcade nurtured him, egged him on, and sort of adopted him as our own sort of firebrand—a loose cannon that we pointed in any direction that we wanted. The Zippies really only coalesced in '72, but in the lead-up to that is Dana was kind of fun in his hair-brained, dangerous—but useful to us—mode. You have to remember that Tom had gotten into a dispute with Abbie over *Steal This Book*. Suffice for your purposes to say it was a business dispute over services rendered—rendered by Tom and disputed by Abbie, and it was basically $5,000.

Dana did try to get close to Abbie and Jerry and become part of the Yippies, and he was rebuffed by them, thus making him sort of a renegade Yippie. He wanted to be loved by Abbie and Jerry, and the masses. The adulation that they enjoyed—rock-star adulation—he craved that, and when he wasn't brought into their inner circle, his disaffection joined together with Tom's became the genesis of the Zippies.

In '72, Abbie, Jerry, Ed Sanders, and a bunch of the Yippie stalwarts endorsed McGovern. The Zippies stood apart from that and, in fact, I even wrote an op-ed piece for the *New York Times*, pointing out that in '72, when the media narrative was sort of, "Oh, look, Abbie and Jerry have joined the mainstream of Democratic politics"—implying somehow that everything they'd done before was somehow invalidated—I pointed out that not everybody was going along with that. And, here was this new group called the Zippies. So, there's a fucking op-ed piece in the *New York Times* written by me. [*Laughs.*] Where I publicly declare, in other words, for the first time in the mainstream press, the word "Zippie" as opposed to "Yippie" is uttered.

OPPOSITE: A. J. Weberman, co-founder of the Zippies. Photo courtesy of A. J. Weberman

RIGHT: 1972 Press Conference, Jerry & Abbie endorse McGovern.

Dana Beal weighed in:

DANA BEAL: At the New Haven protest for Bobby Seale I met Tom Forcade, and he wanted to work with me. So I went to his loft—he was running the Underground Press Syndicate. Next, Forcade and I did a demonstration against the CIA and I got on national television, which led to my arrest. So during this time, Abbie and Tom had a falling out over *Steal This Book*. Abbie gives all the money to the Panther 21; he owes $3,000 to Tom. And Tom got really fucking incensed, overreacted, and started the Zippies.

I get out of jail and I go, immediately, to Miami for the '72 Democratic Convention. I got there, and Abbie said, "if you just denounce Tom, I will make you the leader of the Yippies." And the problem was that Abbie wasn't interested in it anymore. Ed Sanders, Jerry, and him were going to do the book *Vote*, which came out after the fucking election. They got a book contract!

I told Abbie, "Tom came and saw me in jail. Can't we all get along." The Yippies ended up denouncing me, and I have a lot of energy, so I responded. I still wanted to have antiwar demonstrations. The problem was Abbie and Jerry wanted to get along with McGovern, and the Zippies said, "No, this is going to be a mistake." Because we have to keep our distance from him, we have a distinct thing.

David Peel wanted to stay friends with all of them.

DAVID PEEL: Tom Forcade had an altercation with Jerry Rubin. Very ugly war between Jerry and Tom—who kept changing Yippies to "the Zippies." Abbie played along with Jerry and we had the Yippies and the Zippies fighting each other, they had a big breakup because it's all about power brokers and it's all perpetual jealousy. They had a big war going on and I made sure when I played the John Sinclair benefit in Ann Arbor I had both of them with me. Tom Forcade became my security guy and took care of the firecrackers on stage during my set, and Jerry Rubin was the drummer for my set when we played behind John & Yoko for the benefit.

Zippie cofounder A. J. Weberman laid it all out from beginning to end:

A. J. WEBERMAN: Tom Forcade decided that Jerry and Abbie had really burned out after the Chicago 8 trial. Then he didn't like them endorsing McGovern. They also had a contract with Warner Brothers for a book called *Vote*, about the '72 campaign.

So Forcade formed the Zippies. The Zippies were putting the "zip" back into YIP. We had actions. The Rock Liberation Front was part of the Zippies, and we all went down to Miami in 1972 to start a riot down there. Nixon was going to be reelected and I had John & Yoko behind me at the time, so they were financing the nefarious activities down there, but there was a lot of tension. The Yippies were staying at the Hotel Albion, which was a dumpy hotel, and the Zippies were staying in Flamingo Park, camping out in tents.

There were physical fights between Forcade and Abbie. We got into a fight with Abbie—and Ginsberg told me that he's been a pacifist all his life, but if there's one person he'd like to punch in the face it was me for attacking Abbie. You know, that it was all basically "mishegas." Then Jerry said Forcade was a cop. A contract went out on Jerry, so he got set up. Jerry suggested, "Well, let's have a conference in the pizza parlor on Bleecker & MacDougal." When he got there he sat down on this table. And Forcade's henchman Tim Bloom came in [and] kicked Jerry in the back, and the entire table that was anchored to the wall came loose.

After that, Jerry said he was willing to apologize. Right after, we were walking down the street together and we meet these other Zippies. They don't recognize Rubin (standing right next to me) and they say, "Hey, we heard Rubin is in town, let's fuck him up." We tell them, "Nah, be cool, man. Jerry's gonna straighten things out," so he knew that people were after him and he had to retract some of the ugly statements that he made.

Meanwhile, Ed Sanders would get on *The Alex Bennett Radio Show* and call me a cop, so we found out where he was living—and we went there and trashed his Land Rover. We put sugar in the gas tank but the fucking sugar wouldn't go down, we didn't have any water, so I had to piss in the gas tank to get the sugar to go down. I got arrested for indecent exposure. After a while, Abbie and I, we settled our differences and became close friends. It was crazy to fight with each other because Abbie was about to go underground. While he was a fugitive we made up. All of that shit was forgotten.

After the '72 election, the original Yippies went their separate ways and retired the name. The Zippies did what any enterprising Yippie would do. They co-opted the name and used it well into the '80s.

REX WEINER: [After Miami], they had a newspaper called the *Yipster Times*. They took over the mantle of Yippie and claimed it for their own. Abbie and Jerry just sort of washed their hands of it. It's not like they owned it. It'd be interesting to know if there was copyright on "Yippie."

Jerry Makes a Public Apology to the Zippies.

On the fourth page of the October 17, 1974 issue of the *Village Voice*, the headline read *"Jerry Rubin: YIP & Karma."* It was a letter of apology from Jerry to Forcade, Beal, and Weberman. Jerry's letter had the tone of a twelve-step recovery program as a result of the West Coast self-realization movement that he'd embraced after Nixon's reelection.

Jerry explains that he was in Miami hoping to get McGovern elected. His role was more of a journalist than a protester (he didn't participate in street demonstrations). His main focus was co-authoring the book *Vote*, and admits that he, Abbie, and Ed Sanders kept the bulk of the proceeds rather than donating them to YIP. He says that the Zippies went to Miami (in their words) "to make trouble—trouble for McGovern, trouble for Nixon, trouble for all politicians, left or right! . . . I used my relationship with the media to help project the idea that the Zippies were either 'police agents' or 'police provocateurs,' although I did not believe this at the time, or now."

Jerry apologizes for publicly embarrassing Weberman into apologizing to Dylan, in hopes that Dylan would join the anti-Nixon protest tour that he, along with John & Yoko, was attempting to get off the ground. He mentions that, as a guest on a then-recent episode of the *Dick Cavett Show*, when Cavett stated, "There are no more Yippies," he didn't disagree. But he stresses there were still YIP chapters across the country involved in the "guerilla theater and anarchist tradition" that he helped evolve. He makes it clear that he supports their activities, although "I am no longer a Yippie (except in spirit). I ask the media to stop referring to me as a 'Yippie' leader. My current activity is, like most people I know, finding out who I am. And finding out the relationship of who I am to the sociopolitical system we live in. And that makes life exciting enough."

[Almost a month to the day earlier (on September 18), Rubin had participated in a press conference with Allen Ginsberg and Ram Dass, calling for the atonement of Tim Leary's countercultural sins—mainly ratting out his defense attorney to the Federal government.]

ONE THING JERRY AND ABBIE DID FOR THE CITY OF MIAMI WAS TO BEEF UP THE TECHNOLOGY OF THE POLICE DEPARTMENT WITH THAT GRANT MIAMI GOT TO BUY ALL THIS STUFF.

—MCGOVERN STRATEGIST RICK STERNS, TO HUNTER S. THOMPSON

ABOVE: That's Patty Oldenburg between Jerry and Ed—with the white dove of peace.

OPPOSITE: Jerry meets the mayor of Miami, 1972.

I Wanna Go to Miami!

There was a surge of progressive energy at the '72 Democratic Convention. Women's rights were finally being recognized—Gloria Steinem and Betty Friedan were on the floor discussing the Equal Rights Amendment and backing congresswoman Shirley Chisholm for President. Chisholm had the distinction of being the first-ever major party black candidate for President, as well as the first woman to run for the Democratic presidential nomination. In front of TV cameras, feminist icon Flo Kennedy attacked reporters for their limited coverage of Chisholm. Underrepresented groups took her seriously, resulting in a decent amount of electoral votes. She came in fourth on a panel of thirteen.

Although he refused an invitation by Dave Dellinger to meet with the North Vietnamese, primary candidate George McGovern appeared on national television to deliver his key message to prospective voters: "Within ninety days of my inauguration, every American soldier and every American prisoner [in Vietnam] will be . . . back home in America where they belong." However, the convention had run way overtime—and McGovern didn't hit the stage till 3 a.m.!

The Democratic Party offered the Yippies press passes into the Miami Convention Hall. 1968 loomed large, and the Democrats knew they'd be better served by playing ball with the Yippies. Recently indicted for "instigating riots in Chicago," Jerry "was in the perfect position to use the paranoia of the politicians and theatrics of the media to have some electronic fun." Ever the master manipulator, Jerry removed his shirt during a press conference and announced that ten thousand Yippies were going to parade around nude during the Miami Convention.

Reporters didn't doubt Jerry's ability to pull this off; they just went ahead and announced on several local television stations that a nude march was coming into town. People began writing the newspapers, protesting a nude march that was never going to happen in the first place. "I doubt that I could have found five hundred Yippies to parade nude. But TV reporters are interested in drama. The public needs the image of nude Yippies to act out their own repressed fantasies; at the same time, it allows them to play the role of moralists."

Jerry is quick to point out that the manipulation was mutual; a tame image didn't make for good press. Had he "given a sober lecture on the history of Vietnam, the cameras would have been turned off." One Miami journalist told Jerry, "My paper would never print a picture of you smiling. That's *not* 'Jerry Rubin' to them." Despite sentiments like that, the irony that the Yippies were now welcomed into town was not lost on them. Jerry and Abbie wrote in the book *Vote*, "Standing on the floor of the Democratic Convention, surrounded by demonstrators turned delegates, the definition of who's inside and who's outside became blurred. The Democratic Convention in 1972 showed that the people who fought in the streets in the 1960s were right. We were guests within the Convention and Lyndon Johnson was the black sheep of the family. We were in—and [Mayor] Daley was out!"

In 1968, Rubin had declared, "When in doubt, burn. Fire is the revolutionary's god. Fire is instant theater. No words can match fire." Now Rubin's decree was, "Take your parents to the polls. Voting against Nixon unites kids and their parents." The Republicans held their Convention in Miami that year as well. Originally scheduled for San Diego, they changed it to Miami after it was revealed that that International Telephone & Telegraph (ITT) would pledge $400,000 if the Republicans came to San Diego, in exchange for the Department of Justice dropping an antitrust case against them.

They later canceled the Republican convention in San Diego, but at that point, Jerry was going to check things out and wanted a car. So we went to a car rental place in Santa Monica. And this old codger—he looked at the name, he looked at Jerry, and he looks at me. He says, "You're not the Jerry Rubin, are you?" Jerry, very innocently, said, "Who's that? What do you mean?" He goes, "That radical who goes around the country, causing all the trouble." And he said, "Oh no, that's not me." They rented him the car, and Jerry was in hysterics. He said, "You realize that in an hour from now the FBI is going to show up—and ask this guy whether he rented a car to Jerry Rubin?"
— *LARRY YURDIN, FM RADIO PIONEER*

McGovern said that the American people must "Vote for the Vietnamese people who cannot vote regarding the destruction of their own land." Rubin and Hoffman added, "From the street to the ballot box is not that long of a walk." When they arrived for the Democratic Convention, they received a warm greeting from the Mayor of Miami. He viewed them as celebrities who would bring fun and frolic to the proceedings along with the delegates themselves, who party as much as they pontificate. Jerry and Abbie had breakfast with Democratic celebs Warren Beatty and Julie Christie, with the conversation fully focused on the presidential campaigns, and not a mention of anyone's movies. They bonded over their disgust with Vietnam and Nixon.

A younger generation of Yippies showed up in Miami. Gabrielle Schang was part of this next wave and quickly fell in with Jerry, Ed Sanders, and company.

GABRIELLE SCHANG, *BERKELEY BARB* STAFF, PSYCHOTHERAPIST: Abbie, Jerry, and Ed got the money to fund the whole Yippie Youth International Party group to have events [to attract the older retired voters in Miami], and to stay at this rundown hotel, the Albion. The central Yippies stayed there, that was paid for. It was funded from an advance for this book called *Vote* that they were going to write after. I was with Ed Sanders then, so I spent my time with him or with the group of women who were involved. That was a big

time for the women's movement too; I was part of several women's things, demonstrations, making murals.

Jerry realized, "We gotta get a permit from the mayor." So they threw a "getting to know the mayor" party. Chuck [David T. Kennedy] somebody, this white-haired guy, the perfect picture of what a mayor should be. I remember watching Walter Cronkite with Jerry. Because he'd do stuff, and then he'd come back to the hotel, and check if Walter Cronkite's going to cover that.

Jerry had always been into health food. Everybody thought he was really weird, down in Miami, because he would go—it was fun to have dinner with these guys—but if you wanted to go with Jerry, you had to go to a macrobiotic place. He really was avid about this health food stuff, even then.

KATHY STREEM, PUBLIC DEFENSE ATTORNEY: We had a Yippie collective. We had stationery with our names on it. What happened is that all the [original] women in the Yippie movement threw the men out, but then Miami was coming, so the men find Gabrielle and me. We don't understand what's going on, because we're younger. Nancy Kurshan and the other women hated Gabrielle and I; we were these little miniskirt-wearing teenyboppers. But we think these men are cool, *even if you don't [laughs]*. I wouldn't like that, in retrospect.

And so we became . . . three women in this election. We did have some meetings, Gabrielle and Patty Oldenburg and me, but no one was really interested in what we had to say. Patty's ex-husband [sculptor Claes Oldenburg] made our poster; we were more that kind of people. We went to Miami for both conventions. I was interviewed on the TV news, and my parents saw it in New York. They didn't even know I was in Miami. Jerry and Abbie had press passes, so they could go into the convention.

ROBERT FRIEDMAN: I had a press pass through *University Review*. Miami was not violent. While there were arrests and some mayhem, the protests were just way more peaceful than Chicago '68 was. But remember who the Democratic Party candidate was in '72, George McGovern, who was as far left as the Democratic Party ever got. And in '68, it was Hubert Humphrey, who was about as "stuck in the middle" of the party as you could get. And so, the party had definitely moved to the left and therefore was more willing to put up with the Yippies and thousands of protesters outside. They didn't necessarily see it as a threat. And that's not true, obviously, of the Republican Party, which despised the whole notion of everything we stood for. And it's funny, because both of those events took place in Miami that summer.

Let me raise one thing about Stew Albert in Miami. Stew made a mark because part of his strategy was to ingratiate the Yippies and the Left to all the old Jews in Miami Beach. He was great at that. He'd go every morning out to the park in Miami Beach and just talk to people. Being a Jew from Brooklyn, he could relate.

Fellow Chicago 8 defendant Lee Weiner has no fond memories:

LEE WEINER: Seventy-two was a . . . not a good year. [*Laughter.*] We went down . . . I don't know whose lunatic notion it was to go down to Miami, to be at the conventions. I have no notion of why I agreed to go. But we did. And it was bad. There was celebrity, there was drugs, there were women . . . not good. We hung out at some hotel, whose name I can't remember. People were camping out at the parks, not us. What was the fuckin' drug? Quaaludes. 'Ludes . . . Bad fucking drug. And . . . I've never bothered to find appropriate language in relationship to that. I do know that a couple months later, as I told you, I had enough. I took every single name in my telephone book and burned it in an ashtray. Every single name.

In *From Yale to Jail*, Dave Dellinger remembered, "During the 1972 Miami Convention, the government tried to pacify the demonstrators by flooding them with Quaaludes. One of the chief middlemen who received the Quaaludes from the government and distributed them to demonstrators was a Zippie whom I knew. The Zippies were scornful of Abbie, Jerry, and Ed Sanders, who had endorsed McGovern, taking an optimistic view of achieving electorally the antiwar objectives for which they had demonstrated in Chicago four years earlier. This time, they were welcomed on the floor of the Democratic Convention."

Nixon's (Re)election in November '72.

In the end, McGovern alienated many of his left-wing supporters before it was time to cast a ballot. When Election Day arrived in November '72, the voters decided to support Nixon (with 47.1 million votes), who was still promising peace (just as he had back in '68), over McGovern (who received 29 million votes), whose antiwar stance was his main platform. The final tally of electoral votes was brutal: five-hundred and twenty for Nixon and only seventeen for McGovern—Nixon had won forty-nine out of the fifty states. For many, the bottom fell out of the movement when Nixon got reelected that November. Because of the fame he achieved from the Chicago 8 Trial, Jerry was seen as a "rock star" by high school and college students. Now it was as if Jerry's albums had stopped selling and he lost his recording contract.

GARY VAN SCYOC: After Nixon's reelection that was pretty much it for Jerry and me both. It was so deflating. It was so intense, and then it was just like the air went out, you know? For the rest of the '70s, Jerry expressed his frustration at seeing the movement fall apart and his neurotic attempts at trying to resuscitate it with ideas like forming a Dylan/Lennon supergroup that would tour against Nixon's campaign. He blamed his own inabilities as a leader for the movement running out of steam.

NIXON ELECTED IN LANDSLIDE;
M'GOVERN IS BEATEN IN STATE;

DICK NIXON
BEFORE HE
DICKS YOU

LANDSLIDE!

ON ELECTION NIGHT 1972, Jerry held a party in his apartment that should have been a McGovern victory celebration, but turned to disaster as Nixon crushed McGovern in a landslide victory. What transpired became a watershed moment for John & Yoko, with Jerry as a "guilty by association" accomplice. It set off what become known in Lennon mythology as the "The Lost Weekend." John & Yoko split up, and Lennon exited to Los Angeles to explore the decadent high life. It also marked the end of Jerry's close-knit relationship with the couple—although they would continue to socialize together occasionally for the remainder of Lennon's life.

Yoko herself has never shied away from discussing it, and, in the liner notes of the *John Lennon Anthology* box, she describes the scene at Jerry's that night. John was intoxicated, and he invited another woman to have sex in an adjoining room. Someone put on a Dylan album to help drown out the sounds. Another person tried to engage Yoko in a "isn't John wonderful" conversation. She describes how "something was lost that night" in their relationship. She writes, "Jerry thought it was terrible that I couldn't 'forgive' John." They were all "totally devastated" by McGovern's loss, which was why Lennon got so drunk. Later, she told him "that I thought a trial separation would be a good idea."

Lennon's dalliance had been with Jerry's roommate, Carol Realini, which added to the resentment that Lennon and Ono already felt toward Rubin for (in their view) hoodwinking them into joining the Revolution. After that election night party, just the sight of Jerry was a bitter reminder to John & Yoko of Lennon's callous cheating. Carol Realini told Ratso Sloman that Lennon had entered the Election Night Party "raving like a maniac" and "shouting at the top of his lungs." She added that Lennon had thought, up until that very day, that "there was gonna be a revolution," and it "was gonna be led by Abbie and Jerry, these great American radicals who he believed in. Now it seems like it was going down the drain, because here is Nixon getting elected by this huge landslide and here he, John Lennon, is within the same four walls as the leaders of the revolution . . . so he wants them to tell the answer. *What* are they gonna do and *when* is it gonna happen and what can he do to help? And he wasn't kidding.

"Apparently, earlier in the day, the truth started to dawn on him that the revolution wasn't happening. The truth was that he actually was looking at these people as some kind of heroes. *He had heroes!* That day was an epiphany in his life, it really was. He was screaming his guts out that he couldn't have any heroes either, and how could he have been so stupid to be telling his fans that he couldn't be their hero, when in fact he was doing the same thing [his fans] were doing, creating heroes in his own mind, one of whom was Jerry Rubin and sitting there in the room with him. Everybody was dumbfounded, but most of all Jerry. He was completely tongue-tied."

As Realini told Ratso Sloman, "Jerry had John Lennon for a hero, and John had Jerry for a hero." She describes John that night as "having a nervous breakdown," while Jerry remained silent and director Julian Beck and his wife, Judith Malina, tried to calm Lennon down. Realini describes Lennon as "getting more and more sober every second as the realizations were starting to penetrate, that this was like the end of his whole life."

Although it's undated and likely precedes that fateful evening, I found a letter on Apple Records stationery in Jerry's archives. Yoko sent it to him in the autumn of 1972. Referring to him in third person, she wrote, "Though I love Jerry—the fact is that Jerry is violent—basically longing for confrontation: the kind that happened in Chicago, is because his daddy and mommy died and he has the pain of losing them twice—first he was never close to them—second he lost them anyway." She goes on to say, "we can't sacrifice legs, arms and lives of our youth because of his personal pain that he is not aware of. We have to do it the hard way—which is patience and love—even for the ignorant pigs." The top, left-hand corner is singed—Jerry tried to burn the letter, then thought better of it. What makes this letter bemusing is that throughout 1972, Jerry never endorsed violence. He was suggesting a nationwide music tour by John & Yoko. At the Miami Democratic Convention, Jerry showed up with a press pass, eager to socialize with the establishment! As he told Jon Wiener during a 1980s interview, Lennon was the one who would get angry during private discussions and suggest violent acts.

Lennon blamed Jerry for all of his own personal and political follies of 1971–'72.

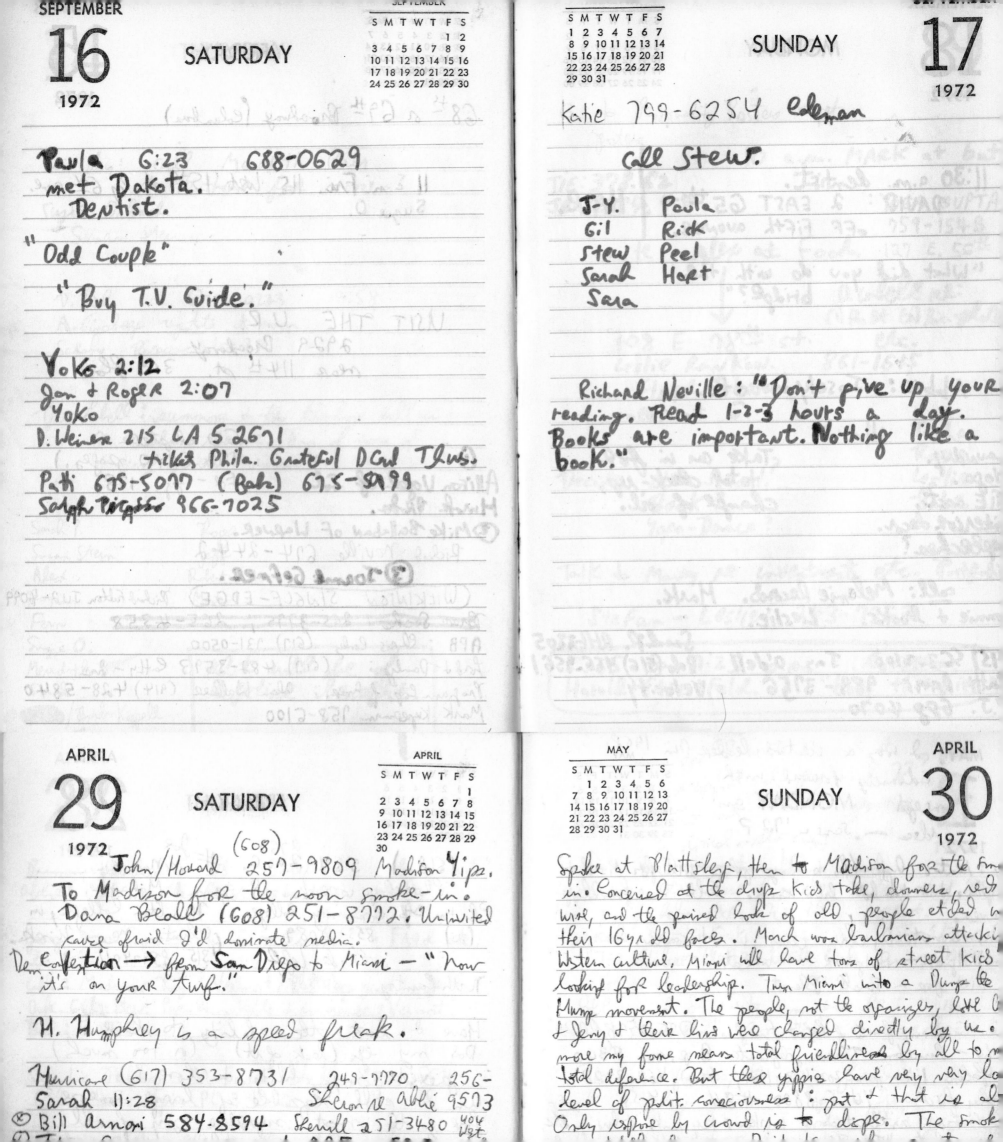

SEPTEMBER 16 SATURDAY 1972

S M T W T F S
1 2
3 4 5 6 7 8 9
10 11 12 13 14 15 16
17 18 19 20 21 22 23
24 25 26 27 28 29 30

Paula 6:23 688-0629
met Dakota.
Dentist.

"Odd Couple"

"Buy T.V. Guide."

Yoko 2:12
Jan + Roger 2:07
Yoko
D. Weiner 215 LA 5 2671
tickets Phila. Grateful Dead Thurs.
Pati 675-5077 (Babe) 675-5999
Salph Pirgador 966-7025

SUNDAY 17 1972

S M T W T F S
1 2 3 4 5 6 7
8 9 10 11 12 13 14
15 16 17 18 19 20 21
22 23 24 25 26 27 28
29 30 31

Katie 799-6254 Coleman

Call Stew.

J-Y.   Paula
Gil   Rick
Stew   Peel
Sarah   Hart
Sara

Richard Neville: "Don't give up your
reading. Read 1-2-3 hours a day.
Books are important. Nothing like a
book."

APRIL 29 SATURDAY 1972

S M T W T F S
1
2 3 4 5 6 7 8
9 10 11 12 13 14 15
16 17 18 19 20 21 22
23 24 25 26 27 28 29
30

(608)
John/Howard 257-9809 Madison Yips.
To Madison for the noon smoke-in.
Dana Beall (608) 251-8772. Uninvited
cause afraid I'd dominate media.
Dem Convention → from San Diego to Miami — "Now
it's on your turf."

H. Humphrey is a speed freak.

Hurricane (617) 353-8731   249-7770   256-
Sarah 11:28   Sharon & Abbie 9573
Bill Amori 584-8594   Sherill 251-3480 404
                                                West

MAY ... APRIL 30 SUNDAY 1972

S M T W T F S
1 2 3 4 5 6
7 8 9 10 11 12 13
14 15 16 17 18 19 20
21 22 23 24 25 26 27
28 29 30 31

Spoke at Plattsville, then to Madison for the smoke-
in. Concerned at the drugs kids take, downers, red
wine, and the pained look of old people etched in
their 16yr old faces. March was barbarians attacking
Western culture. Miami will have tons of street kids
looking for leadership. Turn Miami into a Dump the
Hump movement. The people, not the organizers, like Ed
& Jerry & their lives were changed directly by us.
more my fame means total friendliness by all to me,
total deference. But these yippies have very very low
level of polit. consciousness: pot & that is all.
Only response by crowd is to dope. The smok...

Sarah 11:28   Sharon re Abbie 9573
◯ Bill Arnon 584-8594   Sherill 251-3480   404
◯ Tina Grossman very impt. 795-0598   Wash.
call Abbie very impt. (617) 873-8536   ave.
Larry Sloman 233-6514   John/Howard 257-9809
John Warman 256-6325 tells message to
    Jim Rowen & Sue Rowen McGovern.
Larry Lichter & Anita 257-7960.
Peter Neufeld 256-7435   Yola 255-3874
rev. Ted 251-8772 Wagner   251-6401 Jane
                        7 FRANCIS ct.
Tuli to talk   2 p.m. Yip meet. 10 Langdon
Ruth
Jim Higgins   Arthur Lisch (717) 897-6619
Peter Coyote - introduce someone be fun DI 4-5460
Steve Gebhardt   to call in n.y.   (202) 223-7272
Stew (Carlin Decker Wsh. Post)   234-6168

level of polit. consciousness : yet & that is all.
Only response by crowd is to dope. The smoke-in
was totally lumpen. Don't know who parents are.
But kids are lumpen — & beaten down. Abbie & I
speak to lumpen & to college kids. alcohol beats
out dope.
Dave Ifshin (301) 299-4253 (202) 462-3922 5115 Sumner

Jim Higgins PL 3 1960   after 5 p.m.

Rick STERNS 543-8500 (202)

Change: (1) Repub. move from San Diego to Miami;
(2) fall of Muskie; (3) close fight between HHH & McG.

Abbie & I must visit Miami soon — as well as
Wsh. Make Yippie presence.

MAY I was a creative leader in 1968 1968
advancing forward with   MAY
1 concepts MONDAY and   S M T W T F S
idea — same in '72 ?   1 2 3 4 5 6
1972   7 8 9 10 11 12 13
                                  14 15 16 17 18 19 20
                                  21 22 23 24 25 26 27
                                  28 29 30 31

Pay: rent. Ask Yoko to pay phone bill for March &
April. Wait til both bills come. Call Dave Lubell re
taxes.
Dr. Gonstead, chiro clinic in Wisconsin.
  Bulger — Bulghur — wheat.
Diet for a Small Planet

Tina Grossman, friend of Robert Friedman 795 0598/10:29 a.m.
Cathy — Princeton Thurs. definite 8 p.m. $300
D. Ifshin 1:41 p.m. 202 483-1531; (202) 462-3922
Arthur Lisch YU 6-8800 #811   4:50
McG: link intellectuals & workers; key link & business etc.
In penal note: "The Thieu govt. is corrupt, why we die for
it." Nixon is a cowboy. McG. suit & tie radicalism
expresses what is best for Amer. Ideological election. Nixon
is the minority pres. Encourage trip to China, not bombs in
Hanoi. Loosen the oppression of the Amer. people. JFK good
cause he engage people in a polit. crusade — care more for
drama than content. Same with protest. Yips always serious &
connected to a polit. goal & strategy. What & Wallace say is
not crucial in this elect. camp. cause he releases right & left
the Amer. people. Viet. Vet. most impt. figure in country
today: He knows Amer. a conservative country — NYC blinds
us. Will Amer. let blacks, youth, intellect, college, urban, poor,
take over power from Christ. tough-fighters, white Amer.? McG.
to that. Amer. out to face a big defeat & a loss in
power & view of its role & self-identity, big change

JUNE   In 68 wrote seminal &
S M T W T F S   inspirational papers. In 72 ?   **MAY**
      1 2 3   put out positive
4 5 6 7 8 9 10   TUESDAY political **2**
11 12 13 14 15 16 17   statements.
18 19 20 21 22 23 24   1972
25 26 27 28 29 30   ~~Dr. Neuman appt~~ 10 a.m.

Yippies change politics cause of me & ab. endorsement of McG.
From zap to help McG. No 1968 repeat.
  speak Lay-to-Oak. City: Oak. State Univ.
  Ted Glasser (405) 377-0854. Oak. Univ. Norman.

Abbie and I write an article: "Why We
Endorse McGovern" for Life or someplace ?

The more famous, the less freedom. More
people watching you.   Capit. in Amer. no longer
                   want to be capitalists.
I know I eat food in NYC: nowhere else.
Hard to eat food on the road.

internally within & need for someone to guide through those
changes without bloodshed & mayhem & death. Most. provided
Amer. — now not spitting in Amer.'s face but explaining to people
how change won't hurt them necessarily. Still big role for
Dems. cause they keep the issue alive. For a moment we
give up idea of revol. to see big changes in country: if poor
get pol., cult. diversity, loss of power in World & self-image, socialize,
Diff is: We believe demos. & disruptions & strikes etc.
most impt. part of political process — get attention — force
issue — dramatize — make McG. & delays possible. Create jobs.
Workers, housewives, retirees should demonstrate. Our work
just begin when McG. become Pres. Abbie & I are trying

The Daybook.
Jerry's 1972 daybook shows that he practically moved from Manhattan to San Francisco within hours of the election being called. He shed his Yippie identity and popped up in the Bay Area just weeks later—freshly shaved, with shorter hair, and spouting the virtues of self-awareness therapy. He was burned out, and, arguably, had he remained in the political realm, he may have suffered a nervous breakdown.

DAVID PEEL: After all was said and done and Jerry stopped working with Lennon, we were at a bagel shop on 8th Street. The war in Vietnam was winding down; he said, "There's not really much for me to do and I'm pretty bored right now." I said, "Jerry, look at the other things you can do besides . . . You know, we helped stop the war in Vietnam, we've still got active civil rights going on, we've got the Youth International Party," and that's when he said, "I'm bored. The war is over." He just didn't know what to do and that's when he started, little by little, turning from Yippie to Yuppie.

ABOVE: Gabrielle Schang and the boys at the Yippie office in Miami talking to the Mayor to persuade him to let them use the public golf course for their "events."

Aftermath.
With the reelection of Nixon, Jerry and John Lennon weren't the only ones to see their dreams of a revolution smashed. For many, "the 1960s were over," and it was time to go back to reality.

LEE WEINER: Look. You must understand the refugee status. You know how I got my first credit card? I got it because I was living with a woman who was my direct boss at work. She was able to sign the fuckin' thing. That was part of my reintroduction into the world. Not reality, a *reality*. That transition—I was able to make it because people didn't know my face. Shave my beard—gone. I had accumulated a bunch of real-world credentials. Jerry never did. So in combination with not having those credentials and having his name, I was too cowardly to accept that burden. I've always defined it that way. It was a "cheap out" that I took. Jerry was not gonna have that easy path. Nor did Abbie, nor did many people—if you didn't write well, if you didn't sing well, if you didn't do something . . . nobody survived it. Nobody in that group survived it, although some struggled their way out from it.

Jerry, early on, said, "Nobody will ever hire me. I can't get work outside." By that time, I was already working. I mean, it's true, when I got work, people thought, "Why'd [you] come to work here? To organize the Communist party?" So it was tough, but I didn't have the celebrity Jerry had. So he had a very narrow path. And so, was I going to begrudge him going in the direction he did?

GERALD LEFCOURT: I agree with what you said. When the movement crashed—*and it crashed*, there's no question—nobody knew what to do. Jerry had to find something. And he found est, and Rolfing, and it was therapeutic. We were all in a state of depression beyond belief. And so that morphed into networking . . . and it's really that he had to find something to do. Jerry is a passionate person. And when he found something that intrigued him and he liked, he got involved with it, emotionally.

MARTIN KENNER: Yeah, but it also seemed slightly out of place, too. Jerry was completely floundering, trying to find a role for himself. I always felt lucky—that I was not famous, and I could just naturally glide into another life after the movement. And Jerry, you know, the headlines: *Yippie Becomes Stockbroker!* While Steve Tappis, the ex-Weatherman, could be on the floor of the Chicago Mercantile Exchange, and no one knew who the hell he was. Or I could be a commodity-trading advisor, which I was.

So Jerry had a hard time, and Abbie was underground. Abbie was like the Japanese soldier left on the island after World War II, in the hills. So he missed that, and when he resurfaced, he had a hard time adjusting. Jerry had to do the adjustment in public, and it was hard. And you know, look at some of the others. Rennie flipped out with that thing. And Tom was a bit of a drunk married to a multi-millionaire actress. None of the so-called leaders had an easy transition.

So it's got to be put in that context, too. That when the movement fell apart—*and it fell apart with a thud*—somewhere between '71 and '73. Nixon was smart to end the draft. A lot of these guys were scrambling. Lee Weiner and John Froines were not famous. And I wasn't. We could go on with our lives. And the other people, whether they were famous, or felt they were famous, felt the need for self-justification.

MOE HIRSCH, UC BERKELEY PROFESSOR/VDC ACTIVIST: Yeah, Jerry's one of these people like Mario Savio. They were great at these certain kinds of protest activities, but then after that, they had nothing to do. That was my feeling about Jerry and his "therapist" time. My feeling was that he was kind of lost. It happened to a lot of people. A lot of people were attracted to the whole protest movement, and then when that died down, like you said, they had no place to go. But some of them stayed around. There was a guy named Frank Bardacke, did you run into him?

FRANK BARDACKE, VIETNAM DAY COMMITTEE/LABOR ACTIVIST: [When Jerry went through his various changes] I just said, "that's the same old Jerry," you know. He wasn't that egomaniacal. There are a lot of people who say that, I don't agree with that. I think those people who tell you he sincerely believed in what he was doing are accurate.

RENNIE DAVIS: For me, the movement ended in Ann Arbor [at the John Sinclair Rally in December '71]. All the wind was sucked out right there. The wind you're talking about—the '60s movement, as opposed to the public sentiment. It wasn't that Nixon got reelected, and that's what pulled the plug. It was the fact that we could not go on. That it was over.

See, you have to understand. From the Student Strikes [including the killings at Kent State] of spring 1970 came the "Cooling of America." It was over. Then came this amazing, heroic thing with May Day [May 1971 in Washington, DC]—that just came out of nowhere, and we did it again—one last hurrah. Now it's definitely over. And then came John Lennon [and his plan to tour the country], and I'm like, "Oh my God, we're gonna breathe life into this thing one more time." And when John's plug was pulled [with immigration coming after him], it was over. That's how I feel. If you were out there talking to people, and the base for doing these things, it was over before Nixon's '72 election. If you want to mark the end of the '60s movement, I would say it was after Ann Arbor [December 10, 1971].

I do remember Jerry saying explicitly that, "The '60s are dead, Jonah." Like there was a corpse there, and he wanted to pry me away from my old attachments, and I was still definitely attached. Some people say the '60s ended in December 1969; I don't think that's accurate. The May Day demonstrations were an indication that they went on—they continued into the '70s.
—*JONAH RASKIN*

They Just Saw It from Another Point of View.

LENI SINCLAIR: To me, the movement ended the day those four students got killed at Kent State. That woke up white, middle-class youth to realize this wasn't just having fun, going out on the streets with flowers in your hair. It was much more serious, and then it kind of stopped—but it really hasn't stopped, it just takes different forms.

These days I don't have time to demonstrate. We have too many responsibilities, the next generation has to pick up the bat. And when the whole Occupy movement happened, I was unable to participate. God, I wish I had time to pitch a tent in Grand Circus Park and sleep there, but I have too much to do! [*Laughs.*] We used to go to national conferences, hitch rides with people and go anywhere across the country, but those days are over to afford to do that kind of stuff anymore.

ROBERT FRIEDMAN: I hung around with *University Review* until it went out of business in 1975. Politically myself, Stew Albert, and others stayed focused on the Vietnam War. And that didn't end until '75 or so. I don't think the focus shifted. People were despondent, in many ways, politically. And you had parts of the left splitting off and becoming more violent: the Weather Underground movement. But yet, a large chunk continued organizing demonstrations against the war in Vietnam. And that stayed the focus, as it did for Stew, Judy Gumbo, and for lots of other people.

COUNTRY JOE MCDONALD: There were a lot of people who—it was like the "Flavor of the Day." And people, if you grew up like I did in a union family, a political family, we knew it had been going on for generations and we continued to go on. Just because an ultra-conservative gets elected, there's no reason to pack it in. They come and go.

But then, what did they think when Watergate happened and Nixon got kicked out? Did they think, "Oh, I'll recommit myself"? No! Because you don't actually recommit. What you do is, slogan-wise, *think globally, act locally*. You work every day according to your social, political, moral belief system. It's a day-to-day thing. It's a difficult line to toe. People got killed, but there is a huge rank-and-file of people who are working toward making a better life for everybody and that goes on today. It's never going to end. America's a very peculiar place, as far as freedom is concerned.

Gabrielle Schang, Kathryn Streem, (Rennie Davis behind), Judith Mirkinson, and Jerry in Miami, 1972.

Goodbye to All That.
Robin Morgan became an internationally acclaimed feminist. She authored many books and served as editor in chief of *Ms.* magazine. But while still part of the Yippie brigade, she took "*a pair of needle nose pliers and a blowtorch*" to the radical Left. In 1970, she penned the infamous essay "Goodbye to All That," which ran in the New York underground paper *Rat*. It was quickly reprinted in other papers, followed by numerous feminist anthologies ever since. She declared, "Let it all hang out. Let it seem bitchy, catty, dykey, Solanisesque, frustrated, crazy, nutty, frigid, ridiculous, bitter, embarrassing, man-hating, libelous, pure, unfair, envious, intuitive, low-down, stupid, petty, liberating. We are the women that men have warned us about . . . Goodbye, goodbye forever, counterfeit Left, counterleft, male-dominated cracked-glass mirror reflection of the Amerikan Nightmare. Women are the real Left."

[Author's Note: "Solanisesque" is a reference to Valerie Solanas, the woman who shot Andy Warhol and the author of the radical feminist tract the "S.C.U.M. Manifesto." Solanas was represented by radical lawyer Flo Kennedy.]

Morgan listed many of the key women of the revolutionary movement: *"Free Kathleen Cleaver! Free Anita Hoffman! Free Bernardine Dohrn! Free Leni Sinclair! Free [Judy] Gumbo! Free Nancy Kurshan!"*

Robin also called Nancy "[Jerry's] woman, the power behind the clown." Nancy told me, in 2013, that although the statement wasn't accurate, "I knew what she was getting at," even though Morgan herself "was in a relationship with a man at the time. And at the time, I hated it. It really pissed me off. But, it made me think. *What am I doing?* And I thought and I thought, and I was very uncomfortable, but I think it really helped me change."

Without the support of the women in their lives, many Yippie men were rudderless. When Nancy left Jerry, he called it the equivalent of a nervous breakdown: "The next day I furiously destroyed my apartment, running through it naked, crying, screaming, at the top of my lungs. I alternated between rage and getting down on my hands and knees to beg Nancy to stay. I was mad, insane; I could not bear to be alone and insisted that friends sleep over to keep me company." Aside from the emotional toll, it left him without the logistical support he needed to be a revolutionary leader. In his 1972 personal diaries, Jerry occasionally laments the break up, some two years after it happened.

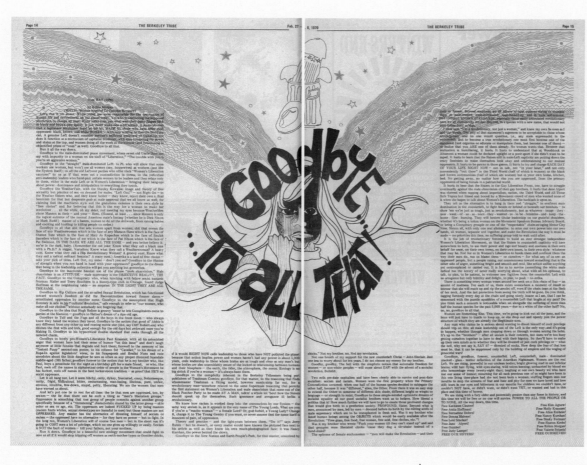

Jerry wrote in his memoir, in 1976, "Women abandoned the male-dominated New Left movement, leaving men without a work force. We were as chauvinistic as the society itself, radicals as far as Vietnam and blacks were concerned, but imitation John Waynes in our personal lives. Without women, the movement was over. Although they were dominated by men and the male image, women were the soul and heart of the movement, and often its fist, brain, and voice."

RATSO SLOMAN: I think Jerry learned a lot from the backlash of the women's movement. Jerry, Abbie, Ed Sanders, all those male chauvinist pig leaders . . . I think they all learned a lot from the backlash from the women in the movement. And I think Jerry became . . . a much more inclusive person, in some respects.

In a 2014 conversation with Tom Miller, he recalled some late-night conversations he had with Jerry, around the time of Jimi Hendrix's and Janis Joplin's deaths in late September and early October 1970. Jerry missed Nancy badly.

TOM MILLER: It was extraordinary because it was a very different personality. It was not the public Jerry Rubin, it wasn't even the private Jerry Rubin, it was somebody baring his soul, like, "What am I going to do without Nancy?" He depended so much on Nancy emotionally—I don't know about intellectually, but certainly he would bounce ideas off of her. Either way, she was his support mechanism, and on the third night—there were nights where we would just go walk for hours, and on one of the nights . . . It wasn't Janis Joplin; it must've been Jimi Hendrix—one of the first major rock drug suicides took place. Without Nancy there was no one there to support him. I remember the phrase he said and it just freaked me because he was so innocent: "Tom, you're my Nance." He didn't even say "Nancy." He just said, "Nance."

One of the things that distinguished Jerry from Abbie, privately and publicly, is that Jerry was willing to embarrass himself and show his vulnerability.

TOM MILLER: Good words, that's exactly what he was showing on those nights we went on walks. He had nothing to rely on. No one to bounce things off of. "Tom, you're my Nance." I've never forgotten that. I've never written it up, either. Anyway, there you are.

In a 2013 email, Robin Morgan agreed that Nancy was a vital part of the movement: "More so than any of the guys, for that matter, in intelligence, quiet accomplishment, and getting things done . . . You can quote me on that."

Women's Lib Stages a Sit-In

Post Photo by Terrence McCarten

Members of Media Women occupy offices at the Ladies Home Journal, 641 Lexington Av, today, where they demanded that the magazine give women greater voice in operations Story on page 38

We Are Everywhere: Jerry Goes at it Alone, Without Nancy.

Nancy Kurshan had left Jerry by the time his second book, *We Are Everywhere*, was being readied for publication, so he sought editing elsewhere. The book was scribbled by hand in the Cook County Jail, and then smuggled out in bits and pieces. It chronicles several incarcerations, along with rants about "a defendant's inside view of The Conspiracy Trial . . . the Weather Underground, the Black Panther Party, LSD, Women's Liberation, Walter Cronkite, Judaism, street fighting, and the coming revolution." Jerry describes working on the book in the Cook County Jail (which is also where Abbie worked on part of *Steal This Book*):

WE ARE EVERYWHERE.

BY JERRY RUBIN

HARPER COLOPHON BOOKS/CN 245/$1.95

For seven hours, until noon, I just poured out my insides until my fingers hurt like hell, my mind felt like a block of wood, my body was exhausted . . . I was scared to death that guard might rip off my notebook so I hid it under my mattress when I wasn't in the cell. I lied to the guards as to what I was doing. Guards told me that if I was writing a book it would be taken away from me and burned when I was being discharged from the jail . . .

Every week my lawyer came to see me and I tore out the pages I had written, hid them inside legal briefs and held my breath as I was searched by guards on my way to a lawyer's conference. Whew! Made it! Then I'd exchange my legal papers with the journal inside. That's how I smuggled the book out of Cook County Jail.

Stew Albert helped whip it into shape, but Tom Miller did much of the heavy lifting.

TOM MILLER: Well, yeah, it's hard to polish Jerry. To polish it simply meant just clean it up. If you took the politics out of it and you took Jerry's enormous ego out of it, it was a series of sentences that had to come to a stop, and then have a new paragraph . . . Although I can't take credit for being the one person who did it. Because by the time I saw the finished product, I said, "Oh, yeah, I don't remember this section, but somebody did a good job on that." The book itself I thought was just dreadful, but it was well put together.

The Federal Bureau of Investigation's War on Yippie Terror.

Although the organization is best known for its actions against the Panthers, Yippies, and other radical groups of the era, J. Edgar Hoover started the COINTELPRO (Counter Intelligence Program) in 1956 to circumvent Supreme Court rulings. He wanted to use subversive tactics on law-abiding organizations. Its original target, the Communist Party, is no surprise. "Expose," "disrupt," and "neutralize" were commonplace terms on internal FBI memos. Whenever the FBI saw a weak link within a group, like the growing divide between Jerry and Abbie or Newton and Cleaver, they were not above forging letters to stir the pot. In those heady times it was easy to fuel paranoia. And of course, the usual array of wiretaps, undercover agents, stolen mail, and planted and fake information was always at COINTELPRO's disposal. The most telling sign of their illegal, wicked ways was when the members of the Weather Underground resurfaced toward the end of the '70s. Many of the charges were dropped (even though they took credit for the bombings), due to prosecutorial misconduct, and the FBI not wanting to reveal their own dirty secrets.

We Are Everywhere is dedicated to the Weather Underground and includes the FBI's Wanted poster of Bernardine Dohrn.

JUST THE MINUTE THE FBI BEGINS MAKING RECOMMENDATIONS ON WHAT SHOULD BE DONE WITH ITS INFORMATION, IT BECOMES A GESTAPO. WE ARE A FACT-GATHERING ORGANIZATION ONLY. WE DON'T CLEAR ANYBODY. WE DON'T CONDEMN ANYBODY.

—J. EDGAR HOOVER

MARK RUDD, THE WEATHER UNDERGROUND COFOUNDER: The WU (including the predecessor, Weatherman faction of SDS) and the Yippies were extremely close. I can speak definitively for the period when I was still in leadership, to the end of 1969. We always considered Abbie and Jerry and Stew and the whole crowd to be brothers and sisters. This began, for me, in the fall of 1967, when I found myself sharing a holding cell with Abbie in the Tombs in NYC. Post–1969, I think the close relationship continued.

I first ran into Jerry at an IHOP [International House of Pancakes] in Berkeley in the fall of 1968. He was with Phil Ochs! Then we hung out a little in NYC, but I remember too little specifics of my time with Jerry and Nancy Kurshan. You may recall the goofy footage in the Weather Underground documentary featuring Nancy doing a press conference after a bombing: 'We didn't do it, but we dug it!'"

Sometime in the late '70s, Jerry stayed with me when he came to speak at the University of New Mexico. I took him for a ride out in the mountains east of Albuquerque, on the Turquoise Trail to be exact. He freaked out, saying he was really spooked to be out in the middle of nowhere. He wouldn't get out of the car to look around; he just wanted to be taken back to the city. *Now there's an urban guy.*

Well before the age of cell phones and emails being scrutinized by the NSA (National Security Agency), government agents were infiltrating antiwar organizations, and landline phones were the target of surreptitious surveillance. Sam Leff, who had known Jerry since his days as a student in Israel in the early '60s, told me about how the FBI's harassment affected Jerry:

SAM LEFF: I hadn't known, when we reconnected with Jerry in 1967, that through his activism in Berkeley it had already put a big mark on his back. [Hence the reason he was called into HUAC the first time around.] But the point is that the FBI was not just investigating. They were very much focused on the leadership of the Yippies. When I first got involved with the Yippies, we had no idea that by my calling Jerry it would put me into a situation of being watched.

Jerry's line was tapped. I've seen the FBI files. And there are things that happened in Jerry's life, thereafter, that were not necessarily his doing. And the same goes for Abbie, and even myself. A half-dozen different government agencies were actively employing people to try to undermine the antiwar movement. And the Yippies were, in their own particular way, the most threatening of the various groups. The FBI had decades of experience of screwing up the Communist-Socialists, the various leftists, what we called "the old Left." But with the Yippies, this was a whole other breed that they didn't know what to do with. And so, the FBI were involved in many different ways. And Jerry had a big mark on his back.

BARBARA GULLAHORN: Rennie Davis flew me out from California to Washington to help organize a demonstration, and one day Abbie called from New York and said he'd be late coming back. We started chatting away but he was calling from a pay phone, and his coins ran out. And all of a sudden, another voice came on, and said, "That's okay, operator, this is so and so number something," and Abbie and I said, "Who are you?" And he said, "I'm an agent with the FBI, and I just couldn't stand it anymore. *I couldn't stand listening to you Commie Pinkos talk about the things you talk about. You should be ashamed of yourselves.*" And the FBI agent went on and on. And Abbie made a quip and we hung up.

In Jerry's 1972 daily diary, he talks about how he can't get a driver's license in New York, because the DMV was harassing him—so he has to get one in Vermont or New Hampshire.

NANCY KURSHAN: And the IRS was harassing us as well.

SAM LEFF: Hoover said, "We want [Jerry and Abbie] to feel like there's an FBI man behind every mailbox." They really went to extremes. Another way of looking at this, was that Jerry and Abbie took a lot of heat for a lot of other people who were very much involved. There were people who were ready to come forward if anything happened. Because we knew Abbie and Jerry were out front, and totally vulnerable. After Abbie got his nose broken because Nixon's thugs went after them, there's a tape recording from the White House: *"We got Abbie, we got Hoffman."* That's what Nixon said. So, people were aware that Jerry and Abbie were really taking the heat. And when you look through the FBI files, you realize how very much they were. And so, in a way, their being a duo was good for them, because it wasn't just one person for the police state to try to kill off, but two of them. That was almost a little bit of protection.

STELLA RESNICK: Jerry and I always joked that our phone was tapped, but who knew. But we were very careful what we said over the telephone. And it exists to this day. [*Laughs.*] Sometimes somebody says something that I don't want to be heard, and I say, "I don't know what you're talking about." And people say, "Stella, come on, this isn't the '60s." I don't care. I just don't trust the telephone. You know Dick Gregory's great line. He was convinced that his phone was tapped. And somebody said to him, 'What makes you think your phone is tapped?' And he says, "*Well, if you're a black man and you don't pay your phone bill, and they never disconnect your phone, you figure your phone must be tapped.*"

Abbie Goes Underground. In August 1973, Abbie was arrested for trying to sell cocaine to undercover police officers. Citing COINTELPRO, Abbie claimed that the drugs had been planted, and that he'd been coerced into making a deal. To avoid what looked like a setup to put him behind bars for a long, long time, Abbie jumped bail, got plastic surgery, and went underground. While Abbie maintained his innocence, recent (anonymous) interviews for this book claim that Abbie *did* deal drugs.

ANONYMOUS: You really have to contextualize all of this, because he wasn't a "dope dealer," but he was a drug dealer. He was justifying it. It was a different time. He [borrowed] from a community Bail Fund to make that cocaine deal where he got busted. Abbie went and got it all [about $10,000] to make this deal, and then was going to return it.

STELLA RESNICK: It was the middle of the night. We were sleeping when the phone rang that he got busted. And we were beside ourselves. We were so scared what would happen to Abbie, he could be thrown in jail for life, such strong laws at the time. And then he got out on bail, and then another call in the middle of the night, sometime later. Abbie said that he was going to skip bail, and he was going underground, and he was saying goodbye to us. And Jerry cried.

TIMOTHY LEARY AND THE YIPPIES.

IN EARLY '68, PAUL KRASSNER asked Timothy Leary to come to New York to discuss a coalition between Leary's "people" (the hippies) and the newly formed Yippies. Krassner explained that he, Jerry, and Abbie dropped acid on New Year's Eve, and "had revelations about margining the entire spectrum of dissenting Americans in a Young People's Party" (Yippies). In Leary's view, their LSD trip "had apparently imprinted an urban-socialist vision, which they expressed in a new style of political theater." In his *Flashbacks* memoir, Leary said, *"The Yippies became the urban political expression of the Baby Boom, the first party not to deal with voting blocs or platforms but with information, media images, neurological campaigning. Guerrilla raids, not on the Bastille but on the Six O'clock News."* Despite being a media whore himself, Leary was not impressed. He considered the Yippies to be Anti-American! He chastised them for their "old-fashioned leftist negativity, a pessimistic ghetto-socialist distrust of what [America] stood for." In the weeks leading up the Democratic Convention, he "argued passionately" with Jerry and Abbie "against moving into enemy turf in Chicago." Leary foresaw a bloodbath and a win for Nixon. At one point, he suggested "a counter-convention in San Francisco," but the Yippies weren't interested. Leary knew that "if Nixon won, especially if he won on the basis of a reaction to youthful violence," then he'd "be in a lot of trouble." With Nixon in the White House, the FBI would tighten a noose that they'd been threatening

him with for years. Ultimately, Leary sat the Convention protests out, but got called as a witness at the Chicago 8 Trial.

During questioning, Leary declared himself "the Democratic candidate for Governor in California," stating his occupation as "a religious ordained minister, and a college lecturer." Leary described meetings with Jerry and Abbie, offering insight into their thoughts about Chicago: *"Mr. Rubin pointed out that since the Democratic Party was meeting here, there was great concern about having police and having National Guard and they were bringing in tear gas. Mr. Rubin pointed out that it could possibly be violent here, and both Mr. Rubin and Allen Ginsberg said that they didn't think that we should come to Chicago if there was a possibility of violence from the soldiers or the police."*

After LBJ stepped down, Leary and the two Yippies spoke again: *"The meaning of a 'celebration of life' on our part, as opposed to Mr. Johnson, was lost since the man we were attempting to oppose was not going to come to Chicago. At that time, Jerry Rubin pointed out that Robert Kennedy was still alive, and many of us felt that he represented the aspirations of young people, so we thought we would wait. I remember Mr. Rubin saying, 'Let's wait and see what Kennedy comes out with as far as peace is concerned. Let's wait to see if Kennedy does speak to voting people, and if Kennedy does seek to represent the peaceful, joyous, erotic feelings of young people.'"*

In early 1970, Leary had been charged with possession of two roaches, which had been reportedly planted by a cop searching the ashtray of Leary's car. The court awarded him ten years for less than a half-ounce of marijuana. Before he landed a gig lecturing at Harvard, Leary had been a research psychologist at the Oakland-based Kaiser Foundation, where he devised a personality test to help classify prisoners, allocating them to different levels of incarceration. When Leary got arrested, he was handed the very test that he had developed years before, and therefore knew how to frame answers that landed him in a minimum security prison in San Luis Obispo, making it easy for him to bust out. With the aid of his lawyer Michael Kennedy, Leary escaped from prison in September 1970 and made his way to Algeria via the Weather Underground. Jerry and Abbie sent Stew Albert (with the blessing of Huey Newton) over to meet with Eldridge Cleaver and pave the way for Leary's appearance.

As Stew Albert listened to Cleaver, he became excited, announcing that he would "return to America with good tidings of the grand alliance, arranging for more counterculture people to join [Cleaver & Leary] in Algiers." October 22, 1970 was Tim Leary's fiftieth birthday, and the Yippies wanted to celebrate with him in style. Jerry and Abbie couldn't leave America because they were out on bond from the Chicago conspiracy charges. So Stew returned to the Mediterranean city with Anita Hoffman, Martin Kenner, Jonah Raskin, and Bernardine Dohrn's sister, Jennifer. Leary and Cleaver greeted this band of outsiders at the airport—and according to Robert Greenfield's Leary biography, he promptly handed Anita a joint and said, "*Welcome to the Third World. I've been trying to get Eldridge to do acid but he's uptight. If we could trip together, we'd be much closer.*" The visiting dignitaries were hoping that "the [white] revolutionary youth movement and the black liberation struggle" could form a bond.

JONAH RASKIN: I got to know Stew Albert in 1970; there was a Yippie delegation to Algiers, when Timothy Leary was there with Eldridge Cleaver. I was on that trip, with that delegation. We all stayed in a Muslim hotel, and Stew and I shared a bed together. No funny business, but it was funny. Stew had not packed a suitcase, or even a backpack. He had a toothbrush. That's the only thing that he took. I mean, I had a suitcase, you know? *He wore the same clothes for a week!*

Stew was definitely trying to mediate between Leary and Eldridge. He admired Eldridge a great deal, and had known him from Berkeley. And was a strong supporter of the Panthers. But, Eldridge was . . . Well, the whole thing was kind of strange. The Black Panthers had this embassy in Algiers. I mean, it looked like any other embassy. The North Korean ambassador would show up in a chauffeured limousine, and Eldridge would meet him. It was kind of nutty, and some of the Panthers were armed. Eldridge had an AK-47, which he used to like to sit down and hold in his lap. He placed Leary under house arrest.

Eventually, the Acid Guru got on Cleaver's nerves. He detained Leary and his wife Rosemary. In a radio broadcast heard across the Bay Area, he declared, "There have been many hippies and Yippies tripping over here to see their god [Leary], and they bring sacrificial gifts to their god, and we want them to know that it's not acceptable to us here and you will not receive a warm or a happy welcome if you show up. What I'm saying here also applies to the Jerry Rubins, the Stew Alberts, and the Abbie Hoffmans, and the whole silly psychedelic drug culture, quasi-political movement, which they are part [of] . . . We're through. We're finished with relating to this madness . . ." At Jerry's funeral in December 1994, Eldridge told the gathered mourners, "Jerry symbolized the aspirations of youth, we all love him and look forward to being with him in another place."

Leary escaped the Black Panthers' compound, landing in Switzerland to record an album with Krautrock band Ash Ra Tempel, titled *Seven Up*. To make an outlaw's story short, he returned to America to serve out his sentence. This where the old cliché "truth is stranger than fiction" really kicks in. Leary demanded a show trial, asking for "Dennis Hopper, George McGovern, Jerry Rubin, and the Rolling Stones" to testify. The government ignored him and kept the trial moving at a brisk pace. Leary was sent to Folsom Prison, and incarcerated in the 4–A adjustment area. Leary recalled, in his 1983 memoir *Flashbacks*, that an experienced prisoner informed him, "That's where they stow the real motherfuckers. Folsom is the asshole of the prison system, and 4–A is the bottom of that!"

Leary had his own cell. Next door was a "guy sitting in the lotus position, looking like Jesus Christ," who wanted to know if he took sugar and cream in his coffee, and if he liked honey. This friendly cellblock mate handed over reading material, including *The Teachings of the Compassionate Buddha*, written by E. A. Burtt; a survey of G. I. Gurdjieff's thoughts; and the old classic for Heads everywhere, *The Teachings of Don Juan*, by Carlos Castaneda, whom Leary knew personally. Over the next week, the generous, as-yet-unidentified friend gave Leary organic honey and graham crackers. Finally, his fellow prisoner began to speak to him: "So you finally made it. I've been watching you fall for years, man. I knew you'd end up here. I've wanted to talk to you for a long time. I wanted ask you how come you blew it. You had everyone looking up to you. You could have led the people anywhere you wanted." Leary "suddenly realized the identity of the only other person that [he] was allowed to talk to"—Charles Manson!

The prison psychologist that treated them both, Edward Wesley Hiler, told reporter John Bryan, "They liked each other very much, but they were both on big power trips. They were both megalomaniacs and both felt they were sort of Supermen." After weeks of dialoguing, Leary asked Manson what his vision was. "Death and time," was Manson's reply. Leary was eager to cooperate with the Feds. He ratted out his lawyer Michael Kennedy (who had supposedly helped orchestrate Leary's prison escape with the Weather Underground), and even petitioned publishing magnate Randolph Hearst to broker a deal in which Leary would be freed in exchange for brokering a truce with the Symbionese Liberation Army for heiress Patty Hearst, who were holding her hostage. Leary was nothing if not inventive. He didn't deliver Patty, but he was let go.

[Author's Note: In the '80s, Manson complained that Rubin had popularized the slogan "Kill your parents," but that he took the fall for

Ram Dass, Ken Kelly, Jerry, Allen Ginsberg at PILL (People Investigating Leary's Lies) Press Conference in San Francisco, November 15th, 1974. Photo © Robert Altman

it. Manson repeatedly claimed that he didn't tell any kids to kill their elders (i.e., the infamous Manson Family murders), and wondered why Jerry and Abbie weren't in prison, as they caused a generation of young people to rebel against their parents, not him. In 1985, he referenced (in an interview on UC Berkeley's KALX radio) Jerry's appearance at HUAC carrying a (toy) M-16. Manson said, "You didn't see that? You don't remember that? You didn't put him on trial. You got Charlie Manson and put Charlie Manson on trial."]

Michael Kennedy was, like other progressive lawyers, tight with the activist Left. In his defense, Ken Kelly of the underground paper *Berkeley Barb* joined Allen Ginsberg, Ram Dass, Jerry Rubin, and Jack Leary, Tim's twenty-four-year-old son, to form an ad hoc collective known as (People Investigating Leary's Lies). Jerry was particularly incensed that Leary had allegedly appeared on video and "named names and pointed the finger at old friends." Jerry's rant intensified as he told a hundred journalists assembled at the ritzy St. Francis Hotel in San Francisco, "This ghost from the past never had a firm grasp where the truth began and the fantasy ended. He used words and sentences for their effect, not for eternal truth." Jerry concluded with an over-the-top statement, even for him: "*I feel sick for the death of Tim Leary's soul.*"

There were some, including Paul Krassner, who felt that Leary should be given a pass on this behavior. Another one was Dr. Eugene Schoenfeld (a drug addiction specialist at the Haight-Ashbury Free Medical Clinic). Schoenfeld felt this press conference was a "kangaroo court," so he arrived wearing a kangaroo mask and suit, which had a lemon meringue pie in its pouch. While Krassner was heckling

Rubin, he saw "Schoenfeld come hopping out" with the intent to "pie face" Jerry. Unfortunately, the pie "had Saran Wrap on it," Krassner recalled to Robert Greenfield.

Ultimately, the press conference served its purpose. Attorney Michael Kennedy wasn't prosecuted for his connection to the Weathermen and Leary's 1970 prison escape. The Feds couldn't present Leary's testimony as credible, but he still got a "Get Out of Jail Free" card. Ken Kelly, who had organized this press conference, clarified in a 1996 interview with Robert Greenfield that a quote he's often credited with was actually Jerry Rubin's. It appeared in the *New York Times*, and was *Rolling Stone* magazine's favorite "quote of the month." As the press conference closed, with the iconic high priest of LSD completely vilified, Jerry cried out, "This is the death of the '60s." The date was September 18, 1974, and Richard Nixon had vacated the White House in shame a month and nine days earlier.

In 2006, Robert Greenfield aptly pointed out that several years before, Rubin became "a businessman obsessed with networking, and many of those who had served with him in the front lines of the revolution began writing memoirs in which they renounced their youthful indiscretions in favor of family values." Similarly, Timothy Leary "turned his back on the counterculture from which he had once drawn all his fame and power."

Leary, not Jerry, was the real villain. And yet, there is one more "can you believe it" punch line to this sordid tale, which is that the Conservative William F. Buckley now supported Leary and threw the power of the *National Review* journal behind him. He called Leary "a good Catholic boy," and offered to help him get a teaching position at a Catholic university.

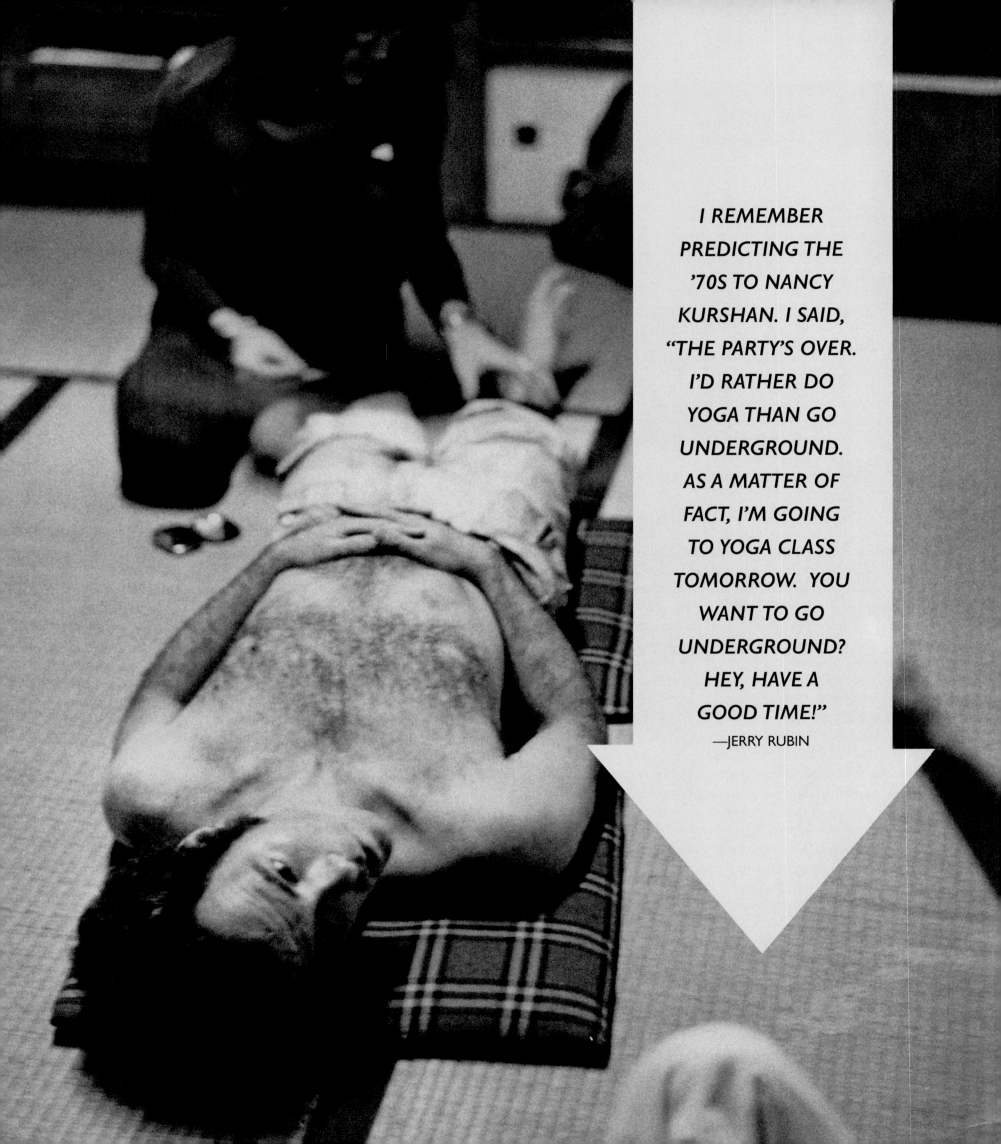

I REMEMBER PREDICTING THE '70S TO NANCY KURSHAN. I SAID, "THE PARTY'S OVER. I'D RATHER DO YOGA THAN GO UNDERGROUND. AS A MATTER OF FACT, I'M GOING TO YOGA CLASS TOMORROW. YOU WANT TO GO UNDERGROUND? HEY, HAVE A GOOD TIME!"

—JERRY RUBIN

BY HIS OWN ADMISSION, at the age of thirty-four, Jerry "felt dead." Younger people had taken to heart Jerry's infamous catchphrase, "Don't trust anyone over thirty." Meanwhile, as the '60s were winding down, the media, more often than not, put Jerry in "Where Is He Now?" articles. He was seen as an aging relic, rather than an essential part, of a decaying revolution—a revolution that pretty much died when Richard Nixon was reelected and people shifted their energies from public protests to personal introspection.

In November 1972, after the election night debacle, Jerry abruptly left New York for San Francisco. Overcome with self-pity and eager to be emotionally reborn, Jerry immersed himself in "body awareness and spiritual consciousness." Away from the cynicism of Manhattan, Jerry let the mellow vibe of San Francisco help him "rediscover [his] body and spirit."

LEE WEINER: Jerry's level of enthusiasm, there was no artifice. Nobody ever thought he's putting them on. Nobody ever thought he was bullshitting. How could he be so fuckin' enthusiastic about something like est? How can these fuckin' vitamins be the world's answer to war and peace? But Jerry believed it. And with Jerry—there was no artifice.

It's the Beginning Of a New Age...

LOLA COHEN: The New Age thing, yes, we were all doing it. Jewish Buddhists.

OPPOSITE: Jerry gets a massage on a trip to Asia.

ABOVE: Jerry makes a smoothie with "Dragon's Milk."

ENJOY THE MOMENT.

YOU'RE HERE.

THERE IS NOPLACE TO GO.

GOING <u>THERE</u> IS GETTING HERE.

YOU ARRIVED.

YOU ARE "THERE."

THERE'S NOPLACE TO GO BUT WHERE YOU ARE.

BELOW: Jerry's astrological chart.

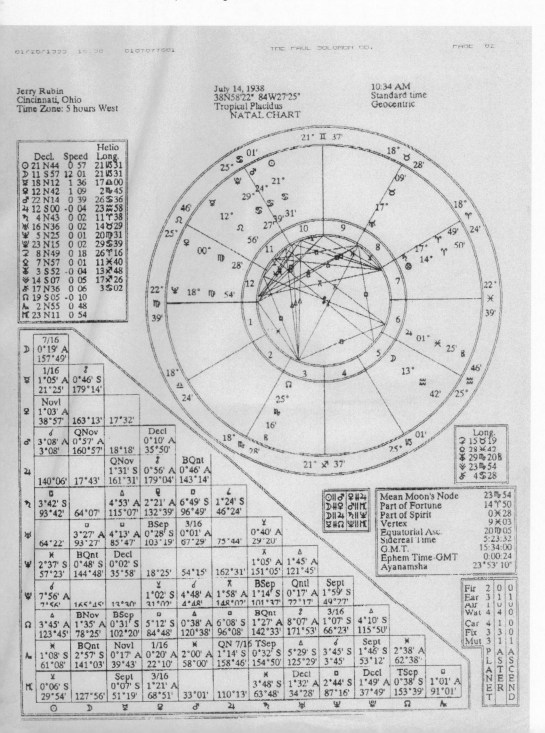

DIANE ROSE, THERAPIST/AUTHOR: Jerry had a tremendous effect on the consciousness movement at the time and on the spirituality that people were just kind of tasting from the whole smorgasbord of Zen Buddhism, Hinduism. People were getting gurus, they were meditating, and that was long before mindfulness became a common word in our vocabulary. So, Jerry was a real pioneer in the Human Potential Movement, *and* he wasn't afraid to go in front of the Congress and say, "Hey, let's just stop all this," and nobody today is doing that. Politically, we have so many issues where we're really frozen. There's no revolutionary thinking coming through from any direction.

RENNIE DAVIS: There was an internal world starting to emerge. And you can say, well, some of the psychedelic influence may have shaped that and maybe it did but . . . it really was a phenomenon. And Jerry was somebody that I could talk to, at least he was receptive. He didn't just close down. In his mind, he was on a similar journey, changing yourself . . . Jerry and I, in that 1970s period, were actually closer than during the Chicago 8 trial.

LEE WEINER: I was done, cooked. Finished. It probably was no later than '73 that I went into therapy. I remember my therapist saying, "Okay, here's the choice; do you wanna go to the hospital, or come see me five days a week?" It was hard, man. Abbie, same thing . . . nobody was healthy. Phil Ochs? C'mon, give me a break. Phil was always so down all the time. I mean, '72 was not a good year for anybody. Jerry was doing it to try to save himself. Everybody tried to save themselves.

RONA ELLIOT, MUSIC JOURNALIST: I just remembered another story. Jerry begged me to sleep with Phil, because he was so depressed. I said, "You sleep with him! I don't like his music that much!"

JONAH RASKIN: Jerry was trying all kinds of the alternative therapies and primal scream . . . he was a pioneer at that time, doing that. I would say that I was still back in the '60s, and he was branching out. Going off in a new direction. So, he did get me to think.

RONA ELLIOT: He was looking in. He was with a woman [Stella Resnick] who demanded that he look in. And I think, when he looked in, it was scary. And that was my experience with Jerry in the entire time I knew him. He was short, and insecure. I loved him and I'm not saying that short and insecure is any different than me being insecure, despite my success. But what ran his motor—when you have that kind of visibility and success, and infamy and fame, if you are not self-aware, you start to think that it's true. I think Jerry, who was nothing if not shrewd and strategic, however he got there, was looking inside. So I could laugh at him, and see his vulnerability, because that's really where I live.

PHOTO © ROGER RESSMEYER

JERRY BECAME A NEW AGE JUNKIE. HE TRIED EVERYTHING: COUNTER-GROUPS, EST, JUST ONE THING AFTER ANOTHER. PUT A PILLOW OVER HIS HEAD SO HE COULD YELL THINGS AT HIS MOTHER . . . ALL OF THESE THINGS.
—PAUL KRASSNER

est. Jerry had fed off the energy of the '60s: eating junk food, doing drugs, and never sleeping. After he settled into San Francisco, he began observing his food intake. He cut out meat, sugar, and carbs, and replaced them with fruit, veggies, and fish. He started practicing yoga, Rolfing, and Gestalt therapy. Much of Jerry's 1976 book, *Growing (Up) at 37*, discusses his newfound interest in diet, exercise, and a quest for self-awareness. Along the way, he encountered Werner Erhard, who had developed a seminar called est (Erhard Seminars Training) that forced its attendees to confront their own fears, take responsibility for their own actions, and not see themselves as helpless victims. Skeptical at first, Jerry quickly realized that he could take control of his life and decide why, how, and when he wanted to feel bad about himself—if ever. After all, why would anyone ever want to feel bad?

SUZANNE PECK, EDUCATOR/AUTHOR: I always loved Jerry's energy and his enthusiasm, and whatever he got into, that's who he was. He did it to the fullest. And he just embraced est. Werner Erhard was really big in San Francisco and he was personally leading est training sessions. He was very captivating. I invited Jerry to come and he totally loved it. I believe I was the person who introduced Jerry to est. But I wasn't the only one. I can think of half a dozen other people who also knew Jerry and were involved.

RONA ELLIOT: I was friends with the great Buddhist teacher, Alan Watts, and he said Werner was just a rogue. But Jerry said, "Rona, I'll loan you the money to do it," and he did.

GIL RUBIN: But you know what's funny, Jerry never went into anything with one toe. He jumped in—so one week it was est, and then the next week it was . . .

LEE WEINER: But you gotta understand the consequence of that to his friends. That is, anything Jerry's doing, he's gonna be fully committed to, but that didn't mean that it was necessarily a hundred-percent-wonderful thing. You see the man with orange legs, and no matter how much he tells you how carrot juice tastes wonderful, give me a break. Similarly, for est.

RATSO SLOMAN: I remember him coming to New York and him taking me to an est meeting. I remember . . . lasting about fifteen minutes. "What the fuck is this? Are you out of your mind?" and leaving. He went into everything he did with such enthusiasm that you had to admire it. And a lot of that was he would sweep you up in it. Until you realize—like with that fuckin' est meeting, this guy's giving you this bullshit. [Laughter.]

est, Erhard Seminars Training

NOVEMBER 15, 1975

JERRY RUBIN
c/o CAVESTANI, APT. 28
917 LARRABEE
LOS ANGELES, CA 90069

DEAR JERRY,

I WANTED YOU TO HAVE THE FOLLOWING AS A QUOTATION
ABOUT YOUR BOOK:

JERRY RUBIN SHARES HIMSELF IN HIS NEW BOOK.
IN READING IT, I EXPERIENCED THE MAN WHO WROTE IT,
THE MAN BEHIND THE DRAMA OF HIS OWN STORIES, WHOM
I KNOW AS A PERSON OF INTEGRITY.

THANK YOU FOR THE OPPORTUNITY TO SHARE WITH YOU AND
BEST WISHES FOR SUCCESS WITH THE PUBLICATION.

Love,
Werner

1750 Union Street • San Francisco, California 94123 • (415) 441-0100

est forced Jerry to take off his mask. He had to dispose with everything he *thought* he was: a know-it-all, a radical, a revolutionary, et al. He stated, "I am responsible for everything that happens to me. If I am miserable, I chose to be miserable. It is up to me."

GERALD LEFCOURT: He was so enthusiastic about this newfound discovery. Rolfing, going to est—he was selling it like he was selling the revolution.

SUZANNE PECK: I remember introducing Jerry to Werner. Jerry loved the message—that you're responsible for creating what you want to be. It fit who he was, thinking about what was next for himself. I wasn't at all surprised that he would reinvent himself and do something really different and embrace it and be good at it.

WERNER ERHARD: When I met Jerry he had come to a crossroad in his life. He was beginning to see that no matter the contribution he might have made [to society during the '60s] . . . his identity, that era was over. Jerry was appropriately combative during the est training, and yet he walked out transformed with the freedom to be and to act beyond the way he had wound up being and acting [as a Yippie]. Personally, I liked his underlying authenticity. Of course, he didn't approve of the organization being a capitalist enterprise, but he acknowledged the value he got from the training. [He said it] "permanently altered my consciousness" and [he] "felt totally free!"

Rubin told the *New York Times* in 1976 that of all the therapies he'd tried, est was the best: "the acid of the 1970s!"

Fame Puts You There Where Things Are Hollow.

Earlier in the week, Jerry Rubin was lunching with Patty Hearst's ex-fiancé, Steven Weed. Weed told him that DO iT! *had been Patty's favorite book. Nostalgia buffs will recall that the book urged children of America's elite to rebel against their parents.*

—ROLLING STONE, RANDOM NOTES 4/10/75

[Author's Note: Patty, daughter of newspaper baron William Randolph Hearst, became famous after she was kidnapped by a radical group, the SLA (Symbionese Liberation Army). She changed her name to Tania (after a woman who fought alongside Che Guevara) and joined them. A photo of her robbing a bank with a machine gun is an iconic 1970s image.]

In *Growing (Up) at 37*, Jerry addressed the trappings of fame. He pointed out that "In the '60s, singers sang protest songs and revolutionaries made revolution. Then protest singers and revolutionaries got rewarded with media attention and money, and they began singing not about inequality, but about over-attention." He saw himself in the same light. He used fame to cover up his insecurities, but he also knew it was an asset. He could telephone just about anyone in America and they would take his call, just out of curiosity. He commented, "every famous person is a groupie. I became famous so I could meet other famous people on an equal basis. They're meeting 'Jerry Rubin' and I'm meeting 'Walter Cronkite.'"

STELLA RESNICK: The first contact that I had with Jerry was on the telephone. He called me out of the blue, said that he had heard a lot about me, and wanted to meet. He said that he was now living in San Francisco, was on a health kick, that he was in therapy, and he heard about my work as a Gestalt therapist. And I was . . . impressed, that it was *the* Jerry Rubin, as he liked to say. His first name was "*The*." We made a plan to meet at my office!

Almost Cut My Hair, It Happened Just the Other Day.

As Jerry went through his West Coast transformation, he realized that his "long hair had been as much a costume as suits and short hair are for the middle class." His attachment to his hair made him a prisoner of his own self-image. He shaved off his beard and got a haircut, which then caused people to say, "you're *not* Jerry Rubin!" when he first met them.

In 1970, Abbie had addressed hair as a political statement in the *East Village Other*: "If I'm flying on an airplane—I don't have long hair now, because they cut it in jail—but when I had long hair, flying in the early morning was strange because it's all executives. And here comes a freak bopping along, so I say I'm with a band. They ask what band. I say the Yippies. Oh sure, they say. It's accepted. It's not threating to them. Their racism can allow nonconformity as long as it knows its place. They feel we wear long hair and freak clothes so we can make money, which is accepted. Sort of—we have to dress this way because our job requires it."

STELLA RESNICK: Jerry was coming up the stairs as my ex-husband was threatening to jump out the window, because he didn't want me to divorce him. And so my husband was on the fire escape, threatening to jump. Then there was Jerry [coming up the stairs]. One man's going out the window, while another one's coming through the door . . . I pictured him as a radical with wild hair and the beard, but here he was clean-shaven, and he was cute. He had a little gold earring in his ear, and that charmed me. He clearly liked what he saw. If he was a cartoon character, his eyeballs would be coming out. *Boing!* So he smiled and he said, "Well, I thought we would have dinner together." So we went to the Spaghetti Factory, and we're talking, and he looked at me, and said, "I'm going to marry you." Not what I wanted to hear. I wanted to be free—and in that moment was the conflict that we had for our entire relationship.

Contrast this freshly shorn 1973 Jerry with the shaggy-haired version who, just three years earlier, was battling the guards at the Cook County Jail in Chicago. Abbie, Rennie Davis, Tom Hayden, and Jerry were told they had visitors waiting for them downstairs. They knew better. Even though they barricaded themselves in the cell, the guards won out and marched the four of the defendants to the barbershop. Abbie struggled, screamed, and fought back. The barber (a black inmate) refused to cut Abbie's hair, given how distraught he was. Jerry was next and began to growl. According to *We Are Everywhere*, Jerry shouted at the guards (who were African American), "Cutting our hair is like taking off your black skin!" "Jerry, I wish we could. *You have no idea how much trouble my black skin has given me.*" The barber then whispered into Jerry's ear that he'd leave as much hair as possible—and he did. Jerry felt: "sheared, humiliated, beaten." By 1973, long hair had become a symbol of a revolution that was now over, and it signaled a major shift in Jerry's psyche to have his hair cut.

STELLA RESNICK, THE SEXUAL REVOLUTION, AND GESTALT THERAPY.

In the course of interviewing people who knew Stella Resnick in the '70s, I was struck by the way people talked about her. Diane Rose described Resnick at that time.

DIANE ROSE: [She was] gorgeous. She looked like Elizabeth Taylor. She became well known by doing innovative workshops all over the country, incorporating different kinds of exercises and practices. She was sunny: a marvelous workshop leader. Definitely one of the top Gestalt therapists, one of the leaders in the Human Potential Movement.

She was sought after: recognized to the extent that Jerry called her out of the blue right after he moved to San Francisco asking to meet her.

RONA ELLIOT: I end up living with Jerry and Stella in her house in the Castro. The Jerry Rubin I met then in '73 . . . wasn't the radical Jerry; this was the vulnerable, lovesick, madly-in-love puppy Jerry. Who is following around the exotic and beautiful and very powerful and narcissistic (*but not in a bad way*) Stella Resnick, who Jerry was both learning from and just head over heels in love with, like an imbecile.

STELLA RESNICK: Being with Jerry was incredible. I read *DO iT!* and I thought it was brilliant. I was doing seminars. And Jerry wanted to do seminars. I was speaking at conferences; I was very popular as a public speaker in San Francisco. Speaking about New Age stuff, and Gestalt . . . And Jerry wanted to do that. So we were perfect. And Jerry would say, "You're a female Jerry Rubin."

I replied, "You're a male Stella Resnick." We had a lot of fun together, but I still wanted my freedom. And, I just found it difficult to be my own person with Jerry. "Now we're doing this, and now we're doing that, and you do this, and I'll do that, and then we'll do that." And I'd say, "Wait a minute. How about 'would you like to, or please?'"

JERRELLE KRAUS, ART DIRECTOR FOR THE *NEW YORK TIMES*, *TIME*, AND *RAMPARTS*.: I got to know Stella very well. She has a lot of the same qualities as Jerry. Stella had the same kind of desire to have a publicist. She didn't specifically ask me like Jerry asked me, I mean, I'm

an artist and I don't think like that. But Stella—I remember one thing she said to me. "It's very important to have people around you—even if they're not on your level." In other words, having acolytes, how important that was. It's been a long time since I've had any contact with Stella, but I understand she's doing well.

Jerry was used to being in charge, but now he'd met his match with Stella and was intrigued by the challenge.

STELLA RESNICK: I was born in Brooklyn in a Jewish and Italian neighborhood. My parents were divorced when I was five; my father was the nurturing parent. He had been orphaned as a little boy in what was called White Russia. He married my mother, who was born in Boston. Neither one of them had graduated from high school. They got married, had me, and fought all the time. Finally, my mother packed my father's bags and threw him out. That was the saddest day of my life at that point, because I was left with the wrong parent. I ended up living with my mother and she remarried three years later to a man who also was uneducated, a cab driver. He totally resented me and became violent with me. Home meant, for me, a place to escape from.

Growing up in a poor neighborhood, coping with an abusive home life, Stella went the route of the bad girl.

STELLA RESNICK: I grew up in a tough section of Brooklyn; I was in a gang when I was a kid. And my boyfriend was the leader of an Italian gang. And when I got pissed off at him, wanting to fight him, I ended up with the leader of the Irish gang. I was a little Jewish girl who was used to gang leaders. I was not afraid of gang leaders, and Jerry was like a gang leader.

Before we moved in together, I remember distinctly, Jerry sitting on the bed. And he was reading to me from an article about himself that somebody had written. And one of the things in the article was, "Jerry Rubin always gets what he wants." And he reads this, and he said, "Did you hear that? Jerry Rubin always gets what he wants. And I want you." [*Shudders.*] Oh my gosh. It was flattering, but it was—gimme a break. I'm a person, too. And I have what I want, also.

With encouragement from her teachers, Stella traded her gang colors for academic robes. She attended Brooklyn College, and got a full scholarship to grad school at Indiana University, where she studied psychology. Ultimately, her studies led her to the West Coast, where she got her PhD at the University of California, San Francisco Medical School, also on scholarship. This was the mid-'60s. Stella was only twenty-four, and she was living in the heart of Haight-Ashbury—ground zero for the hippies and the Summer of Love. She was a PhD researcher by day and a wild hippie chick at night—wandering the streets of Haight-Ashbury in a nightgown, high on LSD. Stella dabbled in the radical scene, crossing paths with Eldridge and Kathleen Cleaver. She never encountered Jerry in the Bay Area during the '60s, although he lived there as well. I asked her to describe the Sexual Revolution for anyone who did not experience it firsthand:

STELLA RESNICK: We know that, during the '50s, sexuality became very closed in. There was a lot of shame associated with sex . . . Virginity was very important, values. Girls were supposed to be virgins until they married; masturbation was never talked about, nudity surrounded by shame . . . After the '50s, with discovery of marijuana and LSD by middle-class and educated people, there was an expansion of consciousness, and the recognition of sexuality, pleasure, and openness as a real value . . . Also, what was different was birth control. We suddenly had birth control pills, and that made a very big difference in being able to experiment . . . The sexuality that came out of the '60s through the liberation of the body, through the liberation of sexuality, through the ability to talk about it, and not to be ashamed, it was a very juvenile, childlike kind of sexuality. It was playful, it was naked, and it was dancing. It was getting stoned and dancing to the music, and rolling around in the mud.

The Sexual Revolution sparked her lifelong mission as a leading proponent of sexual therapy, which she continues to this day. In many ways, her commitment to healing people by repairing their relationship to their own sexuality was one of the most important influences she had on Jerry, who talks about his own repressed sexuality in *Growing (Up) at 37*. He cited sex therapy as a crucial part of his transformation.

STELLA RESNICK: Well, Jerry was very childlike. And he was sexually innocent, in some ways. He was not very experienced, and so that became an issue for us. I was a child of the Sexual Revolution. I found myself in Haight-Ashbury, in '64, wanting to have a sexual awakening. I was sexually open, but I had never really had a lover. I had been married for a year, but the marriage was not satisfying in that way, physically. And so my young husband and I, we decided we would separate. It was the awakening of the Sexual Revolution, and we decided we would separate for a year; we both needed to have sexual experience[s] that would work. I was going off to

San Francisco to do my internship, and he was staying in Indiana, and we were going to have experiences. And so I did. I had some wonderful—actually I had one really great lover, and discovered myself, sexually.

After fleeing Nazi Germany in the '30s, Fritz Perls arrived in New York, where he began the first Gestalt Institute with his wife Laura in their apartment during the 1950s. In the 1960s, he left the East Coast and his wife behind and started workshops at the Esalen Institute. He coined the phrase "I do my thing and you do your thing," which quickly entered into the popular vernacular. Gestalt therapy became the cornerstone of the New Age Movement. In one film, Perls coaches a patient to "kill your mother"—not unlike Jerry's rallying cry of telling young radicals to "kill your parents." Stella eventually got a chance to study closely with Perls during the final year of his life, at his Canadian residential center. She provided therapy for the radical Left.

STELLA RESNICK: Stew confided that he was having heart problems. And that he figured that it was related to having a lot of anger. I said, "It's very important that you get rid of this anger, that you resolve it. You don't need to walk around with a lot of anger in you, it's dangerous."

He said that he wasn't going to go to therapy, and he felt that he needed his anger, that it was a part of who he is, that it motivated him politically, and it motivated him in his writing. I said to him, "You can bang some pillows and yell 'I'm so mad!'" He said, "I'm not going to do that!" So I retorted, "I'll tell you what I recommend. When you go up to Woodstock, chop wood. You're gonna need the wood anyway. Every time you come down, you go [*forceful grunt*]." The next time I saw him, he reiterated, "You know something, Stella, I don't have the anger that I once had. But I do chop a lot of wood."

For those who think that Jerry lost his Yippie sense of humor during his New Age years, I leave you with this tale:

STELLA RESNICK: We did workshops together at Esalen; we did presentations at conferences where we talked about the connection between personal growth and social consciousness, between liberating the mind through therapy and having a healthy body and eating wholesome food. Toward the end of our presentation at the Kohoutek Festival in San Francisco, where thousands came to celebrate the comet as a harbinger of a new way of thinking, Jerry and I wadded up slices of Wonder bread and threw them like snowballs into the audience. We expounded on the virtues of marijuana and just as we concluded our talk, Jerry proudly lit up a joint on stage.

Today, Stella is an author of numerous books on intimacy as well as a noted workshop presenter (often at Esalen). She currently maintains a therapy practice in LA.

I'm a Man, Yes I Am, and I Can't Help but Love You So.

Jerry's father had died at age forty-nine of a heart attack (when Jerry was only twenty-one), which Jerry later attributed to "the neurotic pressures of being a man, the competitive pressures." While self-reflecting, Jerry began to question the role of men in society, realizing that, during the '60s, the men in the movement had been competitive. In a 1976 interview with *Hustler* magazine, Jerry asked rhetorically, "Does a man always have to compete, or can a man be cooperative? Can a man show feelings and cry? Can a man be sensitive?" Jerry demanded "the freedom to be vulnerable, the freedom to let go."

DIANE ROSE: Jerry was a big influence on manhood at that time, because men began opening up more. They weren't taking a nurturing role in the family, and Jerry was a risk-taker, and I think he influenced a lot of men—that it's okay to show yourself in many different colors, hues, and shades as a human being.

PHOTO © ROBERT ALTMAN

Part of Jerry's growth was examining his sexuality. Jerry wasn't a womanizer like Abbie, and felt insecure about his sexual prowess. During this era, he spoke openly about penis size and premature ejaculation—his interview in *Hustler* was titled "Jerry Rubin: Rebel Without a Cock?"

JONAH RASKIN: I remember Jerry was talking about sexual surrogates. I don't know who was helping whom, but he said that he was having sex and it was supposed to be a therapeutic experience, where you're learning how to have a better sex life by having a non-partner.

Ultimately, it was his relationship with Stella—a renowned sex therapist—that opened up his sexuality. Stella recalls helping Jerry work through his hang-ups.

STELLA RESNICK: I already had a reputation for recognizing the importance of sexuality, and self-discovery. And because we had gone through this incredible Sexual Revolution, the values about sex were changing. And yet, people weren't able to bring their behavior and feelings up to date. In terms of what they believed, the head and the body were not together. And so, that was a big part of what I was teaching. To breathe, breathing process, and sensory awareness. Jerry was getting all this from me, he was learning about that. And it was just getting him to loosen up, because he was tense.

An old friend from the Berkeley days remembers seeing him at this time.

MICHAEL LERNER: I went to one of Stella's groups where she had us dancing until we were sweating, it was in the summer, and then she told everybody to take off all their clothes, so we did, and then she said, "Okay, now I want each of you to touch each part of the body of everybody else in the room in a loving and gentle way and saying nothing." That was quite an experience!

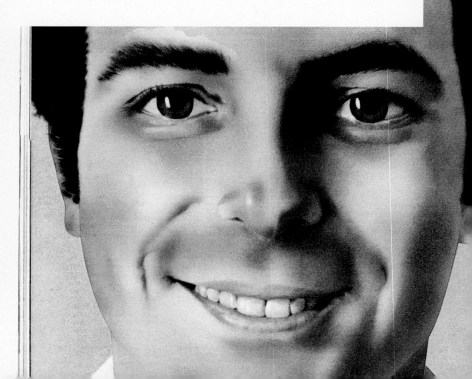

I would hide my cock—hide it from other men in locker rooms and from women in bed.

HUSTLER INTERVIEW

JERRY RUBIN

REBEL WITHOUT A COCK?

If any one person could be said to embody the spirit of individual freedom which permeated the American youth culture of the late '60s, that person would have to be Jerry Rubin. As founder and leader of the Youth International Party (Yippie), Rubin shocked people by urging kids to "kill your parents" and to "make revolution for the hell of it," but his philosophy was really quite simple: Accept no socially-imposed limits on your freedom, define your own morality, and if it feels good—do it! And the kids listened to Rubin's message of liberation.

The darker side of Jerry Rubin's anarchic philosophy was exposed when he and his followers tried to apply it to politics at the Democratic Convention in Chicago in 1968. There, Rubin's vision of personal freedom became chaos, spilling over into a violent, destructive riot in which everybody—kids, cops, and the country—lost, and nobody won. Rubin later stood trial as one of the

"Chicago Seven" for conspiring to incite the convention riots. His outrageous courtroom pranks helped turn the trial into a clownish burlesque of justice which alternately amused and mortified the American public throughout its six-month duration.

Like other radicals who were marooned by the slow death of "The Movement" in the early '70s, Rubin has since turned his attention inward, seeking the source of liberation from within himself. His new book, *Growing (Up) At 37* (M. Evans and Company), contends that only by knowing and coming to terms with his own sexuality, as it has been shaped by himself and his society, can a man "grow up"—be strong enough to liberate himself and that society.

Curious as to what fresh insights Rubin might have in the ongoing struggle of American men to sexually liberate themselves, HUSTLER managing editor Bruce David questioned the aging rebel in New York.

42

HUSTLER

Lecture Topics

1. Growing (Up) at 37
First a conscious graduate school student at the University of California—Berkeley, then the "infant terrible" of the anti-Vietnam war movement and now a proponent of the new consciousness and humane political change, Jerry Rubin discusses his spiritual, intellectual and political growth from the early sixties to the seventies. The journey has been a difficult one but not without its certain rewards. With the background of the 1960's political explosion, Jerry dramatizes what happened to that political energy and then takes the audience on a new journey concerning male chauvinism, men-women relationships, the self and the ego, inter-personal relationships, and the discovery of life goals.

He describes the process of learning to accept and love oneself by dealing with anger and blame, childhood conditioning, and love-and-hate to parents and the parents within. Jerry reveals how he made his body his friend through yoga and meditation. He illustrates the process of self-awakening.

2. "Hell, not We Won't Go!"—political activism in the 1960's.
As co-founder of the Youth International Party (yippie), co-chairman of the Vietnam Day Committee, and a member of the Chicago 7, Jerry will discuss the political goals of the sixties youth movement. It will be a personal story with a historical approach and will answer some of the following questions: What happened in the 1960's? What Was The Student Rebellion All About? What Was At the Core of the Anti-War Movement? Did the Revolution Succeed or Fail? What Is the Difference Between Activism in the 1960's and 1970's. Is Personal Growth Inconsistent with Political Change? What Are Enlightened Politics? Are Politics Obsolete?

3. The New Consciousness
Personal change for the most part is not dramatic. Jerry describes the process of change and the contradictions and absurdities along the lonely and sometimes banal way. His speech is somewhat akin to a Zen experience since the people in the audience will go through their own changes interacting with Jerry. Sharing himself and his experiences, Jerry puts the audience in the position to experience self knowledge through self-confrontation. Jerry criticizes the excessive inward preoccupation of therapy and meditation and reveals how the best of activism and the best of inner awareness can be put together in a new personal political synthesis. He sees the most important confrontation today between macho toughness, gentleness, vulnerability and sharing. As an activist and student of consciousness, he reflects political awareness and the inner awareness of the present.

HOW I LEARNED TO LIKE SEX

ARTICLE BY JERRY RUBIN

THE EX-YIPPIE LEADER USED TO FEEL LIKE A CONSPIRATOR IN BED, BUT NOW HE'S TAKEN HIS LIFE INTO HIS OWN HANDS AND HE FEELS MUCH BETTER, THANK YOU

The most intimate writing in recent years has come from women. Men, on the other hand, believe in maintaining their male image. They have not discussed their emotions and pain publicly. I hope my admission encourages other men to write about the collective pain we experience living in a patriarchal system that oppresses us almost as much as it does women.

I am a typically sex-

ually obsessed American male—obsessed about performance, the size of my cock, competition, jealousy and control. Like other American men, I feel I have to control the woman I am with. If she seems interested in another man, rage and fear roar through my body. Jealousy turns me into an irrational animal. I am always comparing myself sexually with other men.

In bed with my lover, I lay the heaviest

Volume 13, No. 7 (604) Feb. 13-19, 1976

Outside California 50¢ 35¢

LOS ANGELES

FREE PRESS

Jailed Pot Possessors May Be Out of the Joint Soon

The Harrises' Unedited Statement on the FBI

The CIA's Top Gun (cont.)

Jack Anderson: Hoover's Good Side

Plus: Krassner, Bukowski & Expanded Guide to Local Events

Jerry Rubin Discovers:

THE FEMALE IN ME

Published Every Friday. An Adjudicated Newspaper.

THIS PAGE: Men's magazines including *Hustler*, *Oui*, and *Penthouse Forum* printed interviews and essays by Jerry about his sexual vulnerability.

I WAS CREDITED WITH SAYING THAT ALL PARENTS SHOULD BE KILLED. IT'S QUITE AN UNPOPULAR THING TO SAY, AND WHAT I WAS REALLY SAYING WAS KILL THE PARENTS IN YOU.

—JERRY RUBIN, IN *HUSTLER*, APRIL 1976

Kill the Parents in You. As Jerry changed, so did his relationships with many of his old friends. His former colleagues began to criticize him, and that would dog him for the rest of his life.

RONA ELLIOT: I've spent forty years defending Jerry from people who said he's just an asshole. There was a real other side to Jerry. To go off for thirteen weekends and write about your parents and your negative patterns, that was pretty out there. And Jerry was out there. He wanted to get through that, and he was burdened by their dying before they were fifty and that's one of the things that ran his motor.

MICHAEL LERNER: I was watching Jerry move away from progressive politics and towards becoming a New Age guru and that deeply disappointed me. He was moving away from any kind of vision of how to change society, and thought that the counterculture was the vehicle and that it was already winning. I didn't see it that way, and so we drifted apart.

MIMI LEONARD: Jerry showed tremendous courage to discard his [Yippie] "Jerry Rubin" persona. No one wanted him to. The Left, the Light, his friends and family, all wanted him to stay as "Jerry Rubin." In his opinion, 1973 was the year "the music died." Stew was diagnosed with heart disease. Abbie was busted. Rennie had some sort of breakdown or breakthrough, and became a follower of a teenage guru. Jerry went from being best friends with John & Yoko to having a complete break with them, partially over the government's efforts to have John deported. Phil Ochs slid into alcoholism.

So instead of just continuing to do and say the same things over and over again, Jerry asked himself, "What's going on here? Why are things falling apart?" Later, Jerry was on a talk show with the Chicago 8 personalities and he called Bill Kunstler a "broken record." Bill was so angry that he never spoke to him again, although he wrote a beautiful eulogy when Jerry died. Jerry didn't want to be a "broken record." He wanted to wake up in the morning and start from scratch and say, "What do I believe today?" and "What do I want to accomplish today?"

Los Angeles Times Tues., Jan. 13, 1976—Part II **5**

Yesterday's Rebel Becomes Today's Guru

BY JERRY RUBIN

During the past few years there has been such a widespread feeling of powerlessness in our country that people have put aside collective solutions in favor of individual pursuits.

I, too, have experienced these general consciousness changes. Today, I am more apathetic, cynical and individualistic than I was a decade ago. Nevertheless, I am still optimistic, idealistic and a believer in collective action.

Friends ask me, "Isn't your inward growth trip an escape from social reality?" Yes, it's a long way from leading a march on the Pentagon to sitting cross-legged counting my breaths. But there is no contradiction between the two.

We activists of the 1960s eventually lost touch with ourselves. Now, our growth trips are geared to creating a centered individual, who moves politically from a deep place.

The time has come for people to leave their roles and "points-of-view" for a new vision of the human being and society. It is time to apply politically the values of high conscious-

obsession with our power, and transcend our fear. Fear holds America back and perpetuates the very things we are afraid of.

America must go inward to rediscover itself, not to become self-absorbed and isolationist but to share with the world. To do that the American people will have to share more equally among ourselves because we will have less. That requires a power change within the United States away from the large corporations to the mass of the people.

The new movement will base itself on the equality of all human beings, putting into practice the things learned about the body, mind and spirit. A new health philosophy will expand the minds of doctors. A new body awareness will teach people to take responsibility for their own health. A political movement, directly related to peoples' basic needs,

One of the 1960s' most visible activists, Jerry Rubin was head of the Youth International Party (Yippies) and a member of the Chicago Seven. Now living in Los Angeles, he has recently completed a book, "Growing (Up) at 37" (M. Evans and Co. Feb. 27) from which this

few to the many. I don't think that any changes in society can be implemented without collective political change.

Unless the economic sphere is democratized, people have a practical and a psychological motivation to be selfish. But one changes the political-economic level by concentrating also on the personal, spiritual and consciousness level of life.

In the 1960s we postponed all questions on personal growth until after the revolution. But revolution is only as high as the people who make it. I expected the revolution to be apocalyptic, but have since discovered that it is an evolutionary process. *I* am also a process. My personal growth and your personal growth match the growth of mass consciousness.

People out of touch with bodies and souls cannot make positive change. Political activism without self-awareness perpetuate cycles of anger, competition, ego battles.

The potential of spiritual discipline is the ability to break people from programming

Growing (Up) at 37.

Published in 1976, *Growing (Up) at 37* was part self-help guide, part autobiography. Jerry used his own

experiences as a starting point: from the death of his parents at a young age, to the euphoria of being an infamous radical in the '60s, to the crash and burn that he suffered after the movement ended in 1972. It's as revealing as any Hollywood celebrity "tell-all" memoir, but with a twist. Rather than reveal all about the vapid sex and drugs, which frankly wasn't Jerry's experience, he shows the vulnerable scars he carried since childhood; he writes about his failed romantic relationships and the crumbling of his ego once the '60s were well and truly over. His exploration of diverse therapies and self-help techniques during his mid-thirties is inspirational.

A February 11, 1976 profile in the *New York Times* saw dramatic changes in Jerry's persona: "As his previous book *DO iT!* was ferocious, hyperbolic, sloganeering, *Growing (Up) at 37* is gentle, understated, touching, a little naive, very sincere." The article captured the essence of his soul-searching mission: "'Who I am' genuinely obsesses [Rubin], not egomaniacally, but more the way the question used to nag college kids." Jerry was mature to realize that "Before I can change other people, I must change myself."

DAVID SPANER: He asked me if I'd take a look at the book he was working on, which turned out to be *Growing (Up) at 37*. I didn't realize it at the time, but I think that book was a major transitional point for him. In that book, he talks about this ongoing argument he had with this woman he had fallen in love with, a therapist [named Stella Resnick], in which he felt that you couldn't fundamentally change and become a healthy human being in an unhealthy capitalist society. Whereas, she felt you had to change, because unhealthy people couldn't create a new society.

Which, in a way, is the difference between new Leftists and New Agers, the idea that you have to change the system before people can be truly healthy. That's the left-wing ideal. In Jerry's book, he synthesizes both of those things and he comes up with the conclusion that you have to do both. You have to change society, you have to change the system, and you have to change yourself. Later, he kind of dropped the part about changing the system, which I disagreed with.

SHARON SKOLNICK-BAGNOLI, GRAPHIC DESIGNER/RADIO PRODUCER: Jerry asked me to proofread his book that, at that time, he was calling *How to Kill Your Mother and Father*. I didn't like the name. So, he changed it.

DIANE ROSE: I told him, you can't publish the book like this. I said, "You're going to come out really stinking because you've had a love affair with a woman who looks like Elizabeth Taylor and is known as the top Gestalt therapist." He was very transparent about their relationship, their arguments, and I said, "You can't name her. You have to hide her identity, or it's libel."

After talking it through, he felt I understood his life and his desire to change and be transformed, and asked me if I would edit the book and I said I would. He would meet me at the door of his apartment at 8 in the morning, and he'd be smoking a joint. He would give me a chapter and then I'd drive home, pull out my ironing board, and edit his chapter on my ironing board, then bring it back to him first thing in the morning with the edits on it. Changing names, changing identities.

To avoid legal hassles, Jerry took Rose's advice and changed the names of the key women in his life story. For instance, Nancy Kurshan is referred to as "Ruthie." Stella appears as "Rhoda."

While a cynic might view Jerry Rubin as someone who simply jumped on bandwagons (i.e. antiwar protests of the '60s and the New Age health fads of the '70s), one could easily argue that Jerry's ability to change was both a survival technique and a sign of someone who fully embraced the zeitgeist of his times. He didn't just jump on the latest trends; he was a progressive who could see the change coming. His antiwar and civil rights activism started in the early to mid-1960s, well before it was hip. Jerry's desire to publicly discuss his personal issues came well before the deluge of self-confessional autobiographies that have been standard issue for celebrities in the age of *The Oprah Winfrey Show* and beyond.

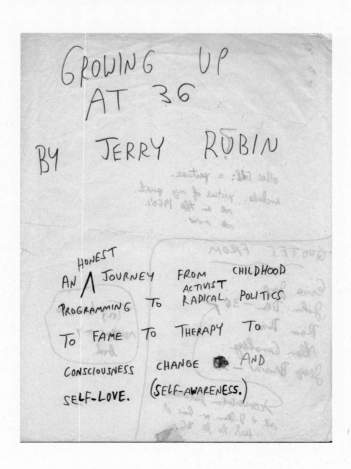

FRANK BARDACKE: In 1972, Jerry came to visit me on the central coast of California. He brought food with him, because he was pure now. Yeah, health food and Quaaludes is what he was into. He's eating pure, and popping Quaaludes! He was intense, he was focused, and he was very much into what he was doing. That's always been true of Jerry. I remember, we took the Quaaludes and went bowling. [*Laughs.*] We just had a great time.

DAVID SPANER: There had been a split within YIP a couple years earlier, based around the Miami convention. There was still an active YIP organization in the '70s, with national conferences. I was asked to go to San Francisco and meet with Jerry to work on a peace statement about the current YIP activists. A lot of the reason I was asked was because I hadn't been at Miami, and I had nothing against either side of that split. So I got along fine with those continuing YIP, and I also respected Jerry and Abbie. We got along extremely well; we're talking about movies, baseball, the counterculture, and our Jewishness. He missed that part of New York. Also, he was still clearly a person of the Left. I asked him if he was interested in getting re-involved with the current YIP? And he said he wasn't interested in organizing around that label, but that he still considered himself to be a Yippie.

RATSO SLOMAN: I found that Jerry getting into health food, est, getting into meditation, yoga, all that shit—I really think that did change his personality, and he was more fun to be with. Absolutely. He was not fun during the Yippie period, too serious, and too in your face, and dogmatic. And to me, while he was doing all this other shit—the networking stuff—he was charming, and fun to be with, and discovered a sense of humor which he never had earlier. So my fondest memories of him are the later years.

SUZANNE PECK: It was early '70s, crazy days in San Francisco. That was the *Rolling Stone* days, and the Werner Erhard days, and lots of parties. And I remember that he was going back and forth to New York. I had his record collection, I had his will. He left everything to his brother, Gil. We were in our thirties then; I didn't know anyone who had a will. It was just handwritten on lined notebook paper. He said, "If I die, everything goes to my brother, Gil." Not, "when I die." "*If I die.*"

Jerry and Stella Call It Quits. While the relationship with Stella helped Jerry grow, it was too stormy to hold together. Though they were passionately in love, their relationship suffered from a power struggle between the two strong personalities. Stella, desperate to maintain her independence, struggled against Jerry's more conventional masculinity and his need to claim her as his own.

STELLA RESNICK: He was just brilliant and beautiful and it was hard not to stay with him. But I couldn't be with a man that was trying to subsume me into himself. It ended badly and was painful. I loved him with great passion. But I was also spiteful. And I was gonna show him that he couldn't control me. And it was painful for him. So we hurt each other. So I decided—during one breakup, I actually threw his stuff out the window. I just opened a window, and tossed his stuff out. In the heat of anger—we had an incredible passion with each other, and I got passionate and threw his stuff out.

Hurt by the breakup, Jerry maintained his distance and avoided a friendship; as Stella recalls after running into him in New York a while later:

STELLA RESNICK: After Jerry and I broke up, I was in New York—and he was crossing the street in front of my car. I was in the passenger seat, my friend Morgan was driving, and I said, "Don't move!" I ran out, and I said, "Jerry! Get in the car!" He said, "No, no, no." "Get in the car!" So he got in, and we drove around and I thought, maybe, because he had such a playful spirit, that perhaps he would get into it and we could be friends. No way. He could not forgive me. That might have been the last time I saw him.

GEORGE LEONARD:
PIONEER OF THE NEW AGE MOVEMENT.

WHEN HE DIED IN JANUARY 2010, the *New York Times* obit headline read:

George Leonard, Voice of '60s Counterculture, Dies at 86

The essay began with, "a former journalist who foresaw the countercultural tides of the 1960s, then dived into them when he helped define the human potential movement at its de facto headquarters, the Esalen Institute." The Esalen Institute was named after the Indian burial grounds on which it had been built (the tribe having been wiped out by smallpox). But before it became Esalen, the grounds were marketed as "Big Sur Hot Springs"—the area was also a haunt of Jack Kerouac, who used it as the inspiration for the novel *Big Sur*. The burgeoning hippie scene along the California coast was captured in the movie *Celebration at Big Sur*—memorable for a scene in which Stephen Stills punches a raggedy hippie for heckling him about the swank fur coat he was wearing on stage with Crosby, Stills, Nash & Young.

While the Esalen Institute credits George Leonard as the "Grandfather of the New Age," the institution was actually founded by two professors from Stanford seeking an alternative to academia, Michael Murphy and Richard Price. Price had suffered a psychotic breakdown in 1956, and his experience with that era's psychiatric care was one motivation for the birth of their sympathetic institution. Michael Murphy's grandmother owned the property. She steadfastly refused to sell it, but she leased it to him.

The Esalen Institute was founded in 1962. Dubbed "A Cape Canaveral of inner space," Esalen "began as a laboratory for new thought, from Timothy Leary's psychedelics, to Carl Rogers's humanistic psychology, to Joan Baez's folk music." In 1965, George Leonard came on board—later describing his first impression of Esalen as "Explosion, catharsis, adventure."

According to Leonard's *New York Times* obit, "Esalen was one of many schools for self-discovery that would lead to the New Age Movement and influence the many yoga and meditation centers that dot the American landscape today, all promoting a belief that human abilities are expandable."

Murphy and Price joined forces with Leonard in founding what they branded "The Human Potential Movement"—now popularly known as the New Age Movement (incorporating yoga and meditation centers across the nation during the 1970s). It was Leonard who insisted on using the word "Movement" to signify it as a societal shift akin to the civil rights movement, in which he had actively participated in the 1960s.

Born in Macon, Georgia, in 1923, Leonard had witnessed the virulent racism of the South firsthand. He later included therapy to help people examine their inner racism as part of the training at Esalen. In the 2002 BBC documentary *Century of the Self*, one of these group therapy sessions shows a young black man confronting the white women in his group about their racist preconceptions.

Century of the Self goes on to talk about how Esalen and the New

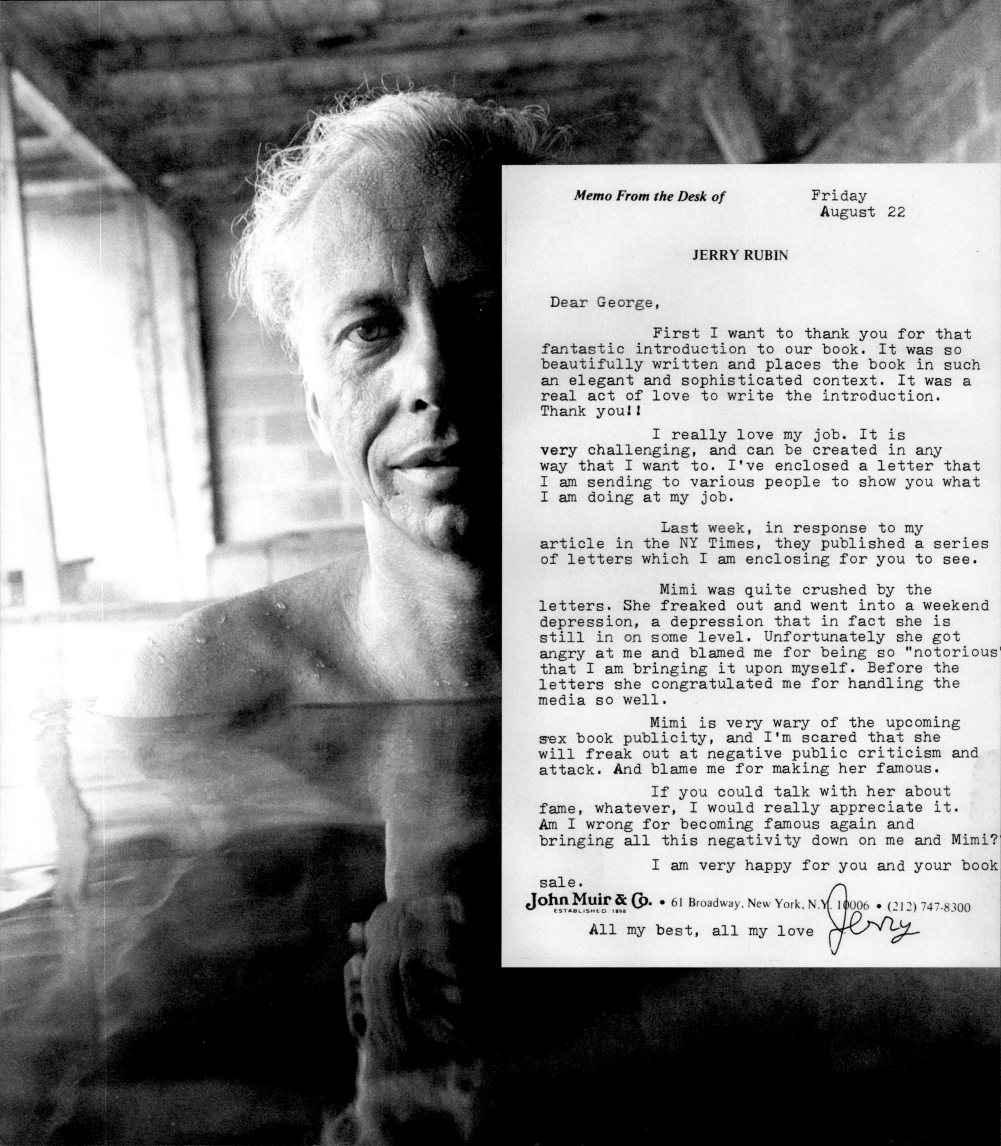

Memo From the Desk of   Friday
                                         August 22

JERRY RUBIN

Dear George,

      First I want to thank you for that
fantastic introduction to our book. It was so
beautifully written and places the book in such
an elegant and sophisticated context. It was a
real act of love to write the introduction.
Thank you!!

      I really love my job. It is
very challenging, and can be created in any
way that I want to. I've enclosed a letter that
I am sending to various people to show you what
I am doing at my job.

      Last week, in response to my
article in the NY Times, they published a series
of letters which I am enclosing for you to see.

      Mimi was quite crushed by the
letters. She freaked out and went into a weekend
depression, a depression that in fact she is
still in on some level. Unfortunately she got
angry at me and blamed me for being so "notorious"
that I am bringing it upon myself. Before the
letters she congratulated me for handling the
media so well.

      Mimi is very wary of the upcoming
sex book publicity, and I'm scared that she
will freak out at negative public criticism and
attack. And blame me for making her famous.

      If you could talk with her about
fame, whatever, I would really appreciate it.
Am I wrong for becoming famous again and
bringing all this negativity down on me and Mimi?

      I am very happy for you and your book
sale.

John Muir & Co. • 61 Broadway, New York, N.Y. 10006 • (212) 747-8300
ESTABLISHED 1898

All my best, all my love   *Jerry*

Age Movement became the answer for a generation disillusioned by a decade of political activism gone sour. For frustrated politicos and burned-out revolutionaries, the journey inward was an attractive alternative. Not surprisingly, Jerry also appeared (posthumously) in the 2002 documentary. He appears in an episode focusing on est.

As Jerry stated in his book, *Growing (Up) at 37*, "Ex-radicals and ex-revolutionaries meet these days in farms, Gestalt groups, therapy retreats, meditation sessions and welfare lines." He described "est [as] an attempt to Americanize Eastern consciousness—to make it available to the majority of the people." The New Age Movement was criticized as an excuse for spoiled baby boomers to become self-centered and self-indulgent. Mainstream media dubbed them "The Me Generation," and they were lampooned in movies like *Bob & Carol & Ted & Alice*, which tells the story of wife swapping masquerading as consciousness.

So how did George Leonard's New Age journey begin? After flying combat missions during World War II, he graduated with an English degree from the University of North Carolina in 1948. He joined *Look* magazine in 1953, and immediately focused on civil rights issues. Among several other journalists (including T. George Harris, a fellow *Look* reporter, who later edited *Psychology Today*), he contributed to "a memorable, hour-by-hour account of the [1962] integration of the University of Mississippi." *Look* was similar in format to *Life* magazine with an emphasis on photojournalism—Leonard was assigned to their San Francisco office in the early '60s.

Leonard's article for *Look* magazine, "Youth of the Sixties: The Explosive Generation" (January 1961), was the first to examine and predict the coming counterculture revolution. He foresaw the "tumult and idealism of the '60s." He wrote that the "quiet generation" of the 1950s "is rumbling and is going to explode"—the following year, he accurately predicted that "that the youth movements would first manifest themselves in California." His 1964 essay, "Revolution in Education," featured the phrase "human potential," which intrigued scores of readers. Leonard's articles may have contributed to Jerry's decision to head westward in the early '60s after outgrowing his hometown of Cincinnati.

Leonard's essays over the years touched on such subjects as the decline of the Sexual Revolution and the collapse of the Soviet Union, long before those events occurred—causing the *San Francisco Chronicle* to declare, "George Leonard has been right so many times about prevailing zeitgeists that you have to wonder if he has a third eye."

As the author of a dozen books on expanding consciousness and achieving potential, he both chronicled and participated in social change and personal growth. At nearly fifty, he began to study aikido (martial arts), quickly achieving a fifth-degree black belt. Just months before his death at eighty-six, he was still "leading workshops on exercise, communication, diet, relationships and understanding." Jerry's evolution from journalist to radical to New Age follower echoed much of George Leonard's work.

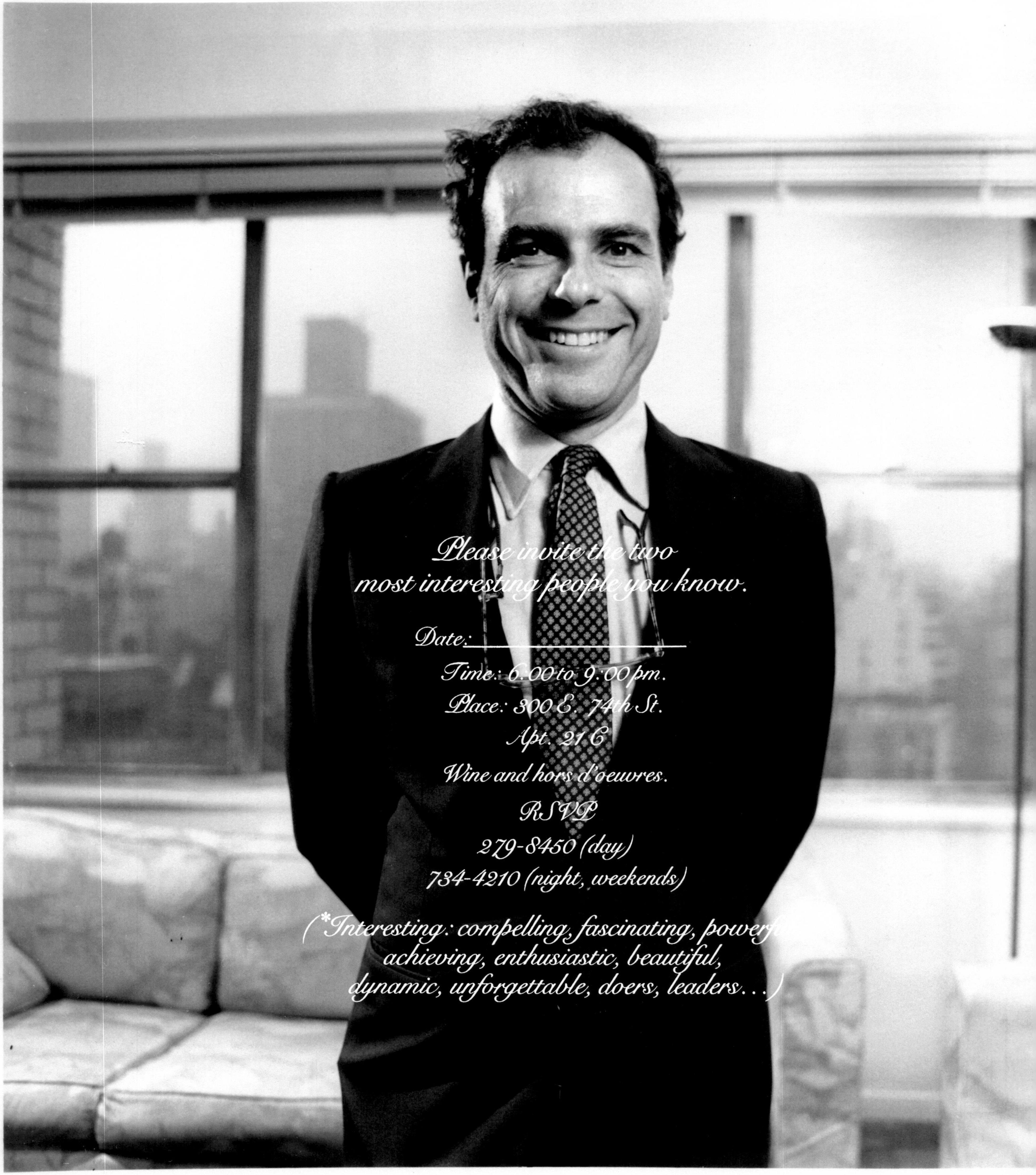

Please invite the two
most interesting people you know.

Date: _____

Time: 6:00 to 9:00 pm.

Place: 300 E. 74th St.

Apt. 21 C

Wine and hors d'oeuvres.

RSVP

279-8450 (day)

734-4210 (night, weekends)

(*Interesting: compelling, fascinating, powerf[ul]
achieving, enthusiastic, beautiful,
dynamic, unforgettable, doers, leaders…)

It was like you're on stage and all of sudden the lights go on and it's very intoxicating to be his spotlight. Things were vivid and colorful and important, that's how it felt. Jerry was very alive.

—MIMI LEONARD

OPPOSITE: Jerry in his 74th street apartment, circa 1988.

Yuppie

When Jerry Met Mimi.   Jerry had been shuffling back and forth between San Francisco and New York for much of the early '70s. By 1976, he was back in Manhattan full time, strategizing. An undated journal entry titled "I Want" was a laundry list; it included notes on having a networking salon one night per week and an "invitation-only brunch or dinner with 20–30 people every week at a great place." He was obviously looking to get back into the game. His list also had this item: "I want a beautiful blond society wife." Mimi Leonard was the beautiful blond daughter of Esalen Institute scholar (and *Look* magazine editor) George Leonard. Because of Jerry's involvement with Esalen, he was already fan of George. Mimi saw him once at the offices of her father's agent.

MIMI LEONARD: It was 1971. I was twenty-one and I was working at the Sterling Lord Agency. Sterling Lord was my father's agent and, as it turned out, he was also Jerry's. Once, when I was sitting there at my desk, Jerry walked in. I just remember he was very disheveled, surrounded by a cloud of marijuana aroma. He looked like a cartoon character; he really did. So, that was my very first contact, and I wrote a paper on him and Abbie later when I was about twenty-five for my social movements class at Columbia.

The two wouldn't cross paths again until December 1976, when Jerry met Mimi.

MIMI LEONARD: I met Jerry when my best friend at the time, Lynn Hollyn, was going out with Greg Mitchell. He was the editor of *Crawdaddy* and friends with Stew Albert, Jerry's best friend. There was a joint birthday party in New York for Stew and Greg. This was December 4, 1976, in the Village.

I was going out with another guy at the time named Ronnie, but I did have a conversation with Jerry. He thought I was attractive, and I was working at BBDO [an advertising agency] as senior marketing analyst, and he said something to me like, "I have some great ideas. I'd love to pitch something to BBDO." And I said, "Well, you know, that has nothing to do with me. I just do scientific research." (Later he said to me, "I knew it had nothing to do with you.")

So then I said, "Maybe you know my father George Leonard?" and then suddenly he just kind of fell back and said, "You're George Leonard's daughter? How is he old enough to have a daughter like you?"

Jerry found out that I was involved with this guy but kept in touch with Lynn and called her every once in a while. When he found out that Ronnie and I had broken up, he called me and I went out with him on February 21, 1977. That was our first date. I was living in a walkup in a brownstone on East 91st Street and 5th.

He came up and before we went out to dinner, he asked me to marry him. [*Laughs.*] I wasn't that interested. But he was very sincere. It took a little bit more time. It took us . . . I don't remember how many dates—it didn't take that long but I think our first date was February 21st and I think we moved in together on April 1st."

Roger Ressmeyer did a photo session with the young couple in the early days of their relationship.

ROGER RESSMEYER: I don't know exactly how they discovered each other. I just know that it was explosively magnetic. They were just so in love and when you see this range of pictures I have—there's probably, in that collection of fifty, about ten of him and Mimi kissing, hugging, posing, smiling.

Jerry and Mimi on their wedding day. Photo © Roger Ressmeyer

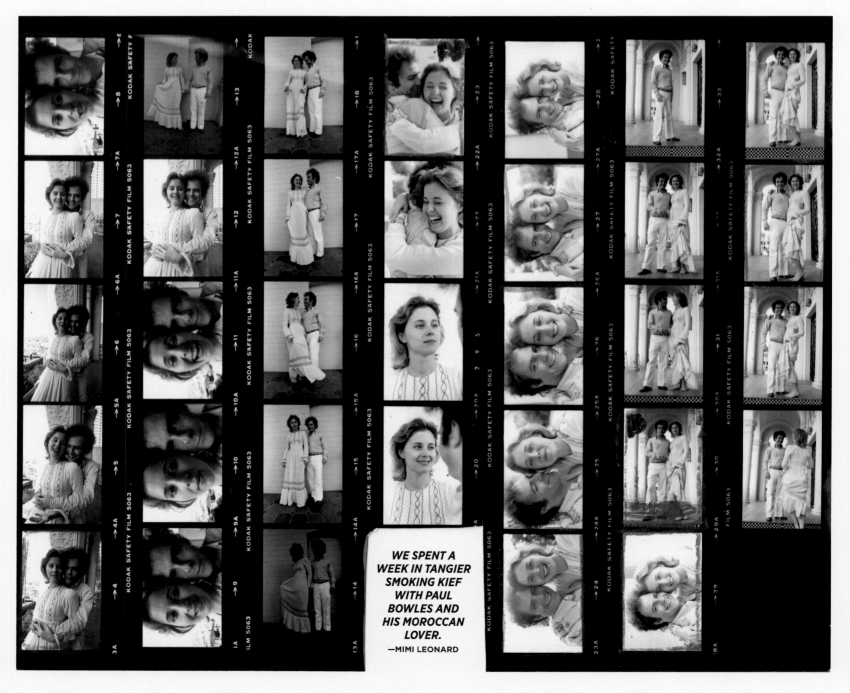

WE SPENT A WEEK IN TANGIER SMOKING KIEF WITH PAUL BOWLES AND HIS MOROCCAN LOVER.
—MIMI LEONARD

When Jerry and Mimi decided to get married in 1978, Jerry went to his old high school friend, Barton Shallot, who had since become a rabbi.

RABBI BARTON SHALLOT: I asked where was he going to get married? Jerry said he wanted to be married in a Temple. I said, "Okay, I can get you the Temple." And he said it was going to be a controversial wedding, with a lot of people there, and he was going to make a big thing out of it. And I said, "Gee, Jerry, I don't know if I really feel comfortable doing that. But I can get the perfect rabbi for you."

I brought him a rabbi named Bruce Goldman, who was a radical also. He led all the riots in Columbia, and caused all this trouble. He was a difficult guy. So I figured they'd be perfect for each other. Jerry told Bruce, "I want you to keep it short." And Bruce did exactly the opposite. "No one tells me how to do what I do, I do it my way." Bruce made it long, and he was obnoxious all throughout. Jerry said, "Why'd you give me someone like that?" I said, "Jerry, because you're like that."

MIMI LEONARD: We went to Morocco for our honeymoon and spent an amazing month driving around the country. We spent a week in Tangier smoking kief with [composer] Paul Bowles and his Moroccan lover, dining at a couple of fine restaurants. And, I remember one evening on a beach eating with our hands out of a pot.

As with so many of the key relationships in his life, Jerry fell into a creative partnership with Mimi. They dreamed big: they wanted to plan celebrity-studded events, write books, and find new ways to take on the world. In November 1978, Jerry and Mimi presented "The Event" in Manhattan, a fourteen-hour "awareness extravaganza" featuring Werner Erhard (of est) and an eclectic mix of notable thinkers of the '70s—self-help advocate Wayne Dyer, comedian Dick Gregory on food and health, maverick visionary Buckminster Fuller, and future Governor of California Arnold Schwarzenegger talking about body and mind control. This was an all-star cast of characters who only could have come together with Rubin's networking skills. The roster proved Jerry's theory about how famous people can always get in touch with other famous people. He told the *New York Times*, "It's a California event in the middle of New York City."

"The Event" was the couple's first collaboration. Mimi recalls how it came together without the benefit of email or the internet.

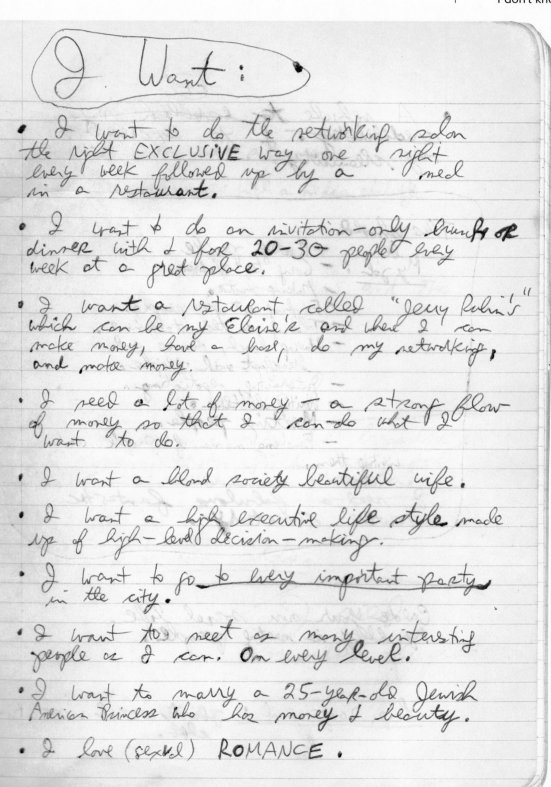

I Want:

- I want to do the networking salon the right EXCLUSIVE way one night every week followed up by a meal in a restaurant.

- I want to do an invitation-only brunch or dinner with I for 20-30 people every week at a great place.

- I want a restaurant called "Jerry Rubin's" which can be my Elaine's and where I can make money, have a base, do my networking, and make money.

- I need a lot of money — a strong flow of money so that I can do what I want to do.

- I want a blond society beautiful wife.

- I want a high executive life style made up of high-level decision-making.

- I want to go to every important party in the city.

- I want to meet as many interesting people as I can. On every level.

- I want to marry a 25-year-old Jewish American Princess who has money & beauty.

- I love (sexual) ROMANCE.

MIMI LEONARD: It was extraordinary how Jerry managed to bring together some of the most influential thinkers of that time as presenters. And they weren't all from our circles. For instance, Masters and Johnson—we didn't have anyone in common with them. And of course, before the internet, all the correspondence was done in stamped envelopes. Jerry's pure enthusiasm and force of personality got them to fly to New York. We thought it was going to be the beginning of a new kind of public speaking forum, and even a new kind of transformational experience. Masters and Johnson were hard to convince but in the end, Jerry's enthusiasm won out and they gave a terrific seminar. Virginia Johnson was sympathetic to Jerry's vision.

We wanted Richard Pryor as our nighttime entertainment. He was the contemporary Lenny Bruce in our minds. When Richard couldn't do it, we turned to George Carlin, who came—asking only for his plane and hotel—giving a hilarious performance. Werner Erhard appeared gratis, as did my father. Some kind of speaking fee went to [the rest]. Arnold Schwarzenegger brought Maria Shriver. They were dating then and she spent every possible moment on Arnold's lap.

Don't Quit Your Day Job. Jerry found himself in another transitional period—one in which he needed to earn a living. As a result, he decided to write a book about the '60s and got an advance from Simon & Schuster. Unfortunately, his interest in reliving those years was nil, so he got Stew Albert to ghostwrite; the manuscript was a disaster. They were both high as kites while writing it, and even worse, they referred to themselves in the third person throughout the text. The publisher felt it was unreadable.

MIMI LEONARD: Jerry had gotten an advance from Simon & Schuster for the book, and they demanded their advance back and no one had ever had to give their advance back in the history of the publishing, but we ended up having to give it back. So, Jerry and I went and got regular jobs. I went and got a job at ABC News.

Mimi quit her day job when the couple got an advance to write *The War Between the Sheets: What's Happening with Men in Bed and What Women and Men Are Doing About It* in 1980.

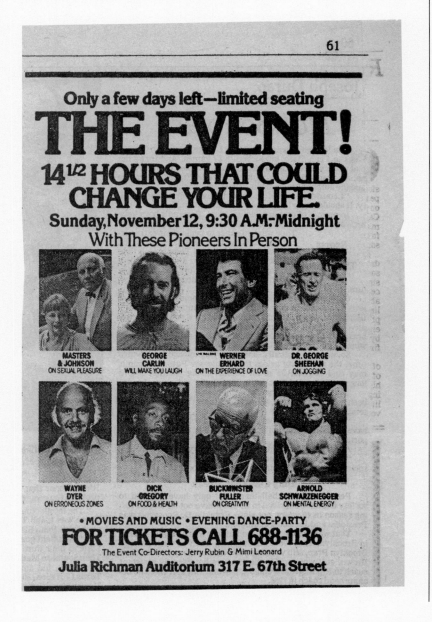

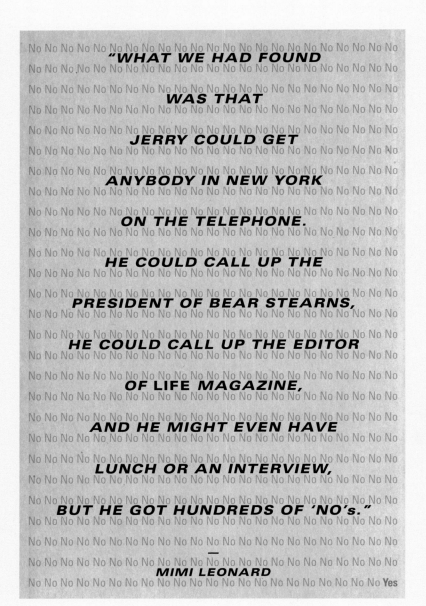

"WHAT WE HAD FOUND WAS THAT JERRY COULD GET ANYBODY IN NEW YORK ON THE TELEPHONE. HE COULD CALL UP THE PRESIDENT OF BEAR STEARNS, HE COULD CALL UP THE EDITOR OF LIFE MAGAZINE, AND HE MIGHT EVEN HAVE LUNCH OR AN INTERVIEW, BUT HE GOT HUNDREDS OF 'NO's."

—MIMI LEONARD

Growing (Up) at 37 had come out fairly recently and he was getting some royalties on that, and there was that chapter in there on male sexuality, and I guess the idea of taking that chapter and making it a book was appealing to Jerry. That was his main idea for moneymaking. He was doing lectures as well, and had an agent named Royce Carlton. —MIMI LEONARD

As he'd done in *Growing (Up) at 37*, Jerry prided himself in total honesty about very personal issues; he frankly discussed impotence and premature ejaculation. But mainly *The War Between the Sheets* was a self-help book for men and women. It was based on hundreds of interviews Jerry and Mimi conducted with both sexes, discussing such issues as "what women really want in bed" and the idea that "men are sexually more vulnerable than women." Once again, Jerry was ahead of the curve, as only *Cosmopolitan* magazine was addressing these issues in the mainstream media then. But, after its release, the book vanished off the public's radar—a good thing, according to Mimi: "After it was published, we suddenly looked at each other and said, 'What in the world did we do?'"

Jerry went back to work; she became a commodities broker. "I guess we both realized we had to go out and get real jobs. I had this idea that being a commodities broker seemed so swashbuckling, so romantic and glamorous. I got a job with ContiCommodity, which was the top firm." Jerry saw Mimi's success, and decided to go to Wall Street.

MIMI LEONARD: Jerry entered into job-hunting with the same enthusiasm and broad vision he did everything. He wrote up a resume and sent it to thousands of people. He made appointments with hundreds. Jerry could get nearly anyone on the phone . . . We were drawn to Wall Street. We had just experienced how unsophisticated and lacking we were in raising money and doing business—having had this spectacular success really with "The Event," but it was a complete flop financially.

Jerry, however, could not get a job. Which I guess looking back at that time, was not surprising. Jerry was wonderful at promoting himself and his own ideas, but was never good at doing anything else. First of all, he was forty-two, which seemed old then, but he was finally offered a job by maverick investment wizard Ray Dirks.

Although Jerry did take and pass the stockbrokers exam, I do not believe he ever acted as a stockbroker. Instead he was named Marketing Director and right from the beginning, his job was to bring in new accounts. He did that by creating his weekly "Networking Salon," for which Ray's firm John Muir paid the expenses—a few hundred a week for wine, light hors d'oeuvres, Jerry's assistant, and a little printing and postage. John Muir was the name of Dirk's firm. They were focusing on ecology and green energy.

Guess Who's Coming to Wall Street.

On July 30, 1980, Jerry penned an article for the *New York Times*: "Guess Who's Coming to Wall Street." It began, "I accepted a position on Wall Street this week. That might strike some people as surprising. I was one of a small group of street-theatre Yippies who stormed the New York Stock Exchange 13 years ago and threw dollar bills from the visitor's gallery. The floor brokers stopped trading and rushed after the falling dollars." He goes on, "We dropped the dollar bills on Wall Street to call attention to a system that we felt had too often separated money and ethics, creating enormous wealth amid mass poverty. Today I have many of the same criticisms and same values. . . But I know I can be more effective today wearing a suit and a tie and working on Wall Street than I can be dancing outside the walls of power. Raising money for projects in the last few years, I have learned that the individual who signs the check has the ultimate power. Money is power. If I am going to have any effect on my society over the next forty years, I must develop the power that only control of money can bring."

John Muir & Company had hired Jerry as a securities analyst, "investigating new companies of the future, including those producing solar and other alternative-energy sources"—i.e., Jerry's job would be to search for small companies that specialized in ecological technology. Then he'd develop financing and marketing strategies for them, ideally turning "socially aware risk-takers" into "tomorrow's titans." Jerry felt that he could help spearhead a new entrepreneurial era in America, one in which depressed areas would receive fresh investment capital. Besides environmental firms, Jerry hoped to uncover new companies with a focus on social change.

JERRY RUBIN COMES TO WALL STREET

By Jerry Rubin

I accepted a position this week on Wall Street. That fact might strike some people as surprising. I was one of a small group of street theater yippies who stormed the New York Stock Exchange 13 years ago and threw dollar bills down from the open visitor's gallery in an action that attracted worldwide media attention. The floor brokers stopped trading and rushed after the showering dollars. The Stock Exchange soon installed a bullet-proof glass between the visitor's gallery and the brokers on the floor making them safe again from the antics of the anti-capitalist comics of the sixties.

A lot happened in the ensuing 13 years. Our nationwide campaign to build public support against the Vietnam war succeeded, and the war ended for us. Yet sadly the war in Asia continues without American military involvement and Russian soldiers are today occupied in Afghanistan. In the United States the radical dream of transforming the system from the outside floundered and then virtually disappeared, although we did reform parts of the system. My friends from that period have splintered into thousands of different, and apparently unconnected, directions.

The reason that we dropped dollar bills on Wall Street was to call attention to a system that we felt had too often separated money and ethics, creating enormous wealth amidst mass poverty. Today I have many of the same criticisms and same values, and with the misery index of inflation and recession, the economic situation is even more disastrous in 1980 than it was in 1968. I know that I can be more effective today wearing a suit and tie and working on Wall Street...

Guess Who's Coming to Wall Stree

By Jerry Rubin

I accepted a position on Wall Street this week. That might strike some people as surprising. I was one of a small group of street-theater Yippies who stormed the New York Stock Exchange 13 years ago and threw dollar bills from the visitors' gallery. The floor brokers stopped trading and rushed after the falling dollars. The Stock Exchange soon installed bullet-proof glass between the gallery and the brokers on the floor, making them safe again from the antics of the anti-capitalistic comics of the 1960's.

A lot happened in the next 13 years. Our nationwide campaign to build public opposition to the Vietnam War succeeded, and the war ended. Yet sadly, the war in Asia continues without American military involvement. In the United States, the radical dream of transforming the system from the outside floundered, then virtually disappeared, although we did reform parts of the system. My friends from that period have gone in thousands of apparently unconnected directions.

We dropped the dollar bills on Wall Street to call attention to a system that we felt had too often separated money and ethics, creating enormous wealth amid mass poverty. Today I have many of the same criticisms and same values, and the economic situation is even more disastrous in 1980 than it was in 1968.

But I know that I can be more effective today wearing a suit and tie and working on Wall Street than I can be dancing outside the walls of power.

Politics and rebellion distinguished the 60's. The search for the self characterized the spirit of the 70's. Money and financial interest will capture the passion of the 80's.

Women today are gaining power by entering the executive marketplace. They are discovering the authority and self-esteem that come with financial independence. Black leaders, too, say the top item on the agenda for

the thousands of people of my ge... tion who want to be effective in th... and 90's by joining — and also d... ing — the same system they one... visions of supplanting.

When I began looking for a j... Wall Street, I expected much di... agement. In fact, one headhunte... it was highly unlikely that the st... stitutions of Wall Street would ta... chance of welcoming Jerry Rubi... I received a job offer in the first... of my job search.

In my job, I will be a securitie... lyst investigating new compan... the future, including those pro... solar and other alternative-e... sources. My task will be to find... lyze and develop financing and... keting plans for those entrepre... nonconglomerate companies th... society desperately needs.

As a radical activist, I could... tively criticize the domination... financial world by huge organiza... primarily through my writin... speaking. As a financial planner... effectively change that reality... covering promising independen... panies and finding the financi... the socially aware risk takers w... become tomorrow's titans.

The challenge for American c... ism in the 80's is to bring the ent... neurial spirit back to America... large organizations have disco... people's expression and am... America needs a revitalization... small-business spirit. Dep... areas especially need an enorm... vestment of capital. Individual... preneurship can create the new... ethic that is so desperately nee... America. To stimulate that... America needs creative finance... and I intend to work to create it.

Today, a person cannot surv... financial challenges of recessi... inflation without financial know... One of the reasons that the r... come richer and the poor po... America is that the wealthy can... the financial information supp... lawyers and accountants. The a... person is unaware of his fin... rights and opportunities. We r... democratize information about... because information is power.

United Press International

Hate Mail. The *New York Times* readership responded with hate mail. The *Times* printed a dozen cynical letters two weeks later. Some of them made jokes that even Jerry could appreciate, such as the suggestion he start a new organization: "The Weather Vanes." Another letter said, "I greet that news [that Rubin is coming to Wall Street] with the same kind of four-letter expletives Mr. Rubin used to hurl at people like me before he saw the light and found bread, butter, and three-piece suits." The most significant response noted it took Jerry only one week to get a job offer from the system that he once ridiculed. An African American writer recalled their mother's words during the turbulent '60s: "When the white children get tired of all this, all they have to do is cut their hair and tell their families and the society they are sorry, and all will be forgiven. They will never forgive your color." The letter writer then asked, "Today, one wonders whether H. Rap Brown would fare as well in his job search, or Angela Davis, or Stokely Carmichael—or even myself, had I pursued Mr. Rubin's path?"

THE NEW YORK TIMES, SATURDAY, AUGUST 16, 1980

Readers Wonder: Is Jerry Rubin Taking the Gravy Train (No. 1) From Wall St.? Or Is It Easy St.?

To the Editor:

Jerry Rubin tells us of his transformation from a radical activist to a capitalist activist ["Guess Who's Coming to Street," Op-Ed page, July 30]. By joining a Wall Street erage firm and getting inside the walls of power, Mr. n feels that he can more effectively work to reform the m he tried so desperately to change in the '60's.

Jerry Rubin is either incredibly naïve or he's just deluded imself to assuage his guilt for joining the corporate Es ishment.

Mr. Rubin may find that his perception of reality will age from his new vantage point.

For instance, I wonder how he will feel about corporate s that result in hindering the growth of companies he represent. Will he have the same compassion for the and disadvantaged who receive benefits from these s?

Mr. Rubin thinks that he will be able to control the sys and mold it to his current sense of values. I think Mr. in will find, if he's really intent on achieving a position wer, that the system will alter his values.

Altruistic people do not last long on Wall Street.

ALLEN COHEN
New Brunswick, N.J.

To the Editor:

Jerry Rubin is going to Wall Street!

greet that news with the same kind of four-letter exple s Mr. Rubin used to hurl at people like me before he saw light and found bread, butter and three-piece suits. And who are the people like me?

m part of the people who spent the last 20 years protect what you sought to destroy. I worked out there in the big, world of business — and even worse, in that narrow, in r, manipulative world of advertising. And guess what?

m glad.

m glad I didn't fight the system.

m glad I tried to make society better from within.

m glad I stood up in board rooms and executive offices said my piece and tried to create new products and serv

m glad I was out there with other hard-working middle s old-values people who tried to effect change from in corporate walls instead of trying to tear down from out

ook, Mr. Rubin, there are a lot of us who've fought for all s of minority representation in the system all our lives. only one of them. And I'll be damned if I'm going to wel e you to Wall Street.

don't care about the nuclear stocks you want to tout. I 't care if you can make lights go on and off at the end of tunnel.

ecause as far as I'm concerned, you not only sat out our , you were the one shooting at us.

ow that you think money is the only power, I can tell you none of my money will knowingly go into your hands. ecause frankly, Mr. Rubin, I still don't trust your mo s.

LOIS WYSE
New York, N.Y.

To the Editor:

erhaps the way for the New Left to spare itself such king debacles as that recently delivered by Jerry Rubin ld be to establish a pension fund for its activists emeri

hat way such persons would be spared the indignity of ing to take degrading and even deleterious employment eir dotage.

JOHN CRAWFORD
New Brunswick, N.J.

To the Editor:

rry Rubin's article certainly illustrates one thing — people cannot effectively protest the Government dur a period of economic instability.

too, fell victim to this — the only reason why I did not oc cupy the Pentagon on April 21 in protest of nuclear energy is because I had to work that day.

If I wasn't so naïve, I would think that the Government had planned it that way — inflation, unemployment, the re cession — all so people would keep quiet, and protest nothing because they are too afraid of starving.

MARIAN P. FRANCOIS
Bronx, N.Y.

To the Editor:

The "old" Jerry Rubin, as Mr. Rubin himself would surely agree, was hardly a model of intellectual rigor. The new one, however, simply sounds pathetic as he tries to convince us (and himself) that the ideals of a radical activist can be easily maintained while doing financial analysis for a firm of stockbrokers.

If Mr. Rubin wants to make money and join the mainstream, that's fine. Let him seek his happiness where he will.

But to say that his new job (promoting the interests of American capitalism) merely continues the work of his old job (promoting the destruction of American capitalism) should offend capitalist and radical alike.

RICHARD EHRLICH
New York, N.Y.

To the Editor:

I stand in an unemployment line this day of July 30 and I tremble with anger. How open-minded of The New York Times, I think, to print this apologia from our own Jerry Rubin.

Why am I so angry, I wonder. I really didn't know Jerry Rubin. I wasn't a Yippie. In fact I wasn't really that politically active.

But I was alive and coming of age in the late 1960's. Around me there were signs of life and change. The Yippies were one kind of vanguard for that change. In their outrageous theatrics, they gave form to my feelings of rage against a system that could indiscriminately slay an un known people in a foreign land or a group of students on a hill in Ohio. Those theatrics were a guide to a struggle. And wasn't this one clear message: that it was the system, based on capital, breeding racism and unemployment and war, the system was at fault.

How bitter betrayal can be. And how neatly explained as result of a simple passage of time.

There is a long article in this same paper about the deplorable state of blacks in this city, their lack of leadership, their experience of racism, their dominant mood of disillusionment.

Congratulations, Jerry Rubin. Capitalism is working for everyone.

On into the 80's.

STAN SALFAS
New York, N.Y.

To the Editor:

I follow Jerry Rubin's varied career with interest. Perhaps Mr. Rubin could found a new society: "The Weather Vanes."

CARL REMICK
New York, N.Y.

To the Editor:

I am a contemporary of Mr. Rubin. In 1968, I was keenly aware of his radical preachings as were many of our peers. Fortunately for him, the vast majority of us decided to ignore those preachings and to make the decision that he made last week. We entered the system and kept it alive for the 10 years he needed to reach the same decision.

In 1970, I took the same job that Jerry Rubin accepted, that of securities analyst. I am today a partner in a successful investment banking firm.

Jerry Rubin says there are "thousands of people of my generation who want to be effective in the 80's and 90's." This is untrue. Most of us have been effective in the 70's.

Would it not be fascinating to throw dollar bills around the Research Department at John Muir & Co. and see who chases them? Probably not the people who have been earning a living for the past 10 years.

JEFFREY L. FELDMAN
New York, N.Y.

To the Editor:

I was present on the floor of the New York Stock Exchange as a member on the day, 13 years ago, when Jerry Rubin and his entourage came onto the visitors' gallery (as millions before him) under the pretext of being a visitor. If he "stormed" the New York Stock Exchange, then my comprehension of the word is sadly lacking. Perhaps he meant "stoned" or "stewed."

It is true that dollar bills were thrown onto the floor of the Exchange, where some entreprenurial clerks, not "floor brokers" "rushed after the falling dollars." Trading was not halted, as Mr. Rubin states, as this practice usually occurs when there is important news pending, not unimportant nuisances pandering.

It follows naturally that, inasmuch as Mr. Rubin has chosen a Wall Street career, this must be the way to have effect on society. Over the next "40 years" he "must develop the power that only control of money can bring."

This 40-year plan may shock historians as well as Wall Street. One might suggest that ideas, not money, are the real power to move mankind.

I never had the opportunity to examine the portfolios of Jesus, Marx, Freud or Einstein, but I could guess that their combined wealth would be less than the royalties Mr. Rubin will make on a future book about the evils of Wall Street.

JEROME WARSHAW
New York, N.Y.

To the Editor:

It must be a great comfort to capitalists to learn that Jerry Rubin has embraced their cause after selling Yippieism in the 60's and self-awareness therapies in the 70's.

The only thing about Rubin that has not changed is his ability for self-promotion and the media's treatment of him as a spokesman for ideas rather than as the huckster he is.

I hope that all of those people who followed his advice to get high, drop out of school and make revolution in the 60's will be as successful as he was in landing a job on Wall Street.

KENNETH J. UVA
New York, N.Y.

To the Editor:

The old adage that "you can't go home again" certainly seems not to apply to all Americans. Jerry Rubin, 60's radical, is a case in point.

I was shocked to find an article on your Op-Ed page written by no less than Mr. Rubin himself extolling the virtues of money and capitalism and, what's more, saying that he will be employed as a securities analyst on Wall Street. It seems he has made peace with the system and it with him. By Mr. Rubin's own admission it took only a week for him to gain employment in the center of America's financial power.

I can only remember other times and places in those heady years called the 60's when people such as Mr. Rubin, Abbie Hoffman and the whole "hippie" movement were roundly criticizing America and particularly its economic and social values. They, coupled with the awakening of a long-dormant black-awareness movement, provided strong and rational arguments to a young black college senior in the 60's. Join in, drop out, was the siren call of that era and one hard to ignore. I can only recall my mother's sage advice in these troubled times: "When the white children get tired of all this, all they have to do is cut their hair and tell their families and the society they are sorry, and all will be forgiven. They will never forgive you your color."

Today, one wonders whether H. Rap Brown would fare as well in his job search, or Angela Davis or Stokely Carmichael or even myself had I pursued Mr. Rubin's path? Abbie, where are you? Wall Street is waiting.

MARTIS J. DAVIS
Westfield, N.J.

WHEN THE WHITE CHILDREN GET TIRED OF ALL THIS, ALL THEY HAVE TO DO IS CUT THEIR HAIR AND TELL THEIR FAMILIES AND THE SOCIETY THEY ARE SORRY, AND ALL WILL BE FORGIVEN.

LETTER TO THE NEW YORK TIMES

A 1960's Rebel Looks to the 1980's

To the Editor:

I was quite surprised to pick up the Aug. 16 Op-Ed page of The New York Times and see myself stoned by a barrage of angry letters. The problem is that the letters were based in part on faulty information because of the parts deleted from my original New York Times article.

The firm I work for is hardly a "Wall Street bastion." I was recruited by Ray Dirks, who broke the Equity Fund scandal in 1973, and who has shown himself willing to challenge the established order of things. I am a venture banker at John Muir & Co., a financial talent scout seeking out new companies, particularly in the area of energy conservation and development. On the lecture circuit over the past 10 years, I've met many enterprising people and I now have a chance to connect them to the world of finance and positive investment.

The emotional letters came from people who expressed either a continuing grudge against me from the 1960's or from people who feel that I in no way can provide any positive service in the financial world, and therefore am deceiving myself and others by saying so. I disagree. I am proud of what I did in the 1960's and I also realize that we are living 11 years later.

This decade, the 1980's, will be a problem-solving era. I believe that I can — and will — make a positive contribution in the world of finance and people.

Lastly, I am somewhat bemused by the view that I am a fad-chaser. I wonder if the government of Richard Nixon tried to imprison me for chasing fads.

JERRY RUBIN
New York, Aug. 20, 1980

GERALD LEFCOURT: I couldn't believe my eyes. Here's a guy who was fighting to change this country in radical terms. And here he was, working for a Wall Street firm, telling me that Wall Street was gonna work for everyone? When he told me years before that Capitalism is designed not to work for everyone. It was very upsetting to Abbie, I must say.

NANCY KURSHAN: The annoying thing about what Jerry did is that he did put himself forward so publicly in an oppositional way to what some of us were still trying to do. Saying, "This is all over." Saying, "You're all being very foolish."

GIL RUBIN: The idea of trying to sell stocks was kind of a sad thing for me. It was almost like Joe Lewis being the doorman at Caesar's Palace. To me it was sad, the enthusiasm there, the suit and tie every day, and clean-shaven. It wasn't the brother I knew.

STEPHEN SMALE: It was great to see him there. He was controversial, because he went into finance. . . became some kind of capitalist, and so on. I was enthusiastic about that. Both of us were kind of radicals, but neither of us were indoctrinated socialists, far from it. So I was on his side, completely, when he became part of this Wall Street culture.

Tuli Kupferberg of the Fugs told Peter Manso:

But if you reflect on it, whatever Jerry's faults were, a lot of them were the faults of the sixties. The movement collapsed, Jerry collapsed. The movement "sold out," in quotes; Jerry sold out, without the quotes. But actually he didn't really sell out. He never bought in. So in a way he's typical of the whole stream of the sixties— the superficiality. Jerry also knew how to work the media, and when I consider that, it throws a frightening thought into me—that the whole sixties thing was a media event. Maybe that's occurred to me once or twice, but I didn't really want to believe it. It wasn't uncommon that the media influenced plans for a demonstration, almost in the same way that the New York Times *sets the agenda of American politics. The President picks up the paper—"What does* The Times *say? What did I do right? Or wrong, what should I do now?"*

Another Op-Ed Piece for the *New York Times*.

By early 1981, Jerry had been promoted to Director of Business Development. In the January 15, 1981 *New York Times*, he wrote, "I hope to actively communicate the opportunities that John Muir presents to the economy, to the entrepreneur and to the investor. Using my knowledge of the media and my communications abilities, I hope to effectively communicate." Jerry also cited that he'd been a reporter for the *Cincinnati Post*, had written several books, and lectured at hundreds of colleges as solid qualifications for his new job title. "I think the process of being active in current events and basically trying to improve the country reveals a commitment I still have. I think the talents I had then, I still have."

In August '81, Jerry had branched out to create his own money management firm. John Muir was a stock brokerage company, and Jerry wanted to diversify into "tax shelters, financial planning, real estate, and venture capital investments." Jerry initiated the change with the cooperation of John Muir & Company, who allowed him to remain as a consultant as well as partnering in Jerry's new firm. The August 24, 1981 issue of *New York* magazine noted: "Ray Dirks, with an innate flair for publicity (he was the star of his own advertisements), flabbergasted the investment community when he hired former Yippie leader Jerry to work for Muir. The wide press coverage of Jerry's conversion to capitalism gave Muir a lot of free publicity. Jerry, who was earning around $50,000 a year at Muir, left recently to start up his own investment service, but continues to be a consultant to Dirks and the Muir firm."

Beatniks Are Out to Make it Rich.

Little known in the mythos of Rubin's supposed sellout is that many of his former friends on the radical Left were also playing the stock market and doing quite well. Still, an argument can be made that calling Jerry a sellout was very much a hypocritical act when one looks at the lives of other, lesser-known radicals after the demise of the '60s.

RON DAVIS: In the '60s, people thought being a revolutionary meant "I'm going to have long hair." Long hair, that's a big breakthrough. So I was thinking that the transition from Yippie to Yuppie is real easy. No problem. You cut your hair, you get a suit. And that's exactly what Rubin did. The changeover is exactly where a lot of the Yippies and Hippies went. They were in the stock market, and they were in the big-time business. Even Peter Coyote [the leader of the Diggers] went on to become a businessman. Another Digger, Chuck Gould, became a millionaire making money from oil wells. A whole bunch of people went on to make money, in the stock market, in the art world, and in Hollywood.

RIGHT: The Yuppie phenomenon exploded with both positive and negative essays, photo-ops, and satire cartoons aimed at Jerry, with Rubin and Ginsberg dancing the '80s away.

Jerry Rubin to Direct Development at Muir

John Muir & Co.

Jerry Rubin, the former Yippie and Chicago Seven defendant who surprised many who knew him by taking a job on Wall Street six months ago with John Muir & Company, has been promoted to director of business development of the brokerage firm. Sounding like a born and bred capitalist, he spoke yesterday about his plans in his new post.

"I hope to actively communicate the opportunities that John Muir presents to the economy, to the entrepreneur and to the investor," Mr. Rubin asserted. "Using my knowledge of the media and my communications abilities, I hope to effectively communicate."

Mr. Rubin, 42,, was an early protester against the Vietnam War and was a member of a group that threw dollar bills from the visitors' gallery to the trading floor of the New York Stock Exchange about 13 years ago. Last week he passed the joint Big Board-National Association of Securities Dealers examination to qualify as a registered securities salesman.

United Press International

Jerry Rubin

Mr. YUPPIE GIVES HIS MESSAGE

By JOHN MACKIE

THE word yuppie may make you sick, but to Jerry Rubin, radical-turned-businessman, it's a godsend. By shaving the fuzz off his face, trading in his tie-dyed shirt for a dark blue suit and closing in "that the language of America isn't English—it's money," the 46-year-old New Yorker has become Mr. Yuppie, a guy who makes muchos money throwing yuppie parties and explaining to non-yups what it is that makes the yuppies sooooo. . . yuppie.

About two hundred well-heeled businesspeople (women in dresses, men in suits) paid $20 to $25 to hear Rubin speak on "how to market to yuppies" at Roboson Square last night. They saw a short (5-5½) man who looks and talks like actor Elliot Gould, a man who doesn't speak so much as he performs, returning to his key themes again and again in a well-designed, rhythmic speech.

He's a quick, commanding speaker who controls the room, resting his arms round the outer edges of the podium like any good politician. He talks in headlines, he talks like an advertising exec narrow-casting his target consumer group, he talks, he talks, he talks.

When he's at his most serious, people laugh. Rubin quickly runs underneath the laugh and grabs their conscience, trying (and

One doesn't know if Rubin has any further delusions of electoral grandeur, but the speech was very political, almost messianic in its defence of yuppiedom.

succeeding) in evoking a "hey, I never thought of it that way before" response. He's a pro.

One doesn't know if Rubin has any further delusions of electoral grandeur, but the speech was very political, almost messianic in its defence of yuppiedom.

He's not as right wing as a lot of his audience — if anything, his political message is. . .liberal.

Essentially, it's an argument for a humanistic capitalism intent on wealth creation rather than distribution; baking a whole bunch of new pies rather than divvying up one already cooked. Democratize the system so that everyone can have their stab at becoming a millionaire.

"I believe that the difference between people and poor people is that rich people understand money and poor people don't really do," he said. "We've got to teach the ghetto kid the language of money — they're not taught how to become rich. Democratize it so that everybody can do it."

These days, Jerry Rubin is big on optimism. He describes himself as an "event creator," a "people person." He is also a master at media manipulation. When he joined a Wall Street investment firm, he didn't hand out business cards at parties — he wrote an article on the op-ed page of the New York Times.

He started his own networking party at Studio 54, Rubin was interviewed by columnist Bob Greene, who coined the term yuppie (as in "Jerry Rubin was leader of the yippies, now he's leader of the yuppies").

While holding a networking party at Studio 54, Rubin was interviewed by columnist Bob Greene, who coined the term yuppie (as in "Jerry Rubin was leader of the yippies, now he's leader of the yuppies").

nightclub in New York.

pies don't drink Perrier for status, they drink it because they care about their health and don't want to poison their bodies with foul elixirs. "The fact is there is a natural health revolution that's going away." This is going away." as the yuppies want the world.

TRANSFORMATION from yippie to yuppie: Jerry Rubin has shed beard and beads for a businessman's dark blue suit

WAITER! ANOTHER ... PERRIER!

JERRY RUBIN IS ON WALL STREET... BOB DYLAN IS SINGING GOSPEL... ALL OF OUR OLD FRIENDS LIVE IN THE SUBURBS... EVERYONE'S SOLD OUT, MAN. YOU AND ME, ARNIE... WE'RE THE LAST OF THE VISIONARIES... THE LAST OF... OF...

CHICAGO 7 1968

FORTUNE 500 1980

JERRY RUBIN
BUSINESS
NETWORKING
SALON ᴿᴹ CARD

PERMANENT · CARD ·

"EVERY WEDNESDAY" AT STUDIO 54

Jerry's Rolodex—the Facebook of the '80s

RATSO SLOMAN: Jerry was the master of the Rolodex. You always knew you could call Jerry, and he would be able to put you in touch with whoever it is, whatever aspect of the world you needed to get in touch with. Jerry's Rolodex was definitely the prototype of Facebook.

MIMI LEONARD: When Jerry talked about the news, he never said that *New York Magazine* wrote about something or another—he'd say, "Marie Brenner," or "Anthony Hayden-Guest," or "Tony Schwartz" wrote it. He had started his radical activities when he was a grad student in sociology at Berkeley, and he was truly interested in sociologically mapping out the people in our world. Jerry's notebooks were always filled with lists of names and phone numbers. It was a currency to him. He could convert those lists into planned outcomes.

ROGER RESSMEYER: He could get anybody on the phone in any office anywhere to talk to him, even if it was in the middle of the night. He would pick up the phone and he could talk his way past any receptionist, secretary, administrative assistant, and get to the person, faster than anybody I've ever known. He *was extremely proficient* at using his voice and the telephone and that was a huge, wonderful thing for me to learn. I never came close to matching his skills at that, but it was quite amazing, and he introduced me to a bunch of people, and took me under his wing. It was very sweet. He was thirty-seven and I was twenty-one and just starting in my career as a photographer.

KATE COLEMAN: After the Facebook thing happened, I looked back at all those years when he had started his meet and greet, or whatever the fuck that thing was—and realized he had preceded Facebook. He really was on to something. And everybody knocked him.

Newswee

December 31, 1964 / $1.75

ARMS CONTROL
The Battle Over Star Wars

THE YEAR OF THE YUPPIE

Newsweek   SPECIAL REPORT

The Year of The Yuppie

The young urban professionals have arrived. They're making lots of money, spending it conspicuously and switching political candidates like they test cuisines.

The Deloons restoring a Chicago town house: Gentrification

NEWSWEEK/DECEMBER 31, 1964

The Birth of the Yuppie.

For better or worse, Rubin helped spearhead the Yuppie (**Y**oung **U**pwardly-mobile [or **U**rban] **P**rofessional) movement, which consisted of twenty- and thirty-year olds that embraced both conservative and liberal values. Socially progressive, many Yuppies supported whichever political party was most helpful in economic growth at any given time. *For the record, Rubin never supported Ronald Reagan or the Republican Party.* He was rooting for Gary Hart as the Democratic candidate before Hart's campaign went south. In 1983, a syndicated newspaper article ran nationwide that mentioned Rubin's networking parties at Studio 54, which featured soft classical music in the background, so people could talk and socialize. The attendees joked that Rubin had gone from "Yippie to Yuppie" and that was used as the headline of the article.

ABOVE: *Newsweek* magazine collaborated with "Doonesbury" cartoonist Garry Trudeau to capture the Yuppie movement.

Fatherhood at Fifty. In 1988, Jerry celebrated his fiftieth birthday, which was a landmark for so many reasons. As cofounder of the "Youth International Party" in the 1960s, he'd infamously said, "don't trust anyone over thirty!" Given that so many right-wingers wanted him dead then, it was somewhat surprising that he lived to see fifty. His birthday bash was covered in the *New York Times*, which described the seventy people who gathered in Jerry's swank Upper East Side apartment as "radicals and former radicals, investment bankers, rock and rollers, lawyers, and Mr. Rubin's personal nutritionist." The party included co-conspirators from the Chicago 8 Trial, as well as a woman who had met Jerry on a blind date a decade earlier. However, the older generation hadn't forgiven him for his youthful escapades; the July 16, 1988 *New York Times* reported, "Staring at the varied assemblage as if it arrived from another planet was Mr. Rubin's mother-in-law, who begged not to be identified, claiming never to have told friends the identity of daughter Mimi's husband."

RONA ELLIOT: I said to Jerry, 'What are you doing with your life?' and he said, "I'm taking Mimi to see a fertility doctor in Pennsylvania . . . Don't say this to her, but I don't want her to be a bitter old woman and at fifty, look back and see that she missed that." It was one of the most insightful things he ever said to me and it demonstrated the depth of his commitment to her, his devotion. It was just shocking; people always assumed that he was shallow, which he certainly could be. But when it came to what was important, he was right there. He wanted to make sure she was happy.

Jerry and Mimi had two children; Juliet in August 1987, and Adam in June 1989.

WALLI LEFF, WRITER, PSYCHOLOGIST: Jerry and Mimi had a naming ceremony and they invited friends to come. And they were so happy, standing on the stage with their two young children. I was seeing this part of Jerry I had never seen much of before.

Jerry Rubin Is 50 (Yes, 50) Years Old

By DOUGLAS MARTIN

Jerry Rubin, the man famous for saying never to trust anyone over 30, just turned 50.

"It scares the hell out of me," said Mr. Rubin, who as a young radical in 1967 dropped dollar bills onto the floor of the New York Stock Exchange and campaigned to elect a pig as President of the United States.

In recent years, he has generated nearly as much publicity by running a business that promotes a pastime called networking — through which people pay hefty fees to go to parties where they might or might not meet someone who can advance their careers.

Tens of thousands have gone to the parties, and only the October stock market crash kept Mr. Rubin from selling $3 million of shares in Networking America to the public.

Uptown Celebration

Thus, it seemed appropriate that some 70 friends from all over the country and [...] ters in Mr. [...] gathered for [...] evening, his [...] loon-bedecked [...] apartment.

There were [...] radicals, in [...] rock-and-rolle [...] Rubin's per [...] There was a f[...] who was deta[...] Rubin in the C[...] linois, and a [...] ered she and [...] try" when the[...] a blind date [...] came friends [...]

Staring at [...] blage as if it [...] other planet [...] mother-in-law [...] be identified, [...] have told fri[...] daughter Mim[...]

"He just is [...] have picked fo[...]

Juliet Clifton Rubin

Eight pounds, thirteen ounces
Twenty one and one half inches

August 19, 1987
2:22 p.m.

Mimi and Jerry Rubin

In the year 2000, Juliet will be thirteen years old.

JERRY AND MIMI RUBIN INVITE YOU
TO THE OPENING NIGHT CELEBRATION
OF THE 1985 NEXT WAVE FESTIVAL
OF THE BROOKLYN ACADEMY OF MUSIC

Diane Keaton
and
Daniel Wolf Co-Chairmen

Bianca Jagger
Opening Night Chairman

Warren Beatty
Mary Boone
Barry Diller
Joan Kennedy
Calvin Klein
Christophe de Menil
Martin Scorsese
Vice Chairmen

Peter Allen
Laurie Anderson
Francesco Clemente
Roy Lichtenstein
Laurie Mallet
Steve Reich
Steve Rubell
Ian Schrager
Willi Smith
Andy Warhol
Artists' Gala Committee

The Weekly Network Party
Tuesday, October 1
at

PALLADIUM

JERRY: yuppie king

NOT even **Jerry Rubin** had any idea how much money he could make with "networking" when he started throwing the business card-swapping parties in his apartment years ago. Turns out he's been grossing close to $10,000 per week for the past three years at the Palladium, collecting 16 percent of the entry fees. Now he and wife **Mimi** have moved to the Limelight with their mailing list of 180,000 names.

The Bubble Bursts with the World's Most Expensive Breakfast.

As the '80s wore on, Jerry and Mimi's networking salons became considerable moneymakers. At their height, the couple were being paid $10,000 a week to host parties at the Palladium. They possessed a mailing list of all the movers and shakers, and nightclubs came to them for connections. But Jerry didn't care to simply accumulate wealth; instead, he wanted to found a chain of networking restaurants and spread the "business networking" experience across the country. Jerry's motto had always been to "Think Big" and now he was doing that. Mark Fleischman, then owner of Studio 54, helped the couple enlist a five-star celebrity panel of investors. The project was about to go public when the lawyers for the group hosted an investor breakfast meeting.

MIMI LEONARD: We had a celebrity panel of Oleg Cassini, Liza Minnelli, and another person, who were going to get a percentage. We were going to go public, and we had a meeting, and I remember we were just so blown away that they served us these wonderful little breakfast pastries and coffee in real china in this gorgeous conference room overlooking Manhattan—and then three weeks later, we got a bill for $35,000 for the first three weeks' of work! Jerry and I looked at each other. "That was the most expensive breakfast we've ever had." We couldn't come up with a name. We couldn't come up with a cuisine. But we finally rented a facility. We were paying for a huge place; it had been the Sea Fare of the Aegean. We were paying lawyers; we went through three different underwriting firms and finally the crash of '87 occurs, so our final, third underwriting, which was in process, crashed. It was all over. We lost probably $250,000.

Black Monday—The Party is Over.

Like the Roaring Twenties, the partying of the '80s came to a halt with the stock market crash of October 19, 1987, Black Monday. In response to Iranian missile attacks on oil tankers and the collapse of OPEC, stock markets around the world crashed, starting in Hong Kong and spreading quickly across the globe. In America, the Dow Jones dropped a staggering 508 points. But it wasn't really political fallout that sent Wall Street into freefall; it was the first selloff to utilize computerized trading. The Stock Exchange's order systems could not handle the volume, which led to more uncertainty as to what was going on, which triggered even more computerized trading. Mimi, discouraged by the loss of a quarter million investment in their proposed restaurant venture, decided to pull up stakes and leave Manhattan for a house in the suburbs, dragging a reluctant Jerry along with her.

MIMI LEONARD: My mother lived in New Haven, so I thought why not be in Connecticut so that she could be near the grandchildren. When we finally found a house and signed the deal, Jerry covered his eyes with his left hand and signed with his right hand. He very much touted the Woody Allen point of view—that he would never live anywhere else but New York City. He was a New York City person. So, why I did that I'll never know. I think I was trying to please my mother. I didn't realize what a bad effect it would have on our marriage.

Jerry the Entrepreneur: Infomercials and Juice.

Though their gig at the Palladium had been wildly successful, they were thrown out when the club realized they didn't have to pay Jerry and Mimi for just hanging out three nights a week. The club was basically paying them to bring the regulars in. Mimi had a team of people who went out and left little VIP cards all over Manhattan at bookstores. The Palladium owners figured that out, got to the marketing team directly, and took them away from Mimi.

MIMI LEONARD: After we lost the gig at the Palladium, we realized we really had to think of something else, and it wasn't going to be a job because Jerry was unhirable. No one was ever going to hire him. He was a handful. He was only good at being Jerry Rubin. The whole infomercial thing was starting and we were thinking of ideas for infomercials. During this time that I was trying to get pregnant, Jerry had become a health nut. He was running and had become a vegetarian.

Jerry read *Life Extension* by Durk Pearson and Sandy Shaw, which was a best seller. Jerry arranged to meet them. We flew to California and we went to their house. Jerry got the rights to their nutritional supplement products, that were kind of a progenitor of smart drinks. And there was actually an effect that you would feel after drinking these things, probably because they were a bit more liberal in the use of caffeine.

Jim Fobair, one of the owners of Omnitrition, went into business with us, and somehow our organization became huge. By the time we moved to California in the summer of 1990, we were making thousands of dollars a month with very little overhead.

[Author's Note: Some of Jerry's critics of have charged that Omnitrition was a pyramid scheme. On March 4, 1996, the United States Court of Appeals Ninth Circuit ruled that "Rubin, now deceased but appearing by the executor of his estate, was alleged to be involved in the creation and promotion of the marketing program." However, "The district court granted summary judgment in favor of all defendants [including Rubin], holding that Omnitrition's program was not a pyramid scheme as a matter of law."]

The End of the Marriage.
The marriage couldn't withstand the Los Angeles lifestyle change, and Mimi filed for divorce, which took Jerry by surprise.

MIMI LEONARD: Jerry was having a lot of fun, but that's when our marriage broke up. I think that being out in California and suddenly having all this money was . . . well, success is dangerous. I didn't want to be in California. I wanted to be in New York. He was a workaholic, and once I was a mom it just didn't work . . . He was willing to change, but never would have. It was also my fault because I let a lot of things happen that I was bitter about that I didn't voice. I mean, the whole country house thing was a huge deal for me and Jerry didn't do any of the caring for the children. Not that he didn't love them, he obviously did, but he was an older

father. We were divorced in September '91. I went back to New York, and put Juliet back in the same nursery school, and just kind of resumed my life. The whole thing was heartbreaking for me and Jerry was very hurt and upset. It was horrible. Jerry stayed out in LA. He had three years by himself.

Mimi is married to Mark Fleischman (the former owner of Studio 54). She currently oversees several fitness studios in Los Angeles, known as The Bar Method (developed by her sister Burr Leonard) and continues to raise her children. Juliet and Adam are both now in their twenties, pursuing their own adventures.

After the divorce, Jerry remained in L.A. and went on with his life, dating younger women and running a very profitable business selling a nutritional drink called "Wow!" Still optimistic, Jerry was looking for new possibilities, even in his romantic life.

RONA ELLIOT: I said to Jerry, "What the fuck are you doing with [your personal life]?" And he said he really wanted a soul mate. So we drafted this crazy document to put in the *New York Times*, offering $10,000 for introducing him to his soul mate. I wrote it. I took notes. I typed it up. We laughed . . .

MIMI LEONARD ON THE EARLY DAYS OF SOCIAL NETWORKING.

MANY PEOPLE INTERVIEWED FOR THIS BOOK suggested that Jerry first popularized the phrase "social networking" decades before it became commonplace on the internet—notice the word "networking" on this cake.

Before Facebook was connecting old friends and making new ones, before LinkedIn was hooking up business associates, before Evite was letting everyone know where the next party was, before the age of emails, Jerry and his wife Mimi were doing it "analog," keeping hand-written lists compiled from landline telephone calls and spreading the word with thousands of snail mail postcards.

For the purposes of this book, Mimi recounted to me how she and Jerry got started:

MIMI LEONARD: Jerry and I actually trademarked the term "Business Networking," after he first came up with it in 1981 and we owned it until we lost interest in it later in the '80s. This is the story of how it started. At that time, the word networking (outside of the world of electronic research) did not exist except as an idea that feminist leaders had come up with to teach women how to break into "The Old Boy's Club." Early in 1981, Jerry came up a "Networking Salon" (we owned that term, too) in which people would do "Business Networking." Once a week, he would invite one hundred people to our 74th Street apartment, asking them to

invite "the two most interesting people you know" to come along. He stationed his assistant at the door, and guests would be asked leave their business card or fill out a card.

And this is where the "networking" idea comes in. Jerry would suggest that all the guests exchange business cards and "network." Obviously, that doesn't seem like a very radical idea now—people think that's always the way it was. But it was totally new then. In that era, it was considered rude to ask someone what they "did for a living." Strange as it may seem today, you were never supposed to talk about your job, but instead your hobbies, the latest play, or world events. So Jerry came up with this idea that not only would people talk about what they did for a living and exchange business cards, they would "network," and figure out how to use each other's services—also something people didn't do openly then.

People considered the idea very gauche when they heard about it. They confided to me how tacky these "salons" were, with people openly social climbing, self-seeking, talking about money, and trying to gain things from each other. My friends said they would never be caught dead at such events. Of course, it turned out just the opposite. *Everyone was dying to go and to be invited back.*

Eventually the other tenants had decided enough was enough. They had been accustomed for nearly a year of a hundred to two hundred people streaming into our building, clogging up the elevators, drinking in the halls, spilling out of the lobby and were, in my opinion, incredibly good-natured about the whole thing. But then we got an eviction notice—seven days to "cure."

Jerry had been methodically keeping a record of all of the attendees of the parties. We had a friend, Lee Lipton, who ran The Underground, on West 14th Street, and Jerry had the idea of doing a party there. We had a list of 2,500 people but the names were not computerized. So we had to hand-address 2,500 invitations and mail them out with the same format—invite two of your most interesting friends, etc. We were astounded when 3,700 people came that first Tuesday night. It was far beyond anything we had hoped for.

Then, Jerry told me that Mark Fleischman had called to offer us Wednesdays at Studio 54. Mark had heard about the numbers at The Underground and wanted us at Studio [54], which he had recently taken over [from Steve Rubell and Ian Schrager]—which was still the most popular, iconic nightspot in Manhattan.

On our first night, we had two thousand people, and we kept that attendance for nearly two years. It was the "Business Networking" concept where—even though it was at Studio [54]—the parties would take place between 5 and 10 p.m., the music would be soft, the lights a little brighter, and people would exchange business cards and network. As the night progressed, the music would get a bit louder, the lights a bit lower, and dancing would begin. Part of the magic was allowing people to go to Studio 54, which was still a highly desirable destination.

But beyond that, we really had to work for the numbers and Jerry was nothing if not a hard worker. We would have themes each week and cohosts, and Jerry would use his genius to make each night more exciting than the previous week. Jerry had converted our 74th Street apartment during the Networking Salon days into a loft-like place—taking down the walls and making it one big room. We began to add desks and telephone lines.

We also decided to create a more exclusive version of the Business Networking Parties and started "The Business Networking 500 Club," which would sponsor more intimate events. Between the two businesses, there were soon ten desks in our apartment; at each was an employee on the phone pitching cohosting opportunities. We would collect every person's business card as they entered Studio [54] (and if they didn't have one, they'd fill out a facsimile), and these were the grist for the mill. Each one of these people would be called and interviewed about who they knew and we would sound them out on potential cohosting opportunities.

I remember around 2 a.m. one night with only Jerry, me, and my sister, Burr Leonard, left in the apartment—there had been an error on our printed invitations, and Burr (who worked with us) had gotten a stamp made to correct the mistake, and was stamping each one of ten thousand invitations with the updated information.

There was not a war raging in Vietnam. A presidency was not about to topple. But working with Jerry made you feel that maybe

there was. Each day was like a tornado of energy and intentionality. Everything was done in an "all-out" fashion. Today, with a computer, it might be different. Emails certainly would have made things faster and neater. We were dealing with pens, stamps, paper, clunky phones with cords plugged into the wall. We had ten different lines, a few with multiple phones. It was hard to walk through the aisles between the makeshift desks without tripping over one of the beige cords, and I can remember toppling over a beautiful vase during one such stroll through the living room.

Eventually their parties ended at Studio 54, but Jerry and Mimi weren't done yet. Mimi contines:

Unexpectedly, in early '85, a nightclub named Visage asked us to do a weekly party. Our lists still worked and we started making money again in the nightclub world. Then Steve Rubell and Ian Schrager, who had long since left Studio 54, asked us to do every Tuesday at The Palladium. The first couple of Tuesdays were only so-so, with about two thousand people attending. The Palladium was huge and could hold five thousand people. Also, the crowd was a little too old, so Steve told us that if we didn't pick up our performance, we'd be cut.

We were out there hustling and dreaming up every potentially good promotional opportunity, and Jerry came up with a knock-out. At that time, there was an annual running event for young corporate executives—Jerry got them to make our Tuesday evening the official after-party for that spring's event. I'll never forget standing there on a glorious spring late afternoon and seeing literally thousands of young, attractive, corporate executives streaming down the streets—with a line literally wrapping around the block. And with all the business cards we collected, we were able to break into the world of young execs in Manhattan and continue welcoming a seemingly never-ending stream of these kids into our Tuesday events. The Palladium could hold five thousand people, and that was the first of many Tuesdays where we filled it!

We were on a roll again with Chambers of Commerce across the country constantly calling asking advice on planning business-networking events in their cities. By 1988, the Palladium dropped us and we had events at other places for a few years, but we knew our club days were numbered and started looking for another source of income. That's when Jerry discovered Durk Pearson and Sandy Shaw's products, and launched our Network Marketing Company, which sold smart drinks.

THE 500 CLUB
Fulfilling the Needs of the 1980s

At a recent Business Networking dinner, Jerry Rubin spoke to members and their guests on the evolution of The 500 Club. The following is an excerpt of his address:
"What is the 500 Club? A lot of people ask me what The 500 Club is, and I usually say it resists definition. But here goes.

"I was a professional public speaker in the 1960s and 1970s, then retired for a few years and have recently resumed doing a lot of public speaking, debating my former partner Abbie Hoffman on college campuses and in nightclubs on the subject of 'Yuppie vs. Yippie'. I find myself having to defend the yuppies or young urban professionals against some people who are still living, thinking and dreaming as if it were still the 1960s. So I feel that I am on safer ground tonight in talk-

Daily News Magazine

The YIPPIE and the YUPPIE

How Abbie Hoffman and Jerry Rubin got to be the best of enemies

By Ed McCormack

While he was underground, Abbie was like a Japanese soldier left on an island after World War II, in the hills. So when he resurfaced, he had a hard time adjusting. Jerry had to do his adjustment in public.
—MARTIN KENNER

OPPOSITE: As the Yippie vs. Yuppie debates crisscrossed the country, newspapers and magazines jumped into the fray.

Yippie Vs. Yuppie

The Return of the Fugitive.   Despite Jerry's new lifestyle and Abbie going underground, they maintained a close friendship throughout the '70s. They even spent Thanksgiving Day together, "on the lam," in 1975. Abbie was in the passenger seat of a white T-Bird, tooling across the vast Texas landscape, with his lady friend Johanna at the wheel and Jerry in the back seat laughing his ass off. Jerry visited Abbie when he could. He brought him an advance galley proof of *Growing (Up) at 37*. Not long after Jerry first met Mimi, they spent a long underground weekend with Abbie and Johanna.

> **WALLI LEFF:** I saw that the tie between Jerry and Abbie remained close, despite their diverging paths, and the way each was living his own life—because there was a basic trust there. Abbie would never, ever, have allowed Jerry to be with him while he was underground had he not trusted him.

Abbie's post–'60s legacy is best remembered for his alter ego "Barry Freed." Although still on the run, he surfaced publically as an environmental activist. While living on the St. Lawrence River in upstate New York, "Barry" very publicly battled the U.S. Army Corps of Engineers, who wanted to change the ecological makeup of the river. Under the "Freed" name, Hoffman enjoyed high-profile acknowledgments from United States Senator Daniel Moynihan and New York Governor Hugh Carey, who thanked "Freed" (*they had no idea what his real identity was*) for his environmental work. Hoffman's Save the River campaign was so successful, he found himself in the nation's capital lecturing to a room full of congressmen. In a truth-is-stranger-than-fiction moment, one of them looked "Barry" right in the eye, and proudly stated: "*Now I know where the '60s have gone—everyone owes Barry Freed a debt of gratitude for his organizing ability.*"

After several public events, Abbie realized that it was better to turn himself in than risk getting caught. Through the efforts of his attorney, Gerald Lefcourt, and many others, a deal was brokered with the authorities—a one-year work release program—and there was a Barbara Walters "Comeback interview" on ABC's *20/20* prime-time news show.

DAVID FENTON, CO-PRODUCER OF THE 1979 "NO NUKES" CONCERTS, PHOTOGRAPHER, NON-PROFIT PR MAVEN: I moved to Ann Arbor and worked on the campaign to get John Sinclair out of prison. Jerry spoke at the 1971 Sinclair Freedom Rally, so we knew each other pretty well. I was also close to Abbie and in fact, I learned public relations from Abbie, which has been my business for the last forty years; I run a progressive public relations company. When Abbie went underground on the cocaine charge I lost touch, but I stayed in contact with Jerry and one night—it must have been '78 or '79—Jerry and his wife Mimi invited me to their Upper East Side apartment. I walked in and they introduced me to a couple who I didn't know. Barry and Johanna Freed, they said they were. They started telling me this story about how they were fighting the US Army Corps of Engineers' plans to super-dredge the Saint Lawrence Seaway between the United States and Canada where they lived. About thirty minutes into dinner, I locked onto Abbie's voice. I recognized his voice. It was really hard to recognize him from his face because he had plastic surgery and altered his nose, but after a while I realized who it was! They were watching to see how long it would take me. I was overjoyed; we spent the whole evening into the wee hours talking. Out of that came the plan to help Abbie turn himself in, because if you turn yourself in you get much less time than if you're captured and at the time Abbie was on the FBI's Ten Most Wanted List. So, we hatched a PR plan, to have Barbara Walters come to Abbie and Johanna's hideout. She did an hour on ABC's *20/20* and it was like Jewish-mother-meets-Jewish-son. It was very positive and so when Abbie turned himself in, he got a very short sentence—that all grew out of that night at Jerry and Mimi's.

The Yin and Yang.

In the January 1969 issue of *Eye* magazine, Anita Hoffman penned an "open letter" under the title "Diary of a Revolutionary's Wife." She wrote that Chicago had inflated Abbie's ego to the extreme, and that he had "more of a paranoid" vibe than before. She saw him truly believing his own myth, and what Abbie obsessed about more than anything else was his relationship with Jerry—sometimes he talked about Jerry in his sleep, which both concerned and amused her.

NANCY KURSHAN: It's funny, because they ended up differently, but initially Jerry was more serious politically. And Abbie was more of a comedian. In the beginning, Jerry thought more about building a movement—while Abbie was more of an individual. I think that Jerry was more capable of working cooperatively with other people. Abbie was this brilliant individualist. They were both really smart; Jerry was great at figuring out how to work with mass actions, setting them up in ways that would be effective and dramatic. I don't think Abbie was particularly good at that.

During the first few years that Abbie was underground, the FBI harassed Anita, hoping that she would lead them to him. She had a hard time finding work and supporting their son, America. Abbie found a new life partner, Johanna Lawrenson, in 1974, and he and Anita did not reconcile when he resurfaced on September 4, 1980. Abbie and Anita remained close, and published a book of letters that they'd exchanged during those years: *To America with Love: Letters from the Underground*. Anita was a consultant for the film *Steal This Movie*, in which Janeane Garofalo portrays her. In the 1980s, Abbie

Jev:

Do you think David Fenton would like to coordinate work on the Committee for Amnesty? Jay's good but seems busy and desperate for money. It's just a thought. I talked with Lynda Obst & she's calling Murray Kempton to do piece next spring on our friend. He's already agreed. So that's taken care of.

You can get Mailer turned on to the R. Stone piece. It'll be helpful though if he sticks to the "unk" topic so to speak.

Ron Kovic will be helpful + Gloria McDonald is asking Lillian Hellman to be on the committee.

I'm looking for:
Paul Michael Glasser
Joe Papp
Julian Bond
Shirley Chisolm (my brother's on to her)
(I've got a list somewhere).

+ Mike Lang is checking out rally prospects.

On other fronts. Talked to Sam Keene who loves idea of me interviewing Carlos + is trying to arrange it. If I can't get him again. (I will have left by time you get letter). He'll contact you. Just pass the note along & I can always zip out there or anywhere to do it. It would be fantastic. Let's keep it quiet.

Adios

+ Jefferson Airplane Starship - will play at the homecoming! It would be good to come back

Letter to Jerry from Abbie discussing plans to resurface, asking if David Fenton could organize an amnesty committee for Abbie. He also suggests Shirley Chisholm would participate and that Jefferson Airplane (Starship) would play his homecoming party.

told Ronald Sukenick that Jerry always referred to his "career," even in the '60s. "Jerry used to always talk about his career—this is good for his career, this is bad for his career . . . and I always used to go, '*Career?!*'"

The February 1980 issue of *High Times* contained a candid conversation between Jerry and Abbie. Jerry told him, "The '70s were a time of changing identity—[and your new autobiography, *Soon To Be a Major Motion Picture*] indicates that—and I want to compliment you on such a creative writing achievement. The ending implied that you have metamorphosed into another person. You *really* did the '70s trip of self-awareness."

After all these years, the debate continues on how Abbie really felt about Jerry in the '80s, and several of their mutual friends told me that Abbie would always respect Jerry for sticking by him while he was underground. Abbie knew that loyalty came at a price, and he appreciated it. When Jerry told Abbie, in a 1980 *High Times* co-interview, that he had shared Abbie's grief at having to go underground, Abbie said, "Thank you. That's why no matter what happens to us down the road, we'll always be close friends." The subject turned to business acumen, and Jerry asked, "Are you insulted if I call you a good businessman?" Hoffman: "Not anymore. Fidel Castro and my father, Johnnie Hoffman, taught me that not only is there no contradiction between being a good businessman, a good man, and a good revolutionary; one *must* be all three, unless, of course, one is a woman."

Rubin and Hoffman. In their 1980 back-and-forth banter in *High Times*, they discuss Abbie's recent memoir, *Soon to Be a Major Motion Picture*. Jerry offers that "it wasn't a book about our relationship. It was a book about your adventures in the '60s, and I thought the things you said about me were—with a few exceptions—pretty appropriate." Abbie said he'd heard through the grapevine that Jerry wondered, before the book was published, if Abbie had talked about how the two men fought? And Hoffman's editor had replied, "No, there's no fighting in there." Then, Abbie said to Jerry, "You wanted me to be a bit more honest?" Jerry retorts, "I say in my current public speeches that there was ego competition between us. It's just human. I mean, it's no judgment or anything. And maybe my insecurity was the source of my competition."

Abbie clearly becomes uncomfortable with such honest communication and declares, "I wasn't competing. I *wasn't* competing with you!" Trying to draw Abbie out, Jerry comes back with, "Well, you're very competitive. You're incredibly competitive." Abbie's fear of this type of discussion, even with a close friend, causes him to deflect with half-baked humor: "Maybe with Muhammad Ali. He said he was the greatest, and I knew I was." Jerry capitulates, "All right," while Abbie continues with more lame sports analogies: "You're the quarterback on this side, and I'm the quarterback on that side, and now that the game is over, we'll go out and have a beer together and make jokes about *all* the spectators. That's the kind of competition that I can understand." Jerry tries one more time to bring about a heartfelt discussion of their lifelong yin and yang. But, Abbie just can't do it, and becomes embittered: "I totally reject that sick shit."

JUDY CLAVIR ALBERT
STEW ALBERT
2854 S.E.Tibbetts St.
Portland, Oregon 97202
(503)236-3431

Dear Jerry and Mimi:

Just a note to let you know that we have moved and are comfortably settled in Portland Oregon at the above address. It is a very large, friendly house and we now have all our various belongings out of storage and with us. Jessica is attending a Waldorf school which she likes very much.

It was fun spending time with both of you in Berkeley, San Francisco and Sausalito. What's all this about Yippie/Yuppie? Are you really going to travel around the country debating Abbie? You mentioned something about speaking with Abbie but you did not say that it would be an adversarial situation. Well, I have grave misgivings about this project. I'm not sure that this is an appropriate way for old friends to earn a living. However, if you are intent on it, I certainly wish you luck and hope you get a lot of bookings and make a lot of money. I would advise you and Abbie to work for a professional wrestler's theatricality with no hard feelings backstage.

Our book The Sixties Papers is coming out in December. As you recall, the book presents sections of readings on the civil rights and black power movements, SDS, the anti-war movement,the counterculture and the Yippies, and women's liberation. Most of the selections are either out of print or very difficult to obtain. We introduce the book with a 50 page overview of the decade.

Do you have any names of people to whom Praeger could send promotional material? We think our book will be very interesting to sixties veterans, academics studying the 1960s especially those teaching social movements courses, and those who missed the 1960s but wished they could have been there. So if you can spare the time, please send us appropriate names and addresses and any suggestions you might have as to where to advertise, how to get it reviewed and anything else.

We hope things are going well for you. You are of course always welcome to stay with us should you come to Portland...And the state of the world seems so unbelievably bad that it's not even worth commenting on.

Much love

Judy and Stew
September 20, 1984

Abbie's mood becomes positive: "Let's talk about a difference that I didn't put in the book that really fascinated me. What are the different kinds of courage?" The two touch on the fact that Jerry mentions his own cowardice in *Growing (Up) at 37* as a "public guerrilla to be feared, and inside is a little boy who's afraid." Abbie recalls, "I played football and other rough sports. So in a certain sense, when things were sort of rough in the streets we rioted in together, I was sort of used to it. I didn't think you were, and yet you kept doing it over and over and I kept saying in my head, 'Why is he doing this? This is so hard. He's working so hard *to overcome this fear*. This is incredibly courageous!'"

In 2013, Jay Levin, founder of the *LA Weekly*, repeated a similar tale to me:

> **JAY LEVIN:** Abbie would say, "People would always tell me I had a lot of guts to take on the cops. And they thought of Jerry as something of a wimp. But the truth is, Jerry had courage, because I was having a ball, it was nothing for me to do it. Jerry was doing it, even though he was scared shitless. But he was doing it. And that's courage.'"

Looking back on what they'd achieved together in the 1960s, Hoffman said to Rubin:

> We were, as you remember, glorious about being action freaks. It was the apocalypse. It was war. We acted on impulse. If you read our books during that period, they are

So to quote a great '60s philosopher, "Why don't we end the bullshit discussions and just DO IT!"

cheering everybody on. Let's go team! Rah, rah! You know, it's not like "this is why we do things," and "this is how we didn't," and "this is because we were doing it!" We were doing it at the moment. Dwight MacDonald, my crotchety old friend, once said to me, "Whatever possessed you people in the '60s? The idea of acting on your ideas is so against the intellectual tradition. It just doesn't make any sense." "Yeah," I said. "that's what it was." The Beatles broke up and I don't think they'll ever be united and I could care less. Jerry and Abbie don't see each other much . . .

AMAZING INSIDE STORY OF ABBIE HOFFMAN ON THE RUN — BY HIS BEST FRIEND JERRY RUBIN

Exclusive interview by MICHAEL MUNRO

For six years they dined in disguise, threw parties — and laughed at the law

The colorful radicals who shocked America

ABBIE HOFFMAN and Jerry Rubin first met in the mid-1960s on New York's Lower East Side and teamed up to become the most famous radicals of the long-haired hippie generation. They formed the Youth International Party in 1968 — calling themselves Yippies — and created a "festival of life" at the Democratic National

JERRY RUBIN, Abbie Hoffman's closest friend and ally since the anti-Vietnam days of the 1960s, has revealed an amazing cloak-and-dagger relationship he and Hoffman shared for the past six years.

With FBI agents spread out all over America searching for Hoffman, the two former revolutionaries enjoyed dinners at restaurants in Manhattan, vacations together in Mexico and Florida, and weekly phone calls to each other.

In an exclusive interview with the STAR, Rubin, now 42 years old and working on Wall Street as an investment banker, said Hoffman's whereabouts while calling himself Barry Freed was a "tremendously kept secret."

"No one ever knew who Barry Freed really was. Even at dinner parties we attended together guests didn't know my identity," Rubin said.

"Abbie and I have remained the closest of friends since he disappeared in 1974. But to continue seeing each other we had to be extremely careful in what we did and where we went."

Gone were the wild days of the Chicago Seven trials and burning dollar notes in front of the New York Stock Exchange. But for nearly seven years Rubin and Hoffman kept in contact.

"There were gaps of several

there or that he was Howie Samuels. They came and asked if I knew a Howie Samuels.

"Of course, I told them I had never heard of the guy and they never came back," he said.

But, Rubin added, the first thing he did was to call Hoffman at his St. Lawrence River home and tell him never to use the name again.

Rubin also told about vacations with Hoffman in Florida and Mexico. "We had some great times together," he said, "but there was always this constant fear of Abbie being caught. That was his greatest worry."

Rubin admitted that he knew more than two months ago of Hoffman's decision to give himself up to narcotics agents. He added: "To me he is Barry Freed. They are two separate people as far as I'm concerned, and he has already

Hi, you may remember me from the 1960s. I led thousands of college students into the streets and Presidents fighting wars quivered at the sound of my name.

I was known and not wanted in many states. I was the cause of thousands of arguments around the family dinner-table between parents and children.

Then I took off my beard and no one recognizes me anymore. So I carry my American Express card with me wherever I go. You can have one too. But first you've got to become a yuppie.

The Public Debates: Yippie vs. Yuppie.

You may remember me from the 1960s. I led thousands of young people onto the streets, and presidents fighting wars quivered at the sound of my name. I was known and not wanted in many states in the USA. The government spent millions of dollars to try and put me and many others in jail for quite a long time. I was the cause of thousands of arguments around the family dinner table between parents and their children—parents warning their children not to be like me. Then came the 1970s and things changed and I shaved off my beard, and, wherever I went, no one recognized me anymore. So today, I never leave home without my American Express card.

Without his lucrative gig hosting networking parties at Manhattan nightclubs, Jerry needed to make money, and he knew that Abbie did too. Both men were unemployable in the traditional sense. Nobody at a "straight company" trusted either of them, not even Jerry in his suit and tie. Jerry suggested the debate idea to Abbie, and he loved it. It was a media circus wherever they went—keep in mind that the '60s had only ended a decade and half earlier—and many tabloids were portraying it like a heavyweight rematch. (After their success came a less compelling debate tour between the infamous G. Gordon Liddy and Timothy Leary.)

In hindsight, we can watch the debates on YouTube and see that, in many ways, Jerry was right. The very things that Jerry was laughed at for—the idea that someday a baby boomer would be president (Bill Clinton) or that a company named Apple would popularize computers, changing everyone's life—turned out to be quite prescient on Rubin's part. When watching the debates, it is interesting to note, that despite their differences in strategy, both men wanted the same things. and neither is advocating a right-wing agenda. Jerry is simply proposing a new tactic: one that we acknowledge today as socially conscious entrepreneurism. Jerry foresaw the possibility of a company that could make money *and* help people—embracing the notion that the two did not have to be diametrically opposed. It would take another decade and the emergence of the internet to make that a possibility.

Yet, even with Jerry's incredibly thick skin, playing the fall guy got tiresome. The cracks appear when he bitterly comments—after getting a pie thrown at him—that Abbie will be shaking the guy's hand later. After a year of playing the straight man, Jerry simply grew tired of arguing about the '60s, and decided to move on with his life. The acrimony of the debates had started eating away at the friendship, and the two men tended to avoid each other offstage.

It was time for their partnership to end, and although Abbie wanted to keep going, Jerry insisted they call it quits. In their last debate, a disappointed Abbie tells the audience that since "*Jerry's announced that this is the last debate, so I want to announce that this is rigged. It is not a difference of opinion; we have been homosexual lovers for sixteen years. This is a sexual disagreement that we have.*"

By the way, in preparing for these debates, I have
100% changed my lifestyle and I wish to tell you how. In the
late 1970s and early 1980s I discovered that marijuana smoking,
my left-over habit from the 1960s, had helped become into an
ineffective and non-productive person.

In 1983 and early 1984 I weighed 160 pounds, ate meat,
ate junk food, did not exercise, and was aging fast. In the
spring of 1984 I began a program of Detoxification. I lost
30 pounds, lowered my cholesterol from 226 to 126, began running
six miles a day, stopped eating meat and chicken and sugar, and
embarked on a serious program of life extension. I plan to live
to the age of 100 without any serious disease.

No issue is more important to the yuppies than physical
health. And the key to physical health is diet. Heart attack and
cancer are preventable diseases preventable by a low-fat, low-sugar
diet. I predict that over the next 10-20 years that the yuppies
as consumers and as businessmen and businesswomen in the food
industry will transform the American diet.

The yuppies, working within the system, will cure cancer
and heart disease in our lifetime. The yuppies, working within
the system, will transform the American lifestyle to one of
health and fitness. The yuppies, working within the system, will
expand the human lifespan.

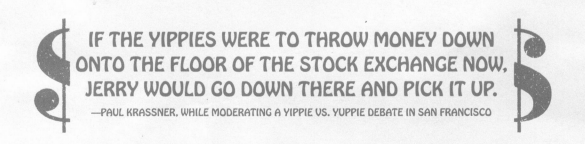

IF THE YIPPIES WERE TO THROW MONEY DOWN
ONTO THE FLOOR OF THE STOCK EXCHANGE NOW,
JERRY WOULD GO DOWN THERE AND PICK IT UP.
—PAUL KRASSNER, WHILE MODERATING A YIPPIE VS. YUPPIE DEBATE IN SAN FRANCISCO

The Yippie vs. Yuppie debates traveled throughout the United States during 1985 and the final
debate occurred in Vancouver, Canada, in '86—
the only one that circulates on video. Although
the rhetoric varied from night to night, the
overall cockfight remained the same—so these
excerpts below are typical. Standing at lecterns,
separated by a large expanse of stage, Jerry is
dressed in a suit and Abbie is dressed casually
in a sweater and jeans. After introductions,
Jerry makes the opening statement.

Yuppie: You may remember me from the 1960s. I
led thousands of young people onto the streets and
presidents fighting wars quivered at the sound of my
name. I was known and not wanted in many states in
the USA. The government spent millions of dollars to
try and put me and many others in jail. I was the cause
of thousands of arguments around the family dinner
table between parents and their children—parents
warning their children not to be like me. Then came the
1970s and things changed and I shaved off my beard
and wherever I went, no one recognized me anymore.
So today I never leave home without by my American
Express card! It's a joke, okay? I gotta announce my
jokes, because people think if you have a credit card
you're in favor of apartheid in South Africa.

Yippie: First, I should say something. I have a confes-
sion to make, because I don't see Jerry much. I don't
see him socially. I only see him on the stage. In fact,
the press will always ask me, "Do you see many of the
Chicago 7?" And I say, "Well, I only see him—but it's
just to yell at him!" He's announced that this is the last
debate, so I want to announce that this is rigged. It is
not a difference of opinion; we have been homosexual
lovers for sixteen years. This is a sexual disagreement
that we have. Anyway, I am the broken record, the has-
been, the one that hasn't changed his underwear in
twenty years. I'm fifty years old this year. I paid my
taxes. I have three kids. I have all the hang-ups of being
a middle-aged, middle-class American, but I still know
shit from shoe polish.

Jerry argues for joining the establishment versus staying
the outside. He tells a hostile audience that someday, the
baby boomers will be in charge.

Yuppie: I predict that in 1988 you will see a baby
boomer-oriented candidate elected President of the
United States.

Jerry wasn't far off. Bill Clinton was elected in 1992. Ab-
counters by equating Jerry's entrepreneurialism with Rea-
omics. He pokes fun at Apple computers, referring to the co-
pany as being over already. The audience laughs in support
the pre-internet, pre-iPhone '80s, the audience can't imag-
why Jerry would promote a company like Apple.

Yippie: I still have not been Big Chilled. Essentially
Jerry's stuck in the 1950s if I'm stuck in the 1960s
He said he's proud of what he did in the '60s, but if you
redo it you'll see he's eaten every single page alive
He's a born-again capitalist. Entrepreneurs are his
new heroes. Just like Ronald Reagan, he goes around
to campuses and tells the Horatio Alger rags-to-riches
stories. Last year it was Apple Computer—two hippies
tinkering with their toy in their garage, make millions
of dollars, all new consciousness. The Apple went a
little rotten, and now it's Ben and Jerry's Ice Cream, o
Rachel's Cookies, or a new pet rock.

Yuppie: What saddens me about Abbie is not only does
he not listen to what I'm saying, because his entire at
tack is not on me, but it's on some phantom vision o
me that is he's inventing for the debate, because it's no
my politics he's talking about. In a sense, three-fourths
of what he said at the end—"We need the will, we have
the technology, all we need is the commitment."—hey
that's what I'm saying!
    The tactics that Abbie and I used in the '60s, that
Abbie still thinks is the only way to change in the '80s
were effective when the issue was racial discrimination, but they're not effective when the issue is who has
the money in society. We do need more entrepreneurs
and young, urban professionals who are politically
active. It's people saying, "Government's not doing it
we're gonna do it ourselves." It's people caring, and
who's doing it? Professionals, successful people, the
kind of people Abbie just spend twenty minutes laugh
ing at and making jokes at.

Yippie: Well, the Yuppies are going to take politica
power. Where's the evidence that this new generation
of rich is going to be any different than the old generation of rich? Where's this younger generation that you
keep talking about? Change does not come about by
generations passing into other generations.

Yuppie: Jesse Jackson led a lot of protests against a lot
of corporations, but he won one protest and that was
against Burger King. What Abbie didn't tell you was a
thirty-five-year-old baby boomer who was active in the
antiwar movement happened to become the Vice Pres-

ing, he immediately called a meeting with Jesse and he gave into all of Jesse Jackson's demands, [including] a certain number of entrepreneurs would be black in the Burger King empire. I think that proves my point; you can protest all you want, but unless we move into the establishment, because if Burger King had the old guard in charge . . . Burger King shows how when the baby boomers move into the corporate structure, they're going to adapt to different kinds of changes.

The debate moderator invited the audience to participate in a Q&A.

Audience Member: Jerry Rubin, you once spoke of being in contempt of money and corporate power, the judicial system and other aspects of capitalism. Now you feel happy to have joined the apathetic death culture of capitalism. We believe you haven't grown up but contracted a premature desire for senility with a desire for security . . . Jerry, we are disgusted at your sellout. We believe you need a righteous pie in the face for your hypocritical stand.

At this point, another audience member runs up on stage and throws a pie at Jerry. Jerry turns away and the pie hits him on the shoulder. The pie-thrower runs off the stage and out the exit door.

Yippie: Okay, that was stupid.

Yuppie: Anyway, let me respond. [Pauses and laughs.] My comment is the following: I think it's actions like that that really convince me that the leftovers of the '60s have very little to say, that they're not gonna make any positive changes. Those tactics are the tactics of the past. They're juvenile, they're adolescent, and they don't prove anything, and it doesn't make any difference—to me it's kind of sad.

Different Audience member: It seems that after listening to you two, that there are only three types of people in the world. There's hippies, yuppies, and baby boomers, and they are either left or right. I'm not any of those. I thought that was kind of dogmatic of both of you.
I'm talking to Abbie now. It seems like the stance that you take is one of a political watchdog, or somebody that decides to pull the brakes on the train after it's run away, and Jerry's stance is one of "let's make the train, let's get it on the tracks, and let's get it rolling." I think there's a give and take there, is what I see; I'm an entrepreneur and one of the reasons I am is because I got sick and tired of having my paycheck taken away by the government. What I'm saying to Abbie is

that I believe that, in this day and age, the pendulum has swung . . .

Yippie: I'm not here barefoot . . . I do have a credit card, I have a VCR, I have a Cuisinart—I'm not interested in having those objects define what my political point of view is. I work with electoral candidates . . . I was the environmental advisor to Jesse Jackson. I gave speeches for him. Jerry supports Gary Hart. He didn't go out and raise money for Gary Hart. Gary Hart had more support from his jockstrap, so this is not a debate about what the strategy is. Jerry is saying that everyone went into business. I believe that. The business of America is business and every one of us—even the rebels—are in business.

Yuppie: The problem is that Abbie really doesn't talk about how we're going to change society. I think Abbie is going to be giving the same speech twenty years from now . . . He's distorting a lot of what I say but I'm not going to go into that—Abbie says that when you go for economic and political power and try to get rich then you're absolutely part of the problem, then you're a sellout and I'm saying no, there's actually something different happening right now. Abbie is just selling cynicism tonight, as far as I'm concerned. Cynicism about people trying to change things.

And the Winner Is...

In the March 1985 issue of *Mother Jones*, David Corn summarized the two debates he witnessed:

As to the big question—who wins?—it's a close call. The young crowds that the two attract appear to favor the ever-rebellious Hoffman. But while Hoffman may appeal to their hearts, Rubin has them by the billfolds. Hoffman scores points when he tells the students that none of them could pass the dress code at one of Rubin's business salons, but both he and Rubin know that in a few years, most of these students will want to dress more like Rubin than Hoffman. Those students rushing toward professional careers are truly Jerry's kids. He tells them what they want to hear: "Do not fear success. Do not fear that because you may become financially successful in America you have to sell out your beliefs or your values." Hoffman's politics seem too far left for many.

But more telling was the automobile ride he shared with both of them on the way to the gig. Corn writes,

And for the entire trip, what do they discuss? Videocassette recorders and television sets. And who gives advice to whom? It makes sense that Hoffman knows where to find the best buy, but he is also a walking Consumer Reports *on video equipment. Rubin, now the self-proclaimed spokesmen of the Yuppies, is paradoxically a video neophyte.*

While still underground, Abbie invites Jerry and Mimi to visit him anytime and expresses love for his new Betamax video recorder and the movies he's acquired. He also includes a list of celebrities who have written letters calling for Abbie's freedom when he turns himself in. Note that Jon Voight was still a liberal then!

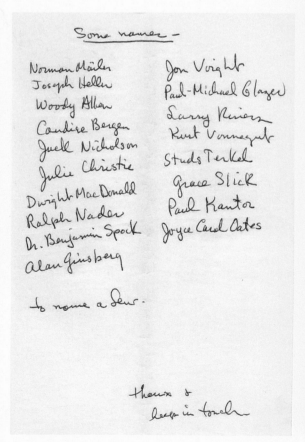

DAVID SPANER: I was at that Vancouver debate! As a matter of fact, I spent the afternoon with Abbie before the event. All I can say is both of those guys changed. You shouldn't assume that just one guy changed. Abbie . . . when I say a more conventional activist, there's a lot of reasons why he became that. A lot of it's changing with the times, a lot of it's changing with him. I'm not saying Abbie's a less creative person, but he did go through those kinds of changes, himself.

GERALD LEFCOURT: And so, Abbie's speaking all over the country, he does the Yippie vs. Yuppie shit. He hates that. He despises Jerry for the things he says. And he walks around saying, "You know, they cheer me, but they're gonna do what Jerry says!" That's what he said.

A. J. WEBERMAN: Abbie wouldn't denounce Jerry in the press because they were both in the Chicago 8 but, on the other hand, he wouldn't hang out with him. He never denounced Jerry. We tried to get him to do it a number of times in the '80s—but Kunstler wouldn't let him do that shit. Solidarity.

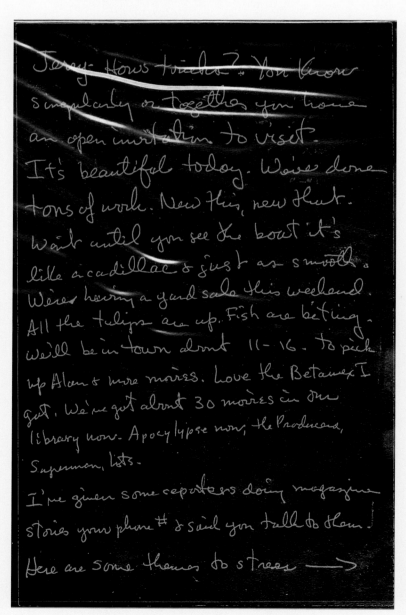

Chicago 7: Out of limelight, on with life

On a snowy day in Chicago 15 years ago Monday, a jury dropped the curtain on the morality play of the '60s.

All of the so-called Chicago Seven were acquitted of conspiracy to incite a riot during Chicago's 1968 Democratic National Convention.

But five were convicted of crossing state lines to incite a riot, and the defendants and their lawyers got jail terms — later overturned — for contempt of court.

Where are these emissaries of the Age of Aquarius?

David Dellinger, 69, an elder statesman of the pacifist movement, is writing his autobiography in Peacham, Vt.

Dellinger, who teaches at Vermont College, will appear Wednesday on a Chicago TV talk show with **Abbie Hoffman** and **Bobby Seale.**

Hoffman 48, co-founder of

By Sahm Doherty, Camera 5

THEN: At a May 1970 rally in Connecticut to free Bobby Seale are, from left, Tom Hayden, John Froines, Jerry Rubin (partially obscured) and David Dellinger (at microphones). Black Panther member Elbert Howard is next to Dellinger. To right of Howard, other former defendants: Lee Weiner, Abbie Hoffman, Rennie Davis. Seale, jailed on murder charges, was freed after a mistrial. Froines and Weiner were acquitted of all charges in the Chicago Seven trial.

WALLI LEFF: Abbie genuinely disagreed with Jerry's position and philosophy. However, he always trusted Jerry, because he'd proven he was trustworthy when Abbie was underground. That was a tie that was never broken. There was gratitude, trust, and recognition that Abbie was absolutely certain about. He felt that Jerry may have sold out in some ways, from the business angle, but that didn't affect his feelings toward somebody that he valued as a friend he could trust. Certainly, Abbie articulated different positions. Both of them were showmen, both trying to attract as big of an audience as they could, so they knew they had to—their disagreements were genuine, but no matter how heated it appeared in public, there was always that common thread that was never broken between them, ever.

PAUL KRASSNER: Abbie would defend Jerry even though Abbie disliked what Jerry had become. Some people got them confused and would ask Abbie, "Are you still a stockbroker?" and Abbie got furious when people got them mixed up like that. But, if they started putting Jerry down, Abbie would defend him, by saying; "You can say that when you lay across the train tracks leading to the Oakland Depot where the soldiers were being sent overseas to die." It was a personality thing, really. And the values, you can't separate that.

I saw the futility of being

cast in the role of the

protester,

    the freaky opposition.

In America everyone

        plays roles.

The Jerry Rubin role

    of the 1960s,

      as exciting and

          experimental

as it was when it was created,

    had become predictable

and much less effective

by the 1970s.

Abbie's Funeral. Suffering from depression, Abbie took his own life on April 12, 1989. A private funeral was held in Massachusetts for family and close friends, followed by a large public memorial in New York months later. Jerry and Dave Dellinger were the only two members of the Chicago 8 to attend the private ceremony. Dellinger stated that the suicide verdict was a conspiracy and lie, while Jerry predicted that Abbie's "spirit would be reborn in the 1990s but in a coat and tie." The *New York Times* reported that most funeral attendees "were more yuppie than yippie" and that "there were more ties than ripped jeans" to hear Pete Seeger's voice and banjo soothe the mourners. In 1970, Abbie had written about the bitter disagreements he and Jerry had had about protest methods on the streets of Chicago: "*We would not let a personal fight upset anything. Besides, we were both so dedicated that I realized that Jerry would cry at my funeral and make the right speech and I would do the same at his.*"

DANA BEAL: I continued to be good friends with Abbie up until he died. I attended his funeral in Massachusetts. Some people told me that a certain part was only for family but I showed up. Abbie was very depressed by that whole Yippie vs. Yuppie thing. That was one of the things that made him depressed. He also went to this thing in Arizona, and the kids didn't want him, they wanted Jello Biafra, it was the faculty that invited Abbie. But he shouldn't have fucking given up. He could have lived a long time.

GABRIELLE SCHANG: I went to Abbie's funeral; I went with Jerry. He was the only member of the Chicago 8 to attend Abbie's funeral. Jerry was really sad. Everybody was. I don't remember Jerry wailing and gnashing his teeth. But, there was a sober, somber feeling. Later, there was a memorial for Abbie at The Palladium in New York, way after his death, so people from the West Coast came. But at his real funeral, it was more people who were from the East Coast. There weren't a whole lot of people that were in the movement there, it was more family.

WALLI LEFF: When Abbie died, there was a huge memorial in New York, I came onstage—it moved along chronologically, different people got on for different parts of Abbie's life, I came onstage for the '60s. A lot of people came on, and we all remained on stage. And believe me, at the '60s point, the audience just went wild. One of the people who came on later was Jerry, and spoke a very beautiful piece about Abbie. He was standing next to me, and when he came on, they booed.

And then he spoke his piece; it was beautiful. So we all went off to great applause, and he got applauded at the end, for what he said. I said to Jerry, "I feel so bad, I know this must be very hurtful for you, it must be very hard for you." Mimi was just about to give birth to Adam, she was about eight months pregnant. She was standing in the wings backstage, and so I went back, and I spoke to them. I could tell he was very hurt. But he was very strong. Jerry had a lot of self-strength. But I think he appreciated that somebody cared enough about him to say something.

Jerry's legacy has been much abused since he first arrived on Wall Street and in the years since his death—Abbie has been the subject of several biographies, while Jerry has had nothing written about his life until now. Abbie is arguably more charismatic and a little more famous. To oversimplify, Abbie didn't change (at least in the public eye), and that's both admirable and tragic—perhaps it was his inability to change that was his downfall.

ABE PECK: Of course, you could argue that Abbie didn't sell out, but several things happened. One was that he got busted. So that changes a lot, because suddenly he had to go underground, he became "a character," he made a character out of that, and did some real good things. I remember getting a call from a friend at the *New York Times* when Abbie died, who told me that Abbie was manic depressive. Maybe because he was, Abbie didn't want to stand down, and he couldn't climb down. He didn't want to be normal or bourgeois. It wasn't over for him politically near the end of his life. Cleaning up the Hudson River was very important for him and that was the best thing he could do under his circumstances.

I'm more close to Jerry; I became a mainstream journalist. Jerry was able to climb down, stand down, transform, and maybe even climb out of it more easily than Abbie could. I'm certainly much less critical of people now than I might have been then. But I think the cartoon of Jerry—the Yippie vs. Yuppie debates that they each welcomed, of course radicals don't have good pension plans—so that was making them dull, and also keeping themselves relevant in a different way.

I think you had more people rooting for Abbie in those debates even if they were closer to Jerry in lifestyle. Abbie's lifestyle continued to be—even with the drug bust, which wasn't romantic—he's a romantic hero who died a bad death. Jerry is something different and it was a different path. If you take a long arc, you come out a different place with Jerry than you would if you'd been writing about Stokely Carmichael living in Africa, answering the phone "ready for the revolution" until he dies. It's admirable, but also a little removed.

David Spaner poses the theory that Abbie changed, not Jerry:

DAVID SPANER: Jerry may not have even changed as much as Abbie. Abbie evolved into, in his later years, a conventional activist—which I'm not criticizing him for, he did some great work then. But what I am saying is that Jerry still kept that kind of thing about wanting to create epic events, do something big. That P. T. Barnum approach to life, which is very Yippie. I think that was always a part of Jerry. He channeled it to progressive politics, because that was a mass movement in the 1960s. I think that if you look at the history of the Left in America, it goes in cycles.

Jerry's brother Gil recalled watching Jerry and Abbie debate:

GIL RUBIN: I went to see Yippie vs. Yuppie at Fairfield University, and I remember sitting in the audience, thinking, "I think Abbie's my brother." [*Laughter.*] I sat there thinking, it's gotta be very painful for Jerry to stand in front of a college audience, and be booed and heckled, while you're giving your spiel. And here's Abbie, being who you were [Jerry was] ten years ago, it's gotta—

how do you stand in front of an audience and do that? To go and be ridiculed, to have your persona ridiculed, by the very same people who once adored you, that's amazing. For me, it was sad to see that. But that was very sad for me to see what happened to Jerry as opposed to what happened to Abbie. Jerry—every couple years, became something else. Whereas Abbie stayed the same, and of course that had its own—obviously, Abbie, in the end, wasn't pretty.

ABBIE DIDN'T WANT TO STAND DOWN ❧ AND HE COULDN'T CLIMB DOWN. ❧
—ABE PECK

Jonah Raskin points out the little-known fact that Abbie was also playing the stock market, and doing quite well:

JONAH RASKIN: Well, at one point Abbie was smuggling and selling cocaine. And then when Abbie and Jerry were doing the Yippie vs. Yuppie debates, Abbie was also investing in the stock market. He kept that secret from the public, but he also claimed privately that he was doing better on the stock market than Jerry. I never saw Abbie's financial records, but he claimed that he was doing very well, that he was working both sides of the street. Which was part of Abbie's trademark: to work both sides of the street. You continue to say that you're a Yippie, and you're true to the Yippie thing, but you also have the other side of you, where you're a Yuppie.

DAVID SPANER: The image is that Abbie stuck to his guns, and that Jerry sold out. A lot of it is simply that people think Abbie deserves more credit because of that. It's as simple as that: why there's been more emphasis, since they died, on Abbie than Jerry. But, as you say, it's complex. Because Jerry didn't change as fundamentally as some people assume. And Abbie was doing all sorts of other things as well, as you're saying.

ROBERT FRIEDMAN: I was always a lot more accepting of Jerry's decisions about those things [attending est, working on Wall Street]—partly because it was self-preservation, although I didn't necessarily agree with him. Jerry and Abbie burned at a very high heat for a period of years, and, in many ways, burned themselves out. I think Jerry, at least, was able to find something that was able to stabilize him and keep him going, and that's much to his credit. Abbie descended deeper into depression and his own craziness, and ended up in a downward spiral. Which is not to say Abbie didn't accomplish anything—didn't have good periods during that time, as well. But, they both burned at a white heat. And that's tough. Nobody, and that included Stew Albert, operated with that kind of intensity.

Also, Abbie had a mental illness. He was bipolar, and I don't think that was something he developed as a result of his working in the movement, but that's something he lived with his whole life, and it just got a whole lot worse. Jerry just didn't suffer from that. He had other issues and problems; I think his personality was a lot more stable than Abbie's was.

FRANK BARDACKE: One thing is, Abbie almost always had to be on. He couldn't turn off being "Abbie"—that must be fucking exhausting.

JUDY GUMBO: That dynamic continued no matter what decade it was. The bitching—Abbie bitching at Jerry, Jerry bitching at Abbie, the rivalry continued. It never stopped. Like two brothers, like Cain and Abel.

STUART SAMUELS: Abbie was the opposite of Jerry—he didn't like getting people together, he wanted to lead people. Abbie didn't want to organize them together. That's why they worked well together, in certain issues. Jerry was the quintessential matchmaker.

The 1979 book *Woodstock Census*, by Rex Weiner and Deanne Stillman, polled a diverse cross section of a thousand baby boomers who had experienced the 1960s in full flight, and asked them a series of questions of what they thought then, what they thought now, and so on. Even in 2016, the results concerning Jerry and/or Abbie are interesting. When the entire group was asked to rank "who in the movement did they admire and were influenced by," Jerry and Abbie each received thirty-five percent of the vote, showing that they were equally popular, with Eldridge Cleaver getting twenty-seven percent of the vote, Tom Hayden twenty-six percent, and the rest split nearly evenly between Rennie Davis and Mark Rudd. The questionnaire participants who classified themselves as "political activists" were asked the same question again, to rank "who in the movement did they admire and were influenced by," and again, Abbie and Jerry came out on top, basically even, with Abbie and Jerry splitting the vote nearly fifty/fifty between them—with Abbie receiving just one percent more.

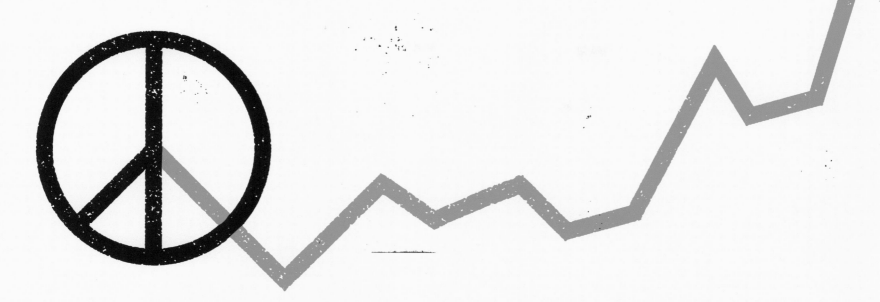

MONEY, IT'S A GAS.

IN THE 1980S, THE JERRY VS. ABBIE competiveness also carried over to money. Mutual friends say that, although he'd never publicly admit it, the Yippie Abbie wanted to make as much money as the vilified Yuppie Jerry. Abbie's broker, Steve Tappis, told Hoffman biographer Jonah Raskin that Abbie "loved the idea of making more money than Jerry Rubin, of being more Yuppie and at the same time more Yippie." Tappis confirmed that Abbie "bought and sold commodities, including crude oil, on the Chicago Mercantile Exchange." Obviously all involved were sworn to secrecy at the time, but Abbie was known to purchase everything from "speedboats to computers," and that sometimes his income was "a hundred thousand dollars per year"—which was a lot of money back then.

Martin Kenner told me in 2013:

MARTIN KENNER: Abbie was playing the commodity market. I had a friend, Steve Tappis, who was on the floor of the Chicago Mercantile Exchange. He had been on the original Weather committee, and he quit the first day the Weathermen took over SDS—he went to graduate school, dropped out, and became a broker. He traded currencies for Abbie, and Abbie would call him up, when Jerry was in the other room during their Yippie vs. Yuppie tours, in the motel. He'd be talking to my friend about Swiss francs and Deutschemarks. There's no doubt that Abbie had a far better business brain than Jerry. I mean, Abbie could have been Don Draper—you know, *Mad Men*—he was an advertising genius. He was good at it. He made his living, when he was underground, betting on horses, betting on games. He was a bookie! That's how he made his living. He was a speculative kind of guy. He liked to take chances, he'd bet on things. Jerry was much more of a straight arrow, conversely, in that respect.

In his memoir *Confessions of a Raving, Unconfirmed Nut*, Paul Krassner tells a number of Yippie vs. Yuppie era stories. In 1988, there was a twentieth-anniversary "celebration" of the Chicago protests held, ironically enough, in the very same venue as the Democratic Convention. As Krassner stood at the podium, he "couldn't help but notice that Abbie Hoffman was sitting exactly where Mayor Richard Daley sat in 1968, when Senator Abraham Ribicoff was on the podium at the Amphitheater saying, 'With George McGovern [as president] we wouldn't have Gestapo tactics on the streets of Chicago.' And then [broadcast live on national television], Mayor Daley shouted from his seat, 'Fuck you, you Jew son of a bitch. You lousy motherfucker, go home!'"

Krassner continues, "And the déjà vu became even more twisted. When I referred to the recent debates between Abbie and Jerry—'It was a Yippie event in and of itself, but it was also a Yuppie event, since they were grossing five thousand bucks a throw'—Abbie started shouting at Krassner: 'That's not true!'" Abbie knew it was true, but he had to be "adamant about not being perceived as performing politically for financial gain." Abbie was occasionally mistaken for Jerry and asked, "Do you still work on Wall Street?" That annoyed him to no end, but Krassner's "outing" made him much angrier. "Why the fuck did you have to do that?" he asked, "I don't want you deciding what's on- or off-the-record."

Krassner's reply was direct: "Abbie, you debated Jerry publicly." On the other side, Krassner was bemused by the fact the man who "once wrote that 'a necktie was a hangman's noose' was now wearing one." Jerry had recently stated, "Money is the long hair of the '80s," and had issued "a press release requesting that the media no longer refer to him as a former Yippie leader." Krassner's wit was spot on: "I envisioned the headline: '*Former Yippie Leader asks not to be called Former Yippie Leader!*'"

I DIDN'T REALLY THINK ANYTHING COULD KILL JERRY. HE HAD MORE OR LESS BROUGHT DOWN THE GOVERNMENT, LBJ, AND NIXON. HE WASN'T GOING TO BE KILLED BY A CAR.

—MIMI LEONARD

14

Last Days

Crossing Wilshire Boulevard. It was late afternoon in LA and Jerry was hungry. He had been talking for hours with Fred Branfman. A Vietnam–era whistle blower in the tradition of Daniel Ellsberg, Fred and Jerry shared a common past as antiwar activists. Now, the two shared an interest in longevity and had spent a long afternoon discussing philanthropy, legacy, and mortality. Hungry and eager to continue the conversation, they ventured out for dinner. Jerry's girlfriend, Tiffany Stettner, joined them.

TIFFANY STETTNER: We had a meeting with Fred Branfman, who was the head of an organization where we'd be part of helping children, disenfranchised black kids in Los Angeles, from the other side. We'd be providing all kinds of creative ways for them to be educated, to help them actualize, and move to a place where they could have every opportunity to do what they love, where there weren't so many boundaries, and there wouldn't be any barriers. We were in a long meeting, and it got very late.

Standing at the corner of Wilshire Boulevard, Jerry was getting impatient. Now in his mid-fifties, the former revolutionary was bored by the '60s and burnt out by the '80s, and looking for something new. Despite his unflagging enthusiasm for life, Jerry was at loose ends. All he knew was that he wanted to return to the spotlight "and stand nationally for something," but he didn't want to just "be famous for being famous." Having earlier backed Gary Hart in a campaign that would be derailed by a sex scandal, Jerry believed a baby boomer would someday be elected president. He knew the time had come for his generation to take over. (Jerry playfully exchanged a long-distance message or two with Donna Rice, the actress/model the media used to derail Gary Hart's presidential campaign in 1987. She's now a well-respected spokesperson for children's internet safety.)

Jerry Rubin of 'Chicago 7' Hit by a Car

□ **Activism:** The Vietnam War protester turned businessman is reported in critical condition after being struck while jaywalking in Westwood.

By ERIC MALNIC
TIMES STAFF WRITER

Former Chicago Seven anti-war activist Jerry Rubin was reported in critical condition Tuesday at UCLA Medical Center after he was hit by a car while jaywalking in Westwood, Los Angeles police said.

Officers said the Yippie turned businessman was crossing Wilshire Boulevard at mid-block between Selby and Manning avenues about 8:30 p.m. Monday when he was struck by a car heading west on Wilshire.

Rubin, 56, who lives in a high-rise Brentwood apartment, was taken by ambulance to the medical center, where he underwent several hours of surgery.

The driver of the car—a 1991 Volkswagen GTI—was not held

Please see RUBIN, B3

Leslie Meyers, another girlfriend of Jerry's from that era, recalls an encounter with Bill Clinton:

LESLIE MEYERS: Jerry's focus was meeting people and networking, and who he could meet that was famous or important. So it was weird: when I introduced him to Bill Clinton and Jerry didn't say who he was . . . just shook his hand and walked away. Jerry had told me, "I want to shake his hand." I was like, "Really? There's five hundred people here." And he's like, "Yeah, let's go wait in line." And I assumed it was because he wanted to say, "Hi, I'm Jerry Rubin." After he walked away, I said, "Why didn't you tell him who you were? I'm sure Clinton would have found that really interesting." He was like, "Oh, no, no, no.'"

Mimi Leonard offered an explanation:

MIMI LEONARD: That's interesting. Well, he didn't want to be a has-been. He didn't want to have people be most interested in what it was like in the '60s. He wanted to be current.

Jerry was fascinated by the emerging computer technology, seeing future possibilities in networking. Tiffany Stettner talked about his idea of using the internet (then in its infancy) to connect people.

TIFFANY STETTNER: I had a laptop, and soon it was his laptop. [*Laughs.*] And I'd be working on it and he'd be talking to me about the laptop and how we could use this to connect with this person and that person. And his ideas were remarkably identical to what Facebook is now. He really predicted that it was our generation, the generation that happened between my age and his age that were going experience it. I absolutely believe if he were sitting here in 2015, he'd be like, "Oh, yeah, that was my idea, that other guy stole it from me!" He'd be laughing at me and pushing his elbows, saying, "Are you gonna tell him it's my idea?" If he was around, he would have flown out to meet Mark Zuckerberg. Whether he was on the tail or the beginning, he would have been right on that revolution.

Jerry was also a dad who worked hard to stay in his children's lives. Stettner recalls taking them to the movies the day before his meeting with Branfman.

TIFFANY STETTNER: We had gone to a movie with Juliet and Adam. It was very typical for Jerry to be with his kids, which usually made him extremely ecstatic. The four of us went to the movies and everybody had a seat at the movie, but they'd sit on somebody's lap. We would switch. One minute Juliet would sit on my lap, then Jerry's, then Adam's. It was just one of those ritual Sundays. It was a very big high—no drugs [*laughs*]—just a really wonderful weekend.

It was 1994, and great changes were in store for the future. But today, Jerry just wanted to get across the street. Having been a New Yorker for most of his adult life, he exercised his God-given right to jaywalk—across eight lanes of LA traffic. Out in the street, Jerry turned to look back at his friends, who were yelling to him to be careful, and was hit by an oncoming car.

TIFFANY STETTNER: Jerry was impatient. And he didn't want to wait to cross the street; the first crossing was enough to stop anyone from jaywalking for the rest of their life. For Jerry, he wasn't fearful. He was just anxious to get his needs met. He was so hungry and who knows what was going on inside. *When you're hungry, you're hungry*. It was just a series of unfortunate events, whatever you want to call it: it was Jerry getting hit by a car, it was him being thrown up in the air so high that, as I said before, it looked like a bird. That's how much my denial system was in play. It's very difficult to see somebody that you care about, that you love, you just can't. Your body will do what it has to do to survive. And my brain said, "*Oh my gosh, what's a bird doing carrying Jerry?*" and so that's the way that I handled it. When he came down—I didn't want him to move. I knew, don't move him . . . I didn't know trauma, nobody does. We just wanted him to get help so between Fred and I, we didn't move him, but we kept the crowd, tried to help with the traffic. I just sat with him just guarding his body.

Mimi had remained Jerry's closest confidante, and was the first to get the call.

MIMI LEONARD: I moved back to LA by then, and we were still doing multi-level marketing. We hung out a lot and were kind of best friends. I was sitting in the bedroom when the phone rang, around 7 p.m. At first I wasn't going to answer it. And then some strange sixth sense came over me, and I said, "No, I should answer this." And it was Tiffany calling to say that Jerry had been injured. I became hysterical and called my husband, Mark.

Then I spoke to a policeman who had been on site after the accident, and I said to him, "But he's going to be okay, right?" because I didn't really think anything could kill Jerry. He had more or less brought down the government, LBJ, and Nixon. He wasn't going to be killed by a car. The policemen paused a long time, and said, "It was pretty bad," then I knew that it might not be okay.

At the hospital, I wanted to make sure that they knew that it was Jerry Rubin who had been hit. I thought that somehow if they knew this was a major personality, the doctors would somehow figure out how to fix the situation. I was not allowed to see him. He was having multiple operations. And when I finally did see him, he was hooked up to machines with so many tubes. It was horrifying and somehow reminded me of some kind of inhumane, experimental testing on animals. He was completely unconscious.

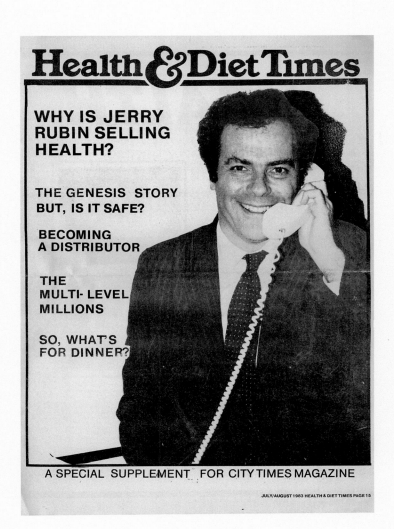

1992 GOALS — Item ④

① To weigh 140 pounds Dec. 31, 1992 + to be ACTIVELY exercising again. (N) (R)
② To be grossing $100,000 a month. (NO)
③ To be out of debt + to have saved $200,000 after taxes in no-risk securities. (ALMOST) ($200K) ($500K)
④ To have been tested all year extensively + to be in perfect health. ④
⑤ To have many friends in L.A. (ALMOST)
⑥ To be "MR. MLM" in USA + be positioned for eventual financial independence. (ALMOST) ④
⑦ Juliet + Adam to be healthy + happy + to have great relationship with them. ①
⑧ To have many girl friends + to be positioned for new relationship starting January 1, 1993. (ALMOST)
⑨ To have more than one source of income by December, 1992. (ALMOST)
⑩ To have "MLM book" out by January, 1993. (NO)
⑪ To have Network Marketing office be breakeven by Sept, 1992! (NO)
⑫ To be "in business" with 2-3 more people by Dec., 1992. (ALMOST)
⑬ To have good, stress-free, friendly relationships with MIMI. (YES)

418
0354

for something in 1992. (NO)
⑮ To have OMNITRITION healthy, in business, + doing $10 mill./month by Dec, 1992. (YES-ALMOST)
⑯ To be making good $$$ with Ralph Oats, Sandy Elsberg, + etc. (50%-YES)
⑰ To have a movie made of my life.
⑱ To dress great + to look great — re hair + skin, etc. (YES)
⑲ To be great "party man" of L.A. (AVG)
⑳ To feel great every day! To have year of fun! (YES)

See GOALS →

GOAL:
① Book + infomercial?
② $200K w/ OMNI.
③ 10 other MLM checks.

Jan. 3
Steinborn re DR. Lewis.

MY SKILLS HAVE IN THE 1980's BECOME NON-FUNCTIONAL.

Society does not reward...
Fantastic political troublemaker.
Great disrupter. Event creator.
Celebrity. Media manipulator.
Anti-cold war philosopher. Story-teller.
Conspicuous writer. Guerilla theater activist.
Psychologically. Host. Public Conference or Model
Excellent. TV-radio guest. Educator
Public Protester. — Political Observer.
Spokesperson — Rebellion. — Personal Health.
Spike leader for — Truth-Telling. Lecturer.
Workshop leader. author.

These no longer useful.

↓ transfer
that into communication and
problem-solving skills and
apply to another interest.

COMMUNICATION
Problem — solver

What are the elemental skills?
I am a professional job-hunter.

C.R. ↔ MIAMI MY SIXTIES
1963 - 1972.
Chapter 1950's. 1963-1967: BAY AREA
Free Speech movt. in Berk. TRIP CUBA
V.D.C.: troop trains Antiwar. Da Protest.
Berk. Antidraft Movt. Mayor. Hip
Hippie S.F. Be-in.
1967-68-69-70
Pentagon demo. Oct. 1967.
Birth of yippie. Yippie coll. dem
Chicago 1968. Woodstock. Alt.
Cons. Trial.
Natl. Demos. all over country.
May Day
Miami.

JERRY'S DAILY JOURNALS

IN THE 1970s, Jerry kept a journal, but in the early '80s, he began to carry around a softbound daily calendar that became more than just an appointment book. He jotted down "thoughts in progress" about work, dieting, personal and professional goals, investments, book and business ideas, and, since his parents had died in their early fifties from health complications, never-ending physical fitness self-diagnoses. In addition to endless doctor's appointments, he kept detailed records of his cholesterol levels. Most people (even with high cholesterol) have it checked a couple of times per year on average. Jerry was getting it checked every month. When I asked Mimi about this, she laughed and said, "That's Jerry—only he could talk a doctor into doing that." After realizing that Jerry had gotten more medical testing done per month (continuously for nearly a decade) than most people would get in a full year, I thought his tombstone should have read: *"I would have gotten even more done, but I was waiting in the doctor's office."*

Nearly every page of his daily calendars are chock full of notes like "Ugh! Never Again Coffee!" "No More Late Night Yogurt." "Call the Doctor." "Call Stew Albert." "Call Marty Kenner." And apho-

risms, like, "Don't Postpone Pleasure," and "Relax—Do Not Move So Fast." These were combined with "resolutions" (his phrase) ranging from "No more salmon steak—only salmon," to "Do not talk to my lawyer or anyone in his office for six months—until November 1st—so there will be no more bills [coming from him]."

Health regimens were repeated like mantras. He was not afraid to list his failures and areas for improvement. Occasionally there was self-awareness—"I am a terrible obsessive"—and he always set goals at the beginning of the year and reviewed them at the end. While many focused on professional and financial success, he also made mention of trying to get along better with friends and family: "Improve relations with Mimi and the children." In 1988, several years before he was hit by a car and died, he had noted on the page for May 16, in all caps:

"BE CAREFULL [SIC] OF ALL CARS WHEN CROSSING THE STREET—ON YELLOW LIGHTS, EVEN ON GREEN, WATCH OUT FOR CARS."

He Ain't Heavy, He's My Brother.

Although the accident didn't kill Jerry, it left him in a coma. Mimi, Leslie, and Tiffany closed ranks around him, becoming his support system while Jerry clung to life. During those last few weeks, many old friends came to sit by his side.

LOLA COHEN: I sat with him and played Phil Ochs's music, and his eyes started to twitch.

MIMI LEONARD: I believe he did regain some kind of consciousness. I think he could hear us, and was somewhat responsive—not exactly physically, but you could tell he was cognizant of what was going on. I remember at one point, big round tears began to roll out of his eyes, and I guess he was realizing that he was going to die and it made him sad. And I'm afraid I was becoming somewhat hysterical, too, and was not a calm influence, but more of a begging-him-to-live influence, which he just couldn't do.

LESLIE MEYERS: When Jerry was in the hospital, what I call the *hippie freaks* came out of the woodwork. It was on the news, so people would come to the hospital and say, "Put this piece of fabric on his left arm, say this word three times, and it will heal him." And on the one hand, how kind and lovely that someone who doesn't even know him wants to help. But on the other hand . . . like, go away. So Mimi said, "Look, no one can just go in to see him."

I'm saying goodbye to Jerry. There's a knock on the door, and there's six-foot-four black man wearing a fez, which makes him like six-eight, and I open the door. And this very handsome presence says, "I know you're an angel, because I can see your wings." And I closed the door. So I'm walking back to Jerry, and "knock, knock, knock." So I open the door and I say, *"Who are you?!"* He said, "My name is Eldridge Cleaver." I said, "That's interesting. Eldridge, do me a favor. I'm saying goodbye; can you just wait? Then I'll help you, so you can go in and see him." I finish up, and I get Eldridge a cap, mask, gown, and booties. And he says, "Will you wait for me?" I said okay. So he goes in, and he comes out ten minutes or so later, and he's crying. Now, it's very hard if you see a man cry. I did not know how to comfort him, as much as I did not know him. I felt very helpless. Here's this man and he's crying about Jerry and what he meant to a generation, and what he did, all of his accomplishments, and on and on.

When Cleaver arrived at the hospital, the staff in the critical care unit had informed him that only family members were allowed to see Jerry. In a move straight out of the Yippie playbook, Eldridge told the nurses that he was Jerry's brother.

BOBBY SEALE: Eldridge called me and said, "I'm sitting here with Jerry in the hospital." I was really sad; I loved Jerry, his energy and his humor.

Like Jerry, Eldridge had undergone a major transformation since the '60s. Eldridge and Kathleen had split up as the Black Panther Party disintegrated. Eldridge became a born-again Christian and a right-wing conservative. He even took his own stab at entrepreneurship, with "cod pants" (a pair of polyester slacks that exaggerated the size of a man's package, and a cringeworthy foray into the fashion world). Myers invited Eldridge to have sushi with her and Timothy Leary that night.

LESLIE MEYERS: I turned to Timothy, and said, "By the way, the reason we're at a bigger table is because we have a surprise guest coming for dinner."

He goes, "Who is it?"

And I go, "There he is now, Eldridge Cleaver." Leary takes the longest drag on his cigarette I have ever seen a human take. His whole face darkened in this weird way I'd never seen, and he looks at me, and says, "Do you know the last time I saw Eldridge Cleaver?"

I'm like, "No, when?"

And he goes, "He kidnapped my wife and I in Algiers when we'd escaped from prison, we'd gone there and been promised safe haven under this little fiefdom he had set up. He kidnapped us and every day, for six months, held us at gunpoint and threatened to murder us and bury us in the desert. The last day I saw him was the day before I escaped." . . . At which point, Eldridge arrives, and he walks in and Tim hugs him very tightly. Then we proceeded to have the most incredible dinner ever.

Eldridge was like watching a tennis match. Either the most fascinating, well-spoken, erudite professor you'd ever seen, or he was like a street person, "Well, I had a gun and I held it up to the mother-effer's head." The two of them were hysterical. They were friends again and it was done.

Meyers had also patched up a long-standing feud between Leary and Jerry. Rubin told her, "Leslie, I haven't spoken to Tim in over twenty years. When Tim was arrested and brought back to the United States, we had a press conference, and got Timothy's son to denounce him too, so that when Tim testified against our friends the Weather Underground, who had helped him escape prison, he would be unreliable. Like, who could trust this guy, even the son says he's a liar, so to speak." Meyers was friends with both of them, so they made up. After Jerry's death, Tim spent time with Jerry's kids as Uncle Tim!

Farewell.

MIMI LEONARD: Jerry was in a coma for fourteen days, and for the first part of the time I was sure he'd live. I talked to Mark about making a room for him at our house in the case that he lived as a paraplegic, and Mark agreed. I was hoping that would be the outcome—better than his death. I was completely convinced somehow Jerry would live. Up until that time in my life, everything more or less turned out fine, and it was incomprehensible to me that Jerry would die. In the end, the doctors told us that there was no hope. It was time to let Jerry go.

On November 28, 1994, Jerry's life support machines were turned off and he passed away—leaving behind his family, his friends, and his two very young children, Juliet and Adam. He was only fifty-six years old. Afterward, doctors discovered Jerry's body was riddled with cancer, and that he wouldn't have survived more than a year at best.

OPPOSITE: Uncle Tim with Adam & Juliet.

ABOVE: Note from Rona Elliot to Jerry, ". . .the enclosed as a very reliable test to determine if there is any cancer presence. . ."

Did He or Didn't He?

Since Jerry was extremely forthcoming with his friends and the media, most aspects of his life are transparent. But there's one question that remains after all these years: did he know that he had cancer when he stepped off that curb and got hit by a car? Tiffany was confident that he did.

TIFFANY STETTNER: Jerry would absolutely want to compete with my cholesterol levels and I [was then] a twenty-something-year-old girl. So he's competitive with his health the way a man could be competitive with a Ferrari or his muscles. Now, reflecting, I see where he was absolutely manic when it comes to his health.

We would go to Cedar-Sinai and the doctor would show me that Jerry had a very high PSA [Prostate-Specific Antigen] level, and it was borderline cancer. Jerry would just constantly watch it and take incredible amounts of antioxidants. He had sworn me to secrecy. He absolutely didn't want anyone to know about all of those issues, due to the fact that he didn't want his children to be worried.

Judy Gumbo has a faint recollection of Jerry calling Stew Albert and inviting them for Thanksgiving, and telling Stew that he had lung cancer. They declined for reasons she can no longer remember, but then wonders, well, if he had cancer, why didn't we say yes? Mimi, who was also in constant contact with Jerry, had no idea.

LESLIE MEYERS: I don't believe he knew he had cancer. My feeling is if he knew, we all would have known. He was not a, "Oh, I'll keep this news a secret, because I wouldn't want to . . ." No, he would want all of us around him, helping him. He would be freaking out.

Rona Elliott didn't know for sure what was going on, but thought he didn't look well, and told him so a few weeks before his accident. Jerry had replied, "That's so funny, I'm going to see the doctor today, I have an appointment." They spoke again after that, but Jerry said nothing.

RONA ELLIOTT: There was a blackout on the news about his death. I called the house, and George Leonard answered. I asked, "What happened?" George said when they opened Jerry up, he was completely metastasized with cancer. So, to me, there are so many different layers to that. One, did Jerry get those results from the doctor? He certainly didn't kill himself, but he certainly wasn't going to go through that thing. He made a vow. He was never going to go out like his parents, and he was [around] his mother and father's age [when they died]. He was fifty-six. So, you can try to run away from your history, and you can handle it sometimes, but—I don't know if he knew. Maybe . . .

LESLIE MEYERS: Everything Jerry did was to lengthen his life, the vitamins, this and that. Stew told me that Jerry was talking to someone about the fact that he hadn't written a will—that he was going to write one, or hadn't, or needed to redo a will. And he jokingly said, *"With my luck, I'll walk outside and get hit by a bus next week."* And that was like two weeks before he got hit by a car!

Los Angeles Times

Mourners Remember Rubin for His Courage and Dedication

■ Funeral: More than 200 attend services for co-founder of Yippies. Friends praise him for his enthusiasm for anti-war causes and his business acumen.

By ERIC MALNIC
TIMES STAFF WRITER

More than 200 friends from a lifetime that ranged from the ragged anti-war street demonstrations of the 1960s to the penthouse luxury of network marketing in the 1990s turned out in Culver City on Thursday to honor the memory of Jerry Rubin.

If Rubin—as described by several of the mourners—was "always in a hurry," those who gathered to pay their final respects at Hillside Memorial cemetery were not. Their eulogies, which offered contrasts in style, lasted for more than two hours.

People such as Eldridge Cleaver, Stu Albert and Sally Kirkland fondly recalled **Please see RUBIN, B3**

Adam Rubin, 5, holds photo of his father that he brought to the funeral services.

Photos by IRIS SCHNEIDER / Los Angeles Times

Former Black Panther leader Eldridge Cleaver performs a traditional Jewish ritual by throwing dirt into grave at Jerry Rubin's funeral in Culver City on Thursday.

Funeral for a Friend. Jerry's funeral was an event attended by everyone from Berkeley to Wall Street. Around the globe, the media noted his passing with a flurry of obituaries and articles. He had survived the turbulent 1960s, only to die in a senseless accident in his fifties. The *New York Times* ran two different-but-similar obits on the 29th and 30th. Jerry would have loved not only being in the *Times* twice, but also in *People* magazine—the apotheosis of mainstream American culture.

MIMI LEONARD: Once Jerry died, there's a media circus—a lot of media at his funeral, and several speakers. I don't know why we loved the fact that the funeral time went over. It was supposed to be an hour, and went for two and half! All the testimonies were too long. It was spilling outside with Jerry's multi-level people, all of his '60s people . . . It was just this huge funeral.

At his funeral, Juliet, who was seven, insisted on seeing him in his coffin. And I brought both Adam and her before the ceremony began to see him lying there. What was amazing to me is that he looked completely different without his soul. After he died, although his body was identical, he looked completely different. Jerry, more than anyone I have ever known, was so animated. His soul was nearly exploding out of him at all times. He had radiance, and the change was astounding when he died. He looked *more* normal. He didn't have that dancing, crazy, funny, all-hell's-broke-loose energy that he carried with him when he was alive. My stepmother, who was standing with Adam at the grave, said Adam looked up at her after people started putting the shovels of dirt in, and said, "*When is he going to get up and come out of there?*" At five, he was unable to comprehend that Jerry was gone and I know it confused him for a long time.

Today, Jerry is still vilified by some of his peers from the golden era, who can't forget—or can't understand—his transition in the 1980s. Journalist Michael Simmons was at a dinner for Jerry's memorial and said that the Yippies sat at one table and the Yuppies at another, ignoring each other.

Jerry's first girlfriend and partner in radical politics got the news while traveling in Egypt.

BARBARA GULLAHORN: When Jerry died, I was in Egypt. I was walking through the streets and saw what was the equivalent of an Egyptian *Time* magazine, and there was a little photo on the front, just a little insert, of Jerry. So I figured, uh-oh, either something very good or very bad has happened, and spent a couple days trying to find out.

KATHY STREEM: I heard about it on the news. I was very sad. I think that might have been the first that I knew he had kids. So, I was out of touch with him for obviously longer than I realized. But, the jaywalking seemed like a Yippie way to go [*laughs*]. You know what makes me feel bad? Stew and Abbie and Jerry, Phil Ochs. They're just not here anymore, and there hasn't really been anybody capable of filling their shoes.

RABBI BARTON SHALLAT: I felt a great loss. It really hurt. He was so needy and so *love*. "Love" is a funny word to use with him, but he would just get your goat so much that he was lovable in his own way. And very frustrating. As my wife said, an unforgettable character. He made a mark; there was nothing about him that was quiet or subdued, tame. In a crowd, he always stood out.

RENNIE DAVIS: Well, it's kind of wild. I can be put in the extreme category on this, but I would say the decision to go out that way, Jerry made before he was born. And that was one hundred percent, not 99.999; it was one hundred percent Jerry's choice. And that's how he chose to go. And that's when he chose to go. And it went perfect. Just like he wanted it. So, it wasn't like some big accident, it never is.

Not long after Jerry's death, Stella Resnick wrote a fourteen-page essay about Jerry—more for herself as a cathartic exercise than anything else. It was never circulated, but she shared it with me during my research. I felt this excerpt was an apt finale to Jerry's passing.

STELLA RESNICK: I've never gotten over Jerry and I never intend to. I learned a lot from him about myself, about politics and social movements, about family, friendship and writing, and about having a good time while doing something meaningful. I know he wanted to make a positive impact on the world during his lifetime and I believe he has . . . One of Jerry's last projects begun just prior to his death—that of teaching inner city kids to become entrepreneurs—might have united all the disparate personas of his life, if he had lived long enough.

Jerry was not a violent revolutionary, but a visionary one. In *Growing (Up) at 37*, he wrote: "The future belongs to the people who have the largest view of the potential of human beings, not to those with the narrowest. A revolutionary must have the most positive view of human nature. Out of that view he acts, creates, and influences behavior . . ."

Knowing Jerry as closely and as intimately as I did, seeing him at his most inspired best and at his despicable worst, I can vouch for his genuineness when he spoke these words and set himself this goal. Like the rest of us—challenged by the life we've inherited, and grappling the only ways we know how to make things better—Jerry was a work in progress. The world is enriched by his having been here. It's all any of us can hope for.

HE WASN'T AN "I THINK THEREFORE I AM" KIND OF GUY. HE WAS MORE OF A "DO IT!" SORT. AND HE DID IT!

JERRY RUBIN

Rubin: from Yippie to Yuppie

Jerry Rubin, radical political activist and founder of the Youth International Party, died in Los Angeles on November 28 aged 56, from injuries suffered when he was hit by a car two weeks earlier. He was born on July 14, 1938.

A "YIPPIE" who, in more materialistic middle-age, became a "Yuppie", Jerry Rubin could lay claim to the dubious distinction of having significantly contributed to the widening of the boundaries of what was politically tolerable both in America and abroad in the 1960s and 1970s.

Having founded an embryo political organisation which he called the Youth International Party — the Yippies — he became a hero of the counter-culture, gaining national and then international prominence for himself and the anti-Vietnam war protest movement by mounting a series of disruptive acts embracing surreal street theatre, anarchic demonstrations and revolutionary diatribes.

After violent clashes between police and anti-war protesters at the 1968 Democratic Party's National Convention in Chicago, Rubin was one of a group charged with inciting the violence during the convention. The group, which included Abbie Hoffman and Tom Hayden, became known as the Chicago Seven. At the trial, the generation gap yawned in all its enormity between the outrageously behaved defendants and the unbendingly authoritarian Judge Julius Hoffman.

Rubin, wild-haired and irreverent, and his co-defendants, used the four-and-a-half-month-long court proceedings as a theatre for their surreal activism and were cited for contempt of court nearly 200 times. In the end, all seven were acquitted of conspiracy charges. Rubin and four others were convicted on intent-to-riot charges but the convictions were overturned on appeal.

Jerry Rubin was a political prankster who delighted in the use of shock tactics to outrage the Establishment. He caused a stir on Wall Street by throwing dollar bills on to the floor of the Stock Exchange and, appeared bare-chested and brandishing a toy pistol and rifle, at a demonstration in the House of Representatives. And although his actions may, today, seem merely curious, in the aftermath of the Nineties and Nineties, it was difficult to conjure up memories of his appearances before Congressional Committees decades earlier dressed in the uniform of a Revolutionary War soldier or Vietcong guerrilla. During his brief tenure with a Wall Street firm and his subsequent creation of a Yuppie hiring hall, it was hard to believe that he was the same man who had once thrown dollar bills on to the trading well of the New York Stock Exchange to evoke an image of corporate greed or had, along with 3,000 supporters, tried to levitate the Pentagon as a protest against his country's tragic adventure in South-East Asia. Frequently, over the years, I have been asked by reporters and others about my reaction to

mass expressions of dissent of 1968 and amid the racial and anti-war unrest of the time, his methods and his agenda were regarded — on both sides of the Atlantic — with considerable alarm.

In his polemical book *Do It! Scenarios of the Revolution* (1970) he said: "You can't be a revolutionary today without a television set — it's as important as a gun. Every guerrilla must know how to use the terrain of the culture he is trying to destroy. Two hundred psychological terrorists could destroy any major university without firing a shot." The Yippies, he claimed, had America on the run. "We've combined youth, music, sex, drugs and rebellion with treason — and that's a combination hard to beat."

Rubin's attempts to introduce his subversive philosophy to Britain in November 1970 were shocking enough to cause the Home Office not to extend his seven-day visitor's visa. He had caused a public furore by taking over the *Frost Programme* on ITV, bursting on to the studio floor, insulting the audience, smoking "pot", shouting abuse and swearing. The media was outraged and an angry Frost reacted by saying that Rubin represented "a tiny minority who discredited the voice of legitimate idealistic protest". After several more media appearances, Rubin left London but, instead of returning to America, he flew to Belfast, where he was arrested and spent the night in a police cell before being put on a plane for New York.

Jerry Rubin was the son of of a bakery driver and both his parents died while he was young. After graduating from the University of Cincinnati he spent 18 months in Israel before starting at graduate school at Berkeley. As a teenager in that city. For six long months, the government tried, by fair means and foul, mainly foul, to convince a jury that these defendants were evil men who had attempted to promote a bloody confrontation in the streets and parks of Chicago in order to bring about the Second American Revolution. Their eventual acquittals proved conclusively that the charges against them were untrue and that their trial was a frantic attempt by the Nixon administration to destroy the protest movement they had spawned and nourished.

Several months before he was fatally injured when he was struck by a car in Los Angeles, he had demonstrated that the fires that had burned in him years earlier had not been ex-

age university student he seemed, at first, fairly typical of his time. He enthused over J. D. Salinger's *Catcher in the Rye* and was captured in a photograph as a clean-cut young reporter in a snappy bow-tie shaking hands with Adlai Stevenson. But Rubin soon left Berkeley and later said he dropped out, not only from graduate school but also "from the White Race and the Amerikan nation". He visited Cuba to sit at the feet of Che Guevara, going back home from there to help found the "Yippies".

Ten years after his rumbustious visit to Britain, however, Rubin had stopped deriding the Establishment and joined it. In August 1980, aged 41 and now smartly turned out in suit and tie, he was a Young Upwardly Mobile Professional, having announced with some fanfare that he had become a Wall Street securities analyst. In the mid-1980s his former Yippie associate, Abbie Hoffman challenged Rubin to a series of "Yippie-v-Yuppie" debates. Rubin admitted that he "missed the sense of purpose" of the days when he was a youth rebel. "But I'm much healthier than I was then."

In 1984 Rubin moved to Los Angeles and was running what he called a Business Networking Saloon, charging clients $8 for the opportunity of meetings with like-minded potential business associates. By 1991 he was a marketing agent for a nutritional drink.

The Sixties, he declared, had been a time of protest and rebellion, the Seventies, an era of internal development (the "me" generation) and the Eighties "the decade of money". His revolutionary philosophy had matured. Power, he said, "really comes out of the cheque book."

California, where he fought against the closing of what came to be known as People's Park, he was the epitome of youthful protest during one of the most turbulent eras of our times. Along with his sidekick, Abbie, he brought young people into the demonstrational process and inspired them to risk their lives, undergo police brutality, and jeopardise their futures in what proved to be a highly successful effort to end the war in Vietnam and eliminate overt racism in America . Now that the United States has turned to the right, his legacy may be more needed than ever before.

William Kunstler

Jerry Rubin, activist, financier,

IN 1969: The Chicago Seven, charg left: John Froines, Tom Hayden, Jerr bie Hoffman. Bottom: Rennie Davis

Rubin: Rebel and dreamer

By Mimi Hall
USA TODAY

At the close of the Chicago Seven conspiracy trial, Jerry Rubin told the judge:

"You are jailing your youth . . . for the crime of dreaming . . . for the crime of idealism."

Years later, the anti-Vietnam War Yippie became a buttoned-down capitalist Yuppie. But friends say Rubin, 56, who died Monday night, remained a dreamer to the end.

"We latest provide the

of heart failure two weeks after he was hit by a car near his home.

"That's typical Rubin — always putting his head down and running," says Lee Weiner, another co-defendant. "He was always in a hurry."

Rubin is the second of the infamous Chicago Seven defendants to die. Abbie Hoffman committed suicide in 1989.

The pair, founders of the Youth International Party — a protest group dubbed

Seale was tried separately, convicted of contempt and sentenced to four years. His conviction also was overturned.

· OBITUARIES ·

me-
t to
e re-
the
. As
eeks
o the
now
aint
lica-

liffi-
any
ory.
ubin
who
y or
and
uch
ote.
urt-
eley,

STATE FILE NUMBER

1. NAME OF DECEDENT—FIRST (GIVEN)	2. MIDDLE	
JERRY	CLYDE	

4. DATE OF BIRTH M M / D D / C C Y Y	5. AGE YRS.	IF UNDER 1 MONTHS	
07/14/1938	56		

DECEDENT PERSONAL DATA

9. STATE OF BIRTH	10. SOCIAL SECURITY NO.	11.
OH	285-32-7441	19

14. RACE	15. HISPANIC—SPECIFY
WHITE	☐ YES

17. OCCUPATION	18. KIND OF BU
OWNER	MARKETIN

USUAL RESIDENCE

20. RESIDENCE—STREET AND NUMBER OR LOCATION
10724 WILSHIRE BLVD., #1102

21. CITY	22. COUNTY
LOS ANGELES	LOS ANGELE

INFORMANT

26. NAME, RELATIONSHIP
MIMI FLEISCHMAN, EX-WIFE

SPOUSE AND PARENT INFORMATION

28. NAME OF SURVIVING SPOUSE—FIRST	29. MIDDLE
-	-

31. NAME OF FATHER—FIRST	32. MIDDLE
BOB	

35. NAME OF MOTHER—FIRST	36. MIDDLE
ESTHER	

DISPOSITION(S)

39. DATE M M / D D / C C Y Y	40. PLACE OF FINAL DISPOSITION
12/01/1994	HILLSIDE MEMORIAL PARK,

FUNERAL DIRECTOR AND LOCAL REGISTRAR

41. TYPE OF DISPOSITION(S)	42. SIGN.
BU	▶ N

44. NAME OF FUNERAL DIRECTOR	45. LICEN
HILLSIDE MORTUARY	FD 13

PLACE OF DEATH

101. PLACE OF DEATH	102. IF HOSPI
UCLA MEDICAL CENTER	X IP

105. STREET ADDRESS—STREET AND NUMBER OR LOCATION
10833 LE CONTE AVE

107. DEATH WAS CAUSED BY: (ENTER ONLY ONE CAUSE PER LINE FOR A

IMMEDIATE CAUSE	(A)	Multiple Traumatic Injuries
	DUE TO (B)	
	DUE TO (C)	
	DUE TO (D)	

CAUSE OF DEATH

112. OTHER SIGNIFICANT CONDITIONS CONTRIBUTING TO DEATH BUT NOT RE

Adenocarcinoma Of Lung

113. WAS OPERATION PERFORMED FOR ANY CONDITION IN ITEM 107 OR

Thoracotomy, Laparotomy, Reduction

PHYSICIAN'S CERTIFICATION

114. I CERTIFY THAT TO THE BEST OF MY KNOWLEDGE DEATH OCCURRED AT THE HOUR, DATE AND PLACE STATED FROM THE CAUSES STATED.	115. SIGNATURE
DECEDENT ATTENDED SINCE M M / D D / C C Y Y	DECEDENT LAST SEEN ALIVE M M / D D / C C Y Y	▶
	118. TYPE ATTE

I CERTIFY THAT IN MY OPINION DEATH OCCURRED AT THE HOUR, DATE AND PLACE STATED FROM THE CAUSES STATED.

119. MANNER OF DEATH

120. INJURY AT

☐ YES

124. DESCRIBE

CORONER'S USE ONLY

☐ NATURAL	☐ SUICIDE	☐ HOMICIDE
X ACCIDENT	☐ PENDING INVESTIGATION	☐ COULD NOT BE DETERMINED

Auto Vs

125. LOCATION (STREET AND NUMBER OR LOCATION AND CITY AND ZIP C

Intersection Of Selby Avenue & Wilshire Blvd

126. SIGNATURE OF CORONER OR DEPUTY CORONER

▶ [signature]

STATE REGISTRAR

A	B	C	D	E

Jerry Rubin, 56, Flashy 60's Radical, Dies; 'Yippies' Founder and Chicago 7 Defendant

By ERIC PACE

Jerry Rubin, the flamboyant 1960's radical who once preached distrust of "anyone over 30," died on Monday night in a Los Angeles hospital where he was being treated after having been struck by a car two weeks earlier. He was 56 and lived in the Brentwood section of Los Angeles.

A hospital spokesman said the cause was cardiac arrest, but Mr. Rubin had been unconscious and in critical condition since he was hit on the night of Nov. 14 while jaywalking across Wilshire Boulevard in the Westwood section of Los Angeles. His former wife, Mimi Leonard Fleischman, said that he had suffered multiple injuries.

As a bearded standard-bearer of the 1960's counterculture and opposition to the Vietnam War, Mr. Rubin carved himself a niche in the history of American radicalism with his energetic and sometimes comic gestures. He was among the founders of the Youth International Party, the Yippies, a militant but loose-knit group with a penchant for political theater. He appeared before a Congressional committee wearing a Revolutionary War costume, and was a center of attention at anti-war demonstrations in his Uncle Sam hat.

Mr. Rubin was prominent in the riotous protests at the 1968 Democratic National Convention in Chicago, which led to the famously unruly trial, in 1969 and 1970, of him and six other radical defendants — the group known as the Chicago Seven. At the trial he showed up wearing judge's robes covering a blue Chicago police shirt.

After the 1960's, Mr. Rubin wrote, lectured, sought self-improvement and then worked in New York on Wall Street and as an entrepreneur. In the 1980's, he became known for his promotion of "networking," bringing together ambitious young professionals at parties at the Palladium nightclub in Manhattan. Transformed from protester to businessman but still demonstrating a flair for the public gesture, he held a series of public "Yippie vs. Yuppie" debates with Abbie Hoffman, another former leader of the Yippies,

Reuters/Bettmann, 1968

Associated Press, 1989

Jerry Rubin went from radical to businessman during a colorful life.

who committed suicide in 1989.

Looking back years later at the 1960's, Mr. Rubin called himself one of "the anti-capitalistic comics of the 1960's" who used street theater to pursue, without much success, "the radical dream of transforming the system from outside."

He once campaigned to elect a pig as President the United States, and in 1967 he dropped dollar bills onto the floor of the New York Stock Exchange.

Though he later renounced his anti-capitalism, he defended his fervent opposition to the Vietnam War. "Our nationwide campaign to build public opposition to the Vietnam War succeeded, and the war ended," he wrote in an article in 1990.

The Chicago Seven trial produced some of the most bizarre courtroom scenes in American jurisprudence. Mr. Rubin and other defendants — Mr. Hoffman, Tom Hayden, Rennie Davis, David Dellinger, John Froines and Lee Weiner — all charged with conspiracy to disrupt the Democratic convention, taunted the iron-willed judge, Julius J. Hoffman. The judge ordered an eighth defendant, Bobby Seale, tried separately because he was so disruptive.

During the trial, which was in Federal District Court, Judge Hoffman aimed sarcastic remarks and occasional tirades at the defendants and their lawyers, including William Kunstler. The defendants chewed jelly beans at first and later screamed insults at the prosecutors and the judge, whom Mr. Rubin denounced as "the laughingstock of the world."

Mr. Rubin and his co-defendants

After that, Mr. Rubin began what was to become a prolonged round of self-improvement, which he was heard to call "a smorgasbord course in New Consciousness." He tried EST, meditation, modern dance, massage, acupuncture and hypnotism. As the 1970's went on, he lectured and did more writing.

In 1978, Mr. Rubin, a son of a Cincinnati truck driver who became an official in the teamsters' union, married Mimi Leonard, a former debutante who worked for ABC-TV in New York. They lived in a posh apartment on the Upper East Side of Manhattan.

With the passage of time, Mr. Rubin became "a buttoned-down entrepreneur for the 1980's," as one cul-

An icon of the anti-war movement who reinvented himself in later years.

tural critic put it. A watershed of sorts came in 1980, when he wrote that while he still had "many of the same criticisms and same values" as in the 1960's, he had learned "that the individual who signs the check has the ultimate power."

"I know that I can be more effective today wearing a suit and tie and working on Wall Street than I can be dancing outside the walls of power,"

aths **Deaths**

n. of Pearl River, 29, 1994. She is sur-usband John Muc-

SHEINBAUM—Fred. Beloved husband of Sydell, dear father of Dr. Roy Sheinbaum and Jill Eliner, Esq. Devoted father-in-law of An

15

JERRY'S A TOUGH SON OF A BITCH. HE'S GOT A HELL OF A FUCKING EGO. ALMOST AS BIG AS MINE, BUT NOT QUITE. THE DEBATE WILL GO ON IN PRINT ONLY, FOR JERRY IS A WRITER. I KNOW I CAN WHIP HIM PUBLICLY BECAUSE I'LL USE ANY MEANS NECESSARY. I ALSO KNOW HE READS HIS SPEECHES. IT'S KNOWING SHIT LIKE THAT WHICH MAKES ME SUCH A COCKY PUNK. ALSO KNOWING THAT I HAVE A FLOWER IN MY FIST HELPS.

—ABBIE HOFFMAN

Jerry's Legacy

ANYBODY WHO KNOWS JERRY KNOWS HE'S ANYTHING BUT CONSISTENT. JERRY HAS NOW FALLEN IN LOVE WITH THE CHICAGO 8 PROSECUTION'S CASE. THE PROSECUTION PORTRAYS YOU AS BRILLIANT, COURAGEOUS, CONSISTENT, AUDACIOUS, IMAGINATIVE. YOU LIKE THE IMAGE. THE DEFENSE PORTRAYS YOU AS A VICTIM, WEAK, NOT ATTRACTIVE.

—STEW ALBERT, IN 1989, TALKING TO JOHN SCHULTZ

MANY OF THE INTERVIEWS FOR THIS BOOK were conducted between late 2012 and early 2015, so current events—like the Occupy Movement and the Tea Party—crept in. Often the interviews turned into conversations, especially when the subject of Jerry's legacy came up. It's complex. There's the Yippie and the Yuppie era, with the New Age period in between. Although the only two people I interviewed together were Lee Weiner and Gil Rubin, it felt natural to present the following as a roundtable discussion.

DAVID SPANER: To give Jerry credit, he was very talented. There's a lot of very good Yippie writers. Abbie and Paul Krassner are good writers, but not just them: later Yippies from Vancouver, Columbus, and New York. But Jerry was probably the best of the Yippie writers—he was able to talk about really substantial subjects with this very engaging, light style. Plus, he was also an extremely good public speaker. *Arguably the best white public speaker of that entire era.* By saying that, I'm quite aware of people like Stokely Carmichael, and others. Jerry was an incredibly good public speaker.

PAT THOMAS: The '60s were a time for activism, and Jerry was on the forefront. The '70s were an introspective time, what they call the "me" decade: Jerry was doing psychotherapy, changing his diet. I wouldn't say he was a leader during that period, but he was certainly

You are cordially invited to

Celebrate

Jerry Rubin's life
July 14, 1938 to November 28, 1994

at

Mimi's

The Century Club

Friday, December 1, 1995

"plugged in" with people who were. And then in the '80s, you have this Yuppie movement, and there he was, again, a bit of a leader.

DAVID SPANER: I think he tended to look at himself that way, as representing the high points of any given decade, human personified. It's interesting to note that all of his books were autobiographies. He tended to look at himself as the kind of personification of what was going on, on the cutting edge of society. And in the '60s, if everybody was an activist, he would be an activist. You explained the evolution of those other decades, and that's sort of how he looked at himself. I would agree with you; he did go through that kind of evolution...

PAT THOMAS: Mr. X drops out of college in 1968, joins the Yippies or SDS, and by 1973 he's back to school, gets his degree, gets married, has a few kids, and he's now working at IBM. But that doesn't mean he's a Nazi, it just means he grew up. I feel that's what Jerry did, but because he was famous he had to take heat for it.

DAVID SPANER: I don't disagree with you. It was a really interesting thing, that movement (Panthers, Yippies, SDS, et al.). How it came along so quickly, so huge, and then disappeared so quickly. But there's a period that's bracketed by the two political conventions—1968 and 1972, which are both high points of Yippie activism, and kind of the high point of the movement—'68 to '72, in which it was a revolutionary movement, and people felt that fundamental change was just around the corner. People openly identified as revolutionaries all over the place.

And for someone who wasn't around at the time, it's hard to explain that this revolutionary fervor existed during that period. But as far as the people who were more anonymous, obviously people go through a transition. People are human beings, and they respond to different things in different ways in different times. They moved on and did different things in their lives; the movement was no longer a mass movement. But they were still progressives, of one form or another . . .

Having said that, I don't think his change was nearly as fundamental as people thought. Some of the changes, like when he got really gung-ho capitalist, I didn't agree with. But at the same time, Jerry never got any further to the right than liberalism, and I don't think that he completely changed everything he believed in—I don't think it went nearly as far as a lot of people assumed.

GIL RUBIN: He has a tremendous legacy. I think that whole group—Jerry, Abbie—really changed the course of humanity, just in terms of the way people see things in terms of theater. The world changed because of Jerry. Throwing dollar bills off the Stock Exchange—maybe not many people remember that exact event, but that way of looking at how to get publicity and change things, people do it now and don't remember that "Wow, Jerry and Abbie started that." I think there's a tremendous legacy there.

The '60s for people of a certain age, were really, more incredible than any other time. Nobody talks about the late '80s. [*Laughter.*]

You can go back into the '60s, and you can remember exactly what was happening then. And so when that ended, '71–'72, that period, you couldn't possibly be anything else except miserable and left out. It's like being thrown out on the street to fend for yourself. But it's a funny thing. No one laughs or begrudges Bobby Seale making barbeque sauce, or whatever he's doing now.

LEE WEINER: Yeah, I do.

GIL RUBIN: They do? Come on, it's good barbecue! Or Eldridge Cleaver for the codpiece and the underwear. *That was a little weird.* Huey Newton, probably, now, would be working for Victoria's Secret. Who knows? He wouldn't be walking around with a machine gun and a belt of bullets. So, everybody moves on. It's just Jerry was such an incredibly polarizing figure that you could have people really love—or really hate—what he was doing.

LEE WEINER: One of Jerry's strengths is one of the reasons why people got so pissed off. When anybody talked to Bobby Seale, he would always reference back to the old days and how it fit in. Maybe it was all bullshit, but it made some kind of sense, because Bobby has not ever presented—no matter how garish his outfit might be, no matter what he's doing—he never presented it as *this is all of me.* This is who I am. It was always who I used to be, and I'm still partly that. Not Jerry. Jerry's *total commitment*, total utter devotion to whatever the fuck he was doing at the present moment, it negated all the previous stuff. And so that pissed people off. That, *"Wait a second. You mean you no longer reference any of that?"*

JUDY GUMBO: I think that Jerry's legacy is changing as the times change. I know for a while, it was that Jerry betrayed the movement, Abbie didn't. Even though Abbie got busted for cocaine, and Jerry didn't. Right? Because Abbie then embraced the environmental movement, so then he got to be okay. And Jerry quote unquote "went to Wall Street." But, I remember a conversation with Jerry about how he was working with gangs in Los Angeles to help them become entrepreneurs. It wasn't this black and white, "Jerry bad, Abbie good." I don't believe that at all.

I think in terms of his legacy, it's "Do it." And I don't mean the book. I mean the concept. The concept of actually going and doing it, that active concept. To the extent that people even attribute it to Jerry, which they don't. I remember when Nike came out with the "Just Do It" slogan. I happened to be in touch with someone who was high up at Nike, and I wrote to him, "Oh, did you know, Jerry Rubin, da da da . . ." and it was like nothing. It was irrelevant to them. I think it's Jerry's legacy, in the "Do It" sense, while it was very important. It may be lost, because it's not attributed to him.

LEE WEINER: It's the difference between Jerry, and Abbie, and "Jerry & Abbie."

GIL RUBIN: That's true, three very different entities. Jerry. Abbie. "Jerry & Abbie."

LEE WEINER: It's three different things. And "Jerry & Abbie" and the people around them, they moved the political needle. But, if you look to their individual legacies . . . [*Sighs.*] Even they came to recognize at a certain point, when they put together those faux . . . debates.

GIL RUBIN: What's the individual legacy of Laurel & Hardy or Abbott & Costello? They were the Abbott & Costello of political theater, and although they were both bigger than life . . . I don't think Abbie would have been as successful without Jerry.

GERALD LEFCOURT: Jerry was at a moment in time, a very important person in this incredibly massive movement to change this country. He was in a key position to lead people away from racism, from war, from destroying the poor; he was a very important part of it. All of them have that legacy. Abbie went on to do other things. Tom Hayden too, in politics. But certainly, they were all part of a mammoth movement that changed this country, that has caused a black president to be president, to have women's rights, childcare, education, end of racism, end of stupid wars, all of that and—women's freedom—sexual freedom, is their legacy. It was a very important thing. *They are the greatest generation. Fuck Tom Brokaw!* They are the greatest generation. They changed this country from bad things, to at least ascribing to good things.

LOLA COHEN: I can't tell you how many times I say to myself, "Jerry, Abbie, Stew, and Phil. Poof." Occupy Wall Street has tremendous debt to those four people. Phil would be there singing. Jerry would be there. There's a tremendous debt owed to the Yippies.

MARTIN KENNER: Jerry should be remembered as a mass organizer of the American youth in revolt against the war in Vietnam. That was very important. And my line today is "white youth are enserfed with debt," and they don't have the opportunity, because they have to pay off their student debt to fight back. Occupy Wall Street was wonderful. But that was a brief, fleeting moment. But Jerry really is out of another era. The '60s was a period of youth rebellion. It was a political rebellion. It was also an era of great—of relative—prosperity, and that gave us a lot of freedom, too.

PAT THOMAS: The youth then certainly had a lot more time on their hands to be idle, but idle in a good way. My generation was the last that could coast a little bit. I arrived in San Francisco in 1987, I was twenty-three, and my share of the rent was two hundred bucks. I didn't need to work a full-time job, I worked part time, and did music. If I was twenty-three now, and I rolled into San Francisco, there's no way!

MARTIN KENNER: Absolutely. I supported myself, but I never had to think about where I'd get money. I could go down to the *New York Times*, got a good job. Go to the UN, got a good job—because they were available. Silicon Valley's ruined everything. *The New Yorker* has a good piece about Silicon Valley. It's just a spoiled rich

Louise Kurshan & Gil Rubin

boy's club, and what a narrow view. They're fighting for immigration reform so they could get high-tech engineers cheaply.

MIMI LEONARD: I always thought one of the things about Jerry was that he could see the unvarnished truth—things that were obvious, but most of us couldn't see because of the layers of convention and rationalizations our lives are filled with. For instance, he was one of the first Americans—and even Jewish American—who saw the Palestinians' point of view. Forty-five years later, it is still a radical thing to say, but it does not compare to saying it in the early '60s, when he lived in Israel. For some unknown reason, he was able to cut through his whole society's layers of reinterpretations on the Palestinian question and see the injustice on what had been done to those people.

NANCY KURSHAN: The Jerry I know was sharply critical of US society and the government, and passionately identified with people who were struggling for a better existence. When I say passionately, I mean *passionately*. And was willing to turn one hundred percent of his life over to try to help transform the world. He was willing to take unpopular positions, and do unpopular things, and really challenge the existing order. And I think he wasn't brave, physically. But he was very brave. There needs to be more people like that.

MIMI LEONARD: One of the things about Jerry is that both of his parents died when he was very young, so he could define himself more freely without worrying about hurting his parents' feelings. I wonder if he could have ever showed up in front of Congress in a Revolutionary War costume if he had been worried about what his parents think.

He talked about the night before that stunt—it was a completely original, never-done-before idea in 1966. He worried whether he would be dismissed as the biggest asshole in the world when he arrived at HUAC. Abbie was still a pharmaceutical sales person, and Jerry was really on his own in the theatrical politics arena. To have found a costume shop, rented the costume, and arrive for his subpoena in the costume, *who has that kind of guts?* He didn't know it would basically halt the whole process and change everything positively.

Later on, his views became less glamorous but he still had the same qualities. His Life Extension product distributors loved his passion, his commitment, his all-out enthusiasm, as much as any of his earlier political followers.

REX WEINER: If the counterculture is part of a continuum of American history, in which the ideals of the founding fathers have been pursued intermittently, what I call the interrupted revolution—the counterculture won, in terms of its very specific and limited aims. But those were very significant, having to do with human rights, women, gays, the disabled, what-have-you. But nobody was saying, "let's overturn the American government" seriously. The proof of that is Jerry's use of American flags, and dressing up as a so-called revolutionary. My point is that Jerry Rubin led the way, in a way that people misunderstood, and today, the counterculture, baby boomers, need to be told that they won. We're all nostalgic about our youth, but it doesn't mean that we failed. *Jerry Rubin's only failure was in getting across Wilshire Boulevard.*

RATSO SLOMAN: Jerry should be remembered for being at the forefront of the Yippies, which doesn't get enough credit for its tremendous ability to nail "the political and the cultural" in a way that nobody else did. For any street kid who had no affinity to SDS, or the Port Huron Statement, didn't give a shit about that, just wanted to get high . . . The idea of being able to politicize hippies . . . Jerry was ahead of the curve, in a lot of cultural events, whether you like it or not. Certainly ahead of the curve in the whole idea that, after being a veteran of the antiwar movement, which was almost like

being a veteran of the war, you had to heal yourself. Jerry took that time, and investigated yoga, vitamins—ahead of the curve on that aspect. Just the holistic idea of taking care of your health as well as having the correct politics. His books were very clever. His books outsold Abbie's, much to Abbie's chagrin; Jerry's books always outsold Abbie's. [*Laughter.*] He put together a very nice package. His books were quality. Graphically, they were wonderful.

PAT THOMAS: I see Jerry as a true American. In the '60s, he's an American revolutionary. He's as American as Paul Revere or George Washington. And in the '70s, he's part of the "me" decade into self-help, self-improvement, health food. He's cleaning up himself emotionally and physically. And in the '80s, part of the American landscape is to be an entrepreneur. America was built on democracy, individualism, and capitalism. So he's a quintessential American across three decades.

STEVANNE AUERBACH, TOYOLOGIST: That's exactly how I feel. If you were writing a play, you've just created the three acts. Jerry and the Yippies stood for what was wrong at that time. And all of the violence in Chicago only represented how wrong the government was in not allowing people to speak freely in what they believed, without violence. That's what happened in the '40s, '50s, with black people in the South. They couldn't vote or couldn't speak out, so they were killed. This is an American tragedy. So the Chicago '68 violence should never have happened, but that's what got people's attention. It took a lot of courage to face what they were facing in those days.

And each phase of these changes from the '70s to '80s were challenges. They were hard, they were tough. Jerry was a strong personality. I don't think he was overbearing. I think he was pushy, like New Yorkers are. That's what I loved about him; I'm a New Yorker. That's part of it; I admired that part of him. So you can look back, and you can say he was pushy, he was selfish, whatever. I don't think that's fair. Those are the wrong ways to judge him.

That's why I told a critic of Jerry's [who knew him during the social networking era], I thought he was full of shit. I said, "You

benefitted from his events. You met a lot of people; you have a lot of business cards that you wouldn't have, otherwise." That was way before Facebook and LinkedIn. Remember, it would have been a lot easier to bring together events like that today, but that was before the computer age. Keeping track of people wasn't so easy. You'll have a good time discussing this book on Twitter.

MIMI LEONARD: Jerry was very sincere. And he was irrepressible. If he had a thought he wanted to share, he would demand attention. He would dominate the conversation until he had thoroughly examined the question from every angle. We were at a party before our son Adam was born. And Jerry was trying to figure out what to name him. The entire conversation the entire evening was on that. He was able to turn everyone's attention to that one subject. We talked about it for hours.

STUART SAMUELS: Marshall McLuhan said that "the artist is the only person who's ahead of the curve. The artist is the only one who could tell the future." And Jerry was an artist in that way. He was Warhol in a way, in that Warhol could tell the future of what was going to happen in the '70s and '80s through his art. Jerry was using networking, using connectivity, using these silos of communication. All the stuff that was emerging. So he was part of that whole notion of the artist as the avant-garde, but also as having the ears and sensitivity to what's coming. He was always looking for what's coming.

I think the way to pull Jerry's legacy together is not through a particular event that happened, but rather a consistency. Jerry never changed his attitudes, his optimism, his humor, his joy. He always wanted to make you laugh. He never was sad, never cried, he's always trying to make you feel up. But what happened comes from two kinds of assumptions that Jerry had, which were consistent through all his activities—and were, in a sense, the groundwork of the counterculture movement. And that is you can transform things by your own individual actions. That if you have an idea, and you gather people around it, and you were consistent, you could do magical things. Whether you were going to levitate

the Pentagon, revolutionize society, or close down a convention. His belief was that the individual actor—leader—could transform society. The notion of revolution was based on that.

And the second part of it was a sense of inherent optimism that went with that, and a lack of cynicism. That was a part of the '60s that became very much part of the '70s and '80s, as cynicism came in. Jerry never bought into the cynicism. He's going toward the end of his life in a process that's about making him live longer. Life Extension, right? So it's the ultimate optimism. No longer for society, but for himself. That was the consistent philosophical glue at work with Jerry. The unswerving optimism made him kind of a fun guy to be with.

ADAM IPPOLITO, OF THE BAND ELEPHANT'S MEMORY: Jerry created networking, I'm talking about before the events in the '80s at Studio 54. He was networking back in the 1960s by bringing people in "the movement" together. He was the master of that, more than Abbie or anyone else.

TIFFANY STETTNER: He was anti-materialistic, but when it came to whatever the healthiest food was, the healthiest vitamin, or healthiest juices, or the healthiest for his children—when it came to buying the things that were going into their bodies, price was never an issue. Jerry was like a kid in a candy store with people he loved. He would get excited by a phone call, or an upcoming event or . . . That's just how Jerry rolled. There was no "medium." It was either ultra-excited, "I love you, I love you, I love you!" Or it was, "I hate you, I hate you, I hate you!" He was a very smart guy because he loved the dramatics of the human condition . . . I think he was misunderstood by many. He was absolutely lovable. And he had something up his sleeve every single time.

WALLI LEFF: His enthusiastic embrace to act upon what he believed in, rather than sit and complain about what the rest of the world was doing. I felt he showed very important leadership, and even if it was flawed, he contributed enormously. At the personal level, he was a person who had more than proven his worth as a friend, and as somebody you could trust and rely on. His legacy is what we all did in the movement, because he was one of the creative engineers of that. And that he was a person that Juliet and Adam could be proud to have as father.

Speaking of Juliet and Adam Rubin: Juliet works at Evite, the modern-day version of what Jerry and Mimi were doing with their social networking parties, and exactly what Jerry predicted would happen with computers. As a vegan, she protests for animal rights (as a member of Direct Action Everywhere). Jerry's son Adam was a reporter at Santa Monica City College, and he's a rapper and videographer. Currently living in Kentucky, Adam shows tremendous potential for the future.

I'm Not Selling Out. I'm Buying In! Jerry's legacy and the debate about whether he "sold out" are inextricably tied. Those who didn't know him cry, "Sell-out!"; those who did were more receptive to his ever-evolving values. Rex Weiner said he never thought Jerry sold out, because he was never an anarchist in the true meaning of the word. In general, Jerry loved the American way, he just didn't like our involvement in Vietnam and the civil rights atrocities on American soil.

In early 1968, while Jerry and Abbie debated their protest tactics in Chicago, Abbie said in an underground paper, "If you can't come away from a demonstration and tell a funny little story about it, it's not going to work." He added, "I hate America enough to run the risk of getting killed." Jerry replied, "No, no, no! You don't hate America the way that any black [person] you can point to does. America has been in large part good to you."

Decades later, in the *High Times* magazine interview, Abbie reflected, "Here we were coming out of the '40s and '50s . . . I accept American culture, its demand for entertainment. Europeans who observed the period of the '60s tell me that [our] contribution to revolutionary theory was to come up with the idea that revolution could be fun. Only an American could have done that."

An excerpt from Jerry's essay, "Self-Portrait of a Child of Amerika" (1970):

I am a child of Amerika. If I'm ever sent to Death Row for my revolutionary "crimes," I'll order as my last meal a hamburger, French fries, and a Coke. I dig big cities. I love to read the sports pages and gossip columns, listen to the radio and watch color TV. I dig department stores, huge supermarkets and airports. I feel secure (though not necessarily hungry) when I see Howard Johnson's on the expressway. I groove on Hollywood movies, even bad ones. I speak only one language: English. I love rock 'n' roll. I collected baseball players' cards when I was a kid and wanted to play second base for the Cincinnati Reds, my home team.

ABE PECK: Jerry did what a lot of other people did later. Of course, Jerry, as was his wont, made an ideology out of his transition. It wasn't quiet. He made a politic out of it, and that's what got pushback. Of course, there were a lot of people who stayed in the movement. Jerry didn't do that, and frankly I didn't do that. I'm into pretty progressive stuff but I don't live in a radical world. A lot of people went in the direction that Jerry went, and in some ways his "crime" was that he was early. But he also did make an ideology out of his transition.

PAT THOMAS: There's a ton of misinformation. He never sold stocks and bonds; he was doing marketing for a firm that was representing opportunities in green energy sources years before anyone else. Another posthumous article claimed he was a real estate baron during his final years. Nope, he was selling health drinks and vitamins.

Jerry's shoes and a tie are his only remaining personal effects.
Photos © Lisa Jane Persky

ABE PECK: I don't even know what's in my stock portfolio. I could have the worst . . .

PAT THOMAS: For all you know, you're building Army helicopters.

ABE PECK: Yeah, I could have the worst portfolio in the world. I didn't go to a values stock firm. Everyone's pot's a little blacker I think.

DAVID SPANER: To be fair to Jerry, he did not become right wing. There were very few new leftists who became really conservative; he was not one of them. His political transformation was closer to Tom Hayden's. He became a liberal democrat, essentially. But it seemed more extreme than other people who became that. Because he was coming from such an extreme place, such an ultra-leftist place.

LARRY YURDIN: Jerry went through life having fun, and to put it less kindly, he was something of an opportunist. He would grab whatever was out there, whatever he thought was cool. He wasn't particularly cynical about it. I just don't think that's the way his mind worked.

PAT THOMAS: One of the things that his close friends have said is that they believed Jerry was sincere with each of the different hats that he put on.

LARRY YURDIN: Yeah! That's what I'm saying. And what I'm also saying is that he wasn't an ideologue, and if something struck him as the right thing to do, he didn't weigh it against previous things he had done, or comments he had made, or whatever. He just thought, at the moment, it was the right thing to do, so he did it.

REX WEINER: There were very few people who were committed ideologically to Marxist Leftism, this was studied only by a few. And those committed to those ideals tended to stay committed to social activism, and there are some who are just fucking misfits and couldn't fit in, and got love for it, and that includes my dear friend John Sinclair. And my sometime friend and jam partner, David Peel. These are people who could not, if you put a gun to their heads, put on a suit and go to work and do the same thing every day, with a long-term strategy.

PAT THOMAS: I love John and, to a lesser degree, David, for who they are, and it was great to meet Nancy Kurshan, who is still an activist to this day. She's gone on to do all kinds of incredible activism, but doesn't blow her own horn. She is a true child of the 1960s because she's still fighting for various civil rights. And it was admirable to see her; she lives in a nice home and made a decent living. Nancy Kurshan shows you don't have to be a dirt-bag and pretend that it's 1968.

REX WEINER: If the free market and capitalism are American values, the '60s were all about that, from the beginning. They were selling dope, weed, and pioneering smuggling routes, and working out prices in the freest market of all, which is the dope market.

JOHN SINCLAIR: Jerry went the wrong way. He was famous, and he wanted to get rich. See, my goal was I wanted to get not famous. [*Laughs.*] Because, to me, famous is not rich. There's no future in that. Everybody hates you, because they think you're rich. And I just thought, "Well, I don't want to be rich, and I certainly don't want *to not be who I am*, in order to be rich." I want to be who I am, I want to carry my ideals forward, which I've done ever since, but I've been totally underground.

RONA ELLIOT: One of the many things Jerry contributed is that you don't have to be attached to who you were. You can give that up. You have to be willing to let go, just because you did your hair that way in the '60s, doesn't mean you need a beehive now. And Jerry made that a business: "I'm not that." But I think it was real to let go of who he was and embrace the next thing. People like Abbie, who got attached to this image, they're still in this same hairdo. But Jerry was the guy who could let go of his whole identity, and Jerry's asshole-ness just added to his charm for me, because anybody who could say to your face, "I'm taking you out of my phonebook." *You've got to be kidding.* That's chutzpah!

PAT THOMAS: I actually see his willingness to change that public persona as brave.

RONA ELLIOT: If you're a Buddhist or you're doing any work on yourself, it's all about letting go, constantly. He was very brave. And taking a stand for it. And not being attached. On a larger level, it's about not being attached to your previous identity. Maybe it was strategic, to make it a better story. I don't know and I don't care. I wouldn't put it beyond him.

STEPHEN SMALE: I think the problem is those people criticizing Jerry. Because they get into some kind of rut about what is right and wrong, and they're unwilling to change with events in the world. That's my own feeling; it shows a kind of crazy ideology that they don't escape from. And a lot of people that were behind our marches and such were in that group of ideological leftists. They were happy to oppose the war, but they always continued to be in this kind of ideological Marxist or socialist setting.

NANCY KURSHAN: So here I am, telling you I never was *done* with the movement. But I also wasn't in the crosshairs in the same way that Jerry was. I didn't have to travel cross-country in prison shackles. I didn't have to stay in Cook County Jail, which is pretty awful. I didn't have my coccyx broken by the police when they threw me around. There were a lot of things that were different. I don't know if that would have stopped me or not. I'm not saying that would have, but I can't say. I wonder if there wasn't a third way, though. Did Jerry have to go on that Yippie vs. Yuppie tour with Abbie, because that was oppositional to those us who continued to struggle, and saying that—I don't know exactly what Jerry said in those debates.

PAT THOMAS: I'm assuming through the years, when someone wanted to drag you into a conversation about Jerry's post-Yippie years with, "he went to Wall Street, he sold out," that you just shooed them away?

NANCY KURSHAN: Pretty much. Because I don't like that conversation, either. A lot of times people were saying that to me, and I reply, "*Well, what have you been doing?*"

Reflection. After Jerry had gone through all his transformations, he was asked by journalist Robert Sam Anson, in the late '70s, to reflect. "We had no time to breathe, to look at each other and ask who we really were . . . In a way, we were really revolting against ourselves. I was the screwed-up, middle-class monster that I was railing against. We were not the new men and women we were talking about."

Around the same time, former White Panther John Sinclair shared similar thoughts in Anson's book *Gone Crazy and Back Again: The Rise and Fall of the Rolling Stone Generation.* "It was a big circus. If I saw anybody doing that sort of thing today, I'd think they were nuts. We didn't know anything. We were déclassé hippies. Can you imagine what would have happened if we had turned the country over to Tom Hayden and Jerry Rubin? They weren't ready. They didn't have any programs."

I thought it would be best to give Jerry the last word, via a 1980s interview conducted by Joan and Robert K. Morrison.

If [the American government] wanted to destroy me, the smartest thing would have been to indict everyone but me [for the Chicago 8 Trial] . . . I don't think I'll ever achieve the energy peak that I had in those periods of time. But the '70s were kind of a burn-out. I had to recharge my adrenaline batteries that had been overloaded by the '60s. [During the 1960s], every six months had to be another escalation in tactics, because of boredom. In a sense we fell into a very American trap: The movement had to produce more and more stimulation for society out there to keep the movement going. Some of our best people went underground, and some of them haven't been heard from yet. I wasn't the kind of person who would enjoy going underground or was built to go underground or who even felt that it was a useful thing to do. I kind of said to myself in the '70s, "Now, wait a minute. There may not be a revolution, and maybe I'd better get healthy." I wanted to prove that there was a "me" that existed outside of politics.

Then around 1977 I started coming out of it. I moved to New York, and decided that I wanted, above anything else in life, an intimate personal relationship. Some people have said that Mimi Leonard made me more capitalistically oriented, but that's not true at all. By the end of the '70s, I had come to the decision that the way to change America is by amassing as much power, financial or otherwise, as one could and then to create a new establishment.

America is not going to be changed from below. Either you live on the edge of society and say, "I'm not playing the game," or you go in and you say, "Well, how do you play the game? I'll play it, and I'll play it better."

LEFT: Adam displays his father's signature.

A Tale of Two Rubins: the Orchid

AL MARTINEZ

GARY FRIEDMAN / Los Angeles Times

Let's clear this up instantly. There are two Jerry Rubins. One is a Venice peace activist, left, who makes $6 an hour potting orchids. The other is a Famous Ex-Radical who paid $85,000 in personal income taxes last year. **B3**

Let's clear this up instantly. There are two Jerry Rubins. One is a Venice peace activist who makes $6 an hour potting orchids. The other is a Famous Ex-Radical who paid $85,000 in personal income taxes last year.

The Venice Rubin is relatively soft-spoken and says please and thank you and had to resort to potting orchids because peace is ruining his paid anti-war activism.

The Other Rubin jumps in your face waving health powders like "Wow!" and displays the kind of relentless energy that drove the Establishment crazy 25 years ago, first when he was a screaming yippie and then a member of the Chicago 7.

When the two Rubins are together, there is no confusing them. The Venice Rubin is tall and curly-haired, wears shorts, a tank top and sneakers and doesn't speak unless spoken to.

The Other Rubin is shorter and neatly trimmed and wears a gray pin-striped suit and red patterned tie and darts around his $5,000-a-month high-rise apartment like a chipmunk in a forest, demanding redress.

The redress he is demanding is clarification. He wants the world to know he is not the orchid-potting Jerry Rubin but the Rubin who, like Ollie North, leaped from the ashes of a former career to achieve success in a new one.

The new endeavor is network marketing in association with a company called Life Extension International, which is about as far removed from political activism as Howard Stern from the Bishop of Canterbury.

Rubin and LEI hustle health potions like the aforementioned "Wow!," an orange-flavored confection which the Famous Ex-Radical urged me to drink, promising it would make me feel stronger and smarter within minutes.

Then he turned to the Venice Jerry Rubin, fixed him with a stare hard enough to pierce armor and said, "I can make you rich."

□

This all began with a nice little column I wrote a fortnight ago about the Venice Jerry Rubin, whom I shall call Rubin #1. He is director of the L.A. Alliance for Survival and made his living taking half of the alliance's profits from its anti-war activities.

But then the Berlin Wall came down, Russia fell apart and the peace movement began going to hell, all of which impacted on the $6,000 a year Rubin was making to live on.

The irony of a peace activist suffering from the agony of peace appealed to me, so I wrote about Rubin, a 50-year-old guy who, by his own assessment, had no skills, couldn't drive and had only $2 in the bank.

Two things happened. Rubin got a job potting orchids for $6 an hour and probably would have been happy potting orchids the rest of his life. But then along comes the Famous Ex-Radical, the 1960s yippie turned yuppie, a description, as columnist Dan Akst says, that runs through his life like a Homeric epithet.

This Rubin, Rubin #2, who is either 47 or 53, depending on whom you believe, moved to L.A. recently from New York and was busily making his bid as Health

Epilogue

Jerry Rubin is alive and well, giving away "Peace Activist" bumper stickers on the Santa Monica pier. "Jerry Rubin" was at the Santa Monica City Hall when he was told that Jerry Rubin had been hit by a car and was at the UCLA Medical Center in critical condition. The two Jerry Rubins had crossed paths a few times before. Al Martinez had written in the *LA Times* that "Jerry Rubin" was broke, relatively speaking. So Jerry called "Jerry" and said, "Gee, people think it's me who's broke. That's not good. I'm running a business and I can't have that perception, so it's time we get together and have this press conference." They had shared a friendly, amicable relationship, but had never had a press conference to clarify that there was an original Jerry Rubin of the Chicago 8, and a "Jerry Rubin" who hangs out on the Santa Monica Pier handing out peace activist materials. So Jerry arranged for KABC radio in LA to air a show in which he declared, "Hey, 'Jerry Rubin,' I'll give you ten thousand dollars if you change your name to anything—and twenty thousand if you change it to Tom Hayden!"

"Jerry Rubin" Explains How He First Met Jerry Rubin.

"JERRY RUBIN": It was back in the early '80s and I was doing a solo protest march from Santa Monica Pier to the Diablo Canyon Nuclear Power Plant in San Luis Obispo, California. It was a couple hundred miles up there. When I got to Santa Barbara, there was a press conference that was taking place at a hotel for President Reagan. I came walking in, wearing shorts and a tank top and a big sign. I had just seen in the *New York Times* that they did this story saying that former Yippie leader, Jerry Rubin, was doing this march.

Somehow through all that I got a lead to contact Jerry . . . He answered, "Jerry Rubin here." I said, "Hi, Jerry. It's Jerry Rubin." [*Laughs.*] "I just wanted to let you know that I'm not going around telling anybody that I'm you." . . . I flew from LA to New York, and I let him know that I was coming into town . . . We sat down and had a great meal. Then the check came. I picked up the check and he grabbed it out of my hand and he said, "No, no, no. Anybody that's getting me so much publicity having the same name as me out there on the West Coast, the least I could do is pay the check!" [*Laughs.*]

Did It!

3 'JERRY RUBINS' TURN UP AT TRIAL

'Chicago 8' Lawyers Charge Confusion on Defendant

By J. ANTHONY LUKAS
Special to The New York Times

CHICAGO, Oct. 3—The defense in the trial of the "Chicago eight" contended today that there were "two, three, many more Jerry Rubins" in and around Federal District Court.

One of them was Jerry C. Rubin, the 31-year-old Yippie, who is among the eight defendants charged with inciting a riot at last year's Democratic Naional Convention here. This Mr. Rubin, dressed in a blue and orange striped polo shirt, sat quietly in court this morning, an impish smile playing around his lips.

The next "Rubin" was a bearded psychology professor named Robert Levin, whom the defense introduced in court today as its first human "exhibit." It contended later at a news conference that Mr. Levin was the man whom a Chicago plainclothes man had mistaken for Jerry Rubin at a demonstration in Lincoln Park during the convention.

At the news conference, the defense produced still a third "Rubin" — a student named David Boyd, who said the Chicago police had shadowed him day and night for six days during the convention under the impression that he was Jerry Rub—

Contending that the Government and its witnesses were totally confused as to who Mr. Rubin was, Rennie Davis, another defendant, told reporters, "Perhaps it is time for the real Jerry Rubin to stand up."

"But instead," Mr. Davis added, "we say, 'Will the Government of the United States please sit down.'"

The Government, in the person of Thomas A. Foran, the United States Attorney, appeared as flabbergasted as the spectators in the courtroom when the introduction of Rubins began this morning.

William M. Kunstler, an attorney for the defense, was cross-examining Sgt. Robert Murray, a plainclothesman who worked as an undercover agent in Lincoln Park during last year's demonstrations.

Yesterday, Sergeant Murray testified that Mr. Rubin had urged demonstrators to attack the police, shouting at the policemen in the park: "Your children are pigs! You are pigs! Get out of the park! Take off your guns and we'll fight you!"

In the cross-examination this morning, Mr. Kunstler tried to pin Sergeant Murray down precisely about what Mr. Rubin was wearing at the time. The sergeant testified that Mr. Rubin had on denim overalls, a shirt and a white football helmet with a blue streak down the center and the numerals "88" in blue on the back.

"Are you absolutely certain the man you saw in the park with the 88 on his helmet was Jerry Rubin?" Mr. Kunstler asked.

"Yes, sir," Sergeant Murray said.

"Then bring in the witness," Mr. Kunstler declared, turning to the doors of the courtroom. Throughs the doors then strode Mr. Levin, dressed in blue

Survey Finds Newspapers

HARTFORD, Oct. 3 (AP)— survey shows that college students believe that many newspaper stories are inaccurate and unfair but that more students believe newspaper than news magazines, television and radio.

The survey, conducted by a committee of the Associated Press Managing Editors Association, was presented at the organization's convention yesterday.

The views of high school students were included in some areas of the survey, and both groups said they spent more time with newspapers than with other news media.

In the survey, 110 college students were interviewed and 36.5 per cent felt that television was the "most interesting" news medium, followed by news magazines, 35.5 per cent; newspapers, 21.5 per cent, and radio, 6.5 per cent.

The interest of 87 high school students interviewed was divided equally among newspapers, television news and news magazines—about 30 per cent for each—with radio being the most interesting for 10 per cent.

When asked what newspaper information was handled inac—

Levin, a 27-year-old native New Yorker with a brown beard and mustache, said he was an assistant professor of psychology at Merrimack College in North Andover, Mass. He said he was among the demonstrators in Lincoln Park on Aug. 25, 1968, the night Sergeant Murray said he had seen Jerry Rubin there. Mr. Levin insisted he was wearing the white helmet all that night.

Miner's Chief Asks House To Strengthen Safety Bill

WASHINGTON, Oct. 3 (UPI) —The president of the United Mine Workers said today that the Senate-passed coal mine safety bill was "a step in the right direction" but provided mine operators too much time to implement the law.

W. A. Boyle, the president, also urged the House to strengthen mine safety measures before final passage.

"The major deficiency in the bill is the length of time given to the coal operators to comply with the dust standards," Mr. Boyle said. "Another is the time permitted the operators to operate their mines as nongassy mines."

The Senate bill sets limits on dust and explosive gases in mines and outlines fines and safety inspection procedures. It also provides campensation for victims of black lung, a disease contracted from breathing coal dust over an extender period, among other things.

Original in Metropolitan Museum of Art

Colonial Sleigh Seat

The next time I heard from him was when he was moving from New York to Los Angeles. He suggested we contact the phone company to do something about our phone numbers and the confusion. I said, "That's a good idea." Steve Harvey, the columnist for the *LA Times*, he wrote something called "Only in LA," and he did a story about how only the Jerry Rubins got to change their phone numbers and got this special exemption from the phone company that usually they never do. I guess because Jerry was such a good salesman. We didn't have three-way calling back then but we did something and we managed to get a special listing which listed him as "Jerry Network/Marketer Rubin," and they listed me as "Jerry Peace Activist Rubin," but that didn't stop the confusion, because of the peace activist thing, people still thought I was the old Jerry. Even though that was my name then and my legal name now; I had "Peace Activist" added legally to my name ten years ago, on my sixtieth birthday.

Just one day before Jerry Rubin died, "Jerry Rubin" was running his bumper sticker table at the Whole Life Expo. They began chatting. "Jerry" asked Jerry to watch his table. So Jerry sat down and started shouting, "Get a peace bumper sticker! Get your hand stamped with the peace symbol. Come on over!" There was a big peace symbol banner hanging behind him that said, "Back by popular demand." When "Jerry" returned, he gave Jerry a hug goodbye. When news got out that Jerry was in a coma, "Jerry" got more than a hundred phone calls at his Santa Monica residence from folks thinking that he had passed away.

"Jerry Rubin": There isn't a day that goes by that someone [who] meets me doesn't say "*Are you the Jerry Rubin from the '60s?*"

The web of myth, rumor, and half-truths is never-ending. There are blogs by people who ran into "Jerry Rubin at the Santa Monica pier." They're angry that the "sell-out" faked his own death and is hawking peace bumper stickers. If only *the* Jerry Rubin had been so lucky. I'm sure he's chuckling that even decades after his death he's still manipulating the public. The Yippie in him would love that.

PHOTO BY NICK UT © AP IMAGES

Gratitude

This journey began in the early 1970s when my older brother, Jerry, turned me on to the Yippies, sparking an interest in the counterculture that become a lifelong obsession. In my early 30's, I read *Growing (Up) at 37* and it struck a chord with me – the search for happiness and transformation – yeah, I can dig that. In the early days of the Internet, before every newspaper and magazine put their archives online, I felt that, despite several Yippie tribute websites, there was a distinct lack of truthful and positive information about Jerry. It was there and then that the seeds of this book began to germinate.

Fast-forward to 2011 and I'm finishing off my degree at Evergreen State College. Professor Chico Herbison said to me, "Why not take a quarter off and do your own thing for credit… What would you like to do?" Without missing a beat I replied, "Write a book about Jerry Rubin." I tracked down Jerry's ex-wife and mother of his children, Mimi Leonard, who greenlighted the project. My publisher Gary Groth agreed to publish the results. I soon moved in with Mimi and her husband Mark Fleischman for several weeks, and they turned me loose on thousands of pieces of paper, photographs, journals, letters, and more. Jerry never threw anything away – and anything reproduced in this book from his archives isn't meant to imply a copyright (the original source of several photographs were not identifiable for example). Other friends and family members allowed the use of materials from their collections as well. People I met on Facebook also sent me items and contributed nuggets of information.

More often than not, Kevin Uehlein scanned the archival items or suggested somebody who could. I crisscrossed the country by plane, phone and email for the next several years interviewing folks like crazy. Along the way, many of Jerry's old friends become my new friends. In the end, I talked to 75 different people, many of them more than once.

Jerry's life-long best friend Stew Albert was no longer around to talk to, but his widow, fellow Yippie Judy Gumbo was a frequent receipt of my speed-dialed calls, as was Jerry's ex and Yippie co-founder, Nancy Kurshan. No subject was off-limits with Paul Krassner, and I don't mean dirt-digging, I mean, the entire 1960s counterculture. Stevanne Auerbach and Stella Resnick were very kind to me. Michael Simmons suggested several of the people that I wound up interviewing in this book.

Along the way, Mimi Leonard was beyond generous with her time and resources and this book would have been impossible without her – she was a constant cheerleader through thick and thin – and introduced me to many people. Jerry's brother, Gil Rubin, was also very supportive.

Kevin Uehlein transcribed many interviews, as did Katie Westhoff, who also explored various research tangents for me.

After all the interviews were transcribed, Kathy Wolf spent months reviewing and editing them into a useful format. As the book progressed, she was hands-on during edits and rewrites, suggesting changes and occasionally writing additional text. She also curated much of the imagery for the initial layout of the book; graphic designer Jacob Covey then picked up the torch and spent months adding and refining and designing – and answering too many phone calls – as did Gary Groth and Eric Reynolds.

Kristin Leuschner supported me during the constant rollercoaster ride this book became (including instigating some inspiring discussions comparing Jerry with Ben Franklin and introducing me to Jeff Smith, who shared insights about Woody Allen and the Chicago 8 Trial). Kristin was beyond tolerant of the countless hours (and years) I invested in this project – also she and her sister Karen provided the use of the old family villa so that I could write for days on end in peace. Kari Pearson compiled the index and, whilst doing so just days before the book went to press, found and amended dozens of typos that other 'eagle eyes' had missed.

Mitch Myers reviewed sections of the text and made edits in the middle stages of the book. Conrad Groth helped in the final stages of the corrections as well as the prep for printing process. Mary Bisbee-Beek signed on as publicist, while Josh Mills agreed to pester music media. Paul Smith made a significant contribution to the promotional fund. Directors Paul Lovelace and Jessica Wolfson are working on a Jerry Rubin documentary with me.

Countless others made donations of time, money, energy, photography and more. I'm especially grateful to anyone who agreed to be interviewed by phone or who answered an email from me. Several of you who heard me complain for hours about this book … You know who you are – and I love you for it.

Dennis McDougal, Jonah Raskin, Aaron Dixon and Ronee Blakley all read advance copies of the book and wrote testimonials; I apologize profusely they didn't appear as I had originally intended.

And yes, all rights reserved by each and every photographer, illustrator, author, writer and interviewee whose work or words appear in this book. If your name is missing anywhere in these pages – trust me, it wasn't intentional.

This book is dedicated to Adam Rubin – long may you run.

"We saw the courtroom as theater; we wanted to make a statement. We knew that we were representing a generation that was making a statement at that time. We wanted to expose the fact that judges have unlimited power and sit in their robes and make statements about people. The gagging of Bobby Seale; here was a black man gagged in an American courtroom, [that image] went across the country. We were very conscious of using the media. When Abbie and I walked into the courtroom wearing judge's robes that day — we were saying defendants have moral authority too. We were in a sense, not defendants, we were offendants! We took the offensive in the courtroom. We used the courtroom to make a national statement. I think that statement really related to so many people's lives in that [time] period and that's why it was so important [then and now]."

-JERRY RUBIN ON <u>GOOD MORNING AMERICA</u> (1987) TALKING TO CHARLES GIBSON

New photography for this book:
Lisa Jane Persky

Archival photography and images courtesy of:
Gordon Gullahorn, Emily Fraim, Burr Leonard, Ethan Persoff (www.ep.tc), Michael Overn, John Jekabson, Leni Sinclair, Gil Rubin, Dave Weller, Nancy Kurshan, Stella Resnick, Judy Gumbo (yippiegirl.com), Truusje Kushner, David Peel, Ratso Sloman, Meegan Lee & Alice Ochs, David Peller, Gabrielle Schang, Rona Elliot, Howard Smith Archive (via Ezra Bookstein), A.J. Weberman, Kate Coleman, Allen Ginsberg Estate (via Peter Hale), Lola Cohen, Mimi Leonard, and the Jerry Rubin Estate.

Licensed photography:
Paul Sequeira, Lisa Law (via Pilar Law), Roger Ressmeyer & Corbis, Nacio Jan Brown, Bob Gruen (via Sarah Field), Robert Altman, John Jekabson, AP Photo/Nick Ut, David Fenton, The Richard Avedon Foundation (via Erin Harris), Oakland Museum (via Nathan Kerr & Michael Lange): 2010.54.787 Unknown Artist, *Vote for Jerry Rubin for Berkeley Mayor, 1966.* Work on paper, 19 x 13.5 in. Collection of the Oakland Museum of California. All Of Us Or None Archive. Gift of the Rossman Family. (page 36)

Archival materials were provided by:
Sean Howe, Barbara Stack, Laurie Charnigo, Norman Mailer Archive (at the University of Texas at Austin via Greg Smith), Jon Wiener (via Brian Deshazor at KPFK), Sara Silverstone, Michael Simmons, Bob Fass (via Paul Lovelace and Jessica Wolfson) and others.

Various odds and ends:
Mary Canning, Peter Davis, Aaron Cohen, Scott McGibbon & Norman Lear, Michel Choquette, Jerry Thomas, M.L. Liebler, John Wilcock, John Eskow, Harper Simon, Alan Baumgarten, Matt Cunitz, J.C. Gabel, Bob Sarles, Ron Mann, Nile Southern, Louise Yelin, Jeff Slate, Brian Deshazor, Barry Simons, Bent Sorensen, Gurbir Dhillon, Norm Kerner, Douglas Hill, John Lynch, David Fenton, Peter Hale, Randy Frisch, John Akomfrah, Leon Kenmen, Alison Martino, Sonia Clerc, Steve Hochman, Chris Estey, Todd Cameron Miller, LeRoy Chatfield, Ben Rinzler, Kenny Shiffrin, Danny Fingeroth, René de Guzman, Chris Morris, Mitch Blank, Matt Sullivan, Susan von Seggern, Todd Cochran, Mike Johnson, Joel Bernstein.

Extra special thanks:
Rex Wiener, Mitch Soloman (*Let's get that biopic made!*), Kate Coleman, Stuart Samuels, Gerald Thomas, Bryan Thomas (for some editing

suggestions), Michelle Nati (organizing the fund-raising campaign), J. Michael Lennon, Daniel Fingeroth, Randy Anderson, David Spaner, Lola Cohen, Ratso Sloman, Martin Kenner, D.W., Beth Hetland, Gregory Smith, Marty Kenner, James Tracy, Mark Fleischman and several others that I'm probably forgetting.

The following people are honorary "executive producers" of this book:
Paul Metsa, Ben Rinzler, Art Eckstein, Debi Ann Scott, Pia Pedersen, Camelia Elias, Marc Weinstein, Andrew Gordon, Bent Sorensen, Stella Resnick, Brad Rosenberger, Randy Frisch, Gil Rubin, M.L. Liebler, Kathy Wolf, Tracy Walsh & Don Kinsella, Michelle Nati, John Armstrong, Terrence Murphy, Otto von Stroheim, Jack & Cynthia Hale, Paul J. Smith, Katharine Starzel, Kurt Statham, Cheryl Pawelski, Nancy Kurshan, Peter Hirschl, Judy Gumbo Albert, Lola Cohen, Michael Doud, Terry Moreland Henderson, Douglas Towne, Michael Clare, Kimberly Wilkinson, Gil Ray, Christian Petersen, Paul Sherman & Susan Gill, Mitch Soloman, Aaron Cohen, Geert Crauwels, Shirley Knolls, Kristin Leuschner, Steve Wynn, Rob Peck, Steve Hochman, David Fenton, Michael Gregory, Dave Weller, Sonya Hunter, Kristian St. Clair, William Kennedy, Stevanne Auerbach, Mark & Stacy Clark.

Where in the city can we go to make friends? Where
can we leap out of our individual prisons and enjoy each
other? The city is full of walls, locked doors, signs saying

DON'T